Local Politics

GOVERNING AT THE GRASSROOTS

Local Politics

GOVERNING AT THE GRASSROOTS

Terry Christensen

San Jose State University

Wadsworth Publishing Company
Belmont, California
A Division of Wadsworth, Inc.

Political Science Editor: Brian Gore
Editorial Assistant: Jennifer Dunning
Production: Melanie Field/Bookman Productions
Designer: Paula Goldstein/Bookman Productions
Print Buyer: Barbara Britton
Copy Editor: Betty Berenson
Illustrator: Richard Sheppard
Cover Design: Paula Goldstein/Bookman Productions
Cover Photograph: Bill Gallery/Stock, Boston
Compositor: Kachina Typesetting
Printer: Arcata Graphics/Fairfield

I(T)P ™

International Thomson Publishing
The trademark ITP is used under license.

Printed in the United States of America

1 2 3 4 5 6 7 8 9 10—99 98 97 96 95

Library of Congress Cataloging-in-Publication Data

Christensen, Terry.
    Local Politics : governing at the grassroots / Terry Christensen.
        p.   cm.
    Includes bibliographical references and index.
    ISBN 0-534-13332-0
    1. Local government—United States.   I. Title.
JS331.C53   1994
320.8'0973—dc20   94-15912
                                                                              CIP

For the students, citizen activists, journalists, and politicians who taught me local politics.

Contents

Preface

When our attention can be turned from the televised drama and glamor of national and international politics to the ostensibly mundane workings of local politics, it can be like removing scales from our eyes. Suddenly we discover a level of politics that affects us daily and intimately, from what happens when we flush the toilet to life in our neighborhoods, traffic on our streets, and the air we breathe. We find a level of politics whose workings we can observe at first hand, without media intervention, learning from the example of our own communities. We see real people participating in the political process and realize that we, too, can do so.

Unfortunately, textbooks about this subject often fail to communicate this immediacy and more often stifle than stimulate interest. Most seem to be written for sophisticated political scientists and graduate students rather than for undergraduates who are just being introduced to the subject, many of whom are not political science majors. *Local Politics: Governing at the Grassroots* recognizes the diversity of contemporary students of local politics and strives to meet their needs. Designed as a primary text for courses in urban, local, or state and local politics, this book is written with an emphasis on clarity, readability, and accessibility. Every effort has been made to make this a real teaching text, not only through its straightforward organization and style, but by emphasizing the nuts and bolts of local politics and by actively encouraging students to learn about local politics by observing their own communities—while simultaneously stressing comparison and generalization.

Local Politics also moves the spotlight a little bit away from the large, Frostbelt cities that are the focus of most discussions of urban politics. That's why the title uses the word *local* rather than *city* or *urban* with all the images they convey. The term local politics more readily implies a variety of communities, including small ones, as well as a variety of units of government, including counties, special districts, and school districts. Frostbelt cities remain an important focus here, but suburbia and Sunbelt communities, where a majority of Americans now live, are also at the center of this book.

As the subtitle *Governing at the Grassroots* implies, *Local Politics* takes a practical approach to its subject, providing a clear description and analysis of the structure and process of local politics. Rather than treating cities as abstractions and reducing readers to passive observers, *Local Politics* encourages them to become aware of local politics in their own communities, not only as a source of concrete examples of the subject under study but also to gain a sense that they can participate themselves. As part of its nuts-and-bolts approach, *Local Politics* includes practical fieldwork assignments in students' own communities at the end of every chapter and has a concluding simulation—a local politics game.

The emphasis of *Local Politics* is not exclusively practical, however. Theoretical and analytical themes, such as political economy, power structures, the politics of growth, race and class, and intergovernmental relations, are also discussed.

Local Politics begins with a discussion of reasons to study this subject and ways of approaching it, with an introduction to the book's practical orientation and its analytical themes. Part I lays the foundations for subsequent chapters by examining the socioeconomic, demographic, and intergovernmental contexts of local politics, paying special attention to suburbanization and the move to the Sunbelt, as well as the role of states in local politics. Part II unveils the formal institutions or structures of local governments in terms of their sources, historical evolution, and general workings. We study the move from machines to reform and counterreform, then consider the balance of power among local legislators, executives, and the bureaucracy. Part III turns to political forces outside government, such as voters, campaigns, the media, interest groups, and community power structures. Part IV examines local politics from the perspective of budgets and selected public policies (with special emphasis on growth and transportation), concluding with a chapter on metropolitan regional government, a subject that directs our attention to the future of local politics.

Many years of teaching, research, and political involvement have gone into this book. Much of the book is informed by the extensive and excellent academic literature on local politics; even more springs from observation of real-life politics and from students, academic colleagues, journalists, political activists, and elected officials. When I began teaching local politics, almost everything I knew came from books. This knowledge was soon challenged by my students. In my very first class were a cop, a city planner, a minority community activist, and a woman who had been one of the early residents of the U.S.'s first mass-produced suburb. Their practical experience sometimes confirmed and sometimes contradicted but always enriched my academic knowledge. Soon they were dragging me along on patrols and to community and city council meetings, and we were inviting elected officials and group leaders to talk to the class. As I became more involved, I came to know many local politicians, activists, and journalists who gave generously of their time and knowledge, again enriching my own. These, then, are the first to whom thanks are due—my students and my colleagues at the university, in journalism, and in local politics.

A few merit special appreciation: Linda Chromik, Larry Gerston, Peter Haas, Ron Sylvia, Steve Van Beek, and my gracious mentor (and newspaper-clipper), Roy E. Young at San Jose State University; Tom Cronin at Colorado College; Thad Beyle at the University of North Carolina at Chapel Hill; and Nick Anderson, Katherine Bishop, Michele Feutsch, Julio Moliné, Mona P. Onstead, and Phil Trounstine. Joelle Rabow, Diane Drew, and Charru Gupta provided invaluable research assistance. Janet Boles, Marquette University; David Covin, CSU Sacramento; Margery Ambrosius, Kansas State University; Keith Hamm, Rice University; Susan Rouder, City College of San Francisco; and especially Robert Horgan, University of Richmond; and Ken Yeager, San Jose State University reviewed *Local Politics* in draft form and made innumerable constructive suggestions and criticisms that made this a better book. Cindy Stormer at Brooks/Cole Publishing initiated and helped shape this project and Diane Honigberg, Melanie Field, and Betty Berenson efficiently guided it to fruition. Several great public institutions and their staffs also gave essential support: a sabbatical leave from San Jose State University sustained the writing and much of the research, and the libraries of New York City, the London School of Economics, San Jose State University, and Stanford University were invaluable resources.

Welcome diversion and reinvigoration were supplied by Don Foster, MP, and his staff at the House of Commons and by the ever-supportive and patient Ray Allen.

Terry Christensen

Local Politics

GOVERNING AT THE GRASSROOTS

An Introduction to the Study of Local Politics: Why We Bother and How We Go About It

Y ou walk into a room where a meeting is in progress. A few of the participants glance at you as you enter; a few are too intent on the business at hand to notice you; most look bored and disinterested; several are reading. A voice is droning on over a loudspeaker. You find a seat and take in your surroundings. If you're in a large, old city, the room may seem a bit like a church, with people sitting in wooden pews facing the front of the room, where some more official-looking people in big chairs sit at desks, perhaps facing one another rather than their audience, which they may outnumber. If you're in a newer city, perhaps in the suburbs or the Sunbelt, the room will be modern and may seem more like a theater, with rows and rows of comfortable seats for the audience and a small group of official types at desks and in padded chairs that swivel, but facing the audience rather than one another.

The official-looking people sitting in the front are mostly men and mostly white. The one who looks most important and official of all sits in the middle and seems to be running the show. Nearby, perhaps below or to one side of the official group, are people shuffling papers or taking notes. Also beneath or to one side of the group is a podium from which a man in a suit is addressing them, his back to the audience. His, you now discern, is the voice on the loudspeaker. Some of the official types seem to be listening to him, but others are whispering to each other, talking on the phone, pouring themselves coffee, reading, or seemingly having an out-of-body experience. The speaker concludes with some ingratiating remarks, and the official in the middle thanks him and calls on one of the papershufflers at a nearby desk. Referring to a report of some sort, this person speaks quickly, using many unfamiliar words and phrases. Then one of the important-acting officials mutters something and the presider rattles out "All-in-favor-all-opposed-motion-approved-the-next-item-is-18c." A few people leave the room looking pleased; others seem to wake up.

Another jargon-spouting official reports, one of the people at the top table gives a minilecture, and a succession of people line up behind the podium. You understand that item 18c involves a housing development. The first speakers, all in suits, proclaim its economic benefits and its contribution to solving your community's dire housing shortage. You are sympathetic. Then, one after the other, people who seem to be average citizens speak. They turn out to be residents of neighborhoods near the proposed development. Unlike the earlier speakers, they are nervous. They do not use jargon, and they sometimes seem a little vague, but they make clear their worries about the project's impact on traffic, schools, and other local services. Some decry the loss of open space and ask for the land to be made into a park. You are sympathetic until some declare that they fear that the "type of people" who might live in the new housing would decrease property values and lead to the deterioration of their neighborhoods. If the proposed condominiums would really cost $150,000, as their developer announced, you suspect it would be people like your own family who might buy them. When the speakers conclude, the officials debate the issue briefly. One or two clearly play to the audience; others seem indifferent. Another quick vote is taken, and the housing is approved. The men in suits leave smiling. The more casually dressed people seem bewildered at first, then straggle out grumbling and frowning, glancing disgustedly back at the officials up front. One comes down to walk out with them, pursing her lips and shaking her head.

"Item 19a," announces the front-and-center official and another paper-shuffler mutters a report, halting abruptly when the doors burst open and a television camera crew sweeps in led by someone in heavy makeup and hair that doesn't move. Blinding lights suddenly bathe the chamber. The person making the report stutters to continue, and all of the important-acting officials now sit up straight and look attentive and concerned. A couple of rumpled-looking people sitting at a table to one side and writing in funny little notebooks smirk. As the made-up person directs the camera, a new set of speakers queues up at the podium. This time they are elderly and gray haired, and you gather that the officials are about to take something away from them. But before they begin their speeches, the bright lights fade, the TV crew sweeps out, and everybody slumps, looking dazed and disappointed. Meanwhile, a group of police officers in uniform enters the room and sits together, right in front.

You need to get home, so you make your way out, noticing too late that you could have picked up a printed agenda at the door. You're surprised to find a crowd in the hall. Some people are talking angrily; you recognize them from the housing debate. A couple of men in suits are huddled with one of the important-looking officials. Some average-citizen types are walking in wearing yellow "Save Our" something-or-other pins.

Mulling it over on the way home, you are surprised that although it seemed boring while you were sitting through it, what you observed now seems sort of interesting, even a little exciting. You've just witnessed a bit of local politics at work: a city council or county board with its mayor or chairperson and supporting bureaucracy along with lobbyists and citizens and a reporter or two. The process, the people, and even the room and building (grand and intimidating or comfortable and accessible) reveal a lot about local government and politics. After another meeting or two, you will discern organizational structures and an operating style. You'll figure out which people, interests, and values have clout. If you go to enough meetings, you'll see most of the elements of local politics in action—elected officials, bureaucrats, interest groups and lobbyists, the media, and sometimes even important members of the local power structure. You may sense the abstract presence of the voters or the public, especially around elections. You'll hear talk of taxes and budgets, of economic development, social issues and services, regional problems, and relations with state and federal governments.

Such meetings will not tell you all you need to know about local politics, but they are a pretty good starting place. They can help you generate questions about how your local politics work and can connect generalizations and abstractions about local politics to real life and to your own life. If you study other communities, you'll find that for all their differences, they have much in common with your own.

Why Study Local Politics?

The most practical reason to study local politics is that they affect us all every day, from what happens when we flush the toilet to life in our neighborhoods, getting along with one another, personal safety, jobs, schools, traffic on our streets, and even the air we breath. Yet much as they affect us, few of us understand how local politics work or how to make them work for us.

National and state politics may deal with bigger issues and seem more glamorous since they get so much more media coverage, but they do not actually touch us as immediately or directly, on such a daily basis. The issues in local politics may seem more mundane, even trivial, but they affect us too intimately to dismiss or leave to others. Moreover, as individuals or small groups we can influence what happens in local politics much more than we can state or national politics because they are so large and so distant. One of the first surprises for students of local politics is how few players actually participate and how easy, with a little energy and ability, it is to become one.

The effects of local politics on our daily lives and their accessibility for our active participation are practical reasons for us as citizens to study them, but they also offer us a great learning laboratory in a more general and theoretical sense. The glamour, drama, and big issues of state and national politics attract our attention, but since most of us do not live in our state capitals or in Washington, D.C., the action is too far away for us to observe in person. Modern media, with cable channels like C-SPANN, are changing that a little, but for the most part we have to rely on intermediaries to pass on information and impressions to us. These include many reputable journalists and scholars, but as excellent as they may be, they filter information and interpret it for us. We learn from them and we need them to help us understand what we observe in our own communities. But even with their estimable assistance, we cannot have the same sort of first-hand access to state and national politics as to local politics. In your own community, you can see for yourself, talk to the participants, judge for yourself. Sheer proximity or convenience is another good reason to study local politics.

We should not, however, allow our focus to fix on just one community. If we did, we might treat it as unique, and in the end we would know only about that one community and its workings, with no greater knowledge about other communities or politics in general. This is a pitfall in studying local politics, but the subject actually contains its own solution to the problem—other communities. Local politics are going on in communities around the state, the nation, and the world, so it is easy to compare what you observe in your community to what others—or you yourself—observe elsewhere. Most metropolitan areas contain hundreds of units of local government, so you don't even need to go far away to begin your comparison. The feasibility of such comparison makes local politics an excellent subject of study, in some ways better than national or even state politics. Most courses and books on national politics focus on just one nation, which is important because a nation affects so many people, but it is, after all, just one nation and as such can offer little scope for comparison. Even comparative politics courses usually contrast only a handful of nations, and state politics is limited to the fifty states, while we can compare hundreds or even thousands of examples of local politics. Maybe there are actually too many to make sense of, but the sheer number impels us to compare and certainly multiplies the potential to do so.

Comparison takes us beyond our individual communities. Comparison enables us to develop generalizations, not only about local politics, but about politics and political behavior at all levels. From generalizations come **theories** or frameworks for explaining how something works—in this case, local politics. But building theories about human behavior is not easy. Researchers make hypotheses (educated guesses) about how they think things might work and then gather evidence to test their hypotheses. These are the building blocks of theories, which help us sort out and understand the perplexing array of phenomena and even predict what might happen in similar cases. To do this, it isn't enough to look at just one community or tell a story about a particular event, as a journalist does. We have to look at many communities or events and find patterns among them.

With so many communities and units of government, many of which are in our own backyard, local politics provides fertile ground for developing our understanding—or theories—not only of local politics itself, but of politics more generally. We can study the relative influence of different individuals and groups and what makes some more powerful than others. We can consider the roles of government institutions and the private sector and their impact on decision making, voting, and public policy.

Our goal is understanding politics through comparison and the development of theories, but your own community is still the starting point. Think of it as the frog you dissected in biology lab. You cut up one frog, not to learn only about that frog but to learn about frogs and anatomy in general. Your frog was unique, as are all living creatures and communities, but it had a lot in common with other frogs and creatures, so you learned about them, too. Remember, though, that the communities we're going to study are not dead. They may change as we study them—and our study can even change them.

What Makes Local Politics Different: City Limits

As useful as the study of local politics is to us as citizens and scholars, we need to be aware of its limitations. Local politics are subnational and subordinate to other levels of politics and to economic and social forces. Some analysts think that these larger powers have now overwhelmed local politics, making them trivial or even irrelevant. Local politicians and many citizens disagree.

Subordinate Governments

For much of human history, communities and eventually cities were the center of political life. Some, like Rome, dominated great empires. Many others functioned as **city-states**—that is, as tiny, independent countries. Each was sovereign or autonomous, governing itself, making its own foreign policy, and raising an army to defend itself and its surrounding territory. Massive walls were also essential to the defense of city-states, but when cannons were invented, the walls fell and so did the city-states. The modern equivalent of the city-state survives in a few places such as Singapore, San Marino, and maybe Hong Kong, but the great city-states of history were absorbed by the nation states that emerged in the past few centuries.

Local governments are therefore no longer sovereign or autonomous. Rather, they are subnational and subordinate—dependent instead of independent. Some are older than the states or nations of which they are a part, yet they gain their right to exist from these now-superior authorities. Their powers to make laws, regulate behavior, decide on land use, tax, spend, or do anything at all come from higher levels of government. In many countries, governmental authority is highly centralized and local governments are essentially administrative agencies for the national government, where all real power lies and where policy is made. There, local politics amounts to little more than choosing who gets to carry out national (or state or provincial) programs, if that. The United States is not so centralized. Power, authority, and responsibility for different programs and policies are divided between the national and state governments through our federal system. State governments, in turn, delegate some of their authority and responsibility to city, county, and other local governments that they create or recognize. This delegation of power may be broad and generous or narrow and restrictive, depending on state politics and the influence of local governments within it. States also limit and sometimes dictate the governmental structures, taxing and spending, land use, and other powers of local governments. Many local governments feel constrained by their subordinate and dependent status, yet they enjoy much greater discretion than local governments in most other countries.

Local governments are empowered to make policies in many areas, and until well into this century state and national governments left the locals to go about their business. The progressive reform movement of the early 1900s instigated greater state and national intervention, and the Depression of the 1930s, World War II, and the postwar years saw ever more active state and federal governments making more and more laws or programs that superseded or affected those of local governments. For although different levels of government have primary responsibility for different services and policies, many overlap. When they do, and when the state or federal government acts, the higher level prevails (subject to the U.S. Constitution). As federal and state involvement in the economy, the environment, education, civil rights, transportation, social services, and other areas expanded, the independence of local governments and the significance of local politics diminished. Local governments have now joined citizens in complaining about state and federal red tape and bureaucracy. Local governments have also grown financially dependent on the higher levels; some are virtual beggars, like the homeless people on their own streets. The state and federal tax burden makes it politically difficult to raise local taxes, which are usually limited by state law anyway, while federal fiscal policy can throw local budgets into disarray with inflation or recession. Land-use decisions are still a primarily local power, but in the past few decades a plethora of state and federal environmental laws have been imposed, adding a new limit to local authority. Even the hiring or firing of their own employees is sometimes dictated by state and federal regulations on civil rights and affirmative action.

Besides all these constitutional, legal, and fiscal constraints, state and federal politics and politicians often steal the spotlight. Their actions and their campaigns are seen as more glamorous and dramatic and push local politics off center stage and sometimes right out of the theater. The decline and displacement of local media, with fewer newspapers and the dominance of television, has added to this.

Economic Forces

The power of economic forces is another limit on local politics. Businesses provide jobs and tax revenues for communities. Without them and without a viable local economy, communities die. Economic interests have always, therefore, had great influence on local politics. They have been well represented in local office and have had a major say in the organization of local governments, their powers, tax structures, and programs. The power of business interests comes from their wealth and their command over employees and associates, but it also comes from their prestige in a capitalist society and the manifest need of communities for the jobs and taxes they provide. When business speaks, government listens, and local government with all its other limits, pays the closest attention of all. Some analysts of local politics, such as Paul Peterson in his influential book *City Limits*,[1] believe that keeping business happy is the predominant concern of local governments.

Like the relationship between local and state and national governments, relations with business have changed in recent years, and not to the advantage of local governments. Bigger government was partly a response to bigger business and the emergence of a corporate economy. Businesses—even big ones—were once locally owned and operated. Their proprietors lived locally and were almost invariably powerful in local politics, despite their rarely holding elected office. But the biggest businesses in most communities are now branch plants of national or multinational corporations. Except in the cities that host corporate headquarters, their owners (now usually shareholders rather than individuals or families) do not live locally. The company is represented by a manager who probably has little connection to the community and hopes to move up the corporate ladder and away. These businesses usually take less interest in local politics than their home-owned predecessors, but when they do, their power is even more heavy-handed because their commitment to the community is clearly not as great. Threats to move their plants to Arizona, Mexico, or Malaysia if they don't get what they want are taken seriously. They probably wouldn't be in a particular community at all if they hadn't been promised just what they wanted. Local governments eager for jobs and taxes often feel as constrained by the decisions of corporations larger and more powerful than themselves as by those of state and federal governments.

Mobility

At the other end of the scale, we as citizens and workers in a nation with a corporate economy add to the debilitation of local politics not only by paying more attention to higher levels but also by our mobility. Americans have always been mobile, but in the past more people really lived in their communities, working, raising families, going to school, shopping, socializing, and dying. Many spent their whole lives in one place along with generations of their families. But most Americans don't live like that anymore. Like corporations, we go where we'll do best economically, moving from city to city and state to state, following jobs. We even hop from city to city in our daily lives, living in one, working in another, shopping and socializing in yet others. We've become virtually temporary residents of our communities—if the places where we live even deserve that term. Most of us don't know enough or care enough to get involved in local politics unless our own neighborhood or job is threatened. This isn't necessarily our fault, it's just the way we live in our corporate economy. It is also a factor in local politics.

Multiple Governments

The pattern of our daily lives—pursuing different activities in different parts of a metropolitan area with different local governments—points to another way local politics is limited. Communities were once geographically separated from one another, each with its own government, self-contained, and capable of solving its own problems. Now communities run into one another, and hundreds of local governments may operate in the same urban area. They have become interdependent, with none capable of solving problems such as traffic congestion, transportation, or air pollution without the cooperation of the others. They also compete with one another for industry or even professional sports franchises in ways that may (or may not) be beneficial to one community while hurting others and being costly for the urban area as a whole. Communities from well beyond a single urban area also join such competitions, further weakening local will power.

What's Left for Local Governments?

All these **city limits** add up to a pretty gloomy picture. "The very heart and soul of local politics has surely died," writes political scientist Mark Gottdiener. Reduced to "form without content," he continues, "local politics has long since passed over into the hands of professional managers, multinational corporations, local capital caught in a predatory jungle of small-business competition, provincial politicians making do on dwindling party resources, and certainly not least, federal interventions promulgated by the long series of crises befalling the country since the 1960s."[2]

Other analysts, such as Clarence Stone, argue that local politics "still matters" and assert that the dichotomy between "structural determinism and local autonomy" implied in the writings of Peterson and Gottdiener is overstated. Stone recognizes the impact of all the "structural constraints," such as state and federal laws and economic forces, but insists that "they are mediated through political arrangements," including the institutions and actors in local government, so "politics matters."[3]

Local governments respond to city limits or constraints in different ways. Will their police force behave like an occupying army or practice community policing? Will they go for growth at all costs or risk losing some economic benefits to preserve their environment? Will they house the homeless or shuttle them out of town? Will they welcome economic and ethnic diversity or seek to be up-scale and exclusive? Will they cater to the automobile or look for alternative modes of transportation? On these and other matters, local governments still make choices, which is what politics is all about. These choices may be diminished, narrowed, even trivialized or marginalized, but they still make a difference in how people live their daily lives, how they feel about where they live, and even whether or not they participate in community life and local politics. Even if only little things are left to local politics, these little things add up to a quality of life. But local governments still make big decisions, too, ranging from building subway systems and stadiums to schools and policing. Many of these decisions are bitterly fought over in local politics (albeit by a minority of residents), which is the best evidence of all that local politics matters, at least to the locals.

The pessimistic prophets of city limits do not necessarily disagree with this. They do not argue that local politics should be forsaken or ignored. Rather, their point is that it operates under powerful constraints that need to be recognized and understood as part of what makes it different. The reasons for studying local politics discussed above, including its effects on us, its accessibility, and its utility as a learning lab, still stand.

Approaches to the Study of Local Politics

The way social scientists think about and study local politics has changed over the years, as the discussion above might suggest. Some of these changes in approach seem to come from changes in intellectual fashion, but others have resulted from the progress of social science, as theory builds on theory and enriches our understanding.

The Institutional Approach

The most traditional approach, which dominated the writings of political scientists until well into this century, concentrates on the institutions of government and the formal political process. The focus is on legal arrangements and constitutions, organizational charts, checks and balances, and separation of powers. In terms of the meeting described at the beginning of this chapter, the officials at the top table would have been the center of attention.

The structural or **institutional approach** to local politics peaked during the progressive reform era, from the turn of the century to the 1920s, when political scientists were actively involved in prescribing the best ways to set up local governments to purge political corruption in the form of strong organizations led by bosses and called machines. The structures they prescribed sometimes worked as intended but more often failed to eliminate the machines as a political force. They also had consequences for local politics that many of their advocates neither expected nor intended. Political scientists realized that institutional structures were not the be-all and end-all of politics and began to widen their study to consider other factors and forces. Primary among them were political parties, interest groups, voters, and elections.

Institutions and structures are not, however, irrelevant. They play an important part in local politics and need to be understood, not for their own sake but in order to comprehend local politics in general. The formal institutions of government allocate power, giving advantages to some and disadvantages to others. They affect what sorts of people sit at the top table at our meeting and who they listen to. They also shape public policy, or what government actually does. The institutions and structures are, however, themselves shaped by forces outside of government, as the reformers who fought the political machines learned.

Power

Even as the progressive reform movement was under way, some political scientists shifted their focus from the formal institutions of government to the study of political parties and interest groups and how they influence government. Although this usefully broadened the study of politics, the researchers were mainly concerned with national rather than local politics. Sociologists wrought a more dramatic shift in the study of local politics with the development of **community power studies.** Unlike political scientists, the sociologists did not assume that power was concentrated in government. By studying individual communities, they concluded that real power was held by business leaders and others rather than by government and elected officials. These findings challenged the traditional institutional focus of political scientists, who, in turn, did power studies of their own, usually concluding that government was, after all, a major, if not exclusive, center of power. The argument is still not completely resolved, but the shift in focus from government to power broadened the understanding of local politics (and politics in general) and provided another helpful way of comprehending it.

Political Economy

More contemporary analysts, some of whom were mentioned above, have built on power studies by examining the relationship between economics and politics. Some apply **Marxist theories** of class conflict, production, and consumption, seeing local government and politics as mechanisms of mediation between economic or class interests.[4] Not all classes and interests are equal, however, so Marxist theories predict that local government will almost always act in the interests of the owners of capital, the rich. Another set of theorists, far removed from the Marxists, take the capitalist economy as a sort of ideal or model for understanding and predicting local politics through the behavior of individuals. Their **public choice theory** views urban areas as marketplaces in which citizen consumers choose where to live based on the tax and service packages offered by competing communities.[5]

For the most part, however, the **political economy** approach to the study of local politics is more straightforward. Political scientist Thomas Dye studied state and local governments and their economic characteristics and found that economic factors were more important than political structures or participation in determining public policy.[6] In other words, much of what local government does can be understood and even predicted just by knowing its economic framework. The political economy approach also tells us that the principal concern of local politics must be economic development. "The interests of local government," Paul Peterson writes, "require that it emphasize the economic productivity of the community. . . . As policy alternatives are proposed, each is evaluated according to how well it will help to achieve this objective."[7] Putting it more flamboyantly, Harvey Molotch insists that "the very essence of a locality is its operation as a growth machine."[8] For Molotch, local politicians and business leaders share an interest in economic development, and their collusion constitutes a **growth machine.**

Critics say the political economy approach is too simple, to the degree that it asserts that economics determine decisions and that politics are irrelevant. However, the critics may be oversimplifying the theory since most contemporary analysts and practitioners of local politics accept the relationship between politics and economics. Some, like Peterson and Molotch, put their emphasis on economics, while others, like Clarence Stone, continue to assert that "politics still matters."[9]

Systems Theory

Another useful approach to understanding politics was also developed over the past few decades. Systems theory was borrowed from the biological sciences and the concept of ecology and is based on the idea of a **political system** as an organism with many parts dependent on one another and existing in a larger environment. Governmental structure is only one part of the system, acted upon and in turn acting upon the society in which it functions.

Thinking of the meeting described at the beginning of this chapter, we might consider the officials at the head table as the government. They make decisions, but not in a vacuum. They are influenced by **inputs,** including the speakers at the meeting, interest groups and lobbyists, the media, voters, and public opinion. Their decisions, which are referred to in systems theory as **outputs,** are public policies that regulate behavior or provide services. These policies usually affect the community positively or negatively and produce a response or **feedback.** Those who like the policies support the decision-makers; those who don't, demand change, completing the circle and taking us back to inputs. This process occurs in an **environment** that includes all the social, economic, and other characteristics of the community and those outside it that affect it, including the national economy and higher levels of government. Figure 1-1 illustrates a political system.

This is, of course, an oversimplified version of systems theory which, like other theories, is itself an oversimplification of what actually happens in real life. Systems theory is worth keeping in mind, however, because it alerts us to all of the elements of politics (not just government) and it emphasizes their interdependence. What happens in one part of the political system may affect others, just as in an ecological system. At the same time, the systems framework does not exclude theories of power or politi-

FIGURE 1-1   A Political System

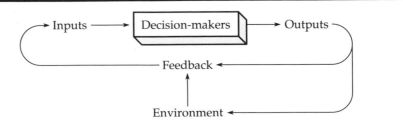

cal economy. If anything, it's a little too general, but that might be an advantage for beginning students of local politics since it includes so much and excludes so little.

A Practical Approach

Our study of local politics will include elements of all the approaches we've discussed, with systems theory as a broad framework. We begin in Part I by considering the socioeconomic, demographic, and intergovernmental context, or the environment of local politics. We move on in Part II to the formal institutions, structures, and political process of local government. In Part III, we turn to system inputs, including voters, elections, the media, and interest groups. We also focus our attention on community power structures as a summary of all we studied before. Part IV takes us to some of the outputs of the political system, including local taxing and spending and public policy issues such as crime, growth, and transportation. Finally, we consider current and future politics in metropolitan areas comprising dozens or even hundreds of local governments, a level of local politics that pertains to institutions, process, power, and political economy.

A few themes will run through our study. You can probably already guess what they are. One is power; another is political economy and the growth machine, which is discussed more in the next chapter. The chapter after that introduces another recurrent theme: the distinctions, conflicts, and competition between central cities and suburbs and between communities in the Sunbelt and those in the Frostbelt. Above all, however, our approach will be practical, emphasizing the nuts and bolts of local political institutions and procedures. The goal is for you to gain an understanding of politics in your own community, both as a student and as a citizen. You should use your community and the others around you as a learning laboratory, testing what this book says against what you observe there and vice versa. You should also gain practical knowledge that will help you as a citizen participant in the politics of your own community. Remember, though, that our aim is not just to learn about local politics where we live, but to learn more generally, so that we know what questions to ask to understand local politics wherever we live or wherever we go.

ESSENTIAL TERMS		
comparison	political economy
theories	growth machine
city-states	political system
city limits	inputs
institutional approach	outputs
community power studies	feedback
Marxist theories	environment
public choice theory	

FIELDWORK 1. Go to a meeting of your local city council or county board and write a description of your impressions. What do the building, the council chambers, and the people tell you? (Don't worry about official titles, who's who, or the details of the discussion, just treat it as theater and write a review. We'll have a more formal look at it later.)

2. If you've taken other political science courses, try to figure out what theoretical approach they took to the study of politics. Do they fit with any of those discussed in "Approaches" in terms of concepts, explanation, or prediction? If not, how do they differ? Could they be applied to the study of local politics or is it too different?

NOTES

[1]Paul E. Peterson, *City Limits*. Chicago: University of Chicago Press, 1981. See also Harvey Molotch, "The City as a Growth Machine," *American Journal of Sociology* 82, no. 2 (1976): 309–331.

[2]Mark Gottdiener, *The Decline of Urban Politics*. Newbury Park, CA: Sage, 1987, pp. 13–14. See also Paul Kantor and Stephen David, *The Dependent City*. Glenview, IL: Scott, Foresman, 1988; or Peterson, *City Limits*.

[3]Clarence Stone, "The Study of the Politics of Urban Development," in Clarence Stone and Heywood T. Sanders, eds., *The Politics of Urban Development*. Lawrence, KS: University Press of Kansas, 1987, pp. 4, 12, 16, 17.

[4]See Manuel Castells, *The Urban Question: A Marxist Approach*. Cambridge, MA: MIT Press, 1979; Susan Fainstein, et al., *Restructuring the City*, New York: Longman, 1986; or William Tabb, and Larry Sawers, eds., *Marxism and the Metropolis*. New York: Oxford University Press, 1978.

[5]See Vincent Ostrom, Charles M. Tiebout, and Robert Warren, "The Organization of Government in Metropolitan Areas," *The American Political Science Review* 60, no. 4 (1961): 831–842.

[6]Thomas R. Dye, "Governmental Structure, Urban Environment, and Educational Policy," *Midwest Journal of Political Science* 11, no. 3 (1967): 353–380.

[7]Peterson, pp. 69, 29.

[8]Molotch, p. 310.

[9]Stone, p. 4.

PART I

The Environment of Local Politics: The Socioeconomic, Demographic, and Intergovernmental Contexts

We begin our study of local politics not with the subject itself, but as systems theory might suggest, with its context or environment. We'll get to local government structures and institutions and to the political process, including mayors, council members, bureaucrats, lobbyists, voters, media, and others, in later chapters. But the environment in which these structures and actors function has such an influence on them that we need to start there.

The environment of local politics isn't just air, water, land, trees, and squirrels, although the physical setting is important. The environment of local politics also includes much more—anything, really, which might have an impact on the political process. We'll concentrate, however, on three broad influences: the socioeconomic, demographic, and intergovernmental environments of local politics. The socioeconomic environment of local politics includes such factors as size, density, diversity, psychology, geography, and economy. The demographic environment is the people who live in particular areas and how they vary from place to place around the country and within urban regions. We'll consider urbanization, suburbanization, and the rise of the Sunbelt as parts of the demographic environment. Then we'll become more explicitly political and turn to the intergovernmental context of local politics, developing the points introduced in chapter 1 about local politics as subordinate to state and national politics.

Studying these environmental elements will help us understand what goes on in local politics. Variation in these characteristics, which scientists call *variables,* may explain why local politics differ from place to place. Some social scientists even think they can predict local political phenomena from voter turnout to education spending on the basis of these characteristics, which we will refer to in later chapters on government structures and the political process.

Most analysts agree that local politics are influenced, perhaps even determined, by their socioeconomic, demographic, and intergovernmental environment. But as in any system, influence works both ways. Local politics, at least to some extent, shape their own environment. Local policies affect their physical and socioeconomic setting, and local political actions have an impact on state and national politics. The components of the system are interdependent, although that doesn't mean their power is equal. If any one element of local politics outweighs the others—and if any one element is overlooked in practical, day-to-day politics—it is surely the environment, which both imposes constraints and provides opportunities.

2

The Socioeconomic Environment of Local Politics: Characteristics of Urban Places

W e begin with the most basic elements of the environment of local politics, the broad and sometimes nebulous social and economic characteristics of communities. The size, density, diversity, social psychology, and economics of places significantly shape their politics, setting constraints and providing opportunities that communities try to control or transcend. Although each of these socioeconomic characteristics will be discussed separately, we should bear in mind that they are interrelated—they affect one another as well as local politics. We should also think of them as variables that, in their variation from one locality to another, help us explain and understand why elements of local politics such as structures of government, voter turnout, and interest group activity differ from place to place. We will refer to these socioeconomic characteristics constantly in the explicitly political chapters to come.

The Basics: Size, Density, and Diversity

The most basic characteristics that distinguish localities are size, density, and diversity. If we put these on a continuum (or line), at one end would be the hermit's cabin in the woods and at the other would be the great cities of the world, large in size and high in density and diversity. In between would be rural villages and towns, small cities and suburbs, and then larger and larger cities. We need not concern ourselves with the hermit, but our interest in local politics should direct our attention to all the others, at least to some extent. The chapters that follow concentrate on large cities and their suburbs, which is where most Americans live, but while these are clearly urban rather than rural places, urbanism is a matter of degree, defined, at least initially, by the variables of size, density, and diversity.[1]

Size

The simple number of residents defines the **size** of a community and, in general, more people mean more complexity, more problems, more politics, and more government. (See Table 2-1 for the largest cities in the United States.) Of course, larger cities also tend to be more dense and more diverse, which adds to their complexity. Whether large or small, however, communities of the same size are not all equally dense or diverse. These characteristics are related but may also vary independently, which is why we need to consider them separately.

Greater size usually means more politics and government because size requires organization. You've seen it in groups you belong to. Three or four people get along without leadership or structure; thirty or forty usually do not. Somebody steps in to set up rules or tell people what to do; they follow, propose an alternative, or drop out. Some people want power; others want a leader; some just want problems solved. Once one or two people get power, others may compete for it. Once one or two get what they want from the group or community, others may try to get what they want, too. That's politics, and some of it comes from increased size.

Density

If increased size precipitates politics and government, density makes them imperative. **Density** refers to the spatial or geographic concentration of

TABLE 2-1   The Largest Cities* in the United States, Ranked by 1990 Population

1. New York City	7,332,600	11. San Jose	782,200
2. Los Angeles	3,485,400	12. Indianapolis	742,000
3. Chicago	2,783,726	13. Baltimore	736,000
4. Houston	1,630,600	14. San Francisco	724,000
5. Philadelphia	1,545,600	15. Jacksonville	673,000
6. San Diego	1,110,600	16. Columbus	633,000
7. Detroit	1,028,000	17. Milwaukee	628,100
8. Dallas	1,006,900	18. Memphis	610,300
9. Phoenix	983,400	19. Washington, DC	607,900
10. San Antonio	935,900	20. Boston	574,300

Source: U.S. Bureau of the Census.
*Adjacent suburbs not included.

population—in other words, more people living closer together. Higher density puts enough people close together to create markets, factories, and social movements, and to support symphonies, head shops, and cafes, not to mention bridge clubs, street gangs, and gyms. In rural areas, people live too far apart to make many of the good (and bad) things of urban life possible. But higher density is also the source of physical and social problems associated with size, such as crime, traffic, and sanitation. If everybody lived far enough apart, these problems would not arise—but then neither would cities. See Table 2-2 for some sample densities.

Political activity and government arise from the need to solve problems brought by growth in size and density. In small communities with low density, people drill wells for water on their own land, but growth, especially if high in density, eventually makes this impossible and a communal water supply must be established, usually by government. In small communities with low density, people dispose of their own waste with latrines or septic tanks, but if growth occurs, too much waste may be

TABLE 2-2 Population Density per Square Mile for Selected World and U.S. Cities and Suburbs, 1990

Hong Kong	297,501
Cairo	97,106
Mexico City	40,037
Tokyo	25,019
Paris	20,185
Toronto	20,420
London	10,429
New York City	24,089
San Francisco	15,502
Jersey City, NJ	15,338
Chicago	12,378
Philadelphia	11,736
Miami	10,072
Washington, DC	9,883
Los Angeles	7,427
Detroit	7,411
San Jose, CA	4,567
Honolulu	4,412
Dallas	2,941
Phoenix	2,816
Arlington, TX	2,814
Palo Alto, CA	2,358
Danbury, CT	1,558
Scottsdale, AZ	808

Source: U.S. Bureau of the Census.

generated to be disposed of in this way since many latrines and septic tanks could pollute the water supply and spread disease. In small communities with low density, one house can burn down without taking all the others with it, but growth and proximity spread the danger. San Francisco burned down six times before 1851 because no one organized a fire-fighting group.

People often turn to volunteerism to solve problems like these. Neighbors get together to put in a water supply or sanitation system or to set up a volunteer fire department. Such solutions work for small communities, but in larger places, the problems are too big for citizen groups to handle and it is difficult to get everybody to participate and pay their fair share. Government is the obvious answer. Most of us are content with that, too busy and peripatetic to help with such basic needs (would a volunteer fire department work in your neighborhood?).

Physical problems such as sanitation and fire protection are not the only ones that increase with density. Social conflict can increase also. In rural areas, isolated residents probably couldn't hear a neighbor's noisy party; and they very rarely vent their anger on total strangers if only because they rarely see them. But in urban places with higher density, noise, crime, and violence are problems.

Intruding on one another's lives is a natural result of density, but conflict is not inevitable. Scientists experimenting with rats living in overcrowded (high density) conditions observed increased antisocial rat behavior, such as fighting, sexual deviance, and eating their own young. But when equally overcrowded rat colonies were better organized, with plenty to eat, one-way paths, and more nest holes, antisocial behavior decreased. The problem was not density but how the density was organized.

The same applies to communities, some of which organize density better than others. Sometimes this is done informally and culturally. Expectations of personal space, for example, are lower in most urban cultures. Personal space is the distance from strangers at which people feel comfortable. Most Americans like 2 or 3 feet, while Europeans tolerate less, and Asians even less, partly because higher densities have taught—or forced—them to. People in dense communities learn to establish their personal space by drawing in upon themselves and avoiding eye contact with strangers in crowded places. When Los Angeles opened its new Metro mass transit system, riders accustomed to the privacy of their own automobiles were given lessons on maintaining personal space in public. When you next ride a bus or subway, observe for yourself how people cope.

Other informal customs also help. In some places, people queue up or get in line for buses, trains, or tickets to movies. It's a way of managing a crowd and it usually comes from the crowd itself, which enforces the rules by informing violators that they're breaking the line. In Britain, people on escalators stand on the right and walk on the left, so those in a hurry can get by. Small signs directing people to do this are posted on most escalators, but strangers learn the rule quickly from observation—or from people in a hurry. Sharing a table in a crowded restaurant or a taxi at rush hour are other informal ways of dealing with density.

All these social niceties are ways of **coping with density** and reducing social conflict. They make it easier—and safer—for people to live in urban places. Significantly, societies with strong cultural traditions of managing density also have lower rates of crime and mental illness. In U.S. cities, where the cultural organization of density is weak, crime rates are far higher than in much more crowded cities elsewhere. The annual murder rates of Japan and Britain, for example, are 1.2 and 3.0 per 100,000 people, while the U.S. rate is 9.4 per 100,000. Some countries with low crime rates may be more authoritarian than the United States; most have gun control laws and less racial and ethnic conflict because they are not as diverse as the United States. But their sophisticated cultural ways of coping with density also mitigate social conflict.

When cultural controls don't work, just as when private latrines and volunteer fire fighting become inadequate, the burden of organizing density and mitigating social conflict may fall on the government. Indeed, higher density generally means more government (and politics). Police were among the first agents of social control established by local governments. Any police officer will tell you that she or he deals not only with crime but with all sorts of social and antisocial behavior. Teachers and social workers perform some of the same functions. Traffic management, from stop signs and traffic lights to one-way streets, pedestrian crossings, and bike lanes, is another governmental way of managing density. So is land-use planning.

Given current antigovernment attitudes, we should note that most local governments were initially created because people wanted help with some basic and urgent problems, often arising from growth in size and density. Many governmental programs were similarly instigated not by government itself, but by citizens demanding services. Once established, the resulting bureaucracy may expand on its own initiative, finding more and more to do even when we don't want it (although somebody else probably does), but before condemning government too vehemently, we should remember that people like us probably created it to provide services we still want.

Diversity

The complexities introduced by size and density are augmented by a third associated variable: **diversity.** Rural communities tend to be populated by people who are more or less alike in terms of race, ethnicity, and culture, but as population increases, so does diversity. Just as communities vary in size and density, so they vary in diversity, from **homogeneous** (similar) to **heterogeneous** (mixed). Besides race, ethnicity, and culture, diversity may include class, occupation, age, sexual orientation, life-style, attitudes, and more. Diversity is what makes cities so exciting, with so many different people to watch and cultures to experience, including a choice of shops, restaurants, and entertainment. But like size and density, increased diversity complicates social life, and communities have to find ways of coping with it.

Some people have difficulty dealing with others unlike themselves. Their intolerance may lead to hostility, conflict, and violence. The cultural ways of dealing with density discussed above may break down when diversity increases because new people with different cultures can be slow or reluctant to learn local ways. Immigration, especially when the immigrants are unlike those who arrived earlier, often causes social strain. Hostility toward the new arrivals may also result from economic fears about greater competition for scarce jobs and low-cost housing. If, as a consequence, conflict increases, then so does the need for formal or governmental conflict management, resulting in more police, teachers, and social workers, and perhaps even traffic signs in different languages.

Segregation—voluntary or mandatory—is another common way of reacting to diversity. Groups of people choose particular neighborhoods for comfort and convenience, to be near people who share their race, ethnicity, religion, or language, or to avoid confrontation with others unlike themselves. We all know of cities with a Chinatown, a Little Italy, a Jewish neighborhood, a gay area, a black ghetto, or a Latino barrio, as well as rich, poor, working-, and middle-class neighborhoods of various races and ethnic groups. Even age groups such as young singles, elders, and families tend to cluster. Most people prefer to live with others like themselves, so often these gatherings are by choice. But choice is limited for many people. In the past, racial and ethnic groups have been segregated by law. These laws have been repealed, although the patterns of segregation they created survive in many places. More perniciously, subtle and informal racial discrimination maintains and increases segregation when minorities are steered to certain neighborhoods by real estate agents, denied loan applications by mortgage lenders, or rebuffed by home sellers. Despite decades of protest and increasing legal protection against discrimination, this problem persists and in some areas is growing worse.[2]

Contemporary segregation results not only from the preferences of groups of people and discrimination, but also from the economics of housing. Local governments zone certain kinds of housing in different areas. Some are designated for high-density apartments, others for single family homes with yards, still others for grand estates. Although the law may say anybody can live in these neighborhoods, the price of housing keeps many out. This is basically **segregation by class,** but since the average income of minorities is less than that of whites, it translates, some say unintentionally, into segregation by race. Only the rich have complete choice about where they live.

This class segregation is strengthened by the way urban areas of the United States are broken down into many local governments. We will return to this subject in the next two chapters, but for now it will do to understand that instead of one big city with one government, encompassing an entire urbanized area, most urban areas have a large city and many smaller ones, each with its own government that inevitably acts to protect its residents—and the racial and class homogeneity of their communities. Even within a highly diverse urban area, communities with their own local government may thus be homogeneous. In short, one way urban areas cope with diversity is by breaking it up into bits that do not have to deal with one another. Many urban dwellers only observe diversity, it has been said, when they drive past it on the freeway.

Even if we'd like to, however, most of us who live in urban areas can't insulate ourselves completely from people unlike ourselves. We have to learn another way of coping with diversity: **tolerance.** In fact, we have no choice. If we as city dwellers yelled insults or ran away every time we saw somebody who was different—in color, looks, dress, manner, language, or whatever—we'd wind up institutionalized. Instead, we learn from experience that the vast majority of "different" people are going about their own business. Experience with diversity makes most of us more tolerant: we cope with diversity by accepting it. At best, this leads us to recognize diversity not as negative and threatening but as positive and stimulating, even to taking pride in friendships with people who are not like ourselves.

Cities in the United States are arguably the most diverse in the world, which makes coping with diversity both more important and more difficult. Tolerance, segregation, and government agents of social control such as police can be overwhelmed, especially if other pressures, such as accelerated immigration and recession, are added to the mix. Urban societies can break under the strain, exploding into riots like those in Los Angeles in 1965 (Watts) and 1992 (South Central). Such strains and explosions usually lead to calls for more government action, thus taking us back to politics.

But diversity adds something to politics besides a need to cope, something more positive. To begin with, if diversity increases tolerance, it enhances democracy. We are more willing to accept the rule of the majority in elections and to protect the rights of minorities—both essential elements of democracy—when we do not fear or hate our fellow citizens. Diversity usually also acts as a stimulant to local politics, as it does with so much else in urban life. In small, homogeneous places, one group dominates. As communities grow, however, other groups emerge, organize, and demand their rights and privileges. Seeing the benefits these groups have gained—

jobs, elective offices, a community center, a special holiday—leads other new or previously unorganized groups to get together and demand their share. Organization and participation stimulate more organization and participation.

As a consequence, politics in heterogeneous communities are usually more competitive and interesting, with more participation by individual voters and organized groups than in homogeneous places. Power tends to be more broadly distributed, too. This could, and often does, mean more conflict, which can become nasty or result in gridlock. But conflict at least means different interests are being expressed and people have some choice. Homogeneous communities tend to be in general agreement or consensus about political matters, which usually brings low levels of participation, the suppression of some interests, low competition, and limited choices. For all the problems that accompany diversity (mostly due to intolerance) it also brings excitement, vitality, stimulation, and greater participation to community life and politics.

Size, Density, and Diversity.   Although these three characteristics or variables have been considered separately, they are closely associated elements of community life. Large cities are usually not only great in size but also in density and diversity; small communities, conversely, are of lesser size, density, and diversity. The impacts of these factors vary accordingly in large and small communities and in those that fall between the two extremes. Their politics vary similarly, as we will see.

Economics and Local Politics

Like size, density, and diversity, the economic structure of communities varies and significantly affects their politics. Rural economies are relatively simple, based on agriculture and a limited number of activities. Urban economies are far more complicated, with elaborate specialization, a high degree of interdependence, massive concentrations of wealth and power, and a more varied class structure. Politics in rural and urban places vary accordingly, as do politics in urban places with different degrees of economic development and vitality. Most urban scholars agree that economics is the reason for the existence of and the key to success for modern cities, and some political economists argue that economic expansion or growth is the key to local politics as well.

Geography

The physical setting or **geography** of places is perhaps the obvious element of their economies. Most of the great cities of the world developed on sites with transportation advantages, such as rivers, natural harbors, or roads that were major trade routes. In the nineteenth century, man-made canals and railroads expanded the network and created other cities, as did freeways and airports in this century. Communities at junctions of any of these systems have a particular advantage. Other cities developed near a valuable natural resource, such as coal, iron, or oil.

But geography can be limiting, too, as the ghost towns of the world attest. The resource that helped build up a city may be depleted or the transportation mode may become obsolete. Physical barriers like mountains and oceans or limited resources like water may restrict expansion, as may the threat of floods or earthquakes. And smog produced by the combination of physical geography, meteorology, industry, and reliance on automobile transportation now threatens the viability of some cities. Yet some places defy their geographic destiny. Los Angeles, the second largest urban area in the United States, is built in a desert smog basin without its own water and with no valuable natural resources except some oil and a lot of sunshine. Its transportation advantages, including its railroads, harbor, freeways, and airports, have all been manufactured. Economic entrepreneurs and politics made Los Angeles, just as they have enabled other communities to transcend their physical settings. This is accomplished in part by the evolution of more complex economic arrangements.

Specialization and Interdependence

In the most primitive rural societies, people take care of most of their own needs, building their homes, growing their food, making their clothing, and entertaining themselves. Of course, such self-sufficiency is rare even in the most rural parts of the United States today, but rural residents remain more self-sufficient than people who live in urban areas. Urban residents specialize in trades and professions and depend on one another to exchange goods and services. We do not build our own homes, grow our own food, make our own clothes, or entertain ourselves. In fact, the better off we are, the more we leave to others to do for us. Almost none of us—not even scavenging street people—are remotely self-sufficient.

The more sophisticated the urban economy, the more industrial or postindustrial it becomes, the more specific and narrow the **specialization** becomes. People do what they do best or what is available for them to do and, hopefully, they earn enough money to buy what they need from other specialists and thrive or at least survive. But specialization requires a diversity of people to provide and use the different specialties. Restaurants, shops, businesses of all kinds, services from resume writing to house cleaning—all need to find their clienteles, and the more people there are in an area, the more likely there will be enough to support them. As generations of sociologists have observed, specialization is intrinsic to cities.

Specialization is a major source of the diversity of urban places, and thus of the delights of urban life. It affects local politics by multiplying the interests that may organize and demand their say. But specialization also affects community life by increasing our **interdependence** or need for one another. In a highly specialized economy, we need one another for the day-to-day exchange of goods and services, but we also need one another for the overall viability of the local economy. Environmentalists who demand local limits on growth almost always win public sympathy until somebody points out that limiting growth will mean fewer jobs in the construction and real estate industries. Maybe that would directly affect only a small percentage of the population, but the other workers and businesses who serve them would soon feel the pinch, too. In a specialized, interdependent economy, what happens in one sector has a ripple effect on others. Individuals and communities thus rally to protect local industry, even at the expense of their own environment or, sometimes, other communities.

Like individuals, cities were once relatively self-sufficient, producing most of what they needed in conjunction with surrounding rural areas. Cities began to specialize long ago, however, and the greatest cities achieved their stature by trading with others. The industrial revolution and modern transportation and communication technology increased trade and specialization. As a consequence, few cities remain self-sufficient, even in combination with nearby agrarian areas, and most specialize to some degree. Detroit makes cars, New York has Wall Street, Los Angeles has film and television industries, San Jose (Silicon Valley) makes computers, Washington has government, and so on. Smaller cities may be so dominated by a single industry that they are, in effect, company towns.

Specialization is a two-edged sword, however. A successful specialty can bring economic boom and well-being, but if a specialty falls out of favor, a boomtown becomes a ghost town. Learning from the lessons of Detroit, Pittsburgh (steel), Akron, Ohio (rubber), the textile manufacturing towns of New England, and others, many cities try to ensure their economic well-being by diversifying, but since the location of industry is decided by private companies rather than local government, their ability to do this is limited. Diversifying also means cities compete with one another for valued industry. Much to the chagrin of the cities of California's Silicon Valley, high-tech industries can locate just about anywhere they please today, with lavish enticements from local governments. Silicon Valley's cities must compete just to keep what they have.

Cities also depend on other cities as markets. That is, cities, like individuals, are interdependent. They need one another to exchange what they make and do; they need one another to survive. But unlike individuals, cities do not function in communities and rarely rally to protect one another's interests. More often, they compete with one another, partly due to tax structures imposed on them by states and partly due to their own internal politics. These forces combine to make local governments into growth machines, a concept that we will return to momentarily.

Wealth, Class, and Power

Urban economies are also characterized by great concentrations of wealth and elaborate class structures, both of which have their impact on politics and power.

Concentrated wealth in rural places is mainly in the form of land ownership, and class structure may amount to little more than the owner and the farm workers. Owners of small farms, shops, and a few professionals such as doctors and teachers fall between landowners and workers in the class structure, but the system is relatively simple. In terms of politics and power, no one can compete with the landowners, whether individual or corporate.

In urban places, land is even more valuable and its ownership is still important. Much local political activity is devoted to increasing land values. Other sources of wealth emerge from some of these developments. The great traders and merchants, such as department store owners and industrialists, join landowners at the top of the local class structure, often exceeding them in wealth. After all, it takes a massive concentration of wealth to build factories, high-rise office buildings, and shopping centers. When these individuals live in the communities where their businesses operate, they almost invariably exercise great power. Even when such facilities are branches of a national corporation rather than locally owned businesses, they are powerful as institutions (usually on a narrower range of issues).

Such massive **concentrations of wealth** affect local politics because they alter the distribution of power. The great economic interests often agree on political issues, generally supporting growth, for example. But as economies develop and diversify, the number of economic powerhouses may grow and diverge on some issues. Landowners, the building industry, retailers, manufacturers, and the service industries, not to mention locally owned and branch-plant operations, have slightly different interests that may affect local politics. Local landowners, for example, may be prepared to accept tax increases to pay for better services, while corporate branch plants threaten to leave town. Downtown high-rise developers and retailers fight shopping malls. Manufacturers push for better planning to provide more affordable housing and better transportation for their workers, while landowners and developers push for unbridled growth. These differences might be small, but there are no differences at all in communities dominated by a single major landowner or industrialist.

Growth and economic expansion alter not only the ownership of wealth in communities, but also their class structures. These, too, become much more elaborate. Whereas the class structure of a simple rural society or company town might amount to little more than owner and workers, that of a sophisticated urban economy comprises many strata. At the top, the wealthiest may be several cuts above land- and factory owners. At the bottom, the street people and urban underclass rank well below the working class. Most significantly, the class in between is usually large and is itself diversified to include a lower-middle, middle, and upper-middle class. These are the office workers, teachers, government workers, small business operators, managers, lawyers, doctors, and others, shading eventually into the bottom reaches of the upper class. Out of these classes come neighborhood, environmental, and other groups that may challenge economic elites and particularly the growth machine, since they do not perceive themselves as being dependent on it.

The elaboration of the **class structure** in large urban places increases diversity and political conflict. Although class consciousness is low in the United States, the classes sometimes perceive and express their differing political interests. The segregation of urban areas by class is an expression of these interests, and class conflict in cities is most visible when neighborhoods defend themselves against outsiders or other neighborhoods, invariably of a class lower than their own. On a larger scale, unionized workers challenged the capitalist upper class in some cities in the nineteenth and early twentieth centuries. The political dominance of the old Yankee upper class in many cities was displaced by the immigrant working class organized by political machines, and the machines were, in turn, deposed by a reform movement that relied on the votes of the burgeoning urban middle class. In both cases, these classes gained advantages, although major economic interests were accommodated by both machine and reform. In more recent years, class has been a factor in the battle to control growth in some communities. The 1980s surge in homelessness and the 1992 riot in Los Angeles, which was as much about class as about race, are other recent reminders of both class structure and politics.[3]

The City as a Growth Machine

In addition to size, density, diversity, and the economic characteristics discussed above, sociologist Harvey Molotch adds that "the political and economic essence of virtually any given locality, in the present American context is growth."[4] According to Molotch, local "land-based" elites seek profits "through the increasing intensification of land use" and "governmental authority, at the local and nonlocal levels, is utilized to assist in achieving this growth at the expense of competing localities."[5] Landowners and builders are in the forefront of this **growth machine,** but they are often joined by other economic interests, such as retailers and manufacturers, who also stand to benefit. The promise of jobs and housing often wins public and governmental support for growth, and local government has its own vested interest in growth as a means of increasing its tax base.

Of course, others also engage in local politics in pursuit of their own interests. People seek to protect the quality of life in their neighborhoods, not to mention the property value of their homes. Minorities and others who perceive themselves as disadvantaged try to get help. Businesses attempt to use local government to increase their profits through lower taxes, improved parking, and the like—and by supporting the growth machine as well.

But while other interests are active and growth is not the only issue in local politics, virtually every community is and must be concerned about its economic viability. Localities act as growth machines because of the political power of local economic interests and the inevitable competition among communities for economic well-being. And state governments add to the growth imperative through the structures of taxation and regulations they impose on local governments.

Thus, we need to be aware of the economic context of local politics, including specialization, interdependence, the concentration of wealth, the elaboration of class structures, and Molotch's summarizing conception of localities as growth machines, a theme that will recur repeatedly in the chapters that follow.

The Social Psychology of Urban Life

The way people relate to one another and their society and the way they think about themselves in relation to society are shaped by the characteristics of communities discussed above, and this social psychology has its own impact on local politics. Urban sociologists such as Louis Wirth (see note 1) look at society in terms of primary and secondary social groups. The former are predominant in rural societies and small towns, while the latter exist in more urban settings.

Primary Groups

Primary groups center on the family—not just the nuclear families of parents and children that most of us are accustomed to, but extended families that include parents, children, grandparents, aunts, uncles, and cousins. Such extended families are most commonly found in rural societies, villages, and small towns, where people know not only their own family but everybody else. Here, people depend on one another, with several family members working together on a farm or in a small business. Even when people in such societies specialize, they know one another not only in terms of their economic roles (as farmer, landowner, merchant, teacher, or student), but as complete people, members of the community with family ties.

Such places have a strong **sense of community** and identity, of warmth and intimacy. People feel they belong and they know who they are. They always greet one another, and when they ask "How are you?" they may really want to know. They keep an eye on one another's kids. They care for each other and take care of members of the community who need assistance. Helping an elderly person carry something is not an anonymous act of good will, but a favor to a classmate's grandmother—*not* helping will mean a lecture on manners. The person passed out on the street isn't an anonymous alcoholic to be stepped around, but the familiar town drunk—the father or uncle of somebody known. Instead of avoidance, people are more likely to help such a person. Members of the community with mental disabilities may also be accepted and assisted rather than institutionalized. Small communities may only have one town drunk or one developmentally disabled person to cope with, which makes it easier, but knowing them as members of the community rather than reducing them to stereotypes based on their disability is even more important.

This idyll has its darker side, however. Such communities can be oppressive and conformist. Everybody knows everybody, and they mind one another's business. Kids don't cut school without their parents hearing about it. The old lady up the road sits on her front porch all day watching traffic—and reports speeders or even loud music to whoever will listen. The way you dress, your haircut, the company you keep, and your behavior will all be observed and commented upon. If you step out of line, the whole town will know. Strangers are noticed, warily watched, and welcomed only if they have a local connection and fit in. Such informal social control reduces the need for government, which may be good, but it also oppresses people who don't follow all the rules or who are misfits. The alcoholic mentioned above doesn't need a social worker or a half-way house, but he won't get therapy, and the community's disapproval will be made known. They only put up with him because he was born there. Others, such as loners, homosexuals, women who want careers, men who don't want to go into the family business, people with different political views—anybody who doesn't fit the cozy norm—are also disapproved of and often isolated. The power of this disapproval and isolation is greater because of the tight-knit nature of the community. People who fit in feel happy and complete; those who do not tend to be miserable or leave.

Cities of Strangers

When societies urbanize, primary groups break down. In the more developed economies of cities, people are not as dependent on one another as they were on the family farm or business. Thanks to specialization, individuals get jobs and support themselves; they rent apartments and get away from the family home. In cities, the extended family shrinks to the nuclear family, and even that may break up. Family members spread out through an urban area or even further. They lose the sense of community and identity of rural places, but they also escape the pressure to conform. People no longer meddle in their lives. Instead, people ignore them. They are free, but alone.

Economic specialization makes the freedom possible and the sense of isolation inevitable. We don't spend our days with our families and other people who know us but with strangers who, despite the occasional "Have a nice day," do not treat us as whole human beings but as roles: students, teachers, customers, check-outs, bosses, workers, passersby. We aren't greeted by everyone on the street; no one really wants to know how we are; we step around drunks and ignore old ladies with heavy parcels. We don't want to get involved; we're all strangers. In a well-known 1991 incident in Los Angeles, a Korean shopkeeper shot and killed a young black woman in a dispute about whether the woman was shoplifting a can of soda. Besides the clash of cultures, these were strangers dealing with one another in an unfriendly city, a situation that wouldn't arise between two residents of a small town.

"Great cities," urbanist Jane Jacobs has observed, "are not like towns, only larger. They differ from towns and suburbs in basic ways, and one of these is that cities are, by definition, full of strangers. In small settlements everyone knows your affairs. In the city everyone does not—only those you choose to tell will know about you. This is one of the attributes of cities that is precious to most city people."[6] Many of us thrive on this freedom and privacy and would feel stifled in a small town. Others feel alienated from the society around them—lost, lonely, unloved, sad, even angry.

Secondary Groups

Secondary groups are a response to these urban social conditions. Whereas people are born into primary groups, they join secondary groups on a voluntary basis because of some shared interest. Such groups may be economic (a union, chamber of commerce, or a network of professional women, for example), or they may be ethnic, religious, cultural, or athletic. They can be anything that interests any two or more city dwellers, and one of the nice things about cities is that they are big and diverse enough to supply people who share almost any interest. These groups give people an identity, a sense of belonging and community to replace the primary-group connection they've lost, but membership is voluntary, not a passive birthright. People can choose—to join, quit, or join another group—but they must act. Cities let people blossom, not only because they are freer, but because they can develop their own interests, whatever they may be— unless, of course, they are too overwhelmed by alienation to act, as many people are.

The Search for Community

The loss of primary group connections is also expressed in a restless **search for community.** People look for places to belong to, such as particular neighborhoods or outlying suburbs, hoping to reclaim some of the benefits of small town life. Both urban neighborhoods and suburban places often call themselves "villages" or "towns," and people often say they are "from" these places rather than from the larger urban entity of which they are a part. Fierce loyalties and rivalries sometimes develop and may be expressed in competition between schools and sports teams—or street gangs. Urban neighborhoods and suburban places, however, often deliver less sense of community than their residents hope for because they are never as intimate as small towns. People do not spend all their time in such places—they work, shop, and visit friends and relations elsewhere—and they don't get to know one another as well as people do in small towns. Some urban areas nevertheless develop a sense of community, especially if they have common meeting places, such as a park, shopping area, or bar, or if lots of people walk or take public transportation and get to know one another that way. Neighborhood newspapers or newsletters also help, and many neighborhood groups consciously work to build community to increase their political efficacy. Some neighborhoods and suburbs may thus offer a good compromise between the oppressive intimacy of the small town and the isolation of urban places. People know one another well enough to pay attention to one another without intrusively minding each other's business.

Segregation.   Less positively, the identity of neighborhoods and suburbs is usually based on segregation, an almost universal response to the alienation of living among strangers. As noted in our discussion of segregation as a way of dealing with diversity, most people seem to prefer to be among others like themselves. Persistent racial and economic discrimination have made segregation a serious problem in the United States, but this phenomenon is not unique to U.S. cities. "Segregation by neighborhoods," declares urbanist Mark La Gory, "is universal in modern societies because it is, in some sense, functional. It maintains order in a potentially disorderly society, . . . makes everyday life more predictable for the city dweller, . . . minimizes the risks of conflict, and promotes social solidarity."[7] Equally, it is discriminatory, oppressive, and a source of social conflict. La Gory's point is not to defend segregation, but to understand its near inevitability.

Government.　Yet another response to the breakdown of primary groups in urban places is increased government. In rural areas and small towns, much social control is informal, carried out by the community itself. People watch out for and help one another, keeping each other in line and providing protection from outsiders. But in a city of strangers, these mechanisms break down. People don't know one another and don't want to get involved; they don't know who belongs and who doesn't. Many behaviors that would be castigated in small towns are ignored in cities, so people are freer. But some behaviors are unacceptable even in cities, so formal or governmental agents of social control, such as police, social workers, teachers, truant officers, and health and safety inspectors, replace at least some of the informal controls of smaller communities. Alcoholics, the elderly, or the mentally ill are institutionalized rather than cared for by their families or communities. Urban social connections have grown so weak that we don't even protect one another from criminals, so police organize neighborhood watch programs, introducing neighbors to one another and asking them to exchange phone numbers and keep an eye on one another's homes.

Thus, cities free us from the oppression of tight rural societies and small towns, but often leave us feeling alone and lonely, without the protection and sense of community such places provide. These differences are the result of the size, density, diversity, and economics of urban places, yet they have their own impact on local politics, stimulating the formation of interest groups, the search for community, segregation, and reliance on government as an agent of social control.

The Socioeconomic Environment of Local Politics

The size, density, diversity, economics, and psychology of communities shape their politics. Variation in these characteristics helps explain why local politics differ from place to place. The characteristics are related, however, usually varying not independently, but in concert. We might, therefore, consider them measures of urbanism—the greater they are, the more urban the community. Urbanism is thus a matter of degree, with communities ranging from rural to suburban and urban, from villages and towns to small, middle-sized, and great cities. See the Glossary of Places that follows for definitions of terms that describe communities. Each place is unique, yet all share some characteristics, with some characteristics being distributed among the different sorts of communities in clear patterns. These patterns will become more apparent as we consider the demographic context of local politics in the next chapter.

A Glossary of Places

Rural: People live in relative isolation in the countryside, with farming the primary activity.

Urban: A large, diverse population living close together with a highly specialized and interdependent economy; describes a social, economic, and cultural, but not necessarily governmental, entity.

Suburban: A smaller, less diverse population living in lower densities on the periphery of big cities and traditionally dependent on them; more urban than rural.

Central City: The dominant city in an urban area—the largest, oldest, and most diverse. It is also self-governing and is the economic center of the region.

Neighborhood: A part of a city with its own distinct identity, but not self-governing.

Suburb: A community adjacent to a central city with less urban characteristics (suburban) and its own local government (as distinct from a neighborhood).

Town: A relatively self-contained community with a population of a few thousand, separate from other communities and probably, but not necessarily, with its own government; in some northeastern states, it is also a unit of local government equivalent to a city or municipality.

City or Municipality: A legal or incorporated local government, created by citizen petition and state recognition (see chapter 4). Primary functions include police, fire protection, land use, streets and traffic, public works, parks, libraries. Suburbs or towns are technically cities or municipalities if they are incorporated.

County: A form of local government created by states to carry out specific functions, usually including elections, justice, welfare, health, and transit, and limited services such as police, fire protection, parks, and libraries for rural areas. Counties may contain several cities. (See chapter 4.)

Urban Area or Metropolitan Region: An urbanized area with many cities and often more than one county, but usually without a single government of its own (see chapter 14).

ESSENTIAL TERMS		
size	specialization
density	interdependence
coping with density	concentration of wealth
diversity	class structure
homogeneous	growth machine
heterogeneous	primary groups
segregation	sense of community
segregation by class	secondary groups
tolerance	search for community
geography	

FIELDWORK 1. Use census data (available at your library) to calculate the size, density, diversity, and extent of economic specialization of your community. Consider what the data you collect might imply about local politics (use only this chapter as a reference).

2. Select a few public places, such as a bus, park bench, shopping center, or just a street, and observe the ways density and diversity are coped with, both formally (by police or traffic signs, for example) or informally (by social custom). If possible, repeat this exercise in two communities with different degrees of density and diversity.

3. Analyze the social arrangements in your own life in terms of primary and secondary groups. How urban are you? Are you typical of your community? What does this suggest about local politics?

NOTES [1]See the classic Louis Wirth, "Urbanism as a Way of Life," *American Journal of Sociology,* 44 (July 1938): 1–24.

[2]See Gary A. Tobin, ed., *Divided Neighborhoods: Changing Patterns of Racial Segregation,* (Urban Affairs Annual Review 32). Newbury Park, CA: Sage, 1987.

[3]Although racial conflict precipitated and pervaded the Los Angeles riot, businesses were often targets no matter who owned them, and the rioters' resentment of the privileged classes was clear, not least to the privileged classes themselves.

[4]Harvey Molotch, "The City as a Growth Machine," *American Journal of Sociology,* 82, no. 2 (1976): 310. See also Stephen L. Elkin, *City and Regime in the American Republic.* Chicago: University of Chicago Press, 1987; Paul E. Peterson, *City Limits.* Chicago: University of Chicago Press, 1981.

[5]Molotch, p. 309.

[6]Jane Jacobs, *The Death and Life of Great American Cities.* New York: Vintage, 1961, p. 126.

[7]Mark La Gory, "The Organization of Space and the Character of the Urban Experience," *Publius* 18 (Fall 1988): 77.

3

The Demographic Environment of Local Politics: Where People Live and Why

The characteristics of urban places discussed in the last chapter are not evenly distributed among localities. Some are larger, denser, more diverse, and more economically complex than others. In this chapter, we will examine the distribution of these characteristics by focusing on the demographic environment of local politics. **Demography** is derived from the Greek word *demos* (people) and means the study of populations. We will consider where particular sorts of people live and why, including how they group into central cities or suburbs within urban regions. These population patterns have such a significant impact on local politics that we might say that for local government, demography is destiny. Population characteristics shape the problems communities face and the resources they have to deal with them, as well as voting behavior, interest group activity, government structures, and who holds power.

Three population movements of enormous magnitude have affected local politics in the United States. The first, running through the nineteenth and twentieth centuries, is urbanization, the movement to cities. The second, occurring mostly in this century, is suburbanization, the movement to the periphery of large cities. The third, a phenomenon of the past fifty years, is the move to the southern and western states of the Sunbelt. Each has its own causes and its own unique social and economic arrangements, and each has its own impact on local politics, in both the individual communities that resulted from the movement and in relations among communities in urban regions, states, and the nation.

Urbanization: The Move to the Cities

Urbanization or the movement from rural areas to cities is an ancient phenomenon. People have been drawn to cities for protection from enemies or a hostile environment, for economic and intellectual opportunities, and for the freedom described in the last chapter. Cities have long been centers of trade, government, religion, education, and culture, as they are today. For centuries, urbanization was slow, however, because economies were based on agriculture, and the vast majority of people in most countries remained in rural areas. Growth in international trade accelerated urbanization in some countries in the seventeenth and eighteenth centuries, but it was technological change and the industrial revolution in the nineteenth century that gave impetus to urbanization and produced the cities we live in now. In 1790, only 5 percent of the U.S. population was urban. In 1990, after two centuries of urbanization, 78 percent lived in urban areas. As in other countries, many Americans left the countryside for the city for economic reasons. But U.S. urbanization was also greatly and uniquely augmented by the arrival of millions of immigrants from other countries seeking both economic and political freedom.

Changes in rural areas and economies made urbanization possible and even necessary. Cities depend on the countryside for food, so rural dwellers must produce far more than they themselves need in order to sustain the cities. The eighteenth and nineteenth centuries brought scientific farming techniques, which increased production, but the huge agricultural surpluses needed for massive urban growth were given even greater stimulus by the industrial revolution, itself an urban phenomenon. The manufacture of farm machinery facilitated more intensive agriculture, while the canals and railroads of the industrial revolution provided more extensive markets because agricultural products could be shipped further, faster, without spoiling. But mechanized agriculture required larger farms with fewer workers, even as the rural population grew due to better health and lower death rates. In the United States, the frontier provided a safety valve for excess rural population for a long time, as people moved further and further west to homestead little farms. But the frontier ran out in the nineteenth century. Some parts of the West were too arid or mountainous to cultivate and others, such as California, were parcelled out in large land holdings rather than small homesteads as in the East and Midwest.

Industrialization

Much as many people might have preferred life on the farm or in small towns, excess rural population and the lack of economic opportunity pushed them toward the city. But the city exerted a powerful pull, too. "Every major urban area is a magnet," says Seattle Mayor Norm Rice.

"Some people come in hope, some to hide."[1] All through history, people have eagerly gone to cities to be free of the oppression and conformity of rural life and to pursue their own interests, including economic opportunity. **Industrialization** vastly expanded such opportunities in cities with millions of factory jobs. Conditions in rural areas gave people a push, while cities exerted the pull of opportunity. Individuals and whole families could find work and make their way, as millions did. New technologies made the factories of the industrial revolution possible and facilitated urban growth in other ways as well. Modern factories needed lots of workers who, at least initially, needed to be near the workplace, which led to higher urban densities. Improved sanitation and taller buildings made such densities possible. Transportation in the form of trolleys, railroads, and buses eventually provided access for workers living further away, enabling the city to expand.

Immigration and Internal Migration

Industrialization and urbanization proceeded apace in the United States after the Civil War. Immigrants flocked to the cities from all over the world, creating in the United States both a unique pattern of urbanization and uniquely diverse cities. Their arrival and the emergence of an industrial working class also produced dramatic political change. Between 1870 and 1890, about 8 million immigrants arrived, and most went straight to the great cities of the northeastern United States, which was the center of the industrial revolution. Foreign **immigration** peaked with 8.8 million newcomers between 1901 and 1910, then declined during World War I and in the 1920s, when strict immigration quotas were imposed. In the 1930s, only half a million immigrants arrived. Big cities continued to grow, however, because an internal migration of Appalachian whites, Puerto Ricans, and especially southern African Americans. Changes in southern agriculture, with large-scale, mechanized farming replacing labor-intensive sharecropping and racist barriers to other options provided the push while jobs in factories and ports (especially during World War II) provided the pull. Millions made the move in what has been termed the Great Migration. By 1990, 30 percent of all African Americans were living in New York, Chicago, Philadelphia, or Detroit.

The Postindustrial City

Together, industrialization and immigration built the great U.S. cities of the early part of this century. Then, in the face of international competition, after World War II, U.S. manufacturing industry began to decline. Blue-collar industrial workers were outnumbered by white-collar office workers and professionals in the United States as early as 1956.[2] In the decades that followed, urban growth was greatest in the service-dominated economies of **postindustrial cities,** which specialized in finance, insurance, government, communications, entertainment, tourism, and trade. New technologies, especially in communications, data processing, and transportation, facilitated the development of these postindustrial cities, many of which were in the South or West rather than the traditionally urban Northeast.

Urban Places and Metropolitan Statistical Areas

The economics and geography of urbanization have changed over the years, as growth shifted to the edges of cities and then to the postindustrial cities of the South and West, but Americans have continued to concentrate in ever greater numbers in urban areas. By 1920, over half of all Americans lived in what the Bureau of Census calls **urban places.** This figure is a little deceptive, however, because the bureau defines urban places as geographic areas with populations of more than 2,500. Some of these are really villages, not cities, and even isolated places with larger populations would be thought of by most of us as towns rather than cities or urban places.

A more useful indicator of urbanization is what the Census Bureau calls **Metropolitan Statistical Areas (MSAs).** These include at least one city of 50,000 or more people and the surrounding area, including other cities and counties with urban populations that interact with the central city and one another.[3] Table 3-1 and Figure 3-1 show U.S. urbanization in terms of MSAs. Each MSA may contain dozens or even hundreds of local governments (the average is 90). Many contain more than one big city and if the Census Bureau concludes that interconnection is sufficient, a hyphenated designation such as Dallas-Fort Worth or San Francisco-Oakland results. Even MSAs are a little deceptive, however. By definition, each comprises at least the whole county in which a central city is located, but some counties in the West are so large that they contain not only a big city

TABLE 3-1 Percent of Americans Living in Metropolitan Areas, 1790–1990

Year	Percent	Year	Percent
1790	5.0	1910	45.7
1810	7.3	1930	49.7
1830	8.8	1950	56.0
1850	15.3	1970	68.6
1870	25.7	1990	77.5
1890	35.1		

Source: U.S. Bureau of the Census.

FIGURE 3-1   Metropolitan Statistical Areas of the United States, 1990

Source: U.S. Bureau of the Census.

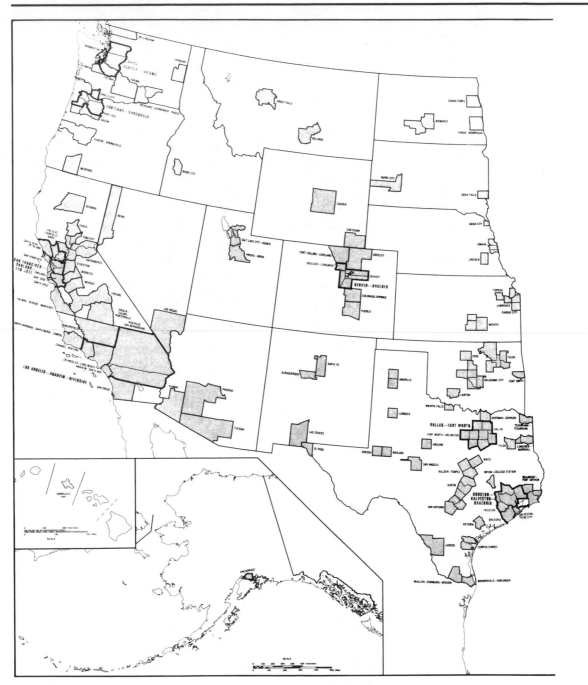

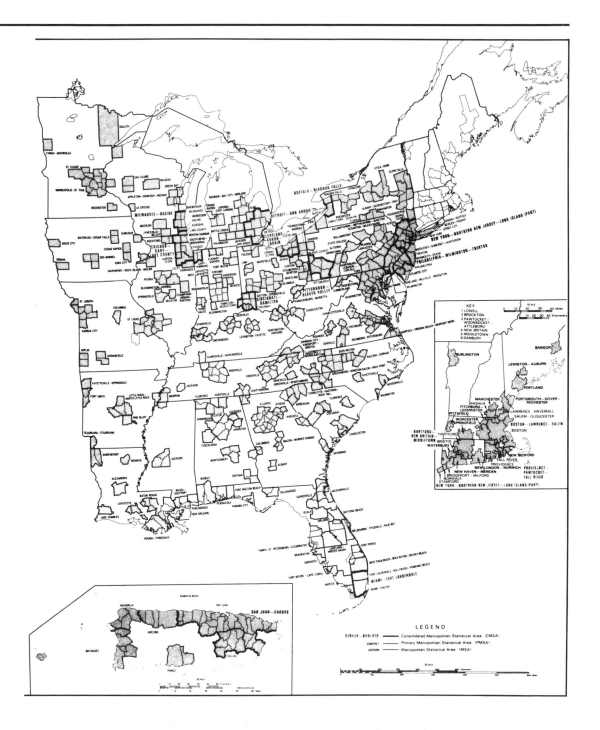

and its suburbs but a lot of rural territory that includes isolated small towns and villages as well. Additionally, some MSAs run right into others, with enough economic and social interaction to make it difficult to know where one begins and the other leaves off. The Census Bureau refers to combined MSAs with more than 1 million people as Consolidated Metropolitan Statistical Areas (CMSAs). The largest CMSA is New York City–Jersey City–Newark, which includes parts of 3 states, 9 MSAs, and 18 million people.

The 1990 Census reported that 78 percent of the U.S. population lives in 284 MSAs and 21 CMSAs. And 49 percent of Americans reside in MSAs with 1 million or more residents and half of these (or 25 percent of the total population) are in just 7 CMSAs, centering on New York City, Los Angeles, Chicago, San Francisco, Philadelphia, Detroit, and Boston. That's urbanization.

Suburbanization: The Move to the Periphery

But urbanization does not necessarily mean movement to big cities. Although Americans have been flocking to metropolitan areas for two centuries, except in the South and West, growth has been greater in the suburbs than in the central cities since the 1940s. **Suburbs** are communities adjacent to big cities, but politically independent, with their own local governments. As their name implies, they are usually a little less than, or "sub," urban—smaller, less dense, and less diverse. Traditionally, they have been primarily residential, with inhabitants commuting to a large, central city for jobs, shopping, and entertainment, although in contemporary metropolitan areas this, too, has changed. Despite their less-than-urban nature, they are an integral part of urban areas, dependent on the other parts and far from self-sufficient. By 1966, more Americans lived in suburbs than in central cities. Today, almost half of all Americans live in suburbs (see Figure 3-2). The causes of **suburbanization** are several and complex, and its impact on local politics has been monumental.

Anticity Attitudes

The superficial reason for suburbanization is simply that Americans prefer it. For decades, public opinion surveys have reported big majorities choosing suburbs or small towns over cities. A 1989 Gallup poll reported only 19 percent of Americans saying that they would prefer to live in a city.[4] **Anticity attitudes** date back to the founders of the nation. "The country life," William Penn wrote, "is to be preferred, for there one sees the works of God, but in cities little else but the works of men."[5] Thomas Jefferson, too, condemned the "degeneration" and "mobs of great cities," which he declared "penitential to the morals, the health, and the liberties of man."[6]

FIGURE 3-2   Percent of U.S. Population by Metropolitan Status, 1980–1990

Note: Percentages prior to 1989 are based on total residential population. Dashed lines indicate definitional changes that influence annual comparability. *Source:* U.S. Bureau of the Census. Reprinted with permission © *American Demographics*, (March, 1991).

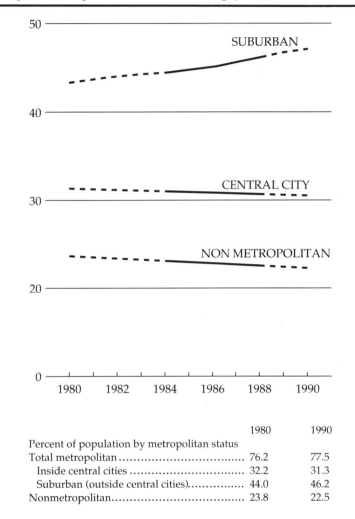

	1980	1990
Percent of population by metropolitan status		
Total metropolitan	76.2	77.5
Inside central cities	32.2	31.3
Suburban (outside central cities)	44.0	46.2
Nonmetropolitan	23.8	22.5

Aside from such moralistic views, U.S. cities are relatively young, so we lack the long and positive urban history of some other countries with their great cities. Frontier, rural, and small town traditions remain a vivid part of America's collective memory and contribute to anticity attitudes. Ask most Americans to free-associate with the words *city* or *urban*, and they will respond with negatives such as dirt, crime, poverty, racial conflict, smog, concrete, traffic, noise, and perversion.

No wonder so many Americans prefer to live in places that are less than urban. Like small towns, suburbs are cleaner and safer than cities, offering more space, bigger houses, and more sense of community. They are also more homogeneous and, as noted in chapter 2, most people prefer to be around others like themselves. The segregation of social groups into suburban enclaves is, as also noted in chapter 2, one way people cope with urban diversity—by isolating themselves from it. Racism and intolerance are thus a factor in our national preference for suburbia. As already noted, African Americans began migrating to cities only in this century. In 1910, 91 percent lived in rural areas; by 1980, 85 percent were in central cities. As blacks migrated to cities, whites moved to suburbs, partly for racist reasons, a phenomenon called **dual migration** or, more revealingly, **white flight.** The concept of dual migration applies to class as well as race, however. In racially homogeneous areas, middle- and upper-class people moved to the suburbs as poor and working-class people migrated to the central cities.

Suburbanization provided a new mechanism for the segregation of people by race and class because state laws allowed suburbs to form their own governments through a process called **incorporation** and thus declare their political independence from the central city. Urban analyst Mike Davis calls this "homeowner separatism," aimed at "putting the more permanent barriers of independent incorporation and exclusive land-use zoning between themselves and non-white or non-homeowning populations."[7]

But despite the retreat from diversity, suburbs have never been all alike. Some are rich, some are middle class, others are working class or even poor; most are white, but some are black, Asian, or Hispanic; in those where the races mix, classes do not. These and other characteristics of suburbs vary considerably, but however much they may differ from one another, most suburbs are internally homogeneous, so if people find the right one, they gain the security of living with their own kind. They insulate themselves from urban diversity and create segregated metropolitan areas. This is accomplished partly through individual choices, but also by economics and discrimination.

The security sought by suburbanites is not only for the psychological reassurance of being around others like themselves, however. Cities are viewed as dangerous places, suburbs as safe. Although often exaggerated—suburban crime rates have risen more rapidly than those of central cities lately—the difference is still real, and it is particularly important to families. Today many singles, childless couples, and elders live in the suburbs, but families have traditionally predominated, and most people say "for the kids" when asked why they moved to the suburbs. Not only are suburbs cleaner and safer, houses there have extra bedrooms and yards for the kids. Most importantly, the schools are newer, better funded, and homogeneous, virtually segregated by race and class. As we will see, local politics in suburbs often center on education for the kids, maintaining the homogeneity of the community, and security—not unrelated concerns. In pursuit of these, suburbanites build fences around their homes, fences around their tracts, and political fences around their communities.

The suburbs are popular partly because they allow people to indulge their life-style preferences and, more subtly, their race and class prejudices. But while over half of all Americans have been able to attain some form of the suburban dream, it is not accessible to all. Many cannot afford the price of admission that involves, in most cases, the purchase of a house and one or more cars. For those who can afford it, however, suburbs may be the perfect compromise—"a reasonable reconstruction of our heritage," according to political scientist Robert Wood[8]—with the feel of a small town but with ready access to an urban economy. Many suburbs are too urban to deliver on the promise of small town life, but that doesn't keep Americans from pursuing the dream. Besides, many of us would find small towns smothering if we really wound up in one. Maybe suburbia is enough.

But race and class, life-style choices, and anticity attitudes only partially explain suburbanization in the United States. The dream is not only American. Other nations have suburbanized, though none so much as the United States. Most are not affluent enough to afford the cars, highways, land, and houses required. Some have proud urban traditions and people there prefer cities and disdain suburbia. The countries of western Europe, for example, are rich enough to indulge in suburbanization and have done so to some extent, but not nearly as much as the United States. Even Canada and Australia, which come closest to the U.S. model, have not suburbanized as much as we have. Several factors then, besides preference and even affluence, have contributed to U.S. suburbanization. These include transportation, housing, taxes, and jobs, and, running through all of these, state and federal policy.

Transportation

The first U.S. suburbs date back to the early nineteenth century, when they were made up of the country homes or summer "cottages" of the rich. Only the upper class could afford these grand homes on acres of land and the private carriages necessary for access. Working- and middle-class people stayed in the cities, to be near jobs and cheaper housing. Even rich businessmen kept houses in town to be near their banks and factories during the week. As **transportation** technology changed, more and more people gained access to the suburbs. Horse-drawn and later electric trolleys or sometimes trains enabled the professional classes to move to the suburbs after the turn of this century. Houses and lots grew a little smaller to accommodate them. Still the streetcar suburbs were mostly an upper class phenomenon, just edging into the upper middle class.

The technological development that made modern suburbia possible was the invention and mass production of automobiles cheap enough for most Americans to afford. Such cars were available by the 1920s, but it wasn't until after the Depression and World War II that auto ownership soared. But cars don't get you far without roads, so suburbanization couldn't have happened without the massive state and federal **highway building** that also followed World War II. Government spending on highways was justified by expected economic benefits, better communications, and, in the case of the federal government, by defense needs (this was just after World War II and the Cold War was tense). But political support for highways was also massive. The driving (and voting) public wanted them. So did cities and local businesses hoping for growth. Landowners and homebuilders wanted them to provide access to the new communities they planned. They joined the powerful highway lobby made up of auto manufacturers, tire makers, oil companies, highway construction firms, and others. No wonder government built highways. The political support was immense, and for many years there was virtually no opposition, except the occasional neighborhood or farmer's objection to a particular route. The impact of highways on the environment and on central cities was realized only in the 1960s, and although opposition is now more common, the highway lobby remains formidable, and usually wins.

Housing

Along with easy access, the other essential for suburbanization was affordable housing. Here, too, federal programs were essential.

Because of the Depression and World War II, many young couples had put off setting up their own homes, so by the late 1940s, an enormous backlog of demand for housing had built up. During the war, with men unable to spend their service pay and many women working, lots of couples built up nest eggs. The postwar baby boom made them even more eager to have their own homes. But having families meant that the sort of home they wanted—not an apartment but a house with a yard—was not readily available. Cities weren't built that way and the price of city land was too high to make such single-family dwelling units economically feasible. Mortgage policies also made buying a home almost impossible for most families. Before the depression, lending institutions required down payments of 40 to 50 percent of the house price, and loans were typically for less than ten years, so big payments were necessary. When home building dropped off during the Depression, the Federal Housing Administration (FHA) was set up to stimulate the economy, encourage construction, and help people obtain housing. Through this and later **housing programs,** (such as Veterans Administration home loans under the GI Bill after World War II), the federal government stepped in to purchase or guarantee home mortgages, either lending the money itself or insuring loans to make banks more willing to lend (since they couldn't lose money).

Government-sponsored mortgages required down payments of as little as 5 percent or sometimes even less, and allowed 30 years for payment. As an added incentive to purchase a home, people were allowed to deduct the interest on mortgages from their income taxes. The combination of pent-up demand and easier mortgages created a huge housing market, and a home-building "industry" emerged, providing cheaper housing through mass production. Instead of relatively expensive and unique individual houses constructed one at a time, builders bought huge tracts of land and threw up hundreds of identical houses with factory-like production methods. **Tract housing** made home ownership accessible to the masses.

But why was this housing built in suburbs rather than in central cities? We've already considered consumer preferences for the single-family housing of the suburbs and the fantasy of small town life-styles. These may be innately American, a throwback to our frontier and small town history, but suburbia was also vigorously sold to Americans through extensive advertising by home builders and the highway lobby from the late 1940s onward. Movies and television helped, too. Their urban stories were (and are) mostly about crime, while tales of suburbia were usually situation comedies that idealized suburbia, such as Doris Day movies, "Father Knows Best" and "Leave It to Beaver." Even Lucy and Ricky of "I Love Lucy," who started the show in a New York City apartment, ended up in suburban Connecticut. Were they reflecting the move to suburbia or encouraging it?

Suburbia did not need a hard sell, however, because there was usually no alternative. Little affordable housing was being built in most central cities outside the South and West. The high cost and limited availability of land in central cities raised the price of what was built and imposed higher densities than families with children wanted. And as the sparkling new suburbs were built, central cities deteriorated, with rising crime and poverty, racial conflict, decaying housing, and little government investment in renewal. To add insult to injury, lending institutions refused mortgages for home purchases in central city neighborhoods, and federal mortgage assistance, readily available for the purchase of suburban homes, was almost impossible to obtain for central city homes until well into the 1970s. Even the few who might have wished to buy a home in the central city were thus discouraged.

Land and Taxes

Cheaper land also facilitated building in the suburbs. Tract housing required big parcels of land, which were generally unavailable in well-developed central cities where land was also expensive, precisely because it was central. Builders thus went to the outskirts, buying up big areas cheaply, which helped keep the price of houses down so more people could afford to buy.

Besides the benefit of an income tax deduction for mortgage interest payments, suburbanites also could expect to pay lower taxes. Local governments depend heavily on property taxes on buildings and land for their revenues, and suburban property taxes were lower than those in central cities because the costs of providing services in new, safe, low-density, healthy suburban communities were lower than in old, crowded, dangerous central cities. Besides, suburban residents had ready access to some of the services of the central city, such as entertainment or sports facilities, so these didn't have to be provided in their own communities. To meet the cost of these services and other, more pressing needs, many central cities had imposed a variety of taxes in addition to the property tax, including sales, utility, business taxes, and sometimes even a local income tax. Most of these taxes could be avoided in the suburbs. It was thus not only cheaper to buy, but cheaper to live in the suburbs. State and federal subsidies for highway building and other infrastructure needs, like sewage treatment facilities, also helped keep suburban taxes low, but the key to lower taxes was the political independence or autonomy of the suburbs. If the new tracts had been developed on the edges of the central city and then absorbed by it, residents would have paid the same taxes as other central city neighborhoods. But state laws allowed suburbs to set up their own governments through the process of incorporation and thus levy their own taxes.

Jobs

The residents of traditional **dormitory suburbs** commute to the central city for jobs and amenities, such as shopping and entertainment. But some of the same things that made the suburbs attractive to individuals also attracted businesses and thus jobs—which, in turn, attracted more people. Today, although many suburbs remain dormitory communities, others are major centers of employment, competing with and envied by the central city.

As early as the 1950s, retailers started moving to the suburbs to be closer to their middle-class consumers. Industry followed. As with housing, land and taxes were major factors in the suburbanization of business. Plenty of cheap land meant that instead of costly high-rises with structural steel, elevators, and escalators, businesses could build low, inexpensive buildings. Outside the costly central city, they could even supply the parking their customers and workers clambered for. Retailers discovered the shopping mall and abandoned downtown business districts. Industry built modern facilities in open fields and left central city factories to decay. Profits were increased by low suburban taxes, which could be as much as 40 to 50 percent less than in central cities. Retailers, manufacturers, and eventually service industries also discovered that the women of suburbia were a ready source of reliable, low-wage, nonunion, unskilled workers.

Eager to attract these businesses for their jobs and taxes, suburban local governments helped with infrastructure improvements and special tax breaks, while the state and federal governments built highways to ensure ready access.

For all these reasons, businesses suburbanized. Between 1947 and 1957, the sixteen oldest and largest cities in the United States "lost an average of 34,000 manufacturing jobs each, while their suburbs gained an average of 87,000."[9] From 1960 onward, more new retail and industrial facilities located in suburbs than in central cities. In the 1970s, new communications technology enabled offices and service industries to join the migration to the suburbs. By the 1980s, well over half of all jobs within MSAs were in suburbs rather than in central cities, their traditional home. By 1990, two-thirds of all the office space in the United States was in the suburbs.[10] The trend continues: in 1991 and 1992, thirty big-name companies moved 11,5000 employees out of New York City and into the suburbs.[11]

New development and the shift in employment have transformed U.S. urban regions so that instead of a traditional single, dominant central city surrounded by a constellation of suburbs, today many metropolitan areas have multiple centers made up of the old central city and other, newer concentrations that have been labeled **edge cities**.[12] Sprouting along freeways, often with gleaming, glass-enshrouded high-rises, edge cities cluster office employment and retail trade in a suburban rather than central city style, with shopping centers, office complexes, landscaping, and lots of parking. People feel safe in edge cities, not only because they provide high-profile security, but because only people who belong there go there. "They don't have to put up with the insecurity and disorder of public spaces," writes journalist William Schneider, because unlike such spaces in traditional cities, these have been "privatized. The difference between a mall and a downtown is that a mall is a private space, a secure environment."[13] Edge cities are homogenized by race, class, and life-style. Some edge cities have housing, but workers often live elsewhere, commuting from suburb to edge city without ever going to the central city. The old commute pattern from suburb to central city and back to suburb has been replaced by "bumper to bumper traffic in both directions."[14]

Jobs, which once drew people to cities, now draw them to the suburbs. As *Edge City* author Joel Garreau writes, "First, we moved our homes out past the traditional idea of what constituted a city. Then we moved our marketplaces out to where we lived. Today, we have moved our jobs out to where most of us have lived and shopped for two generations."[15] Some would substitute *they* for *we* since many central city residents do not have ready access to these jobs, but no one disputes the big change. "Suburbs," political scientist Carl Abbott declares, "are increasingly self-sustaining as economic entities that are able to generate their own jobs"[16]—often at the expense of the central city.

Suburban Diversity

Although the image of the dormitory suburb survives, it is decades out of date due to the massive shift in jobs to the suburbs. Today, only about a third of all suburbs are exclusively residential, while a third mix housing and jobs, and a third are mainly **employing suburbs** or edge cities. Much of the employment in such places is in services and offices, but some older suburbs host manufacturing industries as well. The primary functions of suburbs thus vary considerably.

Suburban life-styles have also diversified. Once dominated by families with small children, today suburbs house many singles, working couples without children, and empty-nesters who still live in the family home although their children have grown up and moved to condos a few suburbs (or states) away. Residential suburbs as a whole have become more diverse in terms of class, race, and ethnicity as well, although individual suburbs are usually internally homogeneous. In other words, the diversity is greater between suburbs than within a single suburb. A majority of residential suburbs are, broadly speaking, middle class, although this covers a wide income range and considerable variety. The best-known suburbs in most areas are the richest, with their multimillion dollar homes, private security systems, and Sunday sightseers. But most metropolitan areas also have working class and poor suburbs. In roughly five hundred suburbs, a majority of residents have incomes below the poverty level.[17] Such places include Florida City (outside Miami), Camden, New Jersey (near Philadelphia), Bell Gardens (Los Angeles), Ford Heights (Chicago), and East St. Louis.

The populations of these poor suburbs are also predominantly minority. Many metropolitan areas have old suburbs where poor blacks and Hispanics have been isolated for decades, although not all minority suburbs are poor. In the 1970s, African Americans and later Hispanics and Asians started moving to the working- and middle-class suburbs in greater numbers. Joel Garreau points out that 40 percent of the African American families in Atlanta are suburbanites and estimates that one-third of the U.S.'s black population is "largely suburban middle class."[18] Altogether, minorities make up about 18 percent of the suburban populace. But while contemporary suburbs are racially diverse, they are not necessarily integrated. With a few exceptions, most are examples of what UCLA population geographer James H. Johnson calls "resegregation"—or **"suburban ghettoes."**[19]

Taken all together, the suburbs of most metropolitan areas are varied enough to provide something for almost everyone: a house they can afford, a community where they fit in and feel safe, the right schools for the kids, a job. The diversity of suburbia gives us choices, but this diversity is tidily separated, while in big cities diversity cannot be avoided. Most Americans seem to prefer the former, as indicated by the fact that over half of us now live in suburbs.

The Suburban Imperative

Suburbanization is a universal phenomenon. Wherever people can afford it, many prefer the low-density housing, automobiles, privacy, and homogeneity of suburbia. But in the United States, greater affluence, a rural past, vigorous marketing, racial intolerance, and economics propelled suburbanization. So did politics, for these forces resulted in federal transportation and housing programs and state laws of taxation and incorporation that made suburbanization public policy in the United States. Suburbanization, in turn, reshaped local politics in the U.S.'s urban areas.

The Impact of Suburbanization: Segregation and Inequity

Despite the increasing diversity among suburbs, the outstanding characteristic of U.S. metropolitan areas is the separation, isolation, and virtual segregation of population groups by race and class (see Table 3-2). Central cities concentrate racial minorities, the poor, the untrained, the unemployed, the old, the uninsured ill, people without cars, and aging, decaying housing. In suburbs, people are predominantly white, wealthier, better educated, employed, younger, healthier (and insured), and younger; they own cars and their housing is newer and better.

These **central city/suburban distinctions** are real and they are increasing, especially in the older metropolitan areas of the Northeast and Midwest. Figure 3-3 shows the pattern in Philadelphia. In greater Philadelphia, America's fifth largest metropolitan area, 85 percent of the richest families live in the suburbs while Philadelphia itself houses 80 percent of the region's poorest families. The city's 1990 population was 40 percent African American, while the region's was half that. Between 1953 and 1982, the city lost 18.5 percent of its population, 24.9 percent of its jobs, and 35.2 percent of its businesses, mostly to the suburbs. Between 1970 and 1990 alone, the city's population declined from 2 million to 1.5 million.[20]

This pattern is typical of the aging cities of the Northeast and Midwest. Southern and western cities have continued to grow and prosper, although even these cities are poor compared to their own suburbs. They also host large minority populations that, in many cities all over the country, are no longer in the minority. In 1990, minorities had become the majority in most of the largest U.S. cities and in 51 of the 200 with more than 100,000 people. Much of the change is due to immigration by Asians and Hispanics, while whites continue to move from central cities to suburbs.

The differences between central cities and suburbs are relative, of

TABLE 3-2 Population in U.S. Metropolitan Areas, 1990

	Metropolitan Areas			Outside Metropolitan Areas
	Total	Central Cities	Suburbs	
Total population (in millions)	192.7	77.8	114.9	56.0
Percent of U.S. total	77.5	31.3	46.2	22.5
Percent white	78.3	66.1	86.8	87.2
Percent black	13.0	22.1	6.9	8.7
Percent Hispanic*	10.5	14.5	7.6	3.8
Percent Asian	3.5	4.4	3.0	0.8
Percent Native American	0.5	0.6	0.5	1.7
Percent below poverty line	13.9	20.2	9.6	9.2
Per capita income	$15,442	$13,839	$16,527	$10,904
Percent homeowners	61.8	49.0	71.0	72.4
Density (persons per square mile)	332	2,820	208	19

*Hispanics may be of any race; percentages therefore do not add up to 100. *Source:* U.S. Bureau of the Census.

course. Suburbs are themselves diverse and central cities are internally diverse almost by definition, with people of all races and classes. The extremes between these groups is usually even greater within the central city than between the central city and the suburb, as bag-ladies harass fur-wearing shoppers getting out of limousines and street people sleep in cardboard boxes far below skyscraper penthouses. Nor are central cities integrated. Race and class groups are generally separated into different neighborhoods and districts. But the diversity of the central city is part of one larger entity, while diversity between the central city and the suburbs or between suburbs is contained in politically separate and independent units. This political independence, achieved through state laws allowing communities to incorporate or form their own government, includes land use powers and a tax structure that make segregation possible, generally legal, and perhaps even inevitable.

FIGURE 3-3 Philadelphia, 1960 and 1990

Source: U. S. Bureau of Census. Copyright © 1993 by The New York Times Company. Reprinted by permission.

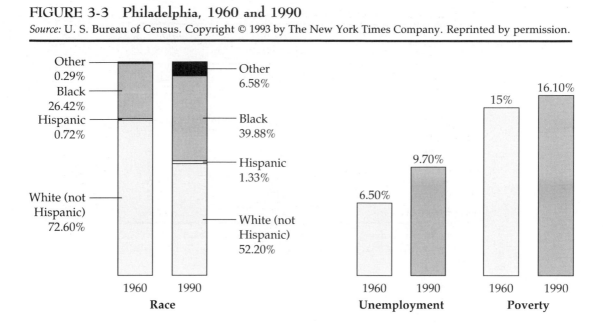

Race   Unemployment   Poverty

How Metropolitan Areas Are Segregated

Initially, the homogeneity of suburbs was guaranteed by local laws and private agreements called **restrictive covenants,** which forbid the sale of homes to members of designated racial and ethnic groups (most commonly African Americans and Jews). Lending institutions and government agencies that guaranteed loans, including the FHA, reinforced these arrangements not only by accepting restrictive covenants but also by refusing loans to minorities who wanted to buy homes in white suburbia.[21]

The civil rights movement challenged housing discrimination beginning in the 1940s and gradually changed public policy. The U.S Supreme Court banned the use of restrictive covenants for purposes of racial discrimination in 1948 (they can still be used to control such things as house size or height or fences). In the 1960s, President Kennedy banned housing discrimination in all federal programs by executive order, Congress prohibited racial discrimination in housing with the Fair Housing Act, and the Supreme Court made discrimination even in private home sales illegal. Most states passed similar policies. By the time these laws were passed, however, suburban patterns of segregation were well established. Open housing laws helped break down these patterns to some extent and blatant racial discrimination is less common today, but Table 3-3 reveals the persistence of segregation in U.S. cities.

TABLE 3-3   Segregation in U.S. Cities

City	Percent in isolation	Change since 1980
Chicago	71	–9.1
Detroit	61	+4.0
Philadelphia	53	+0.1
Atlanta	43	–6.1
Washington, DC	37	–9.3
New York	31	+3.0
Houston	30	–19.5
Dallas	29	–21.6
Boston	19	–5.6
Los Angeles	7	–12.6

*Percent of blacks living in blocks that are at least 90% black. *Source: San Jose Mercury News,* 9 April 1991. Reprinted by permission Tribune Media Services.

More subtle forms of racial discrimination, which may be hard to prove in law, are still around, however, even in the most tolerant communities. Besides the racist attitudes of some realtors and homesellers, minorities still have trouble getting mortgages. A 1990 Federal Reserve study of applications for nongovernment sponsored home loans discovered that low- and moderate-income African Americans were twice as likely as whites with similar incomes to be rejected while rejections for wealthier African Americans were actually 2.5 times higher. Rejections of loan applications by low- and moderate-income Hispanics were 1.5 times higher than for whites, and were twice as high for upper-income Hispanics.[22] As a result of this and other discriminatory practices, housing specialist Joe Darden reports that segregation remains "uniformly high between blacks and whites with equal incomes."[23]

Local control of land use is another mechanism of segregation and suburban homogeneity. When local governments are created through state laws of incorporation, they are granted land-use or **zoning** powers to decide exactly what sort of development they want and where. This, along with the tax advantages already noted, impelled suburban developers and residents to form their own local governments rather than accept absorption by adjacent central cities. Besides lower taxes, they gain control of what happens within their boundaries, so the central city can't build a hospital or low-income housing on their doorsteps. Through their land-use powers, suburbs establish the class of their residents by the sorts of houses they allow. Such **exclusionary** (or snob) **zoning** may require large houses on large lots at specified distances from one another and ban apartments or smaller houses.

Class segregation follows, not by outright banning of working- or middle-class people, but by pricing them out of the community. The rich can buy anywhere; others cannot. And because minority groups, on average, have lower incomes than whites, they are excluded from many areas. Hence the segregation of suburbia. Exclusionary zoning has been challenged in state and federal courts, but in general it has been allowed except where it can be clearly proven that its discriminatory effects are intentional. The New Jersey Supreme Court, however, ruled exclusionary zoning unconstitutional in 1975, and later declared that new developments should include housing at varied prices. Although significant, these rulings were weakened in implementation by the state and its local governments.

Exclusionary zoning is not merely the result of prejudice, however. The structure of local land-use decisions makes it rational and almost inevitable. Imagine you are a council member in a suburban community. A landowner wants to develop a 10-acre property and offers the city a choice of 10 houses on 1-acre lots worth $1 million each or 100 townhouses at 10 per acre priced at $100,000. Which would you choose? However much council members may worry about housing shortages, even the most liberal will opt for the big houses. Why? As noted above, the property tax is a major source of local revenue and its proceeds are based on property values. In this case, both developments will produce properties valued at a total of $10 million, which will generate exactly the same tax income, but council members have to consider spending as well as revenues, and the 100 homes will surely cost much more to service with police, fire protection, sewage treatment, and parks than the 10. The city might actually make money on the 10, but could well lose on the 100. To help the council decide, a group of people who live near the property are at the meeting to testify. Although their own homes are worth considerably less than $1 million, they support the expensive project and condemn the townhouses for their expected effect on congestion, parking, traffic, and the value of their own properties. No one is present to advocate the lower cost homes.

This example is oversimplified, but a council in similar circumstances would have little choice. The resultant zoning would be considered exclusionary and would produce class and race segregation, yet given the relationship between zoning and taxes, the decision is economically rational, not consciously prejudiced or discriminatory. The structure itself—based on local political autonomy, local land-use control, and local property tax—is discriminatory. This structure comes from the state government.

The same structural factors create the local growth machines discussed in the preceding chapters, impelling suburban local governments to pursue shopping centers, offices, and industry for the taxes they will generate, competing with one another and with the central city. Designating land for such developments is called **fiscal zoning** because land use is determined by expected revenues rather than the need for a particular project or its impact on the environment, transportation, or regional balance. As with exclusionary zoning of housing, fiscal zoning creates tax-rich pockets of wealth within metropolitan areas. "Whether led by affluent homeowners or business factions," writes Mike Davis, "the ensuing maximization of local advantage through incorporation and fiscal zoning . . . inevitably produce[s] widening racial and income divides."[24]

The Separation of Needs and Resources

The political autonomy, land use, and tax structures of suburban local governments create a pattern of segregation and isolation in metropolitan areas, with better-off people and economic growth in the suburbs and declining industries and large poor and minority populations in central cities. But the problem is not just the segregation and isolation of social groups, it is also the **separation of needs and resources.**

The central city has the greater need, while the suburbs have the greater resources. Central city populations are more dependent on government services such as welfare, health care, transportation, housing, education, and police as well as recreation programs that they cannot privately afford. Willing workers often cannot find employment because jobs have moved to suburbs that many central city residents cannot reach. Over half of the minority households of Boston, New York, and Philadelphia, for example, do not own automobiles.[25] In contrast, suburbanites are generally economically secure and need fewer public services. They buy their own homes and cars and some join private clubs for recreation and even employ private security. But while the need is in the central city, the tax resources that might pay for the services are greater in the suburbs. With higher home and property values, industries, shopping centers, and edge city office complexes, suburbs have a rich tax base that they can tax lightly because of lower needs or demands for services. Central cities still contain valuable property and prosperous businesses, but these must be taxed heavily to provide higher service levels for large, dependent populations. Central cities are older, too, and their aging infrastructure, including roads and sewers, costs more to maintain. "Big suburban commercial and industrial projects are putting all the tax-base growth in places that don't share the central city's costs in terms of maintaining an older infrastructure or caring for the elderly, the poor, and the sick," says the mayor of Fort Worth, Texas, a relatively well-off central city.[26] Although some states have moved to equalize spending for education, in most these inequities also extend to education, with some school districts—usually those most in need—able to spend far less per pupil than adjacent districts.

Whatever the policy area, the combination of greater resources and less need enables suburbs to tax lightly and still provide good services.

Central cities, with declining resources and greater need, must tax heavily just to try to keep things from growing worse, but they are caught in a vicious circle because their heavy taxes drive industry and commerce away and increase the tax burden on the already overburdened poor. This **needs/resources dichotomy** results from the political independence of the suburbs, which naturally act to maintain and expand their tax bases. They also seek to protect property values for their home-owning constituents and to preserve the racial and class homogeneity of their communities.

The central cities are thus stuck with both a declining tax base and large numbers of people who need public services. Ironically, while many of the people in need are immigrants, others come from the surrounding suburbs where, for various reasons, they are unable to stay. They may be old or ill, or alcoholics or drug addicts, or bad economic times may have made them homeless. Suburbs do not welcome such people or help them stay. Instead, they are absorbed by more tolerant central cities, which then must provide needed services even as their tax resources trickle away to the suburbs.

Worse in the eyes of central cities, as a mayor of Pittsburgh once pointed out, "The people in the suburbs use our facilities but won't pay for them."[27] Suburbanites go to central cities for entertainment, sports, and tourist attractions. They go to the central city to work and shop (though in smaller numbers than previously) and expect public services to ease and make safe their commute and their presence. And edge cities notwithstanding, central cities remain the media, government, legal, and banking capitals of their regions. They are also used by suburbs as dumping grounds for people in need, as noted. In short, neither suburbs and nor central cities can stand alone; they are socially and economically interdependent. As the mayor of Louisville, Kentucky, said recently, "You can't be a suburb of nowhere."[28]

But despite their social and economic interdependence, metropolitan areas are politically fragmented due to the multiplicity of local governments. In some other countries, however, both central cities and suburbs are part of one large governmental entity. In this situation, suburbs, which are still homogeneous, are considered neighborhoods within the larger city rather than being politically independent. Taxes and service needs are shared. In most of the United States, however, metropolitan areas are divided into small, autonomous units. This results not only in the needs/resources dichotomy but also in the fragmentation of government in urban regions. The average MSA has ninety local governments, which may be good for democracy, but which makes solving regional problems like air pollution and transportation almost impossible because nobody is in charge. (See Figure 3-4 for an example of extreme fragmentation.) Only a few central cities, such as Charlotte, San Antonio, and Houston, have managed to avoid this fragmentation by annexing their suburbs, thus retaining a more diversified population and a stronger tax base.

FIGURE 3-4   Municipalities in St. Louis County
Source: St. Louis County Department of Planning, Missouri, Fact Book—1986.

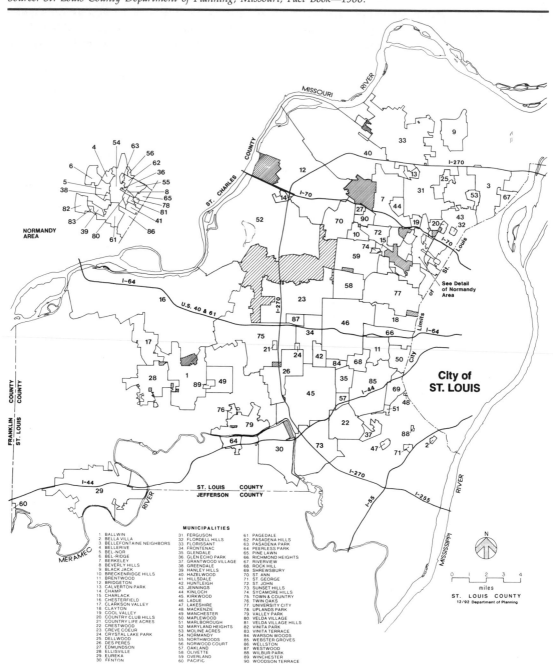

MUNICIPALITIES

1 BALLWIN	31 FERGUSON	61 PAGEDALE
2 BELLA VILLA	32 FLORDELL HILLS	62 PASADENA HILLS
3 BELLEFONTAINE NEIGHBORS	33 FLORISSANT	63 PASADENA PARK
4 BELLERIVE	34 FRONTENAC	64 PEERLESS PARK
5 BEL-NOR	35 GLENDALE	65 PINE LAWN
6 BEL-RIDGE	36 GLEN ECHO PARK	66 RICHMOND HEIGHTS
7 BERKELEY	37 GRANTWOOD VILLAGE	67 RIVERVIEW
8 BEVERLY HILLS	38 GREENDALE	68 ROCK HILL
9 BLACK JACK	39 HANLEY HILLS	69 SHREWSBURY
10 BRECKENRIDGE HILLS	40 HAZELWOOD	70 ST. ANN
11 BRENTWOOD	41 HILLSDALE	71 ST. GEORGE
12 BRIDGETON	42 HUNTLEIGH	72 ST. JOHN
13 CALVERTON PARK	43 JENNINGS	73 SUNSET HILLS
14 CHAMP	44 KINLOCH	74 SYCAMORE HILLS
15 CHARLACK	45 KIRKWOOD	75 TOWN & COUNTRY
16 CHESTERFIELD	46 LADUE	76 TWIN OAKS
17 CLARKSON VALLEY	47 LAKESHIRE	77 UNIVERSITY CITY
18 CLAYTON	48 MACKENZIE	78 UPLANDS PARK
19 COOL VALLEY	49 MANCHESTER	79 VALLEY PARK
20 COUNTRY CLUB HILLS	50 MAPLEWOOD	80 VELDA VILLAGE
21 COUNTRY LIFE ACRES	51 MARLBOROUGH	81 VELDA VILLAGE HILLS
22 CRESTWOOD	52 MARYLAND HEIGHTS	82 VINITA PARK
23 CREVE COEUR	53 MOLINE ACRES	83 VINITA TERRACE
24 CRYSTAL LAKE PARK	54 NORMANDY	84 WARSON WOODS
25 DELLWOOD	55 NORTHWOODS	85 WEBSTER GROVES
26 DES PERES	56 NORWOOD COURT	86 WELLSTON
27 EDMUNDSON	57 OAKLAND	87 WESTWOOD
28 ELLISVILLE	58 OLIVETTE	88 WILBUR PARK
29 EUREKA	59 OVERLAND	89 WINCHESTER
30 FENTON	60 PACIFIC	90 WOODSON TERRACE

ST. LOUIS COUNTY
12/92 Department of Planning

Fragmentation is taken for granted in most metropolitan areas, but it is not inevitable. Segregation, unequal services and taxes, and fragmentation are the results of politics and public policy. The multiplicity of local governments in metropolitan regions is made possible by state laws of incorporation; their land-use and taxing powers also come from the state. Federal programs and private interests also support this system. All reflect the formidable political power of suburban residents and economic interests.

Suburbanization and Local Politics

In addition to its impact on the distribution of needs and resources, suburbanization also has an effect on the internal politics of communities. The differing populations of central cities and suburbs predictably lead to different policy priorities. Central cities worry about decaying infrastructure, public transportation, welfare, AIDS, homelessness, drugs, gangs, and the urban underclass. Suburbs worry about streets, highways, taxes, controlling growth, and maintaining their self-defined quality of life. Both, however, fret about their tax base and schools, although the latter is a particular obsession of suburbia.

Political participation and institutions differ, too. In homogeneous suburbs, where everybody is more or less alike, people agree on most issues. Politics is low key and consensual, with little conflict or competition. As a consequence, voter participation may also be low. Big cities, in contrast, are heterogeneous. All sorts of different people with all sorts of different interests engage in politics, which is often both competitive and conflictual. Voter participation is higher and interest groups are more active. With such differences in political behavior, suburbs and central cities often opt for different governmental structures and institutions, as we will see in chapters 5 and 6.

The Move to the Sunbelt: New Urban Forms

Even as suburbanization transformed U.S. metropolitan areas, a third great population movement was under way—the move to the Sunbelt. By the 1970s, the old central cities of the Northeast and Midwest were losing population and growth because people were moving not just to different parts of urban areas but to different parts of the country, where both central cities and suburbs were growing by leaps and bounds.

The **Sunbelt** is the band of states that runs across the southern United States from Virginia down through Florida and west to California. Along with the less sunny states of Colorado, Oregon, and Washington, this is

FIGURE 3-5 Percent of U.S. Population by Region, 1980–1990

Source: U.S. Bureau of the Census. Reprinted with permission © *American Demographics,* (March, 1991).

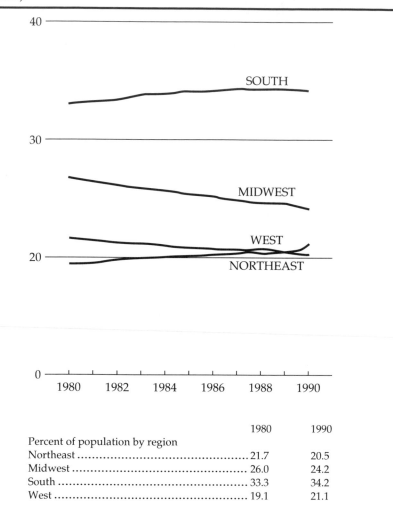

	1980	1990
Percent of population by region		
Northeast	21.7	20.5
Midwest	26.0	24.2
South	33.3	34.2
West	19.1	21.1

the area of the United States that has grown most in the past three decades. In 1960, 53.7 percent of the U.S. population lived in the Frostbelt states of the Northeast and Midwest, while 46.3 percent lived in the South and West. By 1990, those figures had been more than reversed, with 44.4 percent in the Frostbelt and 55.6 percent in the Sunbelt (see Figures 3-5 and 3-6).

Although the Northeast actually lost population during the 1970s, for most of this period the total metropolitan population of the Frostbelt increased slowly. This growth, however, was almost exclusively in the suburbs, with populations in the central cities shrinking, sometimes dra-

FIGURE 3-6   Migration between U.S. Regions, 1980–1988 (in thousands)
Source: U.S. Bureau of the Census.

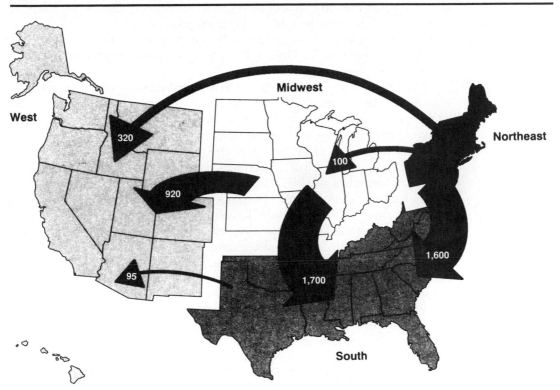

matically. For example, between 1950 and 1990, Philadelphia and Chicago each lost 23 percent of their populations—a total of 1.3 million people! Between 1980 and 1990 alone, Detroit lost 20 percent, Cleveland 13 percent, and Baltimore 8.5 percent. Meanwhile, cities in the Sunbelt boomed, growing at more than double the national rate. San Jose, California, for example, grew from less than 95,000 people in 1950 to nearly 765,000 in 1990. Between 1980 and 1990 alone, San Jose grew by 22 percent, Jacksonville, Florida, by 22 percent, Phoenix, Arizona, by 23 percent, Austin, Texas, by 24 percent, San Diego, California, by 25 percent, El Paso, Texas, by 19 percent, and so on. By 1990, six of the nation's ten largest cities were west of the Mississippi River (see Table 2-1). Unlike the central cities of the Frostbelt, which were boxed in by politically independent suburbs, the relatively young central cities of the Sunbelt were able to grow by expanding their own boundaries through annexation of adjacent areas.

By the 1980s, however, independent suburbs were bringing the territorial expansion of Sunbelt central cities to a halt, too. Most continued to grow, but more slowly, even as growth in their suburbs accelerated. Mesa, a suburb of Phoenix, grew by 89 percent in the 1980s, reaching the sizable population of 288,091. Rancho Cucamonga, a Los Angeles suburb, doubled in size, jumping from 55,250 to 101,409. The Dallas suburbs of Plano and Arlington grew by 78 and 64 percent respectively. Bellevue, a suburb of Seattle (which grew by just 4.5 percent), grew by 17.6 percent. Some of these places are better described as edge cities than suburbs, as are booming Sunbelt areas such as Orange County, California, which has no central city at all.

Most of the people who moved to the Sunbelt were white, but African Americans also moved there. Although rural racism and economic decline had driven many to northern cities, during World War II others were drawn to the Los Angeles and San Francisco Bay areas of California and to the awakening cities of the South. Many Mexican Americans and Mexican immigrants also settled in Sunbelt cities, especially in California and Texas, where 55 percent of all U.S. Hispanics reside. The Sunbelt state of Florida also has a large population of Hispanics, a majority of whom are Cubans who fled there after the Cuban Revolution and who continue to arrive. Asians were also drawn to the Sunbelt, especially during the 1970s and 1980s after the Vietnam War and changes in immigration laws. Today 40 percent of all U.S. Asians live in just four metropolitan areas: Los Angeles, San Francisco, Honolulu, and New York. As in the rest of the country, however, blacks, Hispanics, and, to a lesser extent, Asians have tended to concentrate in central cities, while whites predominate in Sunbelt suburbs.

Some parts of the Sunbelt, particularly in the South, did not enjoy spectacular growth, however, and a few, such as New Orleans, even lost population. Nor did all cities in the Frostbelt shrink; in the 1980s, some enjoyed modest growth. The 1980s also saw the growth of Sunbelt central cities outpaced by that of their own suburbs. By the 1990s, growth had leveled off in California, at least, with new arrivals (mostly Asian and Hispanic) barely equaling those (mostly white) who were leaving. To date, however, Sunbelt growth continues to put that of the Frostbelt in the shade.

Why the Sunbelt Grew

The obvious reason for the Sunbelt boom was its climate, but good weather wasn't new to the region; other factors were even more important. World War II, for example, introduced millions of Americans to the Sunbelt on their way to battle elsewhere. Many liked it and resolved to return. After that war, increased affluence enabled more Americans to take vacations, and tourism, aided and abetted by Walt Disney and other promoters, became a mainstay of parts of the Sunbelt. (Lucy and Ricky vacationed in California even before they moved to suburbia.) Increased affluence along with Social Security and better health also meant that there was a larger population of independent elders, many of whom chose to retire in the sunshine. Natural resources, including oil, uranium, and agricultural land irrigated by federal projects built from the 1930s onward gave Sunbelt growth further impetus.

Tourism, retirees, and natural resources primed the pump, but real growth was stimulated by economic and technological developments. Foremost among these were the electronics, aerospace, and defense industries. These were young industries, free to build new facilities where the economic advantages were greatest—in the Sunbelt. Local workers there were underemployed, low-wage, and, for the most part, not unionized, while cheap housing and good weather drew workers from other regions. Land was cheap and plentiful, so companies could build inexpensive low-rise plants, and start-up costs were low. Energy was cheap and plentiful, too, and warm weather reduced heating costs. The new industries relied on highways and air transportation and on electronic communications, so they did not need to be physically close to the transportation network of ships, barges, and railroads that were the backbone of heavy industry in the Northeast and Midwest.

As with suburbanization, the federal government aided the shift to the Sunbelt with its highway and home loan programs, but other federal spending also disproportionately benefited the Sunbelt. The 1960s and 1970s saw "a massive flow of wealth from the Northeast and Midwest to the fast-growing Southern and Western Regions," led by **defense spending.**[29] With around 10 percent of the U.S. population during these years, California alone raked in as much as 25 percent of the nation's defense expenditures, while aerospace funds went mostly to California, Florida, Texas, and Washington. The new electronics industries of the Sunbelt grew in association with these industries and with federal contracts of their own. These lucrative contracts were not, however, the cause of industrial expansion in the Sunbelt. Rather, new and expanding industries located in the region for its economic advantages, then drew federal spending like powerful magnets and produced further growth.

The cities of the Sunbelt were not passive beneficiaries of these developments. Local growth machines were in high gear, aggressively wooing industry and actively hustling federal spending. Their leaders were confident, probusiness, progrowth, can-do people. They were boosters and their boosting went beyond rhetoric. Federal, state, and local funds provided the infrastructure—roads, sewers, water systems, sewage-treatment plants, and airports—needed by industry. Virtually new cities were built, and built to suit. Meanwhile, the cities of the Northeast and Midwest, saddled with aging infrastructures, expensive land and labor, high taxes, increasingly dependent populations, and competition from their own suburbs, could not adapt to the needs of the new industries and began to stagnate.

New Urban Forms

The Sunbelt phenomenon involved not only a shift in population, but a **new urban form,** a shift, according to Robert Fishman:

> toward urban areas that had been "born decentralized" and organized on new-city principles. The new city lacks what gave shape and meaning to every urban form in the past: a dominant single core and definable boundaries. At most, it contains a multitude of centers, or "edge cities," more-or-less unified clusters of malls, office developments, and entertainment complexes that rise where major highways cross or converge . . . Without anybody intending it . . . decentralization washed over America. . . . The single center had lost its dominance [and was no longer able] to monopolize the life of a region.[30]

The concept of edge cities, a suburban phenomenon in the East, characterizes even central cities in the Sunbelt.

In short, Sunbelt cities are suburbia writ large. Lower in density and diversity than their Frostbelt equivalents, the life-styles and even politics of Sunbelt central cities are more like those of traditional suburbs than big cities. In addition to decentralization, Sunbelt central cities share with suburbs the attributes of predominantly single-family housing, high rates of homeownership, almost total dependence on automobiles for transportation, commuting workers (often to suburbs), and concerns about coping with growth rather than decay. Political priorities differ as well, and local politics is often more consensual than conflictual. Accordingly, voter and interest group participation is often lower than in Frostbelt cities, and government structures vary as well. Even the informal power structures of Sunbelt cities differ from their Frostbelt counterparts. These differences arise partly because Sunbelt cities are new and their political systems have not kept up with their rapid growth. Some still operate with the same institutions and even players as when they were smaller cities. Most, however, are adapting and maturing.

Meanwhile, some very new Sunbelt suburbs, though not part of the central city, do not yet have their own governments. Most are under county jurisdiction, which usually means minimal services. But many new housing or condominium projects with shared public space—called **common interest developments**—have private or shadow governments in the form of **resident associations,** which charge fees in return for security, maintenance, and other services. There are 150,000 of these private governments now serving 32 million residents, further exacerbating the needs/ resources dichotomy and the fragmentation of metropolitan areas.

In the 1980s, as Sunbelt metropolitan areas matured, Frostbelt patterns began to emerge. Cut off from further expansion by surrounding suburbs that were outpacing growth in the central city, many big cities in the Sunbelt found themselves confronted with problems long familiar to those of the Frostbelt, such as racial conflict, urban decay, homelessness, crime, drugs, gangs, and AIDS. Traffic congestion and smog were even worse, and auto-dependent Sunbelt cities lacked mass transit alternatives. The federal bounty they had enjoyed for so long suddenly stopped when the end of the Cold War brought cuts in defense and aerospace spending. Los Angeles alone has lost more than 100,000 jobs since 1986. By 1991, unemployment there was higher than in Pittsburgh or Philadelphia. This pattern was not consistent across the Sunbelt and Frostbelt, but many Frostbelt cities enjoyed a mild revival in the 1980s, partly because their previous decline had made them economically attractive to industry again and partly because Sunbelt cities were beginning to price themselves out of the market. They also found themselves competing with and envious of their own suburbs and facing growing central city/suburban disparities in class, race, and needs and resources.

Although the Frostbelt pattern has asserted itself in the Sunbelt, cities there are still different and so are their problems. They contend with rapid growth and providing services, like suburbs elsewhere, while Frostbelt cities struggle with decay and decline. Compared to Frostbelt cities, they remain well off, growing rather than shrinking, with lower taxes and greater resources. The disparities between Sunbelt and Frostbelt cities are almost as great as those between Frostbelt central cities and their suburbs, so the needs/resources dichotomy now operates on a national scale. The Frostbelt has sought federal aid to redress the balance, but until recently, the Sunbelt has benefited disproportionately from federal largesse.

Megatrends and Minitrends in the 1980s and 1990s

By the 1980s, urbanization, suburbanization, and the move to the Sunbelt, the three U.S. demographic megatrends, had reshaped politics both nationally and locally. As the suburbs and the Sunbelt grew, so did their influence in national politics and elections and their representation in Congress and in state legislatures. More and more, the nation's attention turned away from its central cities. All three megatrends looked set to continue through the 1990s, although none was quite so powerful as before and some minitrends were also under way.

Urbanization proceeded through the 1980s, as metropolitan areas continued growing, especially in the Sunbelt and along both coasts. Central cities in the Sunbelt outpaced those in the Frostbelt, but Frostbelt decline slowed and even turned around in a few places. New York City, which had lost 1.2 million people between 1960 and 1980, actually gained 0.5 million in the 1980s, for a growth rate of 3.5 percent. Rising house prices and wages, along with traffic congestion, drove some industries back to parts of the Frostbelt, such as Boston and Pittsburgh, which decline had made competitive again.

Growth of central cities was also invigorated by foreign immigration, which rose to over half a million people a year in the 1980s. Like earlier immigrants, they flocked to the cities, with New York, Los Angeles, Miami, and San Francisco attracting the most. The rising number of single people and couples without children also stimulated a mild middle-class revival in central cities, with many attractive old neighborhoods being renovated or gentrified, a phenomenon that improved the central city tax base but reduced housing availability for low-income residents. Urban renewal programs built some housing in the central city, too, but more often for the middle than the lower class.

These minitrends continued urbanization, but except for central cities in the Sunbelt and a few modest Frostbelt exceptions such as New York City, they only arrested decline. All across the nation, and especially in the Sunbelt, the greatest growth was in the suburbs. By the 1980s, however, this was due less to flight from the cities than to people moving directly to the suburbs or from one suburb to another. Although more minorities moved to the suburbs (usually to minority suburbs), the pattern of dual migration, with whites going to suburbs and minorities to cities persisted and minorities became majorities in some large cities. This aggravated the suburban/central city needs/resources dichotomy, as did the concentration of jobs in suburbs and flourishing edge cities.

Some demographers predicted there would be a return to the country movement or the deconcentration of population to rural and nonmetropolitan areas because of cheap housing, new communication technologies, and increased numbers of retirees, but except for a blip in the 1970s, the nonmetropolitan population has continued to decline. Smaller metropolitan areas, however, grew in the 1980s, as did many small towns on the periphery of large metropolitan areas. Most of the latter, however, were merely being drawn into an enlarged commuter network. Overall, the pattern of metropolitan and especially suburban growth continues, although Sunbelt expansion showed some signs of abating by the late 1980s, especially in recession-struck California.

These trends are crucial to our understanding of local politics, for the sorts of people who live in a community shape its politics and policies, its needs and resources. And as the community changes so does its politics. We will return to these characteristics, along with the others considered in the previous chapter, through the rest of this book for in local politics, demography is destiny.

ESSENTIAL
TERMS

demography	edge cities
urbanization	suburban diversity
industrialization	employing suburbs
immigration	suburban ghettoes
postindustrial cities	central city/suburban
urban places	distinctions

Metropolitan Statistical
   Areas (MSAs)
suburbs
suburbanization
anticity attitudes
dual migration
white flight
incorporation
transportation
highway building
housing programs
tract housing
dormitory suburbs

restrictive covenants
zoning
exclusionary zoning
fiscal zoning
separation of needs and
   resources
needs/resources dichotomy
fragmentation
Sunbelt
defense spending
new urban forms
common interest developments
resident associations

FIELDWORK
1. Trace the immigration of your own family to where you live today. When and why did your family urbanize, suburbanize, and/or move to the Sunbelt? How does your family history fit with the population trends discussed in this chapter?

2. Study a few months of your local newspaper (at the library) during the 1950s or 1960s. Look at advertisements for houses and cars, editorials, news articles, and entertainment reviews. Was it "selling suburbia"? Do you think the U.S. preference for suburbia is inherent or the product of good marketing?

3. Using census data available at the library, compare the demographic characteristics of the central city in your area to those of its suburbs.

NOTES
[1]Quoted in Jon Bowermaster, "Seattle, Too Much of a Good Thing," *The New York Times Magazine,* 6 January 1991, p. 24.

[2]Daniel Bell, *The Coming of Post-Industrial Society* (New York: Basic Books, 1973).

[3]Some areas lacking a single city with a population of 50,000 are designated as MSAs by the Census Bureau providing they have at least 50,000 inhabitants and a total MSA population of 100,000 (75,000 in New England). Cities and towns rather than counties (see chapter 4) are used to define MSAs in New England.

[4]William Schneider, "The Suburban Century Begins," *The Atlantic* 270, no. 1 (July 1992): 34.

[5]Quoted in James A. Clapp *The City* (New Brunswick, NJ: Center for Urban Policy Research, 1984), p. 191.

[6]Ibid., p. 129.

[7]Mike Davis, *City of Quartz,* (London: Vintage, 1992), p. 164.

[8]Robert Wood, *Suburbia* (Boston: Houghton Mifflin, 1958).

[9]Robert Fishman, "America's New City: Megalopolis Unbound," *Wilson Quarterly,* 14, no. 1 (Winter 1990): 36.

[10]John Lichfield, "No Particular Place to Live," *The Independent on Sunday* (London), 15 November 1992.

[11]*The Economist*, 3 October 1992, p. 61.

[12]Fishman, note 9, p. 28; and Joel Garreau, *Edge City* (Garden City, NY: Doubleday, 1991).

[13]Schneider, note 4, p. 37.

[14]Garreau, note 12, p. 7.

[15]Ibid., p. 4.

[16]Carl Abbott, *The New Urban America.* Chapel Hill: University of North Carolina Press, 1987, p. 188.

[17]*The New York Times*, 10 April 1991. As of 1990, the poverty level was $13,359 for an urban family of four.

[18]Garreau, note 12, pp. 150, 140.

[19]*San Jose Mercury News*, 9 April 1991.

[20]*The Economist*, 1 December 1990, p. 25; 9 May 1992, p. 21.

[21]See Rachel G. Bratt, Chester Hartman, and Ann Myerson, eds., *Critical Perspectives on Housing*. Philadelphia: Temple University Press, 1986.

[22]*San Jose Mercury News*, 23 October 1991.

[23]Joe T. Darden, "Choosing Neighbors and Neighborhoods: The Role of Race in Housing Preference," in Gary A. Tobin, ed., *Divided Neighborhoods: Changing Patterns of Racial Segregation*. Newbury Park, CA: Sage, 1987.

[24]Davis, note 7, p. 169.

[25]John D. Kasarda, "Economic Restructuring and America's Urban Dilemma," in Mattei Dogan and John D. Kasarda, eds., *The Metropolis Era. Vol II: Mega-Cities*. Beverly Hills, CA: Sage, 1990, p. 74.

[26]Quoted in *The New York Times*, 23 February 23, 1991.

[27]Mayor Pete Flaherty, quoted in Clapp, note 5, p. 83.

[28]Quoted in Katherine Barrett and Richard Greene, "American Cities," *Financial World*, 19 February 1991, p. 36.

[29]"Federal Spending: The North's Loss Is the Sunbelt's Gain," *National Journal*, 26 June 1976, pp. 878–880.

[30]Fishman, note 9, pp. 28, 36–37.

4

The Intergovernmental Environment of Local Politics: Creatures of the States and Supplicants of the Federal Government

The social, economic, and demographic forces discussed thus far greatly influence what goes on in local politics, but another primal element in their environment must be considered before we get down to the nuts and bolts of local government, politics, and power. That element is other governments, for nothing is more crucial to local government and politics than their intergovernmental environment. For a start, local governments constrain, compete with, and cause problems for one another. We have already examined the impact of suburbanization; later, we will study this further in the context of regional or metropolitan politics. The federal government also affects local politics, although less today than at some times in the past. But the state is by far the most important intergovernmental influence on local politics.

Local governments have been called "creatures of the state," and rightly so. They are created by the states and may be abolished or altered by the states. They are given their organization, powers, finances, and responsibilities by the states, sometimes generously and sometimes not. Their relations with adjacent or overlapping local governments in the same area also are structured by the states, which formulate the whole, complicated system. Many of the problems faced not only by individual local governments but by regional multiplexes of governments have their source in state politics. First, however, we need to understand the different types of local government, how they are created, what powers they have, and what they do.

Types and Tasks of Local Government

Although it is sometimes hard to distinguish among them, at least six types of local government operate in the United States, with each state making its own choice as to which ones it will have, what they will do, and what they will be called. The division of responsibilities among these governments can be complex and varies greatly from state to state.

Counties

Except for Connecticut and Rhode Island, all states have counties, called parishes in Louisiana and boroughs in Alaska. States subdivide themselves into **counties** for administrative purposes, which is what makes counties distinct from other local governments. The entire territory of the state is divided into counties, whereas other local governments only cover parts of the state, never all of it. Moreover, as administrative agencies for the states, most of what counties do is carry out state programs. That's why they must cover the entire state and also what makes them distinct from other local governments, which administer more of their own programs. Counties are most important in rural areas, where they are the primary local government. Their significance has declined in many urban areas, where their duties have been taken over by cities (municipalities), although in some states, mostly in the Sunbelt, counties continue to provide crucial urban services.

As the principal local government for rural areas, counties usually oversee public health; provide agricultural advice; build and maintain rural roads; keep records on births, marriages, and property transactions; administer voter registration and elections; carry out tax assessment and collection; and operate the state criminal justice system, with a sheriff, jail, and courts. Counties are responsible for land-use planning for areas that are not part of any city and often provide minimal fire protection for these areas. Some counties supply amenities such as parks and libraries. In many states, especially in the West, counties administer state and federal social services, including welfare, mental health, and public hospitals. Urban counties are also likely to operate transit systems. Counties are weakest in the New England states, where older cities handle most of these functions.

Municipalities

What most people think of as local government is, in legal terms, the municipality, but in some states, **municipalities** are called cities, boroughs, towns, or even villages. These are the primary, but not exclusive, local governments of urbanized areas. Although in many states, municipalities have more wide-ranging responsibilities and powers than other sorts of local governments, their authority is still constrained by state law. Nevertheless, municipalities are the most ubiquitous and significant form of local government and will be our primary focus. Although municipalities will be referred to throughout this book as **cities,** they may be of any size and are not necessarily large, urban places.

In most states, cities operate within counties and are created from county territory. The county continues to provide most of its services, such as administration of elections, record keeping, tax assessment, courts, and jails within the city, but the city takes over responsibility for police and fire protection and land-use planning. Cities also handle streets, parks, libraries, sewers, garbage collection, and sometimes other services they choose (but are not obliged) to provide. Some large cities also manage welfare, public health, and schools.

Such arrangements are most common in the twenty-six **consolidated city-county** governments across the country (see Table 4-1). Counties commonly contain multiple municipalities, but in these communities, the county and one or more cities have been combined into one governmental entity for efficiency and sometimes fairness. Such consolidations may also solve the problem of metropolitan fragmentation, although most cover too little territory to do so. Virginia has six such city-county consolidations, but an additional thirty-five Virginia cities operate outside county boundaries and provide both county and municipal services.

Towns and Townships

In twenty states, mostly in the Northeast, local governments called **towns or townships** perform some of the functions of cities and counties. A few in New England still have the sorts of town meetings Americans like to reminisce about, although most are governed by some sort of elected board. Towns in Connecticut and Rhode Island, which have no counties, and in Massachusetts, Michigan, New Jersey, Pennsylvania, and Vermont, function very much like municipalities. In the other thirteen states (with 85 percent of all townships), towns are mostly a vestige of frontier America, existing on paper while their functions have been taken over by municipalities or counties. Some of these towns, however, are still working local governments and some operate as administrative subdivisions of countries.[1]

Special Districts

The most numerous of all local governments are **special districts.** Unlike cities, counties, and some townships, which perform varied functions, special districts usually provide only a single service, ranging from street lighting to cemeteries. They are created when citizens or governments want a particular job done but either do not wish to delegate responsibility to a city or county or wish to service an area that does not conform to the

Table 4-1   Consolidated City-County Governments in the United States

City-County	Date of Consolidation
New Orleans/Orleans County (LA)	1805
Boston/Suffolk County (MA)	1821
Nantucket Town/Nancuket County (MA)	1821
Philadelphia and Philadelphia County (PA)	1854
San Francisco/San Francisco County (CA)	1856
New York/New York County/Brooklyn/Queens, and Richmond Counties (NY)	1874, 1898
Denver/Denver County (CO)	1904
Honolulu/Honolulu County	1907
Baton Rouge/East Baton Rouge Parish (LA)	1947
Hampton/Elizabeth City County (VA)	1952
Newport News/Warwick County (VA)	1958
Nashville/Davidson County (TN)	1962
Virginia Beach/Princess Ann County (VA)	1962
South Norfolk/Norfolk County (VA)	1962
Jacksonville/Davidson County (FL)	1967
Carson City/Ormsby County (NV)	1969
Indianapolis/Marion County (IN)	1969
Juneau/Greater Juneau Borough (AK)	1969
Columbus/Muscogee County (GA)	1970
Holland and Whaleyville Towns/Nansemond County (VA)	1971
Sitka/Greater Sitka Borough (AK)	1971
Suffolk/Nansemond County (VA)	1972
Lexington/Fayette County (KY)	1974
Anchorage/Greater Anchorage Area Borough (AK)	1975
Anaconda/Deer Lodge County (MT)	1977
Butte/Silver Bow County (MT)	1977

Source: Advisory Commission on Intergovernmental Relations, *State and Local Roles in the Federal System* (Washington, DC: U.S. Government Printing Office, 1982), p. 396.

boundaries of cities and counties. Sometimes special districts serve only a part of a city (for example, an industrial zone or the downtown area). Sometimes special districts are formed when cities, most commonly small ones, share providing fire protection, sewage, or other services. Sometimes special districts cover more than one county, usually for services such as mass transit, air pollution abatement, or water quality. These regional agencies add considerably to the complexity of urban governance because their jurisdictions and services overlap those of other local governments.

The most common and important form of special district is the **school district.** Education is a state function in Hawaii and a city or township responsibility in a few states, but in forty-five states it is provided by school districts operating separately from cities and counties.

Private Governments

Although they are not created by the states and are not technically governments, 150,000 private common interest developments now perform some governmental functions in condominium and other self-contained developments, usually with elected directors of some sort. They charge residents fees (equivalent to taxes); provide services ranging from security to buses, gardening, and maintenance; and regulate land use, landscaping, paint colors, and pets. Members are usually required to belong as a condition of residence. This phenomenon is most common in the Sunbelt, but a central city counterpart has developed where some business districts have set themselves special taxes to pay for their own security, street cleaning, or similar services. While these associations get the job done, they further fragment urban areas and insulate neighborhoods and districts, making them even less willing to participate in the larger community, much less pay taxes.

The Multitude of Local Governments

Not counting such associations, the United States had 83,186 local governments in 1987; the number has probably grown since then. As Table 4-2 reveals, the most numerous of these are special districts (especially if schools are included in this category), followed by municipalities. Townships, although numerous, are usually not as significant as the others.

The types and tasks of local governments vary considerably from state to state, which is why this review of their functions may be confusing. Table 4-3, which designates the principal governmental provider of various services, makes the mix clear, if no less confusing. In general, however,

Table 4-2 Local Governments in the United States, 1987

Municipalities	19,200
Counties	3,042
Towns and townships	16,691
Special districts	29,532
School districts	14,721
Total	83,186

Source: U.S. Bureau of the Census, *Census of Government* (Washington, DC: U.S. Government Printing Office, 1987).

Table 4-3   Dominant State-Local Service Provider by Type of Government

	Education	Highways	Public Welfare	Hospitals	Health	Police	Fire Protection	Sewerage	Other Sanitation
Alabama	Sc	St	St	+	St	M	M	M	M
Alaska	+	St	St	St	St	M	M	M	Co
Arizona	Sc	St	St	+	+	M	M	+	M
Arkansas	Sc	St	St	+	St	+	M	M	M
California	Sc	+	+	+	Co	M	M	+	M
Colorado	Sc	St	+	+	+	M	M	+	M
Connecticut	+	St	St	St	St	+	M	+	M
Delaware	Sc	St	St	St	St	+	M	Co	+
Florida	Sc	St	St	+	St	+	M	M	M
Georgia	Sc	St	St	Sp	St	+	M	M	M
Hawaii	St	St	St	St	St	M	M	M	M
Idaho	Sc	St	St	+	St	+	M	M	M
Illinois	Sc	St	St	St	+	M	M	Sp	M
Indiana	Sc	St	St	+	St	M	M	M	M
Iowa	Sc	+	St	St	Co	M	M	M	M
Kansas	Sc	St	St	+	+	M	M	M	M
Kentucky	Sc	St	St	+	St	+	M	M	M
Louisiana	Sc	St	St	St	St	+	M	M	M
Maine	+	St	St	St	St	+	M	+	T
Maryland	Co	+	St	St	+	+	+	+	+
Massachusetts	+	St	St	St	St	+	M	+	M
Michigan	Sc	+	St	+	+	M	M	M	M
Minnesota	Sc	+	+	+	+	M	M	Sp	M
Mississippi	Sc	St	St	Co	St	+	M	M	M
Missouri	Sc	St	St	+	+	M	M	M	M
Montana	Sc	St	St	St	St	+	M	M	M
Nebraska	Sc	+	St	+	+	M	M	M	M
Nevada	Sc	St	St	Co	St	+	M	M	M
New Hampshire	+	St	St	St	St	+	M	+	M
New Jersey	Sc	+	+	St	+	M	M	Sp	M
New Mexico	Sc	St	St	St	St	M	M	M	M
New York	+	+	M	+	+	M	M	+	M
North Carolina	Co	St	Co	St	Co	+	M	M	M
North Dakota	Sc	St	St	St	St	M	M	M	M
Ohio	Sc	+	St	+	+	M	M	+	M
Oklahoma	Sc	St	St	+	St	M	M	M	M
Oregon	Sc	+	St	St	+	+	M	M	+
Pennsylvania	Sc	St	St	St	+	M	M	Sp	M
Rhode Island	+	St	St	St	St	M	M	M	M
South Carolina	Sc	St	St	+	St	+	M	+	M
South Dakota	Sc	St	St	St	St	+	M	M	M
Tennessee	+	St	St	+	St	M	M	M	M
Texas	Sc	St	St	+	St	M	M	M	M
Utah	Sc	St	St	St	+	M	M	M	M
Vermont	Sc	St	St	St	St	+	+	+	T
Virginia	+	St	+	St	St	+	M	M	M
Washington	Sc	St	St	+	+	M	M	M	M
West Virginia	Sc	St	St	St	St	+	M	M	M
Wisconsin	+	+	St	Co	Co	M	M	M	M
Wyoming	Sc	St	St	Co	St	+	M	M	M

Key: St = state; Co = county; M = municipality; T = township; Sc = school district; Sp = special district; + = more than one provider. *Source:* Advisory Commission on Intergovernmental Relations, *State and Local Roles in the Federal System* (Washington, DC: U.S. Government Printing Office, 1982), pp. 32–33.

Parks and Recreation	Natural Resources	Housing Renewal	Airports	Water Transport	Parking	Correction	Libraries	General Control	General Public Buildings
M	St	Sp	M	St	M	St	M	+	Co
M	St	St	St	M	M	St	+	St	St
M	+	M	M	M	M	St	M	+	+
+	St	Sp	M	M	M	St	+	+	+
M	+	+	M	M	M	Co	+	Co	+
M	St	M	M	M	M	St	M	+	+
+	St	+	St	St	M	St	+	St	+
+	St	Sp	Co	M	M	St	Co	St	St
+	St	+	Co	+	M	St	Co	+	+
+	St	Sp	M	St	M	St	+	+	+
+	St	St	St	St	M	St	St	St	St
M	St	M	M	Sp	M	St	M	+	+
Sp	St	Sp	M	St	M	St	M	+	M
M	St	M	M	St	M	St	+	+	+
M	St	M	M	M	M	St	M	+	+
M	St	+	M	M	M	St	+	+	+
St	St	M	Co	Co	M	St	+	+	+
M	St	M	M	St	M	St	Co	+	+
+	St	+	M	St	M	St	+	+	+
Co	St	Sp	St	St	+	St	Co	+	Co
+	St	Sp	St	St	M	St	M	+	+
M	St	M	Co	St	M	St	M	+	+
M	St	Sp	Sp	M	M	+	+	+	+
St	St	Sp	M	Co	M	St	+	+	Co
M	St	Sp	M	M	M	St	Sp	+	+
+	St	+	+	−	M	St	+	+	Co
M	St	Sp	Sp	M	M	St	M	+	+
+	St	Sp	Co	M	M	St	+	+	Co
+	St	Sp	M	Co	M	St	St	St	St
+	St	Sp	Co	St	+	+	+	+	+
M	St	M	M	M	M	St	M	+	+
+	St	M	Sp	Sp	M	St	M	+	+
M	St	Sp	+	St	M	St	Co	+	+
Sp	St	+	+	−	M	St	M	+	+
M	St	+	M	Sp	M	St	Sp	+	Co
M	St	Sp	M	M	M	St	Co	+	+
+	St	+	M	Sp	M	St	Co	+	Co
M	St	M	M	M	Sp	+	M	+	+
+	St	+	St	St	M	St	M	St	+
+	St	Sp	Sp	St	M	St	Co	+	+
M	St	M	M	M	M	St	M	+	+
M	St	Sp	Sp	M	M	St	M	+	+
M	St	Sp	M	Sp	M	St	M	+	+
+	St	St	M	−	M	St	+	+	+
St	St	Sp	+	T	M	St	+	St	St
M	St	M	M	St	M	St	+	+	+
M	St	Sp	M	Sp	M	St	M	+	+
+	St	M	Co	M	M	St	+	+	Co
+	St	M	Co	M	M	St	M	+	+
+	St	M	Co	M	M	St	Co	+	+

cities have more discretion about what they do than other local governments. Although they must supply services mandated by the state, the quality of these services is up to them (subject to their own voters, of course), while counties and special districts are much more constrained by state directives and finance.

But, in practice, these arrangements may remain confusing. Many of these local governments overlap in the complex and governmentally fragmented metropolitan areas, thus exacerbating their problems and increasing costs. A single neighborhood is commonly governed by a city, a county, a school district, and half a dozen special districts. Cities may be responsible for streets, for example, while counties or states are in charge of highways, and a special district builds mass transit. How is the total transportation system coordinated? Often it is not, but a typical response is to create yet another layer of government to attempt the job.

Variation among the states is illustrated by the uneven distribution of local governments among them. As Table 4-4 reveals, some states are extremely frugal about creating local governments while others are profligate. Hawaii, where schools are a state function, has just 18 local governments (1 city, 3 counties, and 14 special districts). At the other extreme is Illinois, with 6627 local governments (1279 cities, 102 counties, 1434 townships, 1783 special districts, and 1029 school districts). Not far behind are Pennsylvania, Texas, and California. These large, populous states no doubt require more local governments than some of those near the bottom of the list, such as Nevada and Alaska, but surprisingly, Kansas ranks fifth in local governments. Population has something to do with these numbers, but New York gets by with half as many as Illinois, and Florida manages with fewer than Colorado (and twenty-six other states). The survival of many largely vestigial townships in Illinois suggests that the numbers have something to do with history. Pennsylvania also has townships, although more active ones. But other states at the top of the list have no such excuse. More than anything else, the proliferation of local governments is bound up with politics.

The Creation of Local Governments

Local governments are not mentioned in the U.S. Constitution. Their existence and functions are left to the states. Most are created by acts of state legislatures or by their constitutions. Counties are created when states divide themselves into units as large or as small as they please, designate them as local governments, and delegate limited authority to them. The states can abolish counties or split existing counties to create new ones by legislative act or by constitutional amendment. Rural parts of urbanized counties sometimes agitate for separation. New counties are rare, however; only five were created in the 1980s, and three of these were

Table 4-4 Number of Local Governments by State, 1987

Illinois	6627	Alabama	1053
Pennsylvania	4956	Florida	965
Texas	4415	North Carolina	916
California	4331	Tennessee	904
Kansas	3803	Mississippi	853
Minnesota	3555	Massachusetts	836
Ohio	3377	Maine	800
New York	3302	South Carolina	707
Nebraska	3152	Vermont	673
Missouri	3147	West Virginia	630
Indiana	2806	Arizona	576
North Dakota	2787	Utah	530
Wisconsin	2719	New Hampshire	524
Michigan	2699	Connecticut	477
Iowa	1877	Louisiana	452
Oklahoma	1802	Virginia	430
Washington	1779	Wyoming	424
South Dakota	1762	Maryland	401
New Jersey	1625	New Mexico	331
Colorado	1593	Delaware	281
Oregon	1502	Nevada	197
Arkansas	1396	Alaska	172
Kentucky	1303	Rhode Island	125
Georgia	1286	Hawaii	18
Montana	1243	District of	2
Idaho	1065	Columbia	

Source: U.S. Bureau of the Census.

in developing areas of Alaska. Townships were created in a similar way, although they sometimes predated states; today townships are most likely to fade into disuse and be abolished by states. Special districts are similarly created or abolished by state governments or, state law permitting, by a pact between local governments or even a citizen petition, although this is rare. School districts are generally determined by states, although this responsibility is sometimes delegated to counties or cities. Large-scale regional governments may result from state action or local pacts, sometimes subject to voter approval.

Incorporation

Unlike most other local governments, cities are formed through a process of citizen petition and voting called **incorporation**. The term is derived from the Latin word *corpus* (or body) and reflects the citizens' determination to become one body—a municipal corporation—for purposes of local government. The process is described in state law, although some old cities predate their states and may have been created by colonial governments. Areas that are not part of any city are governed by counties, but as these **unincorporated areas** urbanize, residents commonly begin to demand more services than most counties can deliver. These typically include police and fire protection, road construction, sewers, water supply, or almost any other service. Residents may also wish to form a city to preserve the identity of their community or to avoid being absorbed by some other city. Affluent areas sometimes incorporate to protect their tax resources or ethnic homogeneity from an adjacent big city and its economic and racial problems.

The process almost always starts with a petition by the community's residents. If the number of signatures determined by state law is obtained, the proposal goes forward for review by the county, state, or special agency created by the state for this purpose. Such reviews were intended to determine whether or not proposed municipalities make sense in terms of tax base, land use, and existing local governments. In the past, however, these reviews were often highly political, with counties and states responding to the political clout of the incorporating area and making decisions that suited themselves. In most states, new incorporations were readily approved because counties and state legislatures dominated by rural and later suburban representatives were happy to allow urban areas to fragment rather than to facilitate the expansion of big cities. More recently, concerns about the environment and metropolitan fragmentation have led review bodies to take their mandates more seriously. If the incorporation is approved by the reviewing authority, the proposal is put to the voters of the prospective municipality. A simple majority must approve. Usually, a city charter (discussed below) is approved and officers are elected at the same time.

The process of incorporation varies considerably from state to state, both in the order of events and in rigor, but the states remain in control of the process and are responsible for its consequences for metropolitan fragmentation. Sunbelt states, except for Texas and Hawaii, have tended to be more lax about the process, at least until lately, but few Frostbelt states have been much more strict. Besides, they aren't growing any more, so the creation of new municipalities is not much of an issue.

How Local Governments Are Organized: Charters

The states recognize the existence of local governments by granting them **charters,** which lay out their boundaries, powers, responsibilities, and organization. Like a constitution, these documents enumerate the selection and powers of local officials and the structure of government, along with its basic tasks, including taxing and borrowing. The authority and procedures for passing ordinances (local laws) is also in the charter. Depending on the state and the particular type of local government, charters may be narrow and restrictive grants of power or may be relatively generous. The state, however, is always in control.

Special Law Charters

Of the three basic types of charters, the most restrictive is the **special law charter,** enacted by state legislatures for specific cities only. Each city must thus apply for its own charter and must return to the legislature for any changes it wishes to make and often for approval of its ordinances or other actions as well, especially with regard to taxes, but sometimes on far more trivial matters as well. The system is restrictive, inhibiting, and inconvenient, as well as very slow. Favoritism and unfairness are likely since some cities will have more effective representation in their state legislature than others. Dating back to colonial times when cities were chartered by monarchs, special law charters were common in the older states of the East and South. Many now have reformed systems, but some cities, mostly in the South, still operate under special law charters.

General Law Charters

Now the most common charter system, under **general law charters,** a state grants all its local governments of a particular type the same basic charter. Counties and special districts almost universally operate under general law charters, as do a majority of cities. General law charters are usually less restrictive than special law charters and, although the state retains control, the problems of inconvenience and unfairness are resolved. Not all cities are the same, however. A single charter may not suit the largest and smallest cities in a state equally well, so most states classify cities by size, with different charters for different classes. As a city grows, it changes classes and may go through a state-specified procedure to move to the next class of charter, giving it broader powers.

Although general law charters are an improvement, problems arise. The classification scheme can be used to revert to virtually special law charters if the classes are drawn to include only one large city, which may be set apart for special treatment. A class of over 1 million, for example, applies only to Detroit in Michigan and Philadelphia in Pennsylvania. Another issue is what happens when cities shrink instead of growing. Detroit now enjoys the charter privileges of a city over 1 million, but the 1990 census shows that its population has fallen below that level. Must it now give up some of its powers to conform to the charter of a lower class of city?

Classification may make general law charters restrictive in some states, but in others, an optional charter system makes it even more generous. Under **optional charters,** cities are allowed to choose their form of government, including the selection and powers of officials, from a menu set out by the state. They can also change the form within broad limits. California, for example, provides a general law charter system for cities of less than 3500 people but also gives them the optional charter advantage of selecting their form of government. Once California cities grow larger than 3500, they may adopt a home rule charter (described below) granting them broader powers. But California's cities are so satisfied with the state's general law/optional system that although most are larger than 3500, only 80 of 468 (among them all the state's largest cities) have bothered to exercise their right to home rule. Thirty-nine states offer charter options.

Home Rule Charters

In the late nineteenth century, cities growing in size and political clout demanded more local discretion. The **home rule** movement introduced a system that allowed cities to write their own charters within broad limits still set by the state. Although the home rule movement dates from the nineteenth century, several states have only recently granted their cities this right, including Massachusetts (1965), North Dakota (1966), Florida (1968), Pennsylvania (1968), Iowa (1968), and Montana (1972). In 1970, Illinois gave home rule to all cities with populations over 25,000 and made provisions for smaller cities to achieve home rule by citizen petition and voter approval. Some form of home rule now operates in over half the states, and two-thirds of cities with populations over 200,000 enjoy home rule, although what that means varies from state to state. Basically, this broader grant of power allows a local government to choose its own form of government and take actions not otherwise prohibited by state law.

Needless to say, local governments prefer the home rule system over any of the others, and the historic trend in the states has been toward home rule, at least for cities. Other types of local governments still operate almost exclusively under general law charters or acts of state legislatures, although a modest home rule movement for counties has been under way for some time. Today, 36 states permit counties some form of home rule, usually more limited than that for cities. But only about 80 of the country's 3052 counties enjoy even such limited home rule. Most of these are large, urban counties; 11 are in California.

Although home rule seems inherently good in terms of democracy and local control, critics point out that it contributes to fragmentation by making small local governments responsible for policies that often have regional implications.[2] Industrial or housing developments in one city, for example, may cause traffic or other environmental problems for its neighbors. Given state fiscal restraints on local governments, home rule may also give them more responsibilities than they can reasonably provide for from their own, limited revenues. The ideal of home rule, however, remains sacrosanct among local governments.

Changing a Charter

Communities change, and charters, like constitutions, also need to change. Organizational structures that worked well in the last century may not be adequate in this one; systems that functioned smoothly in small cities may break down with growth and increased diversity. The next two chapters describe the forms of government laid out in city charters and how they have changed over the years, but at this point we need to note the formal mechanisms for changing a charter.

Besides setting out the charter system, state laws (or constitutions) also describe procedures for **charter amendments.** These, too, vary from state to state. In states or cities with special law charters, any change must be acted on by the state legislature. In general law systems, some changes must be made by the state legislature or by constitutional amendment. To conform to the basic concept of general law charters, each change should apply to all local governments covered by the system, which may make revision difficult. But many general law systems allow cities to revise their charters when population growth moves them to a new charter classification. Besides a formal procedure specified in state law, voter approval is usually required. In states with the optional charter plan, cities may initiate a limited range of charter revision subject to voter approval. Home rule cities may change their charters in any way not prohibited by state law, also with voter approval. In all of these cases, local governments usually originate the action, with a vote of the city council or county board, but in some states, voters may propose charter amendments and get them on a local ballot through an initiative petition.

The process of drafting or amending a charter is political because charters are not neutral documents. As the following chapters will make clear, charters distribute formal political power in a community and, once enacted, they freeze the arrangement until sufficient countervailing powers build up to challenge it. Special and general law charters reflect the power of the state legislature and the local government interests that influence it. Optional and home rule charters mirror the power of more local interests.

Where local governments have the power to draft and amend their own charters, singular changes are usually placed on the ballot by the city council or by citizen initiative. More controversial or sweeping change typically starts with an elite "blue ribbon" committee and culminates in a vote. Charter review bodies are sometimes elected, but more often they are appointed by city officials. Typically, they are the community elite:

business and civic leaders, along with some interest group delegates and academics. Rarely are they representative. Their proposals, however, must be submitted to the voters who are generally skeptical about change. Nevertheless, elites often win because of low voter turnout and consensus among community leaders, including the local press.

Charters need revision from time to time to adapt to changing communities and priorities. Charters that do not adapt stultify elements of the community and isolate the local government. But charter change can become obsessive and get out of hand. San Franciscans, for example, vote on an average of a dozen charter amendments every election. The more they amend their charter, the longer and more detailed it gets, constraining local officials and requiring even more amendments. San Franciscans, however, have little trust in government and rejoice in their hyper-democracy.

How States Create Local Growth Machines

Cities and counties can grow by intensifying land use within their borders, increasing development and diversity. Cities, but not counties, can also change their borders, expanding by annexation. The powers for both forms of growth, however, come from the states.

Land-Use Planning

Probably the greatest power the states allocate to cities and counties is that of deciding how land can be used. These decisions can produce great wealth as well as environmental disasters. Cities exercise land use powers within their borders and counties exercise it in areas that are not part of any city. As a general principal, however, counties are supposed to be for rural and other governmental purposes, not development. Most states want development directed to existing urban areas in cities with service infrastructures. No wonder cities have been labeled growth machines when the power over land and development is one of the few that is clearly theirs and when only they can address the demands of land-related interests. Profligate use of these powers has, however, caused states to impose some controls, such as general plans and environmental impact reports.

The mechanisms for growth within cities and counties are zoning and general planning. Through **zoning,** local governments reserve areas for specific land uses, ranging from single-family, suburban-style homes to high-rise apartments, shopping malls, and industry. Because it limits the rights of property owners to do what they want with their land, zoning was challenged in the courts, but in 1926 the U.S. Supreme Court ruled it a constitutional use of local power,[3] and its use spread rapidly. **General plans,** another innovation of this century, sum up and aim to rationalize all of a community's zones and project intended patterns of future development. Sewers, street plans, parks, and other public facilities are included. The idea is to provide guidelines for future development, although many general plans only reflect what already exists. Changes in zoning or general plans, often sought by developers, keep local governments busy, but these are their main tools for controlling—or encouraging—growth.

Local governments also facilitate or impede growth through capital improvement or infrastructure projects such as roads, storm drains, sewers, and other physical facilities. Without them, growth cannot occur. Private developers can, and increasingly do, pay for such improvements, but local government is charged with seeing that they are provided, one way or another, and has traditionally done so at taxpayer expense, much to the satisfaction of developers.

Annexation

Another way cities grow is by adding to their territory through the process of **annexation.** Only unincorporated areas (not part of any other city) may be annexed; once a city runs up against another city, it can expand no further. Counties have fixed boundaries, however, and cannot annex territory because they are entirely surrounded by other counties (remember, all of the territory of all but two states is divided into counties).

Although unincorporated areas that are already developed may be annexed, most annexations occur when cities want to add land for new development to expand their population and tax base or to gain territory for major public facilities such as airports. Landowners often seek annexation by a city because counties don't want to provide urban services and won't allow them to develop their property. Occasionally, little unincorporated residential areas request annexation to obtain city services, such as sewers or police protection. In some states, the legislature or the courts must approve annexations. Virginia, for example, requires approval of annexations by a special three-judge panel. In some other states, only the city must approve, but in most, the landowners of uninhabited areas and residents of inhabited places must give their approval as well. Landowners are often eager for annexation, but residents equally often use their power to veto absorption by an expanding city out of fear of higher taxes and loss of community identity.

Growing cities, particularly in the Sunbelt, annexed aggressively from the 1950s to the 1980s, doubling, trebling, and quadrupling their territory in some cases. All the land within a city's boundaries may not be annexed, however, either because residents resisted or the city avoided annexation. Areas with physical problems (such as toxic waste dumps) or with poor, minority populations may be skipped over by cities. The unincorporated pockets left behind will continue to be governed by the county, paying lower taxes, but receiving fewer services and sometimes causing confusion in service delivery. Sometimes unincorporated areas are more than just pockets. In Florida and Georgia, for example, unincorporated areas house a majority of the suburban population.[4] Aggressive annexation, especially by Sunbelt cities, has led to sprawling boundaries, competition among cities, and inefficient services in some areas. Strip annexations along a road or even only one side of a road to some desirable land were not unusual. Some states have prohibited such annexations; most have introduced reviews of proposed annexations by special agencies or courts to make sure they are sensible.

Where annexation is relatively easy, however, the problems of metropolitan **fragmentation** are less severe since the central city can absorb emerging suburbs. Thanks to progressive state annexation policy, Charlotte, North Carolina, has been able to do just that. In other areas, emerging suburbs incorporate, forming their own cities to avoid becoming part of the growing central city, which they fear will share its problems with them and raise taxes. Such **defensive incorporation** preserves the racial and class homogeneity of the suburb, but adds to the isolation of the central city and increases metropolitan fragmentation. In general, however, state laws encourage fragmentation by making incorporation easy and annexation difficult. Big cities in the Frostbelt long ago found themselves surrounded by incorporated suburbs and thus unable to expand, with tax- and job-generating growth moving to the suburban fringes. Lately, some Sunbelt cities have hit the same barrier.

Cities sometimes give up territory by the process of **deannexation** or detachment, although this is rare. In the past, minority neighborhoods have been deannexed by cities with white majorities fearing domination by a growing minority vote, but federal courts have firmly rejected such deannexations as unconstitutional. A few cities have given up territory to tidy up irrational borders created by annexation wars dating back to the 1950s. In such cases, states require another city to annex the territory. Both cities and the residents of the area must approve.

Almost as rarely, two or more cities may merge or consolidate, usually when one cannot provide adequate services to its residents. Voters in each city must approve the **consolidation.** A vote is not generally required for school district consolidations, however, and after World War II, states reorganized school districts through this process, reducing their number from over 100,000 to 14,721.

But despite such realignments, most metropolitan areas, as the preceding chapter noted, are characterized by governmental fragmentation and an inequitable distribution of needs and resources. These are a direct result of state policies on annexation and incorporation. If a state wants few local governments and less fragmentation, it can make annexation and consolidation easy and incorporation difficult. Instead of many cities in an urban region, one large one will predominate, with needs and resources pooled and a government that can address problems on a wider scale.

Alternatively, states may encourage fragmentation by making annexation difficult and incorporation easy, so dozens of suburban cities will be formed. Except for a few states, such as Texas, Missouri, and North Carolina, most have policies that encourage fragmentation because state legislators have been more eager to please rural and suburban voters than those of big cities. Serving their short-term political interests, however, has created serious long-term problems for metropolitan regions. Defenders of these arrangements point out that fragmentation provides small-scale, accessible local governments and gives citizens choices.

The States and Local Finance

Another crucial area of state influence over local government is finance. Local governments are heavily dependent on the states, not only for direct financial aid, but also because states set the conditions for local taxation, borrowing, and spending.

Whether a local government can collect a sales, property, income, or other tax is controlled by the state. In most states, only specific types of local taxes are allowed, although the generous home rule charters of some states give cities broad options. Most, however, are strictly limited to a few types of taxes. Principal among these is the **property tax,** which is levied on land and buildings. The heavy reliance of cities on property taxes (forced on them by states) contributes to their propensity to be growth machines, because growth means new development, higher land values, and increased local revenues.

Tax rates are also usually limited or even set by the state. The **tax rate** is the percent of income, property, or other value collected as a tax. A common rate of sales tax, for example, is 5 percent; a property tax rate might be at 1 percent of the property's value. States often fix the rate or set an upper limit below which local governments may choose a rate. Such restrictions constrain the ability of local governments to obtain the revenue they may need and so limit not only tax rates but spending.

States also control the conditions for local **borrowing,** including how much may be borrowed, how and when the money must be repaid, and how it may be spent. Local governments are universally prohibited from deficit spending, but they may borrow for **capital improvement** or infrastructure projects such as roads, buildings, or sewage plants. The total amount a local government may borrow is also set, usually based on the community's total property value since borrowing is ordinarily paid back from property taxes. Some borrowing, however, is paid back by revenues from projects built with the loan, such as airports or stadiums.

State restrictions on tax types, rates, and borrowing are commonly supplemented by requirements for voter approval in **tax referendums.** An extraordinary majority—often three-fifths of the voters—may be required to pass local tax proposals, an amount rarely achieved with today's tax-hostile electorates and one that states rarely require for their own taxes.

Local spending is not as constrained by state law as taxation, but when the states assign different types of tasks (such as police, welfare, education) to the different types of local government, they are directing spending. They also **mandate spending** when they require local governments to do such things as filing environmental impact reports on development projects or when they fix a level of welfare payments but do not supply counties with enough money to meet it without dipping into their own funds. On the other hand, states also help out local governments with grants and shared taxes. About one-third of state spending goes to such **intergovernmental aid,** with up to a third of all local funds and over half of school revenues coming from the states. Much of this money, however, is earmarked for spending on specific services such as welfare and roads.

Financially, as in so many other ways, local governments are creatures of the state.

States Rights: The Bottom Line

Besides the broad powers of states over local governments discussed thus far, states may preempt local action on key policies. Even where local governments were sympathetic, for example, efforts of public employees to unionize were thwarted until state laws were changed in the 1960s and 1970s. Recently, some states have preempted local action to control rents, guns, and smoking with their own laws. "In Illinois," *The Municipal Year Book* reports, "Home-rule powers were preempted on matters regarding consumption taxes, cable television, above-ground storage tanks, the pay of police and fire officers injured in the line of duty, and floodplain and floodway zoning."[5] States also set standards for local services. New York State, for example, sets the caseloads of social workers, thus making staffing decisions for its local governments. In California, such mandates became so burdensome that local governments lobbied for and won a state agreement to institute no further mandates without funding.

All these powers of states over local governments are determined by the state legislatures (or sometimes by the voters) in laws or in state constitutions. Laws or statutes are easier to change and so are more flexible, but many states have fixed the rights and powers of local governments more rigidly in their constitutions, which may be changed, but not so easily. Entrenchment of their rights in constitutions sometimes protects local governments from hostile legislatures, but may also be intended to constrain them.

Like anything in the law, disputes arise and go to the courts. Legal precedent, however, gives states the advantage. Judge John F. Dillon laid it out in 1872 in what has come to be known as **Dillon's Rule:**

> It is a general and undisputed proposition of law that a municipal corporation possesses and can exercise the following powers, and no others: First, those granted in express words; second, those necessarily or fairly implied in or incident to the power expressly granted; third, those essential to the accomplishment of the declared objects and purposes of the corporation—not simply convenient, but indispensable. Any fair, reasonable, substantial doubt concerning the existence of power is resolved by the courts against the corporation, and the power is denied.[6]

In short, local governments may only do exactly what the states say they may do. They have no inherent rights or constitutional status. When disputes arise, the states win so long as the powers they allocate to local governments have been explicitly stated in the law. Exceptions to this strict interpretation have arisen, however, where states have granted local governments a general police power to see to the community's well-being. Some states even give home rule cities the right to do whatever is not otherwise prohibited by state law. For most local governments, however, Dillon's Rule translates to state domination. This shouldn't be surprising, given that states came first and then created local governments. Naturally, the states did not give away all their power in the process. The home rule movement has modified this somewhat, but the fact remains that local governments have no inherent right to exist except at the behest of the states, which can alter their power or even abolish local governments.

Those who have power surrender it only when forced to by countervailing power. Although local governments have gained over the years, they have never accumulated sufficient political clout to force states to grant them broad powers. Their best opportunity came when big cities gained enough population to threaten to dominate state elections. By the 1920s, urban residents were becoming the majority in some states and should have gained control of their legislatures. At about that time, however, rural representatives who still controlled some of these legislatures, ceased the regular **reapportionment** or redrawing of legislative districts to reflect population change. Over the years, the population of some legislative districts grew unequal, with far more people in urban districts than in rural ones. The resultant **malapportionment** enabled rural legislators hostile to the expanding, tax-hungry cities to keep the upper hand. In addition, some states used a federal plan to choose members of the upper house of their legislatures, so their members represented counties (just as U.S. senators represent states) with unequal populations. Rural legislators dominated there, too.

Malapportionment and county representation were ruled unconstitutional by the U.S. Supreme Court in the 1960s on grounds that they denied each person an equal vote ("one man, one vote," was the phrase used by the Court).[7] The reapportionment that followed brought fair representation by population to state legislatures. But reapportionment came too late for big cities. By the 1960s, growth was concentrated in the suburbs, so although cities gained fair representation, the suburbs benefited most, and suburbs are no friends to cities. They incorporated (under conditions made easy by rural legislators antagonistic to cities) precisely to avoid being absorbed by big cities. Suburban legislators formed alliances with rural representatives, and many state legislatures remained anticity, limiting taxes and encouraging fragmentation in metropolitan areas by keeping incorporation easy and annexation difficult. "Historically," says Philadelphia Controller Jonathan Saidel with slight exaggeration, candidates "outside of Philadelphia get elected to the Philadelphia Senate or House by stating in their brochures, 'I promise never to help the City of Philadelphia as long as I live.' "[8]

But suburban and rural legislators were not the only ones pleased to constrain local government. Political scientist Stephen Elkin argues that Dillon's Rule and other legal limitations on cities were the results of "the remaking of urban government in the later 19th and early 20th centuries . . . [in an] effort to create city governments that suited the political actors who had emerged." These actors included merchants, industrialists, landowners, and builders. They were being challenged by social reformers, socialists, and labor unions in many big cities. Dillon's "underlying purposes," Elkin writes, were "the need to protect private property [from the] kind of democracy developing in cities" through judicial and state controls. Such constraints, he goes on, were "congenial to development interests," including "the requirement of balanced budgets, restrictions on how cities can raise money, strict construction of grants of taxing authority, and restrictions on borrowing for other than capital works."[9] In short, these forces used the states and the courts to ensure that cities would be growth machines.

But while the subordination of local governments to the states is well established in the law, its degree varies from state to state. Table 4-5 ranks the states by the degree of discretion they allow their local governments, with substantial variation in evidence. Where local discretion is limited, state legislatures take a very active part in local government, but even where the grant of power is relatively generous, states often intervene. A 1989 study estimated that "about one out of five state measures . . . affected local government," ranging from 3 percent in Hawaii and Mississippi to 67 percent in Alabama.[10]

With so much activity and so much at stake, it should come as no surprise that local governments busily lobby state governments. Legislators from big cities, suburban areas, and rural counties actively pursue the interests of their constituencies, and many cities and counties hire their

Table 4-5   States Ranked by Degree of Local Discretionary Authority, 1980

A. Composite (all types of local units)	B. Cities Only	C. Counties Only	Degree of State Dominance of Fiscal Partnership*
1 Oregon	Texas	Oregon	2
2 Maine	Maine	Alaska	2
3 North Carolina	Michigan	North Carolina	1
4 Connecticut	Connecticut	Pennsylvania	2
5 Alaska	North Carolina	Delaware	1
6 Maryland	Oregon	Arkansas	2
7 Pennsylvania	Maryland	South Carolina	2
8 Virginia	Missouri	Louisiana	2
9 Delaware	Virginia	Maryland	1
10 Louisiana	Illinois	Utah	1
11 Texas	Ohio	Kansas	2
12 Illinois	Oklahoma	Minnesota	2
13 Oklahoma	Alaska	Virginia	1
14 Kansas	Arizona	Florida	2
15 South Carolina	Kansas	Wisconsin	1
16 Michigan	Louisiana	Kentucky	2
17 Minnesota	California	California	2
18 California	Georgia	Montana	3
19 Missouri	Minnesota	Illinois	2
20 Utah	Pennsylvania	Maine	2
21 Arkansas	South Carolina	North Dakota	1
22 New Hampshire	Wisconsin	Hawaii	3
23 Wisconsin	Alabama	New Mexico	2
24 North Dakota	Nebraska	Indiana	2
25 Arizona	North Dakota	New York	2
26 Florida	Delaware	Wyoming	2
27 Ohio	New Hampshire	Oklahoma	3
28 Alabama	Utah	Michigan	1
29 Kentucky	Wyoming	Washington	1
30 Georgia	Florida	Iowa	2
31 Montana	Mississippi	New Jersey	3
32 Washington	Tennessee	Georgia	2
33 Wyoming	Washington	Nevada	2
34 Tennessee	Arkansas	Tennessee	2
35 New York	New Jersey	Mississippi	3
36 New Jersey	Kentucky	New Hampshire	3
37 Indiana	Colorado	Alabama	2
38 Rhode Island	Montana	Arizona	2
39 Vermont	Iowa	South Dakota	2
40 Hawaii	Indiana	West Virginia	1
41 Nebraska	Massachusetts	Nebraska	3
42 Colorado	Rhode Island	Ohio	2
43 Massachusetts	South Dakota	Texas	3
44 Iowa	New York	Idaho	2
45 Mississippi	Nevada	Colorado	1
46 Nevada	West Virginia	Vermont	2
47 South Dakota	Idaho	Missouri	3
48 New Mexico	Vermont	Massachusetts	1
49 West Virginia	New Mexico	—	1
50 Idaho	—	—	2

*Key: 1 = state dominant fiscal partner; 2 = state strong fiscal partner; 3 = state junior fiscal partner. Applies to states in column A. Source: Advisory Commission on Intergovernmental Relations, Measuring Local Government Discretionary Authority (Washington, DC: U.S. Government Printing Office, 1981), p. 59.

own lobbyists in the state capital. Associations of cities, mayors, counties, and school districts also lobby actively.

The Federal Government and Its Local Supplicants

Like the states and other local entities, the federal government is a major element in the intergovernmental environment of local politics even though the U.S. Constitution makes no mention of this level of government and so provides it no rights or status. Indeed, the Tenth Amendment of the Constitution gives emphasis to this absence of status by reserving all power not specifically assigned by the Constitution to the federal government or the states to the states and their citizens, respectively—not to cities or counties. Nevertheless, the federal government has played a significant part in local governance throughout its history, although more at some times than at others.

Legal Relations between the Federal Government and Local Governments

Despite the lack of a direct, constitutional connection between local and national governments, the latter has played a major part in defining the rights and powers of the former, sometimes empowering but more often constraining. The U.S. Constitution and acts of the national government are superior to state and local laws (except for those rights of states and citizens reserved in the Constitution itself). Local acts must therefore conform to these laws. Citizens and interest groups frequently challenge the actions of local governments in court on grounds that their rights have been violated under U.S. law. The **federal courts** hear these cases, and their rulings have greatly affected local governments.

Perhaps the most sweeping of these was the U.S. Supreme Court decision upholding Dillon's Rule in 1923.[11] Judge Dillon was a state judge in Iowa; the federal decision gave his interpretation of state power over local government nationwide application. Two other crucial U.S. Supreme Court decisions affecting local politics have been mentioned: zoning and reapportionment. A 1926 decision recognized the right of local governments to limit property rights by zoning, clarifying a much-disputed power that remains the single greatest discretionary authority of cities and counties,[12] although contemporary forms of growth control still face legal challenges. In the 1960s, U.S. Supreme Court rulings forced state legislatures to reapportion, bringing fair representation to cities and suburbs.[13]

The federal courts have also frequently acted to protect the rights of minorities in local government, applying the Bill of Rights and a series of federal civil and voting rights acts to cities, counties, school districts, and others. Civil rights cases have banned discrimination in public places such as theaters and swimming pools, forced desegregation of schools, and intervened in housing segregation, although this subject is complicated because it overlaps zoning issues. Court rulings easing registration of minority voters have transformed politics in many communities. Some cities and counties have been ordered to change the way they select council members or to redraw council district boundaries when the courts have concluded that either discriminated against minorities. Deannexations have been carefully scrutinized by the courts to prevent unconstitutional expulsions. The rights of minorities and women also arise in current affirmative action and antidiscrimination cases. Criminal justice is another local responsibility much affected by federal court decisions. Local police practices, including reading defendants their rights, have been altered by such cases.

Although courts operate on the basis of precedent (following previous decisions), they sometimes reverse or modify their positions, which may throw local governments into confusion and difficulty. Racially "separate but equal" schools, for example, were approved by the federal courts for a century and then ruled unconstitutional, with local governments obliged to restructure their entire school systems. Recently the U.S. Supreme Court, dominated by conservatives appointed by Presidents Reagan and Bush, has questioned or limited the zoning powers of local governments, affirmative action programs, and some restraints on police practices.

Regulatory Relations

The U.S. Congress makes laws and federal regulatory agencies make rules that affect local governments, which usually comply without the necessity of judicial intervention. For local governments, federal environmental policy may be the most significant emerging area of such laws and rules. Local governments are responsible for sewage treatment and for trash disposal, either of which may pollute water or land, and both of which are now subject to **federal regulation.** Local governments also plan the distribution of housing and transportation systems, both of which affect the use of automobiles and thus air quality, also now subject to federal regulations. Local airports are regulated for both air and noise pollution. Federal standards for safe drinking water, another local responsibility, have also been imposed. All of these are surely good, but to local officials, the erosion of their authority is not.

Policy Impacts

As our discussion of suburbanization and the move to the Sunbelt revealed, federal programs not directly aimed at local governments may affect them. Suburbanization and the decline of central cities were greatly stimulated by federal housing and highway programs. These policies also facilitated Sunbelt growth, along with disproportionate federal spending on aerospace and defense in that region. Conversely, current changes in defense policy have devastated the economies of hundreds of communities as military bases are closed and spending on defense technology is cut.

Federal fiscal and monetary policy also touch local governments when they cause the economy to expand or contract. Like families, cities suffer from high inflation (goods and services cost more) and unemployment (more people on welfare or on the streets), and when recession hits, their tax revenues decline. National tax policy on mortgages, local government bonds (borrowing), and many other items influence local economies, and the national tax burden born by citizens may set a political limit on taxes local governments can impose, even when allowed by the states.

Federal Aid

Most of the federal impacts on local government discussed thus far are limiting and not particularly welcome locally. **Federal aid** programs, however, are popular with local governments because they bring money. Federal aid to local governments dates back to the early days of the republic, when land grants rather than money were given to localities to be used for schools or sold to pay for roads, bridges, harbor dredging or other transportation or communication improvements. In this century, as it ran out of land to give away, the federal government initiated cash grants-in-aid. Not much money was involved until the 1930s when President Franklin D. Roosevelt, elected with the support of urban voters, sought to stimulate the economy and bring the nation out of the Depression through federal spending programs, many of which were directed at the cities. Urban growth after World War II brought an expansion of these programs, with another burst of activity in the 1960s during the presidency of Lyndon B. Johnson.

One common form of federal aid is the **categorical grant** in which Congress designates projects (airports, libraries, and so on) and allocates funding. State and local governments then apply for the funds. If their application fits the project standards set by Congress, they may win a grant. Some local contribution, called matching funds, may be required, but the main task of the local government is to carry out the project according to federal specifications, which include rules on minority hiring and sometimes the participation of citizens in decision making. Federal departments monitor and audit local implementation of all grants. For the federal government, such grants-in-aid are a fast, economical, and handy way of getting what it wants done and pumping money into the economy without having to create new bureaucracies. For hard-up local governments, grants are a way to get money, even if they mean inconvenient paperwork and must be spent for projects that are not high local priorities. Still, local governments have complained about red tape, and critics have asserted that money is wasted on projects that aren't really needed just because the grants are available. Small and middle-sized cities also have grumbled about **grantsmanship,** the way grants seem to go to big cities that play the game best because they have effective representatives and lobbyists in Washington.

Criticism has led to reform, although politics has also been a factor. Urban grants-in-aid are most generous when Democrats are in power, not only because Democrats tend to be liberal and inclined to spend more but because big cities—the primary grant recipients—generally vote Democratic. Republican presidents Nixon, Ford, Reagan, and Bush, all conservatives with predominantly suburban supporters, cut urban grants. One reform was a formula distribution of some grant funds based on population, tax effort, income, or the like. All local governments get a share, so red tape and grantsmanship are eliminated. The money has to be spent on a specified range of programs, but communities can choose their own particular projects. A related reform consolidated groups of grants dealing with a particular policy area, such as transportation or housing, into **block grants** under which local governments gained more discretion about how to spend the money within the block category. Although amounts are set by formula, local governments still have to apply for these. The federal government also, briefly, tried revenue sharing, distributing money by formula to states, cities, and counties with no applications required and no strings attached. Local governments liked getting their checks in the mail (who wouldn't?), but the program was ended by the federal government's own budget problems. Despite reforms, grants-in-aid to state and local governments grew in number from 130 in 1960 to 539 in 1981, including programs for airports, transit, roads, housing, sewers, libraries, parks, flood control, law enforcement, water and air quality control, disaster relief, urban renewal, and many more.[14]

But 1981 was the year Ronald Reagan became president, and he sought to cut spending on domestic programs in general, and liberal, urban projects in particular. Reagan merged some programs into block grants and abolished others, reducing the number of grant programs to around 400. He also decreased spending on such grants for the first time in their history. According to *The Municipal Year Book*, "direct grant assistance declined at a 5.3 percent annual rate between 1980 and 1989."[15] Some areas were cut more than others. The budget of the Department of Housing and Urban Development, for example, was slashed $31.9 billion to $15.4 billion under Reagan and the construction of new public housing projects ground to a halt—just as homelessness in the United States increased. According to the *Financial World*, total federal grants to cities alone was "$10.8 billion in 1978–1979. Had that aid grown proportionately to the rise of city expenses, [by 1991] it would [have totaled] over $22 billion. In fact, it totalled just a third of that—a scant $7.3 billion in 1988–1989."[16] In Philadelphia alone, federal aid fell from $250 million in 1980 to $54 million in 1990. In Los Angeles—the site of the worst urban riots in U.S. history in 1992—federal aid for subsidized housing dropped by 82 percent between 1981 and 1992; for job training and employment by 63 percent; and for community development programs by 40 percent. During those years, big city budgets, on average, doubled while the federal contribution declined from 17 to 6 percent.[17]

President Reagan also introduced the **new federalism,** which devolved responsibilities, particularly for social services, to state and local governments without increasing their revenues. Federal mandates requiring state and local action on air quality and other environmental issues also added to local costs, again without funding. Local governments turned to the states, which took up part of the slack from their own budgets. Some states sought alternative revenue sources for local governments or assumed greater responsibility for traditionally local concerns such as education.[18]

President George Bush carried on the Reagan tradition, but when Democrat Bill Clinton was elected president, hopes for a revival of federal aid to local governments rose, especially among big city mayors, most of whom had supported his candidacy. His appointment of former Denver Mayor Federico Pena as Secretary of Transportation and former San Antonio Mayor Henry Cisneros as Secretary of Housing and Urban Development encouraged them, as did the promise of welfare and health care reform, which would especially help big cities. The massive federal deficit prevented a major turnaround in federal aid programs, although President Clinton attempted to increase funding for housing, transportation, and education. The ongoing problem of the deficit makes it unlikely that aid will rise to past levels, however.

Besides categorical grants, the federal government also allocates massive sums to states for unemployment and welfare programs, mostly Aid to Families with Dependent Children (AFDC). As of 1990, 41.1 percent of all federal aid to state and local governments was spent on public welfare (as compared to 15.5 percent for education, 9.7 percent for highways, 8.4 percent for housing, and 25.3 percent for other programs).[19] The states supplement these welfare funds, set standards of need and payment, and then assign the cities or counties to deliver the programs, usually further augmented by local money. Medicaid, the federal program to provide medical services for the poor, operates under the same basic arrangement: federal funds filtered through the states for programs implemented by local governments. In both cases, the local governments are obliged to carry out the programs of the higher levels of government with little local discretion and usually at some local cost over which they also have little say.

Federal Urban Policy

Although the United States has been an urban nation since at least 1920, the country has failed to develop or even seriously consider a cogent urban or metropolitan policy. Instead, the federal government has responded to crises: the Depression of the 1930s, housing shortages after World War II, drugs and crime in the 1980s, and urban riots in the 1960s and 1990s, although the latter produced little but hand-wringing. Some federal policies, such as those that encouraged suburbanization and the move to the Sunbelt, actually exacerbated the problems of big cities, despite federal urban renewal programs. The contradiction between these two—urban renewal for central cities and policies that stimulate suburbanization—illustrates the absence of a federal urban program. Local governments are reduced to being federal supplicants, making their case in court, in the lobbies of Congress, or in the regulatory agencies and departments that administer federal programs, all on a piecemeal basis. Members of Congress assist the cities in their constituencies in these efforts, although many local governments employ professional lobbyists in Washington, and big city mayors lobby individually and through the U.S. Conference of Mayors. State constraints on the taxing and spending powers of local governments encourage them to turn to the federal government, but until recently it has been turning away from them.

The Intergovernmental Context of Local Politics

The home rule movement, beginning in the nineteenth century and surviving today (mostly for counties) has struggled to wrest power and authority from the state and federal governments to expand local discretion with some success, at least until recently. For the past decade or longer, home rule has been more and more constrained by state and federal laws and court decisions. Higher governments have also devolved more responsibilities to local government without providing funding. Indeed, federal assistance to local government has contracted while the states (usually by voter initiative) have set new limits on local taxation. Despite increasing home rule and state aid, local governments in general feel that their relations with their state and federal superiors fall well short of what *The Municipal Year Book* defined as "the optimum situation," with "both high levels of discretion and high levels of assistance."[20]

If this picture seems gloomy, we should remember that similar circumstances affect local governments everywhere. Government in most other countries is far more centralized than in the United States or any of its states. By comparison to their coequals elsewhere, U.S. local governments enjoy a remarkable degree of home rule. Other countries usually impose the same organizational structures on all their local governments, while U.S. cities and, to a lesser extent, counties are allowed some choice, as we will see in the next two chapters.

ESSENTIAL TERMS		
counties	deannexation
municipalities	consolidation
cities	property tax
consolidated city-county	tax rate
towns or townships	borrowing
special districts	capital improvement
school district	tax referendums
incorporation	mandated spending
unincorporated areas	intergovernmental aid
charters	Dillon's Rule
special law charter	reapportionment
general law charter	malapportionment
optional charter	federal courts
home rule	federal regulation
charter amendment	federal aid
zoning	categorical grant
general plans	grantsmanship
annexation	block grants
fragmentation	new federalism
defensive incorporation	

FIELDWORK   1. Research the creation of your city (or another city of your choice) at the library or the city clerk's office at city hall. Who wanted the city incorporated and why?

2. Find out what type of charter your city has. Most cities publish their charters in booklet form, although general law cities may not since their charter is found in state law. Find out how your city's charter can be amended and study a recent amendment. How did the amendment change the charter? Who proposed the amendment and why? Check newspapers to see if there was a campaign for and against the amendment. Who took which side and why? What was the voters' decision?

3. Go to your city or county clerk's office and check how much of your local government's money comes from the state and federal governments. Look at one or more budgets from at least 5 years past and see if the proportion has changed.

NOTES   [1]G. Ross Stephens, "The Least Glorious, Most Local, Most Trivial, Homely, Provincial, and Most Ignored Form of Local Government," *Urban Affairs Quarterly* 24, no. 4 (June 1989): 501–512.

[2]See Sho Sato and Arvo Van Alstyne, *State and Local Government Law*, 2nd ed. (Boston: Little, Brown, 1977), p. 143.

[3]*Village of Euclid* v. *Ambler Realty* 272 US 364, 1926.

[4]Vincent L. Marando and Robert D. Thomas, *The Forgotton Governments: County Commissioners as Policy Makers* (Gainesville: University Presses of Florida, 1977), p. 22.

[5]David R. Berman, "State Actions Affecting Local Governments," *The Municipal Year Book* (Washington, DC: International City/County Management Association, 1989), p. 129.

[6]John Dillon, *Commentaries on the Law of Municipal Corporations* (Boston: Little, Brown, 1922), p. 448.

[7]*Baker* v. *Carr*, 369 US 189, 1962; *Reynolds* v. *Sims*, 377 US 533, 1964.

[8]Quoted in *The New York Times*, 8 October 1990.

[9]Stephen Elkin, *City and Regime in the American Republic* (Chicago: University of Chicago Press, 1987), pp. 19, 20–21, 50.

[10]David R. Berman "State Actions Affecting Local Governments," *The Municipal Year Book,* (Washington, DC: International City/County Management Association, 1990), p. 55.

[11]*Trenton* v. *New Jersey*, 262 US 182, 1923.

[12]*Village of Euclid* v. *Amber Realty*, 272 US 365, 1926.

[13]*Baker* v. *Carr*, 369 US 189, 1962; *Reynolds* v. *Sims*, 377 US 533, 1964.

[14]U.S. Bureau of the Census, *Statistical Abstract of the United States, 1983* (Washington, DC: U.S. Government Printing Office, 1983), p. 296.

[15]Frank Shafroth, "The Reagan Years and the Nation's Cities," *The Municipal Year Book* (Washington, DC: International City/County Management Association, 1989), p. 115.

[16]Katherine Barrett and Richard Greene, "American Cities," *Financial World*, 19 February 1991, p. 24.

[17]David R. Morgan and Michael W. Hirlinger, *Urban Affairs Quarterly* 29, no. 2 (December 1993), p. 257.

[18]See Berman, note 10, pp. 55–70.

[19]Advisory Commission on Intergovernmental Relations, *Significant Features of Fiscal Federalism*, Vol. 2 (Washington, DC: U.S. Government Printing Office, 1992), p. 62.

[20]Berman, note 5, p. 131.

PART **II**

Official Decision-Makers:
Inside City Hall

We now turn from the social, economic, demographic, and intergovernmental contexts of local politics to the content of the charters that create and empower local governments. In these chapters, we will examine the structures, institutions, and forms of local government, concentrating on cities with asides on counties and special districts.

Charters and forms of government allot power formally, but we must bear in mind that formal power, or authority, is only one kind of power. This sort of power comes with office or position. Its holders may order us to act in certain ways and prohibit others with legal sanctions such as fines or imprisonment to back them up. But informal power, such as the influence of political parties, newspapers, chambers of commerce, neighborhood groups, or even single individuals who hold no public office, also operates in every community alongside the formal authority allocated by charter.

The informal structure of power, discussed further in chapter 11, reflects the social, economic, and demographic environment of each community and, in turn, shapes the formal distribution of power in its charter—along with state law, as we saw in the previous chapter. People with informal power seek to institutionalize that power in city and county charters through the formal structures of government they advocate, either in state or local politics. If they succeed—and if they are real power holders, they do—power is frozen for a time, to their advantage. For, as we will see, structures of government are not neutral. They give advantage to some and disadvantage others; they affect who has access to positions of power and who gains those positions; they make some more likely to win and others more likely to lose, not only in campaigns for office but on issues; and they influence the substance of public policy, or what government does.

But communities change, and so do their informal power structures. New powers, perhaps economic interests or recently organized minorities, emerge and expect access. If the formal distribution of power is too rigid to absorb them, if they fail to gain attention or office, they may conclude that governmental structures are holding them back and seek to change those structures. If the community and its informal power structure have changed enough—if the new interests are really powerful—such a change will occur. The formal allocation of power will be brought into line with informal power, at least until the community changes again. This interplay between formal and informal power will be apparent in the following chapters, as we view three basic forms of city government along with the forces that created them.

5

Forms of Government: From Weak Mayors and Machines to the Beginnings of Reform

The oldest form of local government in the United States is the town or township meeting of all local voters, usually held annually. At these meetings, local officials are elected and laws and taxes are approved. This system, which dates from colonial times, operates only in some New England states and has become rare because few communities are small enough for it to function well, even though it remains a U.S. ideal. When a town gets to be more than a village, more elaborate structures are usually adopted.

Since the days of the town meeting, U.S. communities have grown and developed, increasing in diversity and complexity. The forms of government they adopted also changed. Town meetings were gradually replaced by elected, representative government. In the early days of the republic, the weak mayor system predominated, and it still survives in some communities. But by the mid-nineteenth century, spurred by economic growth and immigration, corrupt political bosses and machines had subverted the weak mayor system and set in motion an urban reform movement. The initial result of reform was the strong mayor form of government, although by the turn of the century, reformers were ready to propose more radical change. Meanwhile, change has generally left counties behind, operating under something like the weak mayor system without the mayor.

The Weak Mayor Form of Government

The oldest major form of local government in the United States is the weak mayor system, forged by the American Revolution. Having just over-thrown an authoritarian monarch, Americans were unwilling to grant their own executive officers much power. At the national level, the Articles of Confederation set up a feeble government with virtually no executive. States and cities at least had governors and mayors, but their powers were strictly and elaborately limited by even more checks and balances than those that would appear in the U.S. Constitution in 1787.

The Mayor.   The mayor in the **weak mayor system** is only a nominal chief executive. The city council (the local legislature) and other appointed or elected executive officers also hold substantial power. Initially, the mayor was appointed by the council from among its members and served mainly as a presiding officer. Some weak mayor cities still operate this way, although after 1820, many began to elect their mayors directly. The weak-ness of the office comes from limits on the traditional executive powers of appointment and administration.

The Council.   **City councils** in this form of government also reflect the democratic values of its founders. They tend to be large in size, numbering fifteen to fifty members, and are elected by wards or districts. Each district covers just a part of the city, ensuring every neighborhood its own council member, although in large districts members may represent several neigh-borhoods. Besides acting as the legislature, the city council in a weak mayor form of government plays a prominent part in the normally execu-tive functions of appointment, administration, and budgeting. Council powers are enhanced by the inability of the mayor to veto or reject its actions. But power is not centralized in the council, either. As the demands on city government became too great for councils to handle, some responsibility was devolved to commissions or boards. Usually with around five members appointed by the council or mayor or both, or sometimes elected, these commissions run certain city departments.

The Long Ballot.   In the 1830s, Jacksonian democracy brought the election of other members of the executive branch, including the city attorney, city clerk, treasurer, and department heads such as the police chief (see Figure 5-1). The **long ballot** resulting from the election of so many officers is highly democratic, but it also fragments executive authority. Even where charters give mayors some responsibility for the operations of the city departments, their administrative powers are severely limited by having to deal with independently elected department heads with constituencies of their own. To compound the problem, other officers, boards, or com-missions are appointed by the city council to run departments. The best a

FIGURE 5-1 The Weak Mayor Form of Government

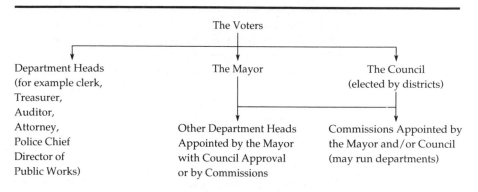

weak mayor can usually hope for is the power to appoint some of these officials, often subject to city council approval and rarely with the power to remove appointees from office.

The Weak Mayor System

The weak mayor system, with mayors denied the veto and with their administrative and hiring and firing powers severely constrained, accomplished the political goal of its postrevolutionary framers, who wanted to avoid dictatorial executives. But the cities they wrote their charters for were small, and their electorates, confined to white male property owners were smaller, with clearly shared interests. The weak mayor system likely worked very well in such circumstances since all its participants were similar and easily agreed on city policy. But cities grew and became more diverse, with expanding populations demanding access to local offices and disagreeing more about what should be done. From the 1820s onward, the ideals of Jacksonian democracy gradually brought wider participation and more elected officials within the basic weak mayor system.

The goal of Jacksonian democracy was greater citizen participation but, unfortunately, the system didn't always function ideally. Power was fragmented, with authority widely distributed among a large number of officeholders, making it hard to get things done and often failing to deliver effective, efficient local government. Political leadership could not surmount this fragmentation because the office of mayor was, by the very nature of the system, little more than titular. No one person was clearly in charge.

Even the democratic values of the system were subverted by the absence of accountability—when things went wrong, the voters didn't know who to blame. For example, if crime increased in a neighborhood, the voters could go to their district council member, who could claim to have raised the issue only to have been ignored by the police chief, the mayor, and the rest of the council. The police chief and the mayor, representing the same voters, might blame the problem on one another or on an ineffective council representative. Short of throwing them all out, which is difficult for a single neighborhood to achieve, the discontented constituents could only mutter among themselves and bolt their doors.

The weak mayor system works reasonably well in small, homogeneous cities where people are in general agreement and don't expect a lot from their government. When they need something done, informal, personal relationships can cut through the fragmentation. So the weak mayor form works best when local government doesn't need to do much, as was the case at the time of its creation. Industrialization, immigration, and growth put the system under strain, however. Diversity increased and social homogeneity was reduced. Disagreements and conflicts arose as new interests and groups wanted a piece of the action. The informal, personal contacts of small communities no longer function in big cities, where social relations are formal and impersonal. Growth also brings bigger problems, from sewage to traffic and crime, which need action and which a leaderless, fragmented government simply cannot solve. Local growth machine interests often feel that inefficient government is holding them back. For all these reasons, the weak mayor form of government today operates mostly in small, relatively homogeneous cities, mostly in the Northeast and Midwest. Only a few large cities, including Atlanta, Chicago, and Los Angeles, still soldier along with weak mayor systems, often with considerable grumbling.

Los Angeles, the second largest city in the United States, is case in point. The mayor of Los Angeles has a high profile, but limited power. Most of the city's sixteen departments, including police and fire, are run by independent commissions that hire the department heads and oversee their budgets. Commissioners, who serve 5-year terms, are appointed by the mayor with council approval, but a mayor who stays in office long enough can pack them with allies. Tom Bradley, Los Angeles' first black mayor, was elected to an unprecedented five 4-year terms, which enabled him to gain considerable influence over the city's commissions. But even Mayor Bradley, an ex-cop, could not control his city's police department. Even with city council support, Mayor Bradley was unable to fire the city's controversial police chief after the videotaped beating of a black citizen by police officers in 1991 outraged the city. The chief, appointed by the police commission rather than the mayor, enjoyed the added protection of civil service rules, a reform adaptation of the weak mayor system. "I cannot conceive of a city like Los Angeles where the mayor does not have the power to appoint or dismiss department heads," said Bradley. "It's a terrible system."[1] A bad situation turned worse in 1992 when the white officers who were videotaped doing the beating were found not guilty by a predominantly white jury, and rioting broke out in Los Angeles and elsewhere. Only unrelenting political pressure finally forced the disgraced police chief to reluctantly resign. Los Angeles voters then revised their charter to limit their police chief to a 5-year term (subject to one reappointment by the mayor), and a new, black, community-oriented chief took office. Los Angeles, with urban problems of mind-boggling complexity and 3.5 million people of astonishingly diverse backgrounds (40 percent are Hispanic, 37 percent Anglo, 13 percent African American, and 9 percent Asian), is a city that has clearly outgrown a weak mayor charter written by and for a white, business-dominated community in 1924.

Many other cities, experiencing similar if less dramatic problems, have moved beyond the weak mayor system. But charter change is not the only solution to these problems. Political organization outside the formal structures of government can be an alternative way to make awkward systems work and, in most communities, such organizations preceded structural reform.

Bosses and Machines: Coping with Fragmentation

The weak mayor system created a vacuum in leadership and authority when cities grew large. Sometime in the nineteenth century, local politicians began figuring out a way to fill the vacuum, overcome the fragmentation, and make local government work, although not necessarily efficiently or fairly. All they had to do was fill the multiple offices of the weak mayor system with allies who would cooperate with one another. With many officials elected on long ballots, campaigns and candidates had to be carefully coordinated. This was easy in small, homogeneous cities, but it became difficult when the cities grew large and diverse, with many competing groups.

Slate-making

The problem was solved by **slates** or lists of approved candidates for various offices, from coroner to city council, mayor, governor, and even president. These lists were agreed on by political party activists who cut deals at meetings, in bars, or in smoke-filled backrooms. A single candidate was chosen for each office and the candidates and their supporters all agreed to support one another. A successful slate would include candidates from different neighborhoods, ethnic groups, and other constituencies, thus pulling diverse interests together to support rather than compete with one another by providing something for everyone. Once the slate was selected, it had to be taken to the voters, and elaborate organizations evolved to do just that.

But what could hold such an organization together? Shared values or ideology might be one way, but, as analysts of political culture tell us, the United States is more pragmatic than ideological, preferring problem solving and getting things done to philosophical or theoretical debate. The particular responsibilities of local government make a practical orientation even more appropriate at that level than others. After all, local government is about streets and sewers, not war and peace or even economic systems. Besides, the diverse groups that made up the slates probably disagreed about ideological values. Political parties proved a somewhat better unifying force, at least in the past, but Americans are not particularly partisan, often voting for candidates of different parties.

Political Machines

Political parties, however, provided the emerging urban political organizations with a unifying label, even if it amounted to little more than a front. To sell its slate, organizations needed a stronger glue. They found it in greed, combined with the real and serious needs of many recently arrived immigrants in the nineteenth century industrializing cities. The slate-making organizations distributed rewards to win and hold support. These rewards were, as political scientists Edward C. Banfield and James Q. Wilson, have pointed out, "both specific and material."[2] They were specific in that only supporters received these benefits, and material in that they involved jobs, contracts, and other, often minor, favors, ranging from a turkey at Thanksgiving to a drink on election day. These rewards were distributed so efficiently that the organizations came to be called **machines.**[3] Insiders got jobs at city hall and with businesses allied with the machine. Many such businesses also profited enormously from their association with machines. Ordinary citizens could go to the machine for help (although often, the machine went to them) when they needed a ticket fixed or had problems with housing or jobs or when the kids needed a new pair of shoes. And the machine could punish as well as reward. Enemies as well as those who merely failed to support the machine were not only denied benefits but often made to suffer. They could lose jobs or contracts, be harassed by police or health inspectors, or be subjected to social abuse by neighbors.

The distribution of both rewards and punishments in exchange for support is called **patronage,** or the spoils system, based on the old saying "to the victor belong the spoils," and the machines exploited it with a vengeance. To them, local government was little more than a way of making money, not in a growth machine sense, but more immediately, out of its daily operations.

Industrialization and Immigration. In a way, the weak mayor form of government with its vacuum of power made machines inevitable, but other factors were also essential to their success. Machines have operated in homogeneous, small cities and rural communities, but they had their heyday in the growing industrial cities between about 1880 and 1930.

Before that, in smaller cities, informal, personal contacts cut through the structural inefficiencies of the weak mayor form of government and Yankee cultural values, disdainful of corruption and selling votes, predominated. But the industrial revolution transformed U.S. cities. Millions of immigrants arrived from all over Europe, often bewildered and in need of help. These urban immigrants supplied the machines with a dependent, manipulable voting base.

Ethnic identity was used as a building block by the machines, many of which were dominated by particular ethnic groups, especially, but by no means exclusively, the Irish and Italians. Saint Patrick's or Columbus Day parades became as much celebrations of political power as of ethnic traditions. Other European ethnic groups were allies, taking their places on electoral slates and enjoying their share of the machine's rewards. Newly arrived immigrants, lonely and far from their native lands, welcomed the solidarity and community the machines shrewdly provided.

How the Machines Helped. But as cynically manipulative as the machines may have been, they provided genuinely needed psychological reassurance and other, more tangible services as well. They helped assimilate the immigrant masses to U.S. society, giving them a sense of belonging to something, teaching them some aspects of U.S. culture. That is, in an immediate and practical sense, the machines were the social workers of their day. Arriving immigrants were greeted by machine operatives who spoke their language and helped them settle into the appropriate ethnic neighborhood—a sort of segregation that was useful to the machine for organizing but was also comforting to the strangers in a strange land. Housing could be found, jobs could be obtained, and the children could be placed in schools, where they quickly Americanized. If the family fell on hard times, the machine stepped in to help.

Organization of the Machines

To accomplish all this, the machines developed an elaborate organizational structure, operating under the aegis of a political party and associated with city government, but not part of it. At the top was the leader, or **boss,** with other party chieftains. These leaders might or might not be elected officials. They didn't need to be officials because their power came from the machine, not government. Government officials were sometimes merely the machine's carefully selected minions, carrying out orders. City council wards or districts provided the next organizational unit, each with its own constellation of ethnic neighborhoods and its own leader who, like the bosses above him (they were virtually all men), probably was a full-time organizer rather than the district council member. Beneath the ward boss was a network of precinct or block captains who knew everybody in their neighborhood, kept track of supporters, made sure they voted, and distributed the benefits and punishments of the machine. Once called **ward**

heelers because of the shoe leather they wore out making their rounds, they were the machine's eyes and ears in the neighborhoods, its enforcers as well as its social workers. More than that, however, they personalized the machines by being part of the communities they organized. They lived in and hung out in the neighborhoods, drinking in the bars, chatting on street corners and doorsteps, going to funerals and weddings. They knew everybody's name, from children to grandparents, and took part in their lives, providing help when it was needed. All they expected in exchange was votes, or in the case of those who got jobs and contracts, a little kickback for the campaign treasury.

For the immigrant poor and working classes, this was not a bad deal. Coming from undemocratic countries, their votes may not have meant much to them, but even if they did, why wouldn't they support the people who had helped and nurtured them? For the machines were not just organizations, they were people. The machine's representatives personalized politics and government. They were seen as friends by many of the constituents they helped (and kept in line). Was this such a bad deal? Machine supporters got something in return for their votes, which is more than many of today's voters feel they get. Those in need were given assistance and treated with dignity and respect because they had something the machine wanted, while even the most deserving welfare recipients today often feel insulted or humiliated by impersonal, bureaucratic welfare agencies.

Business and the Machines

Although the poor and working classes supplied the mass voting base for the machines, business interests benefited, too. Lucrative contracts for building city facilities or for goods and services purchased by the city were awarded to machine supporters, usually with an expected kickback. Millions were made and wasted in such deals. Some business allies won highly profitable licensed monopolies, or franchises, as the exclusive operators of gas, electricity, water, or trolley companies. Other businesses, such as gambling, prostitution, and speakeasies (during Prohibition) were protected by the machine, which made sure the police overlooked the operations of their pals and tormented their competitors.

Even businesses less directly connected to the machine willingly accepted its rule and sometimes used its services. Many newspapers were well connected to machines, which could help with (or create) union or distribution problems as well as supply readers. Small businesses, such as restaurants, might appreciate a lax health inspection. Industrialists or merchants might want quick zoning decisions. The machine could cut through the complexities of fragmented government and guarantee results for those who cooperated. With so much money involved, even banks acquiesced.

Urban and Rural Machines. These sorts of machines were most common in the big, industrializing cities of the Frostbelt. Among the most notorious and long-lasting machines were those of New York City, Albany, Boston, Philadelphia, Jersey City, Hoboken, Baltimore, Cincinnati, Indianapolis, and Chicago. Machines were less prevalent in the Sunbelt states, where industrialization and immigration were slower. Powerful machines nevertheless took root in New Orleans, Memphis, Savannah, Charleston, Augusta, Chattanooga, Montgomery, Jacksonville, Tampa, and San Francisco.

Machines also arose in rural areas and small cities all over the country, suggesting that masses of immigrants were not crucial to their development. The bosses of rural and small town machines could be just as ruthless and corrupt as their urban counterparts. The most famous of the urban machines were associated with the Democratic party, but in rural areas and a few big cities, such as Philadelphia, some were Republican. The entire state of California, including big cities and rural counties, was run by a Republican political machine dominated by the state's monopoly railroad from about 1880 to 1910.

Corruption, Favoritism, and Inefficiency

The machines made government work and provided an important social connection for people who might otherwise have been lost and alienated in the impersonal societies created by rapid urbanization. But their benefits were outweighed by their shortcomings. The machines were notoriously, publicly, even boastfully corrupt. "I see my opportunity and I take it," said a leader of New York's machine.[4] Taxpayers' money was stolen and legitimate business profits were drained away by machines. Local government services such as transit and utilities cost more because the minions of the machine were on the take. And these higher costs were driven even higher by inefficiency. After all, the machine was more concerned that its supporters got jobs and contracts than it was with their performance. Whether or not an applicant for a job as health inspector knew anything about sanitation or a contractor could build a sound bridge or supply well-made goods at reasonable prices was less important than their loyalty to the machine. This was the glue that held the machine together, but it almost guaranteed inefficient, amateurish, and corrupt government.

Those who benefited directly and personally, even if only occasionally and in small ways, were satisfied as were those who identified with the machine socially. But others were left out. Some ethnic groups were excluded, either because they wouldn't play the game or because they weren't invited because of prejudice. Ethnic animosities from old country homelands kept some out. Jews were excluded from some machines, but rose to leadership in others. Asians, Hispanics, and African Americans were often spurned, although in cities such as Chicago and Memphis, minority organizations operated as subsidiaries of the dominant machine.

But the largest group that was left out by the machine was the rapidly growing urban middle and upper-middle classes. These included lawyers, merchants, managers, bankers, doctors, teachers, and other professionals. Some individuals among these groups were associated with the machines, at least occasionally, but for most, the machine had little to offer. They didn't want a job at city hall or, with some exceptions, a contract either. Some didn't mind a favor now and then (such as having a ticket fixed or a zoning regulation changed), but most believed that government should take care of its responsibilities fairly and efficiently, not playing favorites and not spending tax money on inept city staff and graft. The very principles of the machine violated their professional, middle-class values, and its toleration of gambling, prostitution, and rum-running was an affront to middle-class morality. To the mostly white, Anglo-Saxon, Protestant (WASP) upper and middle classes, the machines didn't seem very American, not only in their values but also in their composition. These classes also disapproved of the way the machines bought votes by handing out favors. As educated professionals, they thought votes should be cast intelligently, for the good of the community rather than for personal benefit. But they were also apprehensive of the machine's immigrant support base, which, unlike their own immigrant forbears, was mostly Irish or eastern or southern European and Catholic. These "foreigners" were taking over "their" cities. Thanks to assimilation accelerated by the machine itself, some of the children of these foreigners joined the ranks of the middle-class malcontents.

Bigger economic interests also grew discontented at the wastefulness and inefficiency of the political machines, with which most had played along when it suited them. Some businesses wanted a more stable, reliable, and tax-efficient local government and worried about the machine's role as an intermediary with their workers. Local growth machine interests were also discontented with the political machines. Many landowners, builders, and others who sought benefits from more rapid growth concluded that the machines were holding them back. Physical improvements to the cities, such as street lighting and sewers, were not happening fast enough or competently enough. The big financial institutions that loaned cities money (through bonds) for such works were reluctant to do so when cities were notoriously corrupt. Emergent national corporations were unwilling to locate new plants in such places. Growth machines felt stymied and turned against their one-time allies in the political machines.

The Collapse of the Political Machines

The urban political machines have been dying since the turn of the century. The obvious cause of their demise is the reform movement created by the dissatisfied middle class and business interests described above. Some of the structural reforms introduced wounded the machines deeply, but such reforms could never have been achieved if other changes hadn't made them politically feasible. The reform movement and its agenda will be discussed in the next section and, in greater depth, in the next chapter, but, first, we need to consider some other forces that weakened the machines.

The reform movement would never have been possible if demographic change had not enlarged the class base for reform and weakened the machines in other ways as well. As immigrants assimilated culturally and economically, they were less willing to accept the values of machine politics and needed its jobs and help less. Many became middle class; some moved to the suburbs. Ironically, their assimilation and cultural advance was assisted by the machines, which thus contributed to their own decline. To survive, the machines needed a constant influx of needy, new immigrants, but the flow of European immigrants was cut off by national legislation introduced by antimachine reformers. Immigrants were still arriving in the cities, but by the 1920s, these were mostly African Americans from the rural South, who many racist machines refused to include—at their own peril. With a growing middle class and changed patterns of immigration, the demographic base of the machines was shrinking.

Then the Great Depression of the 1930s brought mass unemployment and hardship, slowing the rise of the middle class but not helping the machines. Although they had long exploited such conditions among the urban working class and poor, the Depression expanded the scale of their needs beyond what the machines could meet. With the support of the urban machines, Democratic President Franklin D. Roosevelt introduced the social welfare programs of the New Deal. But the new welfare system eventually hurt the machines because assistance was taken out of their hands and provided by a new welfare bureaucracy on the basis of objective need rather than political affiliation. Some machines managed to control the new bureaucracies, but over the long run, the new system they helped bring about hurt them all.

Even before the mass unemployment of the Depression, however, other urban problems had grown increasingly complex and beyond the capacity of the corrupt and technically amateur machines to solve. Industrialization and population growth increased both need and demand for improved housing, transportation, public safety, and sanitation, and the expanding middle class called for good schools and for amenities such as parks and libraries. Many machines simply could not cope with it all.

After World War II, other social changes helped finish off the machines. With the economy booming, people needed the machine less, and suburbanization proceeded apace, draining away the third or fourth generations of machine families. Radio and then television kept people indoors and at home, rather than on the stoops and in neighborhood bars and other public gathering places where the machine's operatives could socialize with them. Home visits increasingly meant that favorite TV programs were interrupted or that much time was spent silently watching them with the families.

In sum, the machines were weakened by social changes, some of which they helped bring about. The reform movement, which would have been impossible without these changes, merely hastened the process. The strength of the machines, however, is manifested by the fact that their demise took well over 50 years. Like Freddy in the Elm Street movies, many machines survived waves of change and reform to live, fight, and win again. Some fought their last battles in the 1950s, and Chicago's machine hung on until the death of its boss, Mayor Richard J. Daley, in 1976 (his son, Richard M. Daley is now mayor, but not boss, of Chicago). Although most are now history, the vestiges of machines are still important if not dominant political factions in such cities as Albany, Chicago, and Hoboken. In others, including several cities in New York and New Jersey, their style of favors in exchange for support still operates.

Today, journalists and other people often refer to the "machine" of this or that politician, but usually they only mean the organized backers of an individual, a group that is not like the old machines, either in structure or in strength. The organizations of today's politicians are mostly loyal to a single person, but the loyalty of the old machines was to themselves, whoever the leaders were. Bosses were important, but the machines survived changes at the top. Today "machine" is usually a figure of speech, as in the concept of growth machines introduced in chapter 1.

The First Reform: The Strong Mayor Form of Government

Opposition to political machines is as old as the machines themselves. After the Civil War, crusading journalists, who came to be known as muckrakers, exposed corruption and campaigned for change, joined by many upper- and middle-class, often anti-immigrant, citizens. Aroused opponents of the machines soon emulated them, putting together slates of candidates and sometimes successfully winning local office. They rarely gained complete control or stayed in office long, however, because the ideals that held them together were not as binding as the machine's rewards.

The opponents of the machine claimed they just wanted good government, not for themselves personally, but, they insisted, for the community as a whole. Their perception of the public good was often confused with their own class interests, but few seem to have entered politics to gain individual benefits. Unlike their machine counterparts, most did not see themselves as career politicians and expected to go back to their own businesses and professions after a term or two in office. But well meaning as they may have been, they usually found themselves unable to achieve their goals.

The machine was not easily beaten. Its operatives hung on, gaining advantage where they could. Perhaps they could win just a few of the offices on the long ballots. Under the fragmented weak mayor form of government, these offices might be enough to stop the reformers from doing much. Or they would simply outlast the reformers. Maybe it would take an election or two, but the promise of personal reward kept their workers loyal while they waited for the reformers to go back to their businesses, more likely frustrated than satisfied with their accomplishments. One machine politician called the reformers "mornin' glories,"[5] because they bloomed briefly, then wilted. When they did, the machine made its comeback.

Soon the advocates of good government concluded that winning occasional elections was not enough. They needed to change not only the personnel of local government but also its structure. After all, the nation had moved beyond the Articles of Confederacy to stronger government barely a decade after the revolution. Many states had similarly reformed their governments. Now it was the cities' turn.

The **reform movement** was born, and its first product was the strong mayor form of government. The concepts of reform and strong mayor may seem contradictory since the reformers were fighting powerful bosses. But the bosses' strength came from their command of the machines or party organizations, not the office of mayor. As noted, many bosses never held elective office. The idea of the reformers was to put enough power in the hands of a single, strong executive to get something done once they won an election.

The Short Ballot.   Instead of a long ballot with several elected executive officers and department heads, under the strong mayor form of government only one executive, the mayor, is elected. On this **short ballot,** the city council is also usually smaller, so voters elect fewer officials and can more easily hold them accountable. As Figure 5-2 suggests, this much-simplified structure of city government revolves around the chief executive.

The Strong Mayor.   The office of mayor was modeled on that of the U.S. president. The mayor is elected for a 4-year term and can be reelected for unlimited terms in a pure **strong mayor system** (term limits were introduced later in some cities). As chief executive, the mayor formulates the budget, recommends policy, and oversees the day-to-day administration of city programs. The mayor appoints and removes department heads,

FIGURE 5-2 The Strong Mayor Form of Government

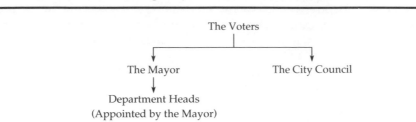

usually without the approval of the city council, although mayoral appointment of some officials, such as the city attorney and the city clerk, may require council approval or, in some cases, these are still elected positions. Members of city boards and commissions are also appointed and removed by the mayor, but usually with council consent.

The Council. The city council in a strong mayor form of government is a more purely legislative body with less involvement in administration. Nevertheless, the council must approve the mayor's budget and programs and often some appointments. Council actions, however, may be vetoed by the mayor, with a two-thirds vote by the council required to override the **veto.** While weak mayors usually preside over council meetings and vote with the council, strong mayors generally do not. As with the national government, the executive branch is clearly separate from the legislature.

The Strong Mayor System

The benefits of the strong mayor form of city government include leadership, clear accountability to the voters, and better coordinated government more able to deal with complex urban problems. The fragmentation of the weak mayor form of government is resolved—government can govern. Political scientists generally advocate the system for these reasons. Mayors like it, too. But activists in many communities worry about a single individual having so much power (an issue that strangely arises for mayors but rarely for the far more powerful U.S. president). Checks and balances are provided by council approval of the mayor's budget and policy proposals, but some cities have modified the pure strong mayor form of government with additional checks, including term limits and council approval of selected appointments.

Another common concern about the strong mayor system has been that although the chief executive must be a skilled politician to get elected, there is no guarantee that he or she will have the management skills to run a highly complex administrative apparatus (another concern that doesn't seem to arise with the presidency). Mayors who want to stay in office or advance may also pay more attention to winning elections than to mundane matters of administration. To address this problem, most cities with strong mayors have changed their charters to allow the mayor (usually with council approval) to appoint a **chief administrative officer** (CAO). The CAO is supposed to be a trained administrator, charged with overseeing the technical operations of the city, answerable to the mayor and under the overall policy direction of the mayor and council. San Francisco introduced the CAO in 1931 and many cities have adopted it since then. Some, including New York and Los Angeles, have more than one of these officials and call them deputy mayors.

Overall, the strong mayor form of government is most commonly found in large cities, including Baltimore, Boston, Cleveland, Detroit, New York, Philadelphia, Pittsburgh, St. Louis, and San Francisco, and mostly in the Northeast and Midwest, where the U.S. big cities first emerged. Few cities, however, have systems as pure and simple as the one presented in Figure 5-2. Most have chosen to introduce at least modest limits on executive power. Such limits are the result of the chronic mistrust of executives in local government—a mistrust far greater than that of state and national executives. The bosses and machines created the distrust and went on justifying it, for if the strong mayor system made it easier for reformers to gain control of local government and get things done, it also made it easier for the machines. Their slate-making was simplified and their command of government was often more thorough thanks to this reform.

Efforts to make the office of mayor more powerful started in the 1880s and continued through the turn of the century, a time when enough of the social changes described above had occurred to produce a reform movement, but not to destroy the machines. Far from being vanquished, they survived and even thrived under the strong mayor form of government. Their frustrated opponents reacted by escalating their demands for reform.

Counties: Anachronism in Action

While city government has gone through the changes described above and the more radical ones that followed, county government has mostly remained as it began, something like the weak mayor form of government without the mayor (see Figure 5-3). Typically, a three- to five-member legislative body called the **county commission** or the **board of supervisors** is elected on a long ballot that includes from three to over a dozen department heads. Other department heads are appointed by the county commission or board. The legislative body dominates and, as with the weak mayor form of government, the county system tends to result in fragmented government and unclear accountability for the voters, especially when the number of directly elected executive officers is great. Even where only a few executives are elected, the multiple membership of the county board or commission can result in conflict and deadlock rather than leadership.

This anachronistic system survives because, as we learned in chapter 4, counties, even more than cities, are creatures of the state. Unlike cities, they function as administrative agencies of the state, carrying out its programs and policies. As such, the states keep tighter control, but leadership and accountability may also be less urgently needed than in cities, and fragmentation less of a problem. Moreover, in many states, counties are primarily responsible for local government in rural areas with homogeneous populations that make few demands—a little like the cities of the early United States, when the weak mayor form of government worked well enough.

Bosses and machines ruled counties just as they ruled cities. In fact, rural counties with few immigrants may have had the strongest and most ruthless machines of all. The reform movement rarely gained momentum in the counties, however, perhaps because of the power of their machines, but more likely because of the absence of a middle-class constituency for reform. Some reforms were introduced, but with counties so closely controlled by the states, the battleground was usually the state legislature rather than the county government. Counties did not, however, follow cities in adopting a strong mayor form of government. Even now, over a hundred years since that reform was introduced in cities, only a few dozen counties have an elected chief executive (weak or strong). (Many of these, including Denver, San Francisco, New Orleans, and New York, have consolidated city and county governments.) Some urban counties have introduced other reforms to cope with increasingly complex problems and diverse populations. Nevertheless, more than 2700 of the 3042 counties still have the basic form of government shown in Figure 5-3. In some states, such as Texas, they are given no alternative.

FIGURE 5-3   County Government

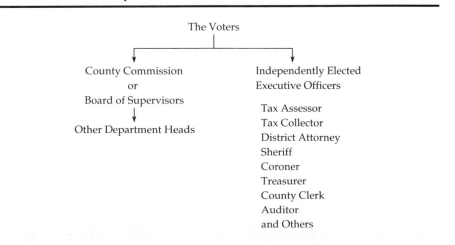

The Voters

County Commission
or
Board of Supervisors
↓
Other Department Heads

Independently Elected
Executive Officers

Tax Assessor
Tax Collector
District Attorney
Sheriff
Coroner
Treasurer
County Clerk
Auditor
and Others

Change and Reform

As we noted, U.S. cities emerged in the nineteenth century, burgeoning with growth brought about by industrialization and immigration. And this growth also brought political change. The old order, the WASP elites, lost control of local politics to the bosses and machines who skillfully organized and controlled the immigrant masses while cutting deals with business interests. Working class and poor voters benefited from the machine in small, personal ways, but machines never really spoke for their class interests or advocated serious social reform. In fact, it was in the machine's interest to keep its supporters dependent. But change continued, with an emerging urban middle class and, eventually, reduced immigration, the Depression, New Deal social welfare, and suburbanization. The base of the machine started to crumble and the reformers launched their challenge, first electorally and then structurally with the strong mayor form of government. Neither defeated the machine, which lived to fight another day, and often to win. But the reformers were not easily discouraged and, as we will see, history was on their side.

ESSENTIAL TERMS

city council
weak mayor system
long ballot
slates
machines
patronage
boss
ward heelers

reform movement
short ballot
strong mayor system
veto
chief administrative officer
county commission or board of
   supervisors

FIELDWORK

1. Research the political history of your community at the local library. Has a political machine ever operated there? What was its base, who was left out, and how long did it last? (If you live in a suburb or other relatively new municipality, pick a large, older city nearby.)

2. Research the form of government of your county and of a large city in your state. Compare and contrast these forms of government with one another and with the weak mayor and strong mayor models described in this chapter.

3. Go to your county office and research the governmental structure of your county. Is it like any of the systems in Figures 5-1, 5-2, or 5-3?

NOTES

[1]*The New York Times*, 31 March 1991.
[2]Edward C. Banfield and James Q. Wilson, *City Politics* (New York: Vintage, 1963), p. 115.

[3]For studies of political machines, see John M. Allswang, *Bosses, Machines, and Urban Voters* (Baltimore: Johns Hopkins University Press, 1986); Alexander B. Callow, Jr., ed., *The City Boss in America* (New York: Oxford University Press, 1976); Harold F. Gosnell, *Machine Politics: Chicago Model* (Chicago, University of Chicago Press, 1937); Milton Rakove, *Don't Make No Waves, Don't Back No Losers* (Bloomington: Indiana University Press, 1975); Mike Royko, *Boss* (New York: Signet, 1971); J. T. Salter, *Boss Rule* (New York: McGraw-Hill, 1935).

[4]William L. Riordan, *Plunkitt of Tammany Hall* (New York: Dutton, 1963), p. 3.

[5]Ibid., pp. 17–20.

6

Reform Politics: The City Manager Form of Government and Beyond

The reform movement that emerged in the 1880s and 1890s picked up steam at the turn of the century and won many victories through the 1920s when it became less prominent, perhaps because much of its agenda had been enacted or because the reform mentality had become ingrained in U.S. municipal politics or because the Depression and World War II were more pressing concerns. But although reform has not occupied center stage in most communities since the 1920s, it continues to play a part in local politics. Vestiges of reform organizations endure in many places, just as vestiges of machines survive in some, albeit like nearly extinct species. The influence of the reformers also survives in the mind-set or style in which local politics are conducted. More significantly, however, the reform movement left a legacy of governmental structures that shape politics in most communities today, nearly three-quarters of a century after they were first enacted. In some cases, these reform institutions had effects that were not intended; in others, the intended effects have frustrated elements of the communities and have been challenged by a new and different generation of reformers.

The Reformers and Their Agenda

The municipal reformers were predominantly middle and upper class, with the former providing the votes while the latter took the lead in most communities. Upper class, however, is a relative term, here referring not to mega-rich we see today on "Lifestyles of the Rich and Famous" but to local elites, such as prominent lawyers, department store owners, manufacturers, bankers, landowners, automobile dealers, and even undertakers. These were the people who formed "blue-ribbon" committees to campaign for "good" government. Some had held their noses and gone along with the machines when they had to, but when the potential antimachine constituency grew large enough, they grabbed the opportunity to overthrow the inefficient and corrupt machines and increase their profits. They were often joined by the more middle-class clergymen, academics, and journalists. In many communities, women were also prominent in the reform movement, which coincided with the national campaign for women's suffrage.

Conservative Reform

Although women activists gave it a social conscience, the municipal **reform movement** was essentially conservative, seeking to protect and advance the interests of its upper-class leaders and middle-class supporters. They scored a public relations coup when they seized the reform label, which to most Americans is a positive term meaning change and improvement. They did bring change and improvement, but mainly for themselves and not for the urban poor or working class.

Machines, however, were also essentially conservative political institutions. Although they relied on the votes of the poor and working class, they reciprocated only with small, personal favors (nevertheless appreciated by those in need), and not with more sweeping social reforms that might have benefited their constituents more in the long run but also made them less dependent on the machine itself. The working class was carefully controlled and contained.

In some places, however, the attack on the machines focused on what political scientist Stephen Elkin calls "the casualties of the industrial city,"[1] demanding more radical **social reform**. Concerned about slums, poverty, crime, appalling working conditions, and other issues, the social reformers, including socialists and radical labor leaders, attacked big business, local economic elites, and machines. Around the turn of the century, they elected mayors in Cleveland, Detroit, and a few other cities, and tried to improve living conditions, provide better and cheaper local services, and raise taxes on business. In most communities, however, social reformers were denounced as dangerous radicals, isolated, and edged out by the more conservative municipal reformers described above.

Social reformers nevertheless remained a factor in local and national politics until the 1930s. Along with the conservative municipal reformers, they were part of the national Progressive movement that helped to elect presidents Theodore Roosevelt, Woodrow Wilson, and, later, Franklin D. Roosevelt. The Progressives successfully campaigned for state and national regulations on monopolies (trusts) and corporations, and for improvements in industrial working conditions, including child labor laws, compensation for work-related accidents, and safety inspections. These programs reflected the agenda of the social reformers, but conservative municipal reformers were more enthusiastic about the Progressives' **limits on immigration**, which they saw as a way of cutting off the voting base of the machine. Liberal labor unions also supported immigration controls, to keep out cheap competitors for their jobs. Earlier, racism had led to limits on Asian immigration, but in the 1920s, Congress passed laws setting strict limits on other immigrants as well, especially those from southern Europe. An average of half a million immigrants a year had arrived between 1870 and 1920, mostly going to cities, but the new laws allowed just 150,000 per year. The ethnocentric WASP elite had struck a significant blow against the machines—and immigrant minorities.

The Municipal Reform Agenda

But long before immigration controls took hold, the municipal reform movement had concentrated its attention on the inefficiency, corruption, and backwardness of the machines. The upper-class reformers condemned the machines for delivering poor services at high cost, thus inhibiting growth and hurting business. The machines, they asserted, took advantage of ignorant immigrants, who some reformers disdained as foreigners, as well as the outmoded structures of local government.

The municipal reform movement that resulted from these criticisms of machine politics was based on three essential beliefs, each of which is open to question. First, the reformers postulated that the job of local government was to serve the common good or public interest—not the self-interests catered to by the machines. All would benefit, not just a few, and politics would be based on agreement or consensus, not conflict and selfishness. Pursuit of the common good is a worthy goal, but it is easier to state than to achieve. The very concept of a common good assumes people and their needs are similar enough to reach consensus on the responsibilities and services of local government, but, at least in large cities, they are not. As we know, diversity is part of the very nature of urbanism. If people and their needs are not the same, they are unlikely to agree on the common good. For the upper- and middle-class reformers, for example, the public interest meant cheap, efficient local services such as streets and sanitation, but the poor and working classes might have preferred social programs and protection from exploitative employers. In fact, the reformers confused their own interests with the common good; to the extent that others accepted their view, they won another public relations victory.

The second basic belief of the reformers was that they could get politics out of government. They wanted to replace machine politicians operating in their own interests with skilled administrators and technicians running local government on the objective principles of scientific management. The business of local government, the reformers argued, was to provide basic services, such as street maintenance, garbage collection, and sanitation. To the reformers, these were not essentially political matters. "There is no Republican or Democratic way to pave a street," they liked to say, insisting that local government could be run like a well-managed business, with party politics and even politics in general extracted. Their thesis had great appeal (and still does) but, in fact, politics cannot be taken out of government any more than it can be taken out of life. Even the simplest decisions allocate benefits and costs—whose street is to be paved first? who pays? does paving come before parks, housing, or schools? Government constantly makes choices, and while the reformers' insistence that they be made objectively is a worthy goal, politics always plays a part.

And, finally, the reformers thought they could achieve their aims and transform politics and power by changing the structures of government, by replacing the weak or strong mayor systems with more efficient and incorruptible institutions. (They succeeded to some extent, although they also learned that changing structures doesn't solve problems unless the politics and power in a community also change.) Basing their actions on these beliefs, they proceeded with considerable political skill to campaign for and enact an astonishing array of structural reforms. Virtually no U.S. community was untouched by their efforts.

Reforming Elections: The Pursuit of the Common Good

The reform movement focused on changing municipal charters, the constitutions of local government discussed in chapter 4. In some cities, sweeping reform packages amounting to virtually new charters were proposed by blue-ribbon commissions dominated by the reformers themselves. In others, reforms were introduced piece by piece in individual charter amendments. In either case, the voters had to approve and usually did. Sometimes, however, the reformers took the battle to the state level, pushing through laws or constitutional amendments that imposed changes on every city in the state. These statewide changes usually concerned elections, while the structures of the local government themselves were left to be locally determined.

The full extent of the reform package is outlined in Table 6-1, with the structures and institutions that preceded reform listed in the middle column and those of reform in the column on the right. The most ardent reform cities enacted the full reform package; others adopted only selected elements; and those most resistant to reform accepted only what the states imposed. Table 6-1 can be seen as a sort of menu from which cities make choices, suiting their own needs and tastes—but not necessarily in any

Table 6-1 The Municipal Reform Package

	Before Reform	*After Reform*
Elections	Caucus or convention	Primaries, runoffs
	Partisan	Nonpartisan
	District	At-large
	Long ballot	Short ballot
	Concurrent	Isolated
	Representative democracy	Direct democracy
Executive	Mayor (and others)	City manager
Personnel	Patronage (spoils)	Civil service
Contracts	Patronage (spoils)	Competitive bidding

particular order. the components of the reform package were conceived at different times (some as early as the 1890s, some as much as two decades later), so many cities proceeded with reform bit by bit. Only after about 1910 could they contemplate the full package, and many did.

Initially, reform at both state and local levels concentrated on the electoral systems the machines so skillfully manipulated. The reformers sought to break the slate-making power of the machines by altering the way candidates were nominated, removing political parties from local elections, isolating local elections from state and national politics, and more. Although they were the most widely adopted of all the reform ideas, these electoral innovations had a less devastating effect on the machine than the reformers expected, and they also had negative consequences that were probably not anticipated.

The Direct Primary

Before reform, candidates for state and local office were chosen by political parties in caucuses of leaders or in conventions (somewhat larger gatherings of party activists). Power was wielded in infamous smoke-filled rooms, as bosses cut deals to agree on slates of candidates. This control was essential to machine politics, but left voters a narrow choice between the slates of two parties, one of which was usually dominant. In short, the real choices were made by bosses in backroom deals. The reformers therefore introduced **direct primary** elections in which the voters of each party—not just the bosses—select the nominees themselves in elections held weeks or sometimes months before a final or general election. Anyone who collects a few signatures and pays a small fee can run for a party's nomination for any office. Voters choose among the candidates and the one who gets the most votes becomes the party nominee for a particular office, running against the nominees of other parties, also chosen in primaries. Direct primaries make elections more democratic and weakened the slate-making capacity of machines. The survival capacity of the machines was formidable, however. They were soon cutting their deals in time to ensure victory for their candidates in the primaries.

Nonpartisan Elections

The reformers escalated their attack on party machines by moving to eliminate parties from local elections altogether, forbidding party recruitment and endorsement of candidates and banning party labels from local ballots. In **nonpartisan elections,** candidates are listed on the ballot only by name and sometimes occupation, with no indication of party affiliation. Some cities with nonpartisan elections have primaries to narrow the field of candidates and ensure that whoever is elected has a majority. If one candidate wins more than 50 percent of the primary vote, he or she is declared elected. Otherwise, the top two vote-getters face each other in a runoff.

Nonpartisan elections are perhaps the most widespread of all reforms—with 72.6 percent of all U.S. cities and 94 percent of those in the West having nonpartisan elections. The system is least popular in the Northeast, where nonpartisan elections are used by only 21 percent of the cities—and where the machines lasted longest and were perhaps most powerful. Alaska, California, Idaho, Minnesota, New Mexico, and Wyoming give cities no choice: nonpartisan local elections are required by state law. Only a few states impose nonpartisan elections on counties (including Wisconsin and California, the two states where the progressive movement was most powerful), but 85 percent of all school board elections are nonpartisan.

The job of the machine was made more difficult by nonpartisan elections because the party couldn't officially select or formally endorse candidates, and machine voters were denied the useful cue of party labels on ballots, but many machines figured out ways of instructing their voters. City council elections in Chicago, for example, are nonpartisan, yet the last vestiges of the United States' most notorious and long-lasting political machine survive there even now, particularly in white ethnic neighborhoods. In 1989 they were an important part of the coalition that helped elect Mayor Richard M. Daley 13 years after the death of his father, Richard J. Daley, one of the most powerful bosses in U.S. history. Between the Daleys, reform politicians such as Harold Washington, an African American, won the office of mayor, but they never completely vanquished the machine.[2]

At-Large Elections and Short Ballots

The progressives also attacked the machine's organizational structure by changing the way city council members were selected. The existing system was by wards or districts, with each member representing a specific area of the city. The reformers saw wards as the building blocks of the machines and also argued that district representation was narrow and parochial, ignoring the needs of the city as a whole. Instead of the common good, reformers believed council members articulated only the interests of the neighborhoods and the ethnic groups in their districts, resulting in conflict, obstruction, and deal making. To break down the machines' neighborhood organization and lessen the parochialism of local politics, the reformers instituted **at-large elections,** through which the whole city elects all members of the council. In some at-large systems, all candidates run against one another for half the council seats in each election and the top vote-getters win, creating a sort of free-for-all that is an advantage for well-known or well-financed candidates and that can be confusing to voters. To provide better focus, other cities give at-large council seats numbers, and candidates select which one they will run for (and who they will run against); usually, if no one gets more than 50 percent of the vote, the top two face a runoff. A few cities, recognizing that neighborhood connections have some merit, require that candidates for particular at-large seats live in specified districts of the city; sometimes the primary election is conducted in the district with the city as a whole choosing between the top two candidates in a runoff.

Whatever the details, the reformers felt at-large elections wouldn't work with the large city councils common in the nineteenth century because each voter would be expected to select all members of the council—which could number fifty or more. The reformers therefore reduced the size of city councils to, on average, five to seven members. Districted councils are usually at least twice as large (for example, the Los Angeles city council has fifteen members, while Chicago's numbers fifty and New York City has fifty-one). Besides making at-large elections feasible, reformers expected less conflict and more agreement on smaller councils. The short ballots resulting from electing fewer council members and other city officials also gave the machines fewer positions for their slates and thus fewer ways to pay off allies.

Today about 60 percent of U.S. cities elect their council members at large and another 27 percent elect some at large and some by district. Most large cities, however, especially in the Northeast and Midwest, elect council members by district, as do counties. School boards, however, are mostly chosen at large.

At-large elections and shortened ballots made it harder for machines to organize ethnic groups and neighborhoods and to make slates. They also somewhat shifted the focus of city councils to broader, citywide issues and lessened conflict since each member represented the same constituency. But adept machines coped with this reform, too; some even found that it simplified their tasks.

Isolated Elections

The reformers also worried about the influence of state and national campaigns on local politics. With balloting for all three levels held at the same time through *concurrent elections,* candidates for local office sometimes won on the coattails of their popular allies for governor or president, even though what motivates voters in state and national races may have nothing to do with local issues. Reformers thought this distorted local politics and aided party machines, so they moved to separate local elections from state and national contests by holding them on different dates. With **isolated elections,** the reformers hoped to concentrate voter attention on strictly local concerns. More than 60 percent of U.S. cities and most school districts use isolated elections, which may focus more on local issues, but which also result in lower voter turnout because the stimulus of state and national campaigns is removed. Those who do vote tend to be less representative of the community as a whole, with higher proportions of affluent, conservative voters (the same constituency that supported reform). Machines were thus weakened not only because they couldn't coordinate local campaigns with those for higher office but also because their supporters were less likely to vote.

Direct Democracy

Just in case the machines survived all these reforms, the reformers introduced **direct democracy** as a sort of insurance. Instead of leaving policy making to elected representatives, citizens were given the right to make laws by the **initiative** process. If a specified number of voters sign an initiative petition, a proposed law is put on the ballot and is enacted if it wins a majority. Through the **referendum,** another form of direct democracy, citizens may petition to revoke an act of the council; referendums are also required for charter amendments or borrowing money. Finally, if voters grow discontented with their representatives before they come up for reelection, they can petition for a **recall** election through which the representative may be removed from office.

Direct democracy thus provides a means of expressing the public interest other than through elected representatives. It also allows citizens to make policy and remove corrupt officials when the machines managed to win elections despite all the reforms, as they often did. For while the machines were weakened by this astonishing array of electoral reforms, many reconciled themselves to change and endured; some even thrived. The reformers proved equally resilient, however. Despite their social conservatism, they were nothing less than radical about structural change. Even before completing their transformation of local elections, they were experimenting with innovative forms of government.

Taking Politics Out of Government: The City Manager System

As we saw in the last chapter, the early reformers endeavored to replace the weak mayor form of government with the strong mayor system and the shortened ballot. But when they saw the bosses and machines taking advantage of that modification, they sought more fundamental change.

The Commission Form of Government

When the city government of Galveston, Texas, seemed incompetent to guide rebuilding after a catastrophic hurricane hit the city in 1900, a group of business leaders more or less took over. They persuaded their state legislature to approve a new charter with a radically different form of government for Galveston. Instead of a traditional executive and legislature, Galveston combined both functions in one body—a commission. Voters elected just five commissioners; together they acted as the city council, but each also headed a specific department, such as public safety, public works, parks and libraries, or finance. This streamlined system worked well for Galveston and was soon adopted elsewhere. Before 1920, nearly five hundred cities adopted the **commission form of government,** usually along with at-large, nonpartisan elections and direct democracy.

But the disadvantages of the commission form soon became apparent. Some commissioners proved better at getting elected than at administering their departments. Commissioners tended to compete with one another and to protect the interests of their own departments, but the system provided no leadership to overcome these tendencies. Because of these problems, it soon lost popularity. Houston gave it up in 1942; San Antonio in 1951. Today, less than 5 percent of U.S. cities are governed by commissions. Most of these cities are small. Among large cities, only Portland and Tulsa still use the commission form, both with adaptations to include a nominal mayor.

The Council-Manager Form of Government

The commission form of government may also have fallen into disfavor because another new system was even more appealing—the council-manager form of government. First introduced in Sumter, South Carolina, in 1912, by 1920, more than a hundred cities had adopted the new form and today it is second in popularity only to mayor-council systems. The **council-manager system** was modeled on modern business practices, with

Figure 6-1   The Council-Manager Form of Government

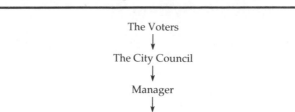

the voters as the equivalent of corporate stockholders, the council as the board of directors, and a professional manager responsible for operations (see Figure 6-1). This innovative arrangement couldn't have suited the reform mentality better.

The City Council.   On the ultimate short ballot, with nonpartisan, at-large, isolated elections, voters choose only a small **city council,** usually numbering five to seven members. Initially, the system had no mayor at all, but now mayors are elected or chosen by the council from among its members in most council-manager cities. The mayor's role, however, consists largely of presiding over council meetings. Council members are expected to serve only part time, linking the public to its government and defining broad policies that the city manager and administration implement. The most important task of the council is appointing the city manager to oversee the operations of the city. The council may also appoint the city attorney, who gives the council legal advice; the clerk, who keeps its records; and the auditor, who checks city finances. With nonpartisan, at-large elections and administration in the hands of a professional manager, the influence of parties and the parochial interests of neighborhoods or ethnic groups are as far removed from government as possible and the pursuit of the public interest proceeds unhindered. In the ideals of the council-manager system, politics stop with the council, although reform electoral structures limit politics even there.

The City Manager.   Based on the reform theory that the business of local government is to provide basic services of a technical nature and should therefore not be political, the council-manager system is at the heart of the reform effort to take politics out of government. The political element of the system, the council, hires and fires the manager, usually by majority vote. In doing so, the council is expected to make its decisions on the basis of the technical, administrative competence of the candidates, not on their political views or connections. **City managers** are expected to be neutral, skilled professionals—experts in administration who can efficiently carry out policies set by the council. Unlike political leaders, managers can come from outside the community. In fact, outsiders are often preferred since their lack of local connections would enhance their objectivity.

Where are such individuals to be found? Initially, the pool of professional candidates was small, and communities often subverted the system by hiring locals. Many of the first city managers were engineers, but eventually a national pool of professional administrators grew. Council-manager cities now advertise job openings and get applications from all over the country. To hire locally is considered bad form (with political overtones), and professional managers advance their careers by moving from city to city, with the largest council-manager cities at the top of the ladder.

As chief executive, the manager appoints department heads, including police, fire, public works, planning, parks and recreation, and others. The department heads, under policy directives from the council and supervision by the manager, oversee the delivery of city services. The council plays no formal part in hiring, firing, or disciplining department heads and may be forbidden from communicating with them except through the manager, to whom they answer. The manager is also responsible for the budget, a crucial role in shaping city services, although the council must approve the manager's budget proposals.

The council-manager system, so modern sounding and so consistent with reform theory, spread quickly. California's reformers made it that state's general law form of government, and it operates in all but a few of its 468 cities. In Virginia, state law requires the council-manager form of government for all cities. Almost half of the cities in the United States with a population of more than 25,000 now use the system, but the only large cities that employ it are Dallas, Phoenix, San Antonio, San Diego, and San Jose.

Like all reform nostrums, the manager plan has its drawbacks, tending to insulate government from the public and to prevent the expression of legitimate differences of opinion. Nor does it truly remove politics from government since administrators have views and biases of their own and may still be susceptible to some political influence, usually that of business elites. More alarming for the reformers, machines adapted even to this innovation. The Pendergast machine continued in Kansas City,[3] for example, and in Asheville, North Carolina, the local boss merely had himself appointed manager.

Civil Service. Another important reform associated with the council-manager form of government was the introduction of **civil service** or merit hiring, first instituted in New York in 1883, but not widely adopted until after 1920. Workers had previously been hired and retained on the basis of loyalty to the machine rather than their qualifications or performance on the job. When control of city hall changed hands in elections, a whole new set of workers would be hired. This patronage or spoils system provided rewards for supporters of the machines, but resulted in inefficient and amateurish city services. To increase competence among city staff and strike a blow at patronage, the reformers initiated a hiring system based on ability to do the job rather than party loyalty.

All city employees except the department heads appointed by the manager (or the mayor in a mayor-council system) are in the civil service system, although managers, mayors, and department heads sometimes may appoint a few deputies. In a civil service or merit system, personnel departments set specifications for jobs. Educational qualifications, written exams, and interviews then sort out job applicants, with the top candidates (not the relatives and friends of current staff) winning employment. Once hired, workers go through a probationary period and, if they perform their job well, gain job security through a form of tenure, and can be fired only for proven incompetence at the job—not just because a new mayor and/or council are elected.

The system protects workers from political interference on the job, and it dealt a serious blow to the machines, although some adapted even to this reform, merely taking over the system and manipulating it by fixing exam results or selling passing scores. Today, many people worry that civil servants have so much job security that they don't have to pay attention to their clients (the taxpayers) or even to do their jobs well to keep them. It is important to remember, however, that their job security was intended to solve the even more serious problems of political interference and in-competence.

Competitive Bidding.   The corrupt and inefficient doling out of contracts for city purchases, services, and construction projects to the machine's allies was another part of the spoils systems the reformers attacked. Their solution was **competitive bidding,** a system by which professional admin-istrators set and advertise the specifications or requirements for a purchase or project and any interested company can put in a formal, sealed bid for it. The lowest bidder who meets the specifications wins the contract—not the boss's pals. Selection of any but the lowest bid must be justified. Under some competitive bidding arrangements, stipulations requiring locally based companies, union employers, or minority businesses may be ap-plied, and small contracts are generally excepted from the process.

Naturally, the machines found ways to cheat. They manipulated specifications so only certain companies could qualify, leaked competitor's bids, or accepted artificially low bids and allowed cost-overruns later. The system has been widely adopted, however, especially on large projects and, although sometimes imperfect in operation, it dealt a serious blow to the machines. Competitive bidding and civil service hiring take away the major components of the spoils system. In cities where they function as intended, traditional political machines have never revived, whatever other reform structures are adopted (or revoked).

The Consequences of Reform: The Bias of "Good Government"

From the turn of the century to the 1950s, few cities were immune to the reform movement, although it struck at different times in different places, and with varying degrees of success. The tide had turned against the machines, as immigrants assimilated, new immigration from abroad was curtailed, a new welfare system was set up, and the middle class expanded. The machine's power base shrunk and a constituency for reform developed, readily endorsing the movement's good government rhetoric featuring the public interest, professionalism, and getting politics out of government. The structural reforms imposed on city government altered it radically, but despite the lofty ideals, reform institutions (like all institutions) have a bias. Not surprisingly, the **bias of reform** favored the reformers themselves.

Weak Parties

The direct primary and nonpartisan, at-large, isolated elections hurt the machines, but they also weaken political parties, lower voter turnout, change the composition of the electorate, and make it easier for some sorts of people to get elected. Direct primaries reduce the ability of bosses to control the nomination of candidates and increase democracy, but because anybody can run for and win the party nomination, personalities count for more than policies, and parties may end up with unwanted candidates who do not agree with their programs. Such independence has its merits, but it dilutes the meaning of the party label and makes it harder for voters to know what candidates stand for and to hold them accountable. Nonpartisan elections enhance this tendency. They also cut off the lower rungs of the party ladder, so candidates for higher office are less likely to serve apprenticeships in local politics.

However wishy-washy U.S. political parties are, most voters believe a party label gives them clues about candidates. But no such clues are provided in local government primaries and nonpartisan elections, so how do people decide? Some choose which candidates to vote for by the ethnicity of their names (would you be more likely to vote for a candidate with a really foreign-sounding name or one with a name a little more familiar?). Some choose by the candidate's occupation (business people, teachers, and police officers usually do well). Other clues may include religion, military service, or status as a local sports hero or media star. These characteristics tell voters something, but not much. Party labels tell more, including whether candidates are inclined to be liberal or conservative. They are especially useful for candidates who are a little outside the mainstream because they may reassure voters that even though the candidates are not quite like them (male/female; majority/minority; heterosexual/homosexual), they are okay because they are Democrats or Republicans.

Parties are more than labels, however. They are also campaign organizations. When they are absent from campaigns, other elements gain influence. Incumbents or anyone whose name is well known do better. Newspapers gain importance because they can make candidates well known or ignore them. Campaign contributors become more influential because they can pay for the campaigns previously provided by the parties. Candidates who are white businessmen usually do best because the traditional voting majority is comfortable with them and also because they can more easily raise campaign funds and count on newspaper support. Women, minority, and working-class candidates have a harder time selling themselves to voters, campaign contributors, and newspaper publishers.

At-large elections increase the structural bias against these candidates. Instead of running in a district made up of a few neighborhoods, they have to run citywide. Such races cost more, which hurts candidates, especially minorities, without ready access to contributors. Minority candidates also have a tougher time precisely because they are members of minority groups and will need to win votes from whoever makes up the city's majority, whereas with district elections their own group might be enough to elect them. In big cities, women are sometimes hindered by at-large elections, too, mainly because their community work tends to focus on neighborhoods and schools, so they have weak citywide connections. Women have done well in at-large elections in small and medium-sized communities, however. And despite the disadvantages of the system, many minority and women candidates have managed to win at-large races in recent years,[4] thanks to their own hard work and declining racism and sexism among some voters.

Low Voter Turnout

Voter turnout is also affected by reform electoral structures, declining precipitously with nonpartisan, isolated elections. The parties aren't actively hustling voters, and local elections separate from state and national balloting often get little publicity and stimulate little interest. Having an appointed manager instead of an elected mayor also leads to decreasing voter interest. On average, 30 percent of voters participate in such elections, less than half the turnout in cities with partisan, concurrent elections. Reformers don't worry about this much, however, because they assume (with some justification) that those who do not vote are not well informed about local matters anyway. But the electorate is not only smaller under reform, it is different and less representative of the city as a whole. Those most likely to vote are better educated, more affluent, and more conservative; they elect people like themselves. Minority and working-class people are least likely to vote or to be elected, except where they are themselves the majority.

The Winners

In most communities, reform election structures increase the electoral chances of white (or WASP) businessmen and decrease those of others. The primary beneficiaries of these reforms are the very people who were the reform movement. Did they intend to institute such bias? In a way, they did. In their view, the system they replaced had been biased against them and helped ethnic, working-class candidates. Many reformers were hostile to such people, although most were more concerned about the corruption of the machines. In attacking the machines, however, they also lessened the participation and electability of some of their constituents. For the most part, this probably was not intentional, and most reformers would say the system is open and fair to all. They are reluctant to acknowledge that it works best for people like them—and that everybody isn't like them.

When the reformers won elections, what sort of person did they appoint as city manager? And what policy guidance did reform councils give? What sort of standards were set for civil servants, and what sorts of people were employed? Again, the reformers created a system in their own image, with middle- and upper-class professionals getting elected and hiring other, similar professionals. They homogenized city government and actually made it less representative of their communities as a whole and more representative of themselves. Those not like the reformers—the ethnic immigrants and working class in the machine age and later, African Americans, Hispanics, and Asians—have little chance of winning elections or even attention. Council members can ignore minorities and their neighborhoods as long as the predominant, usually middle-class voting majority of a city is satisfied. City managers answer to the council, not the voters. They are careful not to alienate majorities, but may ignore minorities with impunity. Modern civil servants have job security, and insulation that protects them from political interference, but that also enables them to ignore public pressure. They need not rush to please their clients or, it sometimes seems, even bother to be courteous.

Majority Rule

The reformers didn't take politics out of government, they only made it less responsive to interests other than those of the majority in any community. The common good or public interest turned out to be nothing more than what the majority wanted. Majority rule is democratic, of course, but it isn't always good government if it means some people and some interests—those not consistent with the majority—are left out. Reform dogma failed to recognize that people are not all alike and that they might want different things from city government. Working-class neighborhoods, minority groups, or other components of urban diversity often have very different needs and interests than those of the majority, yet under reform structures, these are almost inevitably ignored. However, those who are unrepresented are not always working-class or racial minorities. In some cities, these groups have become the majority, and white, middle-class people find themselves left out, for the reform system is biased in favor of any group that constitutes a majority and against any group that is a minority.

Besides strengthening majority rule, reform also gave advantage—or spoils?—to the upper class and business elites who were its leaders. Reform structures, with low voter turnout and council members and professional administrators who thought like themselves, suited businessmen and their interests very well. They wanted low taxes and efficient city services, with social programs put on a back burner (or left to the state and federal governments). But more, they expected reform governments to bring progress through growth, generating jobs, profits, and taxes. Through the reform movement, business interests narrowed the focus of local government to basic services and growth, guided by business-oriented professionals.[5] The growth machine replaced the party political machine.

The Counterreformation: Back to the Future

Eventually, however, disenchantment with the narrowness and unresponsiveness of reform structures brought a counterreformation in many cities. Like the reform movement itself, the challenge to reform was brought about by changes in the cities themselves. As we saw in chapter 3, by the 1920s, the primary immigrants to large cities were minorities, first black, then Hispanics, and later Asian. After World War II, white flight to the suburbs started eroding the reform constituency of big cities, even as minorities approached majority status there. By the 1960s, a critical mass of people who felt excluded from city politics was emerging. The black civil rights movement showed the way, demanding voting rights and full participation for all. The federal government responded with civil and voting rights legislation and by funding community organizing through the War on Poverty and related programs. Hispanics emulated African Americans in organizing and demanding their rights. Then the women's movement took hold, followed by the political mobilization of gays and lesbians. In the 1970s, a neighborhood movement swept the cities, with groups forming not only in minority neighborhoods but in others as well. Many complained that they had no direct council representation and were shocked to learn that a majority of at-large council members lived in just one part of town (usually a rich neighborhood with high voter turnout). All these interests felt that local governments dominated by white, upper-middle-class males (from managers and mayors to council members and civil servants) neither represented nor responded to them. At about the same time, environmentalists and antigrowth campaigners began criticizing city development policies and a deeply antibureaucratic tax revolt took hold.

Like the "morning glory" reformers before them, these dissatisfied groups first put up candidates and attempted to win office. Some were successful, and by the late 1960s most city councils had at least token women, minority, and environmentalist representatives. Unfortunately, these candidates, driven by the need to win majority support to be elected, often alienated their own initial constituencies. Even more often, they found they could change little in city government when they managed to get elected. To these critics, white elected officials and bureaucracies protected by the civil service system (especially the police) continued to be insensitive to the needs of minorities, women, and neighborhoods. The growth machine ground on, ignoring social needs, neighborhood services, and environmental concerns.

Like the earlier reformers, those who felt excluded sought to change the structures of local government. The primary goals of the **counterreform** movement were to make government more representative and more responsive. They wanted more participation. They wanted local government to pay more attention to all of its constituents. They wanted more sensitive and better controlled local bureaucracies. Rejecting the basic assumptions of the earlier reformers, they argued that there could be no single public interest in communities because people are not all alike. Varied needs and views should be represented in local government, not only by elected officials but in bureaucracies. They accepted the inevitability of political conflict that such representation would bring, insisting that reform structures had only artificially created consensus by suppressing different points of view. To accomplish these goals, they went back to the future, selectively reviving or adapting traditional political structures and introducing a few new ones.

District Elections

Primary among the goals of the counterreformers was to replace the at-large system of council selection with good, old-fashioned **district elections.** Each part of the city would gain direct representation, they thought, and responsiveness to neighborhoods, many of which had never had direct representation on their city councils, would improve. Minorities, if they were concentrated in particular districts, would be more likely to win election. So would women and working-class people, because their net-works tended to be localized rather than citywide. District elections would also cut campaign costs, the counterreformers thought, and thus enhance the electoral prospects of all these groups.

Although most big cities in the Frostbelt had never changed from district elections, many growing Sunbelt cities went back to districts in the 1970s and 1980s, including Albuquerque, Dallas, El Paso, and San Jose. In some, the change was wrought by community organizations forcing a referendum or initiative (devices made available by the earlier reformers). In others, including Dallas and Birmingham, the reform was imposed by federal courts that concluded that at-large elections denied minority representation under federal voting rights legislation.[6] According to Sunbelt author Carl Abbott, "One-third of the cities in the Confederate South with significant black populations" had shifted back to district elections by 1986.[7] The at-large systems of many communities have been successfully challenged in the courts since then, including some cases brought by white minorities.

Wherever district elections have survived or been revived, more minorities, women, and neighborhood candidates have been elected and these groups are more satisfied with city government than under the at-large method.[8] Opponents of districting worry about conflict, parochialism, and a lack of attention to citywide issues, but the evidence suggests that while district representatives are more oriented to the neighborhoods and services than their at-large counterparts, they are still (disappointingly for some) sensitive to citywide concerns.[9]

Empowering Councils

To fight bureaucracies, city managers, and mayors, some counterreformers recognized that the more representative councils they had wrought with district elections would need to be more powerful. Reform council members had been expected to be part time and were paid accordingly. But the counterreformers and some traditional reform groups such as the League of Women Voters advocated raising council salaries enough to allow representatives to do the job on a full-time basis; higher salaries would also broaden the range of candidates who could run for office since only the affluent or certain sorts of professionals such as lawyers could afford to take on the job for only token wages.

In some large cities, **empowering councils** meant that council members were also allowed to hire a personal staff so they wouldn't have to rely exclusively on what their executives and bureaucrats told them and so they could respond more efficiently to constituent concerns. Some councils were allowed to hire budget analysts or auditors to advise them as a group, again to counterbalance the executive and bureaucracy.

Stronger Mayors

Mayors gained power in the urban counterreformation, too. The council-manager system had initially omitted mayors altogether, although most cities soon changed their charters to allow the council to designate one of its members as mayor to preside over meetings and perform some ceremonial functions. Eventually, some cities realized that councils were too fractious and managers were too bureaucratic to provide the sort of political leadership that was often needed. As a consequence, 65 percent of council-manager cities now elect their mayors. Just being elected doesn't really give a mayor much power, of course, but being the focus of public and media attention, as mayors are, does bring power to those who know how to use it. Many cities have also taken other actions to achieve **stronger mayors,** including higher salaries, much-expanded personal staffs, and, more substantively, greater budgetary and appointment power.

Other Electoral Reforms

To buttress council representativeness and mayoral leadership, some reformed cities returned to concurrent elections because they could save money by sharing election costs with higher levels of government and because isolated elections depressed and biased voter turnout. This little shift vastly increased voter participation and representativeness. Nonpartisan elections also came under attack, but because they are usually enshrined in state constitutions, change proved difficult. In California, however, counterreformers challenged nonpartisanship in the courts and won a 1989 U.S. Supreme Court ruling[10] (based on freedom of speech) allowing parties to endorse candidates as community groups could.

Controlling Bureaucracy

The insulation and unresponsiveness of civil service bureaucracies were also a major target of the counterreformers. They tried **controlling the bureaucracy** by allowing elected officials mayoral and council staffs, auditors, and policy analysts, as well as special budgeting systems. They also demanded affirmative action hiring to ensure that a broader cross section of people would gain employment with local government—not just the white males that the white male bureaucracy seemed to hire. If hiring was biased, the counterreformers argued, so were city services because an unrepresentative bureaucracy could not be sensitive to its diverse constituency.

Some cities tried to assuage the discontent of those who felt excluded by increasing direct citizen participation in local government through boards, commissions, and committees. Cities such as Boston and New

York attempted to break down their rigid bureaucracies and increase responsiveness by decentralizing local government through neighborhood city halls or more formal community control of some services by neighborhood representatives. Bureaucracies, however, proved resistant to all these reforms, although where demographic change gave minorities greater clout, they gained jobs in the civil service and even came to dominate some departments.

The Tax Revolt

Minorities, women, and working-class neighborhoods were in the forefront of the counterreformation as discussed so far, but in the 1970s, other antagonists to the status quo appeared. Middle-class neighborhoods and environmentalists supported the counterreformers on some issues, such as district elections, but their primary concern was controlling growth to assure better local services. Their challenge to the growth machine was supplemented by a broader **tax revolt** that set strict limits on local revenues and thus, to some extent, on growth. Unlike the counterreformers, the homeowners who dominated the tax revolt were conservative and fundamentally antigovernment. In the late 1980s, they campaigned for term limits to restrict the number of times mayors and council members could be reelected. More turnover, they asserted, would prevent these officials from succumbing to the values of the status quo, lobbyists, and bureaucrats.

The Continuing Counterreformation. The counterreformation in local government structures is still under way in many cities, but it has already transformed community politics in some. Many more women, minorities, homosexuals, and working- and middle-class people have been elected, and bureaucracies, while retaining most of their power, have been changed. Diversity is more widely recognized and accepted; local government is more representative and responsive. The antigrowth movement and the tax revolt have also made their mark.

The Distribution of Forms of Government

The institutions of local government have evolved over 2 centuries of history and change, through industrialization, immigration, urbanization, suburbanization, and the move to the Sunbelt, from the mayor-council form of government to reform and the council-manager system and beyond. Some cities have gone through all these changes; others have experienced only a few. This variation accounts, in part, for the current use of different forms of government by different cities today, although other factors also shape the **distribution of forms of government.** Historical development, region, size, and demography all play a part.

The mayor-council system is most common in the Northeast and Midwest, where cities developed in the nineteenth century when that form of government predominated. Most of the largest cities in the United States, whether Frostbelt or Sunbelt, use the mayor-council form, not just because they are older cities but because of the need for political leadership in such diverse places (see Table 6-2). At least one study has demonstrated that cities with large ethnic minority and working-class populations are more likely to use the mayor-council form.[11] Large cities in the Frostbelt incline to the strong mayor form, and big Sunbelt cities, while not always adopting the pure weak mayor form of government, tend to restrict mayoral authority. Surprisingly, a majority of cities with less than a population of 10,000 also use the mayor-council form. Mostly in older, Frostbelt states

Table 6-2 Form of Local Government, 1992

Classification	No. Reporting (all)	Mayor/ Council No.	Mayor/ Council Percent	Council/ Manager No.	Council/ Manager Percent	Commission No.	Commission Percent	Town Meeting No.	Town Meeting Percent	Rep. Town Meeting No.	Rep. Town Meeting Percent
Total, all cities	4,967	2,201	44.3	2,371	47.7	94	1.9	260	5.2	41	0.8
Population											
500,000 and over	10	8	80.0	2	20.0	0	0.0	0	0.0	0	0.0
250,000–499,999	32	13	40.6	18	56.3	1	3.1	0	0.0	0	0.0
100,000–249,999	100	31	31.0	67	67.0	2	2.0	0	0.0	0	0.0
50,000–99,999	255	86	33.7	164	64.3	1	0.4	0	0.0	4	1.6
25,000–49,999	517	168	32.5	327	63.2	9	1.7	3	0.6	10	1.9
10,000–24,999	1,128	421	37.3	603	53.5	29	2.6	58	5.1	17	1.5
5,000–9,999	1,228	550	44.8	563	45.8	26	2.1	86	7.0	3	0.2
2,500–4,999	1,311	765	58.4	431	32.9	21	1.6	88	6.7	6	0.5
Under 2,500	386	159	41.2	196	50.8	5	1.3	25	6.5	1	0.3
Geographic division											
New England	530	75	14.2	165	31.1	0	0.0	258	48.7	32	6.0
Mid-Atlantic	713	417	58.5	263	36.9	31	4.3	0	0.0	2	0.3
East North Central	952	558	58.6	366	38.4	20	2.1	2	0.2	6	0.6
West North Central	558	334	59.9	204	36.6	19	3.4	0	0.0	1	0.2
South Atlantic	640	199	31.1	433	67.7	8	1.3	0	0.0	0	0.0
East South Central	282	199	70.6	72	25.5	11	3.9	0	0.0	0	0.0
West South Central	502	192	38.2	308	61.4	2	0.4	0	0.0	0	0.0
Mountain	263	133	50.6	130	49.4	0	0.0	0	0.0	0	0.0
Pacific Coast	527	94	17.8	430	81.6	3	0.6	0	0.0	0	0.0
Metro status											
Central	382	168	44.0	207	54.2	6	1.6	0	0.0	1	0.3
Suburban	2,663	1,125	42.2	1,299	48.8	47	1.8	158	5.9	34	1.3
Independent	1,922	908	47.2	865	45.0	41	2.1	102	5.3	6	0.3

Source: The Municipal Year Book (Washington, DC: International City/County Management Association, 1993). Reprinted with permission.

(except New England), they seem content with their original weak mayor systems. Unlike large, diverse cities, these small, homogeneous communities experience less political conflict and few complex problems, so they can get by without strong mayoral leadership and executive authority.

The council-manager form is most common in cities that matured after the turn of the century, especially in the Sunbelt and most of all in the western United States, where the reform movement was strongest and where political parties were, and remain, weakest. Suburbs, again especially those in the Sunbelt, also incline strongly to the council-manager system. Reflecting this, a substantial majority of middle-sized cities use the manager form (see Table 6-2). These communities tend to be relatively homogeneous, so political consensus is easy to reach and fewer people feel left out by the majority-oriented reform system. When reform cities grow, they become more diverse, and political conflict increases. Professional administrators such as city managers are often unable or unwilling to respond to the increasing demands placed on them. As a result, most large Sunbelt cities have strengthened their mayors and altered other institutions as well.

Besides the basic forms of government, associated structures and institutions are similarly distributed. District elections, for example, are more likely to be found in larger cities and in the older cities of the Northeast and Midwest, while at-large council representation is more common in smaller and middle-sized cities and in the Sunbelt and suburbia (see Table 6-3 and Figure 6-2). The regional pattern is also evident in use of nonpartisan elections, with only 21 percent of northeastern cities as compared to 94 percent of western cities requiring nonpartisan elections.[12] Although the number of cities adopting the council-manager system with its associated reform structures has risen steadily since it was first introduced, as cities grow, they generally find increasing diversity and conflict necessitate stronger leadership and broader representation and adapt accordingly.

As a consequence, few cities can easily be categorized as weak mayor, strong mayor, council-manager, reformed, unreformed, or re-reformed. Most have adapted their systems to particular needs at particular times, picking and choosing the electoral or governmental structures that suit them and that satisfy the political forces of the moment. Each form and institution has advantages and disadvantages; none is best in the abstract. Mayoral systems, for example, bring better leadership and accountability and are more democratic. They probably work best in large, diverse cities with conflictual politics and a need for leadership and conciliation. But a manager system seems to work well in small or middle-sized homogeneous cities with clear, consensual majorities. The manager form is also thought to be best for professionalism and efficiency, although at least one statistical study found "no apparent difference in the efficiency levels of the two [major types of] municipal structures."[13]

Table 6-3   Method of Election, 1992

| Classification | No. Reporting (all) | Election Method | | | | | |
| | | At-Large | | District | | Mixed | |
		No.	Percent	No.	Percent	No.	Percent
Total, all cities	4,314	2,544	59.0	506	11.7	1,264	29.3
Population							
500,000 and over	8	3	37.5	1	12.5	4	50.0
250,000–499,999	31	8	25.8	3	9.7	20	64.5
100,000–249,999	88	40	45.5	11	12.5	37	42.0
50,000–99,999	232	110	47.4	23	9.9	99	42.7
25,000–49,999	459	242	52.7	61	13.3	156	34.0
10,000–24,999	994	556	55.9	114	11.5	324	32.6
5,000– 9,999	1,063	631	59.4	137	12.9	295	27.8
2,500– 4,999	1,111	702	63.2	138	12.4	271	24.4
Under 2,500	328	252	76.8	18	5.5	58	17.7
Geographic division							
New England	443	333	75.2	14	3.2	96	21.7
Mid-Atlantic	630	457	72.5	79	12.5	94	14.9
East North Central	854	447	52.3	134	15.7	273	32.0
West North Central	479	202	42.2	108	22.5	169	35.3
South Atlantic	550	302	54.9	52	9.5	196	35.6
East South Central	232	120	51.7	36	15.5	76	32.8
West South Central	418	164	39.2	38	9.1	216	51.7
Mountain	232	132	56.9	26	11.2	74	31.9
Pacific Coast	476	387	81.3	19	4.0	70	14.7
Metro status							
Central	349	119	34.1	56	16.0	174	49.9
Suburban	2,313	1,583	68.4	198	8.6	532	23.0
Independent	1,652	842	51.0	252	15.3	558	33.8

Note: Survey results for this question were coded as follows: jurisdictions with all council members nominated and elected at-large were coded "at large." Jurisdictions reporting all council members nominated and elected by ward or district were coded "district." Any other jurisdictions that indicated the use of more than one method were coded "mixed." Jurisdictions reporting that all council members were selected by other means but that did not specify the means were excluded from this analysis. *Source: The Municipal Year Book,* (Washington, DC: International City/County Management Association, 1993). Reprinted with permission.

In short, the needs of a particular city determine which form of government is best. By mixing elements of the different systems, cities can refine their forms of governments to their own needs. Nevertheless, it is important to remember that the different forms are never neutral. Those who have power at a particular time choose the form of government that gives them advantages. Others may feel unrepresented and ignored, but if they organize and increase their own power, they may challenge and sometimes change the system.

Figure 6-2 Election Methods and City Size, 1986

Source: Municipal Year Book (Washington, DC: International City/County Management Association, 1988). Reprinted with permission.

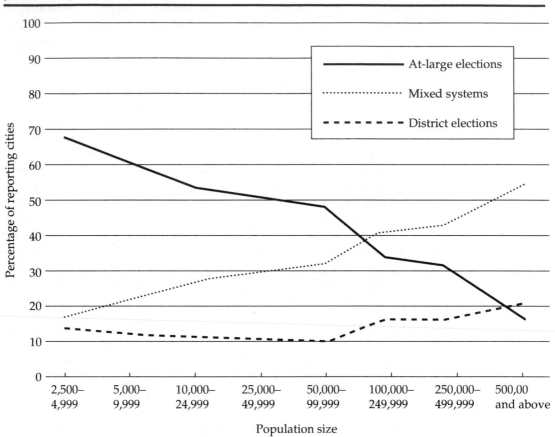

Counties and Special Districts

Most of our discussion in this and the preceding chapter has focused on forms of city government. Government in counties and special districts varies much less and has changed less over time.

Counties, in particular, have been little affected by reform. The states create counties as their administrative agents and generally dictate their institutions of government, although thirty states allow counties to make some local adaptations. As noted in the last chapter, most county governments remain roughly similar to the weak mayor system without the mayor. Eighty-five percent of the nation's counties continue to operate with the traditional elected board or commission and an assortment of elected department heads. The main change in county systems has been the addition of a professional **county administrator** or executive similar to a city manager.[14] Urban counties made the move first but, as of 1992, such officials functioned in about 23 percent of all counties. Often recruited from the same pool as city managers, they are appointed by the county commission or board of supervisors and bring technical and management expertise to the increasingly complex business of county government. Like city managers, they have difficulty when political conflict is great and leadership is needed.

School districts are governed by elected or sometimes appointed boards of five to seven members who hire a professional manager or superintendent of schools to oversee school operations. The system is similar to a council-manager form of government, but school superintendents tend to be even more powerful than city managers because school board members are often less professionally knowledgeable or politically astute than council members and rarely have as much time to devote to their duties. When disagreement arises, the most common response is to replace the administrator, although sometimes the governing boards are replaced instead, either by recall or normal elections.

Special districts operate in a similar fashion, with powerful administrators and often amateur, part-time board members. Their boards, however, are usually appointed by governors, mayors, or other elected officials, so they are not subject to regular elections or recall. The public thus has little control over these agencies—and most citizens don't even know they exist.

Filling the Forms

The structure of local government is influenced and sometimes dictated by state law as well as by the changing characteristics of the communities themselves. They are molded by those who have power and, in turn, they shape access to government as well as public policy. But while institutional structures have their biases, nothing is absolute in politics. Within any of these forms of government, the balance of power among mayors, managers, city councils, bureaucracies, and voters may change, altering not only the form of government, but the way it works. Moreover, real people occupy the positions and offices we've discussed. The way they are chosen affects the sort of people they are and who they are affects what they do, as we will see in the next chapter.

ESSENTIAL TERMS		
reform movement	council-manager system
social reform	city council
limits on immigration	city manager
direct primary	civil service
nonpartisan elections	competitive bidding
at-large ballots	bias of reform

concurrent elections   district elections
isolated elections   empowering councils
direct democracy   stronger mayors
initiative   controlling bureaucracy
referendum   tax revolt
recall   distribution of forms of
commission form of government   government
counterreform   county administrator

FIELDWORK   1. Research the political history of your community at the local library. Has
               it had a reform movement? What reform structures were introduced?
               Who were its leaders? What were their occupations (your local librarian
               can help you find out)? Were they like the reformers described in this
               chapter? (If you live in a suburb or other relatively new municipality,
               pick a nearby large, older city.)

            2. Check with your city clerk on any revisions in your city's charter since
               1960. Would they be characterized as reform or counterreform?

            3. Study your city's charter (available from the city clerk). Can it be char-
               acterized as reformed or unreformed? Which elements of the charter are
               reformed? Which are not?

NOTES   [1]Stephen Elkin, *City and Regime in the American Republic* (Chicago: University of
            Chicago Press, 1987), p. 28.

            [2]Robert T. Starks and Michael B. Preston, "Harold Washington and the Politics of
            Reform in Chicago: 1983–1987," in Rufus P. Browning, Dale R. Marshall, and David
            H. Tabb, eds., *Racial Politics in American Cities* (New York: Longman, 1990), pp.
            88–107.

            [3]Alfred Steinberg, *The Bosses* (New York: Mentor, 1972).

            [4]See Susan A. MacManus and Charles S. Bullock, "Minorities and Women Do Win
            At Large!" *National Civic Review* 77, no. 3 (May–June 1988): 231–244; or Susan Welch
            and Timothy Bledsoe, *Urban Reform and Its Consequences: A Study in Representation*
            (Chicago: University of Chicago Press, 1988).

            [5]See Clarence Stone and Heywood T. Sanders, eds., *The Politics of Urban Develop-
            ment* (Lawrence: University Press of Kansas, 1987).

            [6]See for example, *Rogers* v. *Lodge*, 458 US 613, 1982; *Thornburgh* v. *Gingles*, 106 S. Ct.
            2752, 1986; or Susan A. MacManus and Charles S. Bullock, "Racial Representation
            Issues," *PS* 18 (Fall 1985): 759–769.

            [7]Carl Abbott, *The New Urban America* (Chapel Hill: University of North Carolina
            Press, 1987), p. 255.

            [8]See Peggy Heilig and Robert J. Mundt, "Changes in Representational Equity: The
            Effect of Adopting Districts," *Social Science Quarterly* 64 (June 1983): 383–397.

[9]Susan Welch and Timothy Bledsoe, *Urban Reform and Its Consequences: A Study in Representation* (Chicago: University of Chicago Press, 1988), pp. 77–78.

[10]*Eu* v. *San Francisco County Democratic Central Committee*, 87–1269, U.S. Supreme Court.

[11]Thomas Dye and Susan MacManus, "Predicting City Government Structure," *American Journal of Political Science* 10 (May 1976): 257–272.

[12]*The Municipal Year Book* (Washington, DC: International City/County Management Association), 1988, p. 17.

[13]Kathy Hayes and Semoon Chang, "The Relative Efficiency of City Manager and Mayor-Council Forms of Government," *Southern Economic Journal* 57, no. 1 (July 1990): 176.

[14]Vincent L. Marando and Robert D. Thomas, *The Forgotten Governments: County Commissioners as Policy Makers* (Gainesville: University Presses of Florida, 1977), pp. 30, 33.

7

Legislators and Executives: The Balance of Power

The forms of government discussed in the preceding chapters substantially determine how local governments operate and what sorts of people gain positions of power. In each form, power is shared. In city halls and county courthouses across the nation, legislators and executives grapple for control of programs and policies, sometimes cooperating, sometimes in confrontation, sometimes even in gridlock. Formal authority, such as the veto or power of appointment, gives the protagonists advantages or disadvantages and is therefore itself sometimes the subject of power struggles. But most of the time, legislators and executives play by the rules of the game, using whatever political resources they command. These include not only the formal powers granted to them in charters, but also calling on allies, manipulating the media, or rallying the public to their causes, if they have any (many are content to maintain the status quo). Their own personalities and political styles affect their power and how they play their roles, too. Go to a meeting of your city council or county commission and see for yourself.

Legislators and executives are not the only players, however. Bureaucrats are significant participants, as are committees and commissions appointed by councils or mayors or both to advise them and sometimes exercise independent authority. Voters, interest groups, and powerful individuals outside government also greatly influence what happens in city hall. All these may be allies for legislators or executives in their power struggles, while the division of power within local governments gives these other elements a way around a resistant council, mayor, or manager.

Besides the clash of policies and personalities, local politics is also about the way governments operate and the values they emphasize. In the first half of this century, the reform ideals of professionalism and efficiency predominated, but since the 1960s, the counterreform goals of responsiveness, accountability, representativeness, and leadership have come to the fore. These two sets of values are not mutually exclusive, of course, and both are desirable. Communities must seek their own balance between them, but this process itself injects another layer of tension in local governments, for the outcome of the contest can subtly or substantially shift the balance of power.

Local Legislators: Representation without Power?

Today's **city councils** tend to be small, part-time, poorly paid, and dependent on the executive branch for information and guidance. This hasn't always been the case, however, and in many communities, councils have become more assertive in recent years, gaining greater influence, although still at a disadvantage in relation to the executive.

For much of the nineteenth century, councils dominated city politics. City charters gave them substantial budgetary and appointment powers and kept the executive branch feeble and fragmented under the weak mayor form of government. Early councils were large, numbering fifty or more members in some big cities, and many were bicameral, with an upper and lower house like the U.S. Congress. With **district elections** and small constituencies, representation and responsiveness were ensured, but these unwieldy bodies were not strong on leadership, much less on efficiency or professionalism. Bosses and machines solved some of these problems by amassing the diffuse powers of the weak mayor system so that action was possible, although the city councils often remained the focal point of local politics. Decisions were made by logrolling: you support my boondoggle and I'll support yours. Brokerage politics—making deals—were a way of life. Those who supported the machine were assured representation, responsiveness, accountability, and leadership. Those not aligned with the machine were left out, however, and professionalism and efficiency were beyond the pale.

Many of the reforms that followed focused on city councils. Bicameralism was eliminated, and councils were reduced in size to an average of just five to seven members chosen in at-large, nonpartisan elections. The reformers also took away some logrolling resources by introducing civil service and competitive bidding and shifted the balance of power toward the executive, with the strong mayor and council-manager forms of government. As part of their quest to get politics out of local government, they restricted the powers of what they saw as its most political element, the legislature. City council members were expected to serve part-time, providing policy guidance and leaving administration to experts. The reforms increased efficiency and professionalism but often at the expense of representation, responsiveness, and accountability.

✓ *At-Large versus District Elections*

Smaller councils make agreement easier, but the associated reform of **at-large elections** also helps build consensus and has probably affected who gets elected to city councils and how they behave more than any other reform. At the peak of their popularity in 1981, at-large council elections were used in 67 percent of U.S. cities, but today that figure has declined to about 59 percent; only 12 percent select their councils by districts, and 29 percent mix the two systems (see Table 6-3).[1]

Reformers hoped at-large elections would shift the focus to citywide rather than parochial interests and help achieve consensus, since every council member would be elected by the same constituency—usually a majority of the city's voters. The system does work well in small or middle-sized, homogeneous communities, where people are pretty similar to one another and are in general agreement on what the city should do. In large, diverse cities with lots of political conflict and competition, at-large elections often leave minorities underrepresented and frustrated. Most of the nation's largest cities never implemented this reform and as others, such as Atlanta, Phoenix, San Antonio, and Laredo (Texas) have grown large, they have returned to district elections under political pressure from minorities and neighborhoods. Some have done so when federal courts ruled that their at-large systems denied minority representation. This group includes small cities, such as Watsonville, California; middle-sized ones such as Springfield, Illinois; and large ones, such as Dallas. In 1987, the white minority in Birmingham won district representation in a court case. Several cities mix at-large and district elections in hopes of retaining a citywide perspective while increasing representativeness and responsiveness. Rochester, New York, for example, elects four council members by district and five at-large. Dallas mixes eight district council members with three, including the mayor, at-large. Atlanta, Buffalo, Denver, and Houston use similar combinations. In San Diego and Oakland, California, council members are nominated in district primaries, then elected at-large. In the past decade, more cities have switched to such mixed systems than to pure districting.

Impact: Who Gets Elected.   Just how much real difference these methods of representation make is disputed but, in general, at-large elections produce moderately elitist councils of older, white, Republican businessmen.[2] They focus on citywide issues, support growth, and worry more about efficiency and basic services than neighborhood and minority needs or little things that make a difference in people's daily lives, like a stop sign or a crosswalk. Council members are cooperative and consensual (most votes are unanimous) and the government they oversee, from mayor or manager to the cop on the beat, shares the characteristics of the council members, who generally support their associates in the bureaucracy. District representatives, on the other hand, are usually more diverse, with more minorities and less-affluent people. They tend to trust the bureaucracy less, to emphasize neighborhood and minority issues and services (including little things that matter a lot to some people), and to be skeptical of growth because it might hurt their neighborhoods. Council politics are more conflictual, with more split votes and longer meetings, although this usually reflects city politics rather than district elections. Conflict may be muted, however, because council members tend to defer to one another on district issues (condemned as logrolling by critics), and community frustration may be mitigated by council members' insistence that the government bureaus they oversee are more representative.

Community activists are sometimes disappointed that local politics aren't changed more by district elections, but their expectations may be too high. After all, the same political forces are active in a community after a change in representation. Although district campaigns are cheaper than at-large races, district candidates still need to cater to the traditional contributors and may remain captives of the growth machine, despite their neighborhood ties.

Impact: Styles of Policy Making. Political scientists have more modest expectations of these electoral structures. In theory, at-large council members are expected to act more as **trustees,** doing what they think best for the community, while district representatives function as **delegates,** following the wishes of their constituents. But in reality, most council members, however they are elected, declare themselves to be trustees,[3] perhaps because they prefer to be seen as independent thinkers rather than as mere mouthpieces or because they have no idea how their constituents might want them to vote on most issues. One survey of council members concluded that "the impact of political structure on policy views of council members appears to be quite small."[4] Yet, the same study found more conflict and pork-barrel politics (getting goodies for their own districts) as well as a greater "service orientation" on districted councils.[5] Another study reported that where cities mix district and at-large elections, council representation of "different constituencies causes a wider range of policy issues to be discussed at council meetings . . . , increases citizen participation—at council meetings and polls . . . , [and] increase[s] the likelihood of responsiveness through council coalition building."[6]

These differences may seem marginal, yet anyone who attends a council meeting can tell from the behavior and comments of members whether they represent districts or not. And it is undisputed that minority representation increases dramatically under districting, at least when minority populations are concentrated (or segregated) into certain districts. In every city that has recently instituted district elections, the representation of minorities (and sometimes women as well) has increased. In cities with long-standing district representation, minorities (such as Hispanics in Denver) have achieved "much greater . . . political representation, incorporation, and responsiveness" than in comparable cities using at-large elections, according to political scientist Rodney Hero.[7] Recently, however, minorities and women have done better in at-large elections because of increasing tolerance, good organizing, and, in some cases, because minorities have become majorities (and new minorities now complain about at-large elections).

The struggle for representation continues, for even if these systems make little real difference in policies, as some researchers assert, people need to feel they are part of the government of their community. Such reassurance encourages participation and may, eventually, change policies.

Council Dependence

Whether elected by district or at-large, councils are weak in relation to the executive branch. Although at-large council members represent the entire city, their precise constituency is vague and may be defined to suit a council member's own interests and ambitions. An at-large member, for example, may pay attention only to some neighborhoods or interest groups or only to those that will help them advance to higher office. On the other hand, when a city has both an at-large council and an elected mayor, council members are not easily intimidated by the mayor since they are elected by the whole city, too.

District council members have more clearly defined constituencies to hold them accountable. This is a source of strength, but their narrow viewpoints and the fact that they represent only part of the city usually mean more power for the city executive. City managers can play district council members off against one another, pleasing just enough to retain majority support. Mayors can do the same, with the added advantage of being the only citywide elected official, so they get more media attention and can claim to speak for all of the city, not just part.

Both at-large and district representatives, however, experience **council dependence** on executives and bureaucracies for information. In a council-manager system, the council is supposed to make policy and leave implementation to the manager and bureaucracy. In a mayor-council system, the council shares policy-making responsibilities with the mayor, who also oversees implementation. But the council needs information to make policy, and although citizens and interest groups provide some, most comes from the city administration, whether headed by a mayor or a manager. This is a major source of power for the executive since information can be manipulated or even withheld. Study any council agenda or listen attentatively at any meeting and executive control of information is obvious.

Asserting Legislative Authority

Many councils work comfortably with their executives and bureaucracies, especially in small or middle-sized, homogeneous cities with reform structures. But in other, usually larger, cities, councils often distrust the city administration and seek ways to depend on it less and to assert their own authority more. In some of these cities, counterreformers have sought ways to strengthen the council in relation to the executive.

The reformers expected council members to serve only part-time and paid them accordingly, which ensured dependence on the executive. But better paid council members can work full-time, helping their constituents more and providing a counterbalance to administrators. "It's ridiculous," says a Sacramento council member who is paid $20 per meeting, "to expect people with full-time jobs to also handle full-time council responsibilities."[8] Higher salaries also mean a wider variety of people can afford to hold public office—not just those with other means of support. **Council pay** in most cities is still minimal, however. In Dallas, where council members are expected to work part-time, they are paid $2400 a year; Bridgeport, Connecticut, pays $250; and Little Rock, Arkansas, pays its council members nothing at all. Denver and Cincinnati, however, are more generous, paying their charter-designated "part-time" council members $28,839 and $37,238, respectively. Full-time council salaries range from $37,700 in Milwaukee to $94,774 in Los Angeles.[9] County commissioners or supervisors are more likely to be full-time and are usually better paid than their city counterparts, averaging annual salaries of $18,864 in 1991.[10] School board members are usually unpaid, although some receive small stipends for each meeting they attend.

Another way to enhance legislative independence is to allow council members to hire their own support staff. Some, such as an auditor or budget analyst, may work for the council as a group. Others are hired by individual council members; they assist with constituent services, research, and public relations. Whether hired by the whole council or by individual members, much of what these staffers do is aimed at criticizing the proposals and practices of administrators.

City councils also assert themselves through committees. Instead of always functioning as a full council, with each member a generalist on all the things a city does, they form smaller groups that can specialize on particular policy areas. Typical **council committees** include budget, public works, and planning or environment. In committees, council members are able to spend more time studying and considering proposals and may develop sufficient expertise (with their own staff assistance) to challenge the executive. They report to the full council, which usually follows its own committees' recommendations.

Pay, staff, and committees make city councils stronger and more professional, providing balance to the power of executives and bureaucracies and enabling council members to represent their constituents more effectively. According to political scientist Rodney Hero, having a relatively **professionalized council,** with pay, staff, and a formal committee structure is particularly helpful to minority representation. Hero cites the achievements of Denver's Hispanic minority compared to minorities in cities without such council support.[11]

Other devices help councils, too. In the pure reform structure of the middle-sized, suburban city of Sunnyvale, California, for example, a bright and able council asserts control over the direction of the city by an annual session to set priorities, review its general plan for growth, and project its budget 10 years into the future. The council may still be dependent on the executive and bureaucracy, but these exercises provide both guidance and checks.

That's really about the best that can be hoped for by a city council. Even if professionalized, legislative bodies are always prey to disagreement, conflict, and disarray. They can never really compete with the authority a single executive, whether mayor or manager, has over the city bureaucracy or the hundreds of experts at the executive's command, nor can they hope to supervise or even direct what city workers do in their offices and on the streets. Besides, some citizens are wary of professionalized councils, which they see as a waste of time and money. Council members in some cities have therefore been limited to two or three terms of office, ensuring constant new blood, but also guaranteeing councils full of amateurs at the mercy of the executive branch.

The Council Members' Job

Despite recent improvements in council representation, the vast majority of council members in the United States are middle class and most are white males. As noted, many are paid little and must make professional and personal sacrifices to serve. Although in most communities the job is intended to be part-time, many council members, especially in larger cities, find themselves spending 40 to 70 hours a week on city business. Besides their weekly council meetings, much time is taken up in committees and meetings with constituents and lobbyists. Preparing for these weekly meetings often requires the assimilation of masses of reading material and reports with little assistance. The people they represent also expect council members to help with their problems, so much time is devoted to constituent service. Such efforts help with reelection (another demand on council members' time), so constituent service is usually taken on willingly and even eagerly. In addition to all this, effective council members need to **"work the halls,"** talking to colleagues, administrators, and executives to pick up support for their pet issues. They must be careful about this, however, since city charters often forbid direct contact between council members and administrators other than the manager and mayor, and most states have **open meeting laws** that require public access to any gathering of a majority of council members except when they are discussing legal or personnel matters.

With so many demands on their time—plus the private jobs part-time council members must retain—most feel lucky just to keep up with the press of city business. For the most part, this means that they react to proposals and policies put forward by the executive, the bureaucracy, or businesses and interest groups, rather than initiating programs on their own. In other words, they tend to be followers rather than leaders.

Why do they do it? Surveys of council members report that the main motivation is community service and the spirit of volunteerism.[12] Most actually want to do good for their cities. Some are propelled by concerns about particular issues, such as growth or neighborhood or minority problems. Most get a boost out of being a local VIP, and many enjoy the exercise of power—or at least the illusion thereof. Some may expect to further their personal careers, although not usually in politics. Except for big city mayors, most local politicians do not advance to higher office. They may, however, enhance their law practices or get better jobs through the connections they make as council members, perhaps as consultants or lobbyists or with developers. For the vast majority, however, being a council member brings little personal reward and remains primarily a way to serve their communities in the great U.S. tradition of volunteerism.

Managers: Authority without Accountability

In contrast to council members, **city managers** are among the most powerful and least visible actors in local politics. Although the average manager may sit quietly, perhaps even wordlessly, through a city council meeting, virtually every item on the agenda will have been put there by the manager and his or her staff and virtually every decision will follow their recommendations. Sometimes a city manager takes a higher profile, lecturing the council and behaving more like a mayor than a manager, but although such publicly domineering managers were once rather common, they are now rare. Most modern managers work behind the scenes, prudently letting the council take the lead in public.

The Council-Manager System

That's more or less what the reformers who created the council-manager form of government intended. The council is to be the political element of local government, providing policy guidelines, representation, and accountability. (We've already seen that the reformers' part-time councils, elected at-large, have difficulty achieving these goals except in homogeneous cities, where representation and agreement on policy are easy.) The city manager, appointed by the council, is to be the objective, professional administrator, overseeing the city bureaucracy as it carries out council programs competently and efficiently. Most council-manager cities have a mayor, but unlike the executive mayor in the mayor-council form of government, the mayor in a council-manager system is basically a presiding officer who sits and votes with the council and has no separate powers.

In theory, the council-manager system concentrates power in the city council, with no checks and balances or separation of power. Although the manager is in charge of administration, the council provides policy guidance and, more importantly, exercises the ultimate power to hire and fire the manager. Political scientist James Svara concludes that "the council ultimately wins all battles with the manager."[13] Battles, however, are not common in council-manager governments, where cooperation is the norm. Most issues are resolved before they ever reach the council, perhaps because its wishes are anticipated or because contemporary city managers are so skillful at building consensus. Then again, cooperation and consensus are common in the small- and middle-sized communities that most frequently use the council-manager form of government. These communities tend to be homogeneous; even if they are not, reform electoral structures ensure a council that reflects the dominant majority, manufacturing consensus by suppressing disagreement and discord.

Professionalization

Having the right manager is crucial to making the system work. Reformers intended the position to be held by a neutral professional with expertise in administration who could oversee the technical details of delivering city services. Such professionals were rare when the council-manager system was initiated in 1912, and for a long time most managers were professionals only in the sense that they had skills and knowledge beyond those of politicians and were not themselves politically active. Some were professors, doctors, and merchants, but most were engineers: A 1934 study reported that 77 percent of managers with university degrees had studied engineering.[14] Most were locals, and few regarded city management as their life's work.[15] Although reality fell short of the reform ideal, the first managers seem to have been satisfactory. More and more cities adopted the council-manager form of government and, unlike the commission system, most stuck with it. The engineer-managers who dominated the profession from 1912 to after World War II proved up to their jobs, partly because at that time cities concentrated on the provision of basic, physical services, such as streets, sewage, garbage collection and disposal, and public safety.

After World War II, local government and the **profession of city management** changed. Cities raised and spent more money and took on more responsibilities, including some social services. Federal programs and grants also expanded city activities. Growth, having been held back for nearly two decades by depression and war, went into high gear, adding planning complexities to city operations and also adding many new local governments in the suburbs, most of which opted for the council-manager system. With the growing number of jobs and increased responsibilities, a true profession of city management emerged.

The International City Management Association, a professional organization for managers founded in 1914, provided support, information, and training, and universities developed courses and degrees in public administration. A national pool of career managers with administrative rather than only engineering expertise grew, and by the 1950s and 1960s, city councils were selecting the sort of nonlocal, professional managers the reformers originally intended. Although the number of such professionals has constantly risen, a 1989 survey reported that over half of all city managers were not employed in local government when they were hired.[16] However, more and more career managers work their way up through the ranks, starting in civil service positions or in manager-appointed jobs, eventually becoming a deputy manager or department head. The next step is to manage a small city, then on to bigger cities with bigger budgets and higher salaries (see Table 7-1). As of 1991, the average pay for a city manager was $61,401, but cities with populations between 250,000 and 499,000 averaged $102,107.[17] Larger cities paid even more. Salaries for county administrators, usually recruited from the same professional pool, reflect this range.

Professionalization of city managers has not brought diversity as yet. Like other professions and like the reformers who conceived the city manager system, its practitioners are straight out of the traditional U.S.

Table 7-1 Salaries of City Officials, 1994

City	Mayor	Manager	Police Chief	Council Member
Boston	$100,000	—	$76,699	$45,500
Charlotte, NC	14,800	$124,000	88,766	8,000
Chicago	110,000	—	105,000	55,000
Dallas	2,400	134,000	92,207	2,400
Houston	133,004	—	110,000	37,000
Miami	6,000	160,261	94,408	5,000
Oklahoma City	2,000	102,606	79,323	1,200
Philadelphia	104,500	—	80,750	65,000

elite: As of 1991, 87 percent were male and 94 percent were white.[18] Nearly all were college educated and most were middle-aged. About equal numbers identified themselves as Democrats (25 percent), Republicans (27 percent), and Independents (26 percent).[19] County executives have similar characteristics.

Hiring the Manager

City councils in manager cities now hire mostly from among these professionals, announcing job vacancies and selecting from a pool of applicants, often supplemented by professional headhunters employed by councils to seek applicants. Current city employees hoping for promotion may also be included. The council reviews the resumes of the job seekers, interviews a few, and finally agrees on one. The choice is perhaps the most important decision a council makes and reflects its priorities. Councils that hire outsiders are usually pushing for administrative change, James Svara argues, while those that hire from within the city government hope to consolidate existing arrangements.[20]

Traditionally, the **hiring of managers** was open-ended, subject to termination at the pleasure of the council. In the early days of the system, some managers stayed on for decades, but as of 1989, the average tenure was 5.4 years.[21] Managers in cities with less than 10,000 people have the shortest tenure, but most probably move to advance their careers, not because they are fired or because local politics in such places are too hot to handle.[22] Political pressure may account for managerial turnover in larger cities, but even so, more resign when they see such trouble coming than are fired. Nowadays, many managers are employed under a contract with a fixed term of years. Some managers feel that a contract secures their rights and at least guarantees pay for a specified period, while some councils like contracts because they provide a fixed date to review the manager's performance and a way to get rid of an unwanted manager gracefully. Outright firing can look too political, getting the council in local political trouble and giving it a bad national reputation among professional managers.

Managers at Work

The basic job of the manager is to implement council policy and oversee the operations of the city. Most substantial among a **manager's powers** are hiring and firing department heads and developing and administering the budget. With these tools, a manager can shape city government and set its agenda. The manager is usually also responsible for putting together the agenda for council meetings, including staff recommendations on various items, and, of course, the manager and his or her staff are present at the meeting to advise the council and take its direction. According to the ideals of this form of government, the manager is strictly subservient to the council, providing information, carrying out its decisions, and remaining neutral on policy and politics, especially elections.

Most managers and council members, however, readily acknowledge that such subservience and neutrality are little more than fantasy. Studies of managers and council members show that most expect the manager to play a part in policy making. In a 1989 survey, 37 percent of managers said they initiated policies and 75 percent reported participating in policy formulation.[23] This shouldn't come as a surprise since the manager is an expert and she or he employs other experts. As such, they provide information to the council, and they usually accompany their information with a policy recommendation that the council almost always approves. Of course, shrewd managers consult council members before major decisions, and most know their councils well enough to anticipate reactions to recommendations without consultation. The reformers' idealized line between policy and administration is pretty fuzzy in practice.

Managers and Councils

When councils and managers disagree, the council usually wins due to its power to hire and fire the manager, although in rare cases managers have taken their cases to the voters and survived. But such direct confrontations are unusual in the cooperative culture of the council-manager system, with its clear council majorities reflecting clear community majorities. Managers usually have no trouble discerning what is expected and delivering it. In the process, however, they may exercise considerable influence, and, in subtle ways, their power may be greater than that of the council—or the voters.

Managers have substantial formal authority. Their administrative command of the city bureaucracy is virtually unhindered by the council, which is usually prohibited from even talking to city staff except through the manager. Department heads can be hired and fired by the manager without council consent. Managers generally calculate the council's reaction, knowing that if the members don't like an appointment, they can fire the manager, but getting together a majority for such an action is difficult. Usually the council reasons that few department heads are actually crucial, and they may also be afraid that their intervention could be seen by voters as political meddling. The manager's budget power is a little more constrained, with formal council approval required, yet even there, councils are limited in time and expertise.

These, along with their professionalism, are the primary **political resources of city managers.** While the council is part-time and amateur, with only general knowledge, the manager and the bureaucracy he or she commands are full-time and impressively expert. They can dazzle the council with information presented in such a way as to justify their recommendations. Many council members lack the time and expertise to read staff reports critically; most don't bother, putting their trust in the professionals. The public and interest groups are competing sources of information, but they are tainted by amateurism and bias, as compared to the purported professional objectivity of city staff. Besides, the manager and staff will have presented their reports and proposals to the council in advance of meetings and so have a head start on the public and often on lobbyists as well.

Council agendas are composed almost entirely of items from the city manager's office, including reports and recommendations. The council almost always unanimously approves whatever the staff recommends. The same process applies to the budget, the council's most important annual decision. The manager and a full-time staff work on it through the year, presenting a bulky document to the council about a month before the deadline for approval. The council pokes at the document, holds public hearings, shuffles a little money around, then approves.

There's nothing wrong with this if the manager's recommendations are objective and reflect the wishes of the council and the community, as they usually do. Managers who overtly thwart the will of the council and community don't last long. Yet managers exercise great power and not necessarily neutrally. Every recommendation made to a council is a choice. The manager's own biases (and those of her or his chosen staff) influence these choices. After all, managers are human. Some are liberal, others conservative; some are racist, sexist, or punctiliously politically correct. These attitudes may show in their recommendations and actions. "Despite professional norms that deny such influences," one study concluded, "the political ideology of city managers plays a significant role in influencing council policy."[24] But other biases come from the profession of city management itself. Perhaps because of its roots in the reform movement and the early engineer-managers, the profession tends to see local government functions as limited and physical rather than social. It also apotheosizes expertise and quantifiable facts over intuition and sometimes unquantifiable social values. Moving traffic, for example, is given a higher priority than preserving the social fabric of neighborhoods. The former can easily be counted; the latter cannot. Managers and their minions often show contempt for citizens and even council members who may instinctively know what is right but are unable to provide charts and data.

Nor do managers stay as scrupulously out of politics as the reformers expected. In a 1985 survey, managers said they spent 17 percent of their time on politics.[25] Most keep a low profile during elections (supporting losers is fatal), but may nevertheless provide incumbent council members with crucial information or defer controversial decisions until after the election. More commonly, managers meet with community groups, give speeches, and confer with newspaper editorial boards to sell their proposals. "If you view your job the way we used to do it, shuffling papers and having meetings, you miss the boat," says Camille Barnett, city manager of Austin, Texas. Barnett considers herself a negotiator and facilitator, bringing together diverse groups to reach consensus. Reformers would have assumed this was the city council's role, but Barnett's council, far from being upset, takes credit for the change. "We're always telling the manager to bring all the interest groups together in a room and work something out," says one Austin council member.[26]

Other managers acknowledge their growing role as political brokers, balancing not only members of the council, but also community groups. The bottom line for managers, however, is keeping a majority of the city council happy. "I run for reelection every Tuesday night [when the council meets]," says one manager.[27] In a way, this is another source of power, for managers can play different council members against each other to prevent a majority for firing. If those who wish to get rid of the manager have different reasons, the manager can make concessions to one or two and stay in office. Community groups are trickier for managers to keep happy because managers are professional administrators, not politicians. Except for a few like Austin's Barnett, most managers prefer to keep their heads down and confine their political maneuvering to the city council. This may exacerbate the frustration of community groups that feel the manager and city government are not responding to their demands. These groups may grow angrier when they learn they have no way to hold the manager accountable. Since the manager is not elected, she or he cannot be recalled. Only the council can remove the manager, and it is difficult, if not impossible, for community groups to persuade a majority of the council to do so. Antimanager groups may be described as political fanatics, while the manager enjoys the protective cloak of his or her purportedly neutral professionalism.

Evolving Systems

Such conflicts rarely arise in the generally homogeneous cities that have council manager governments, but when the populace diversifies and political conflict increases, the council-manager system tends to break down. Sometimes, as in Austin, the solution is a more politically active manager, engaging in negotiation and brokerage among various interests. However, managers can get into trouble doing this. When that happens, more radical reform is likely. The mayor is almost always the beneficiary of such reforms.

In some cities, the council-manager form of government is retained but the mayor's powers are enhanced. The mayor is expected to provide leadership, while the manager may be reduced to the status of a chief administrative officer, managing the bureaucracy while the mayor directs policy. In such cities, the mayor is directly elected, presides over and votes with the council, and may set its agenda as well. A full-time salary and staff are likely. Some mayors also gain the power to propose the budget and a special role in appointing the manager and possibly department heads. Mayors in 13 percent of council-manager systems even have veto power over council actions. Almost all large cities that still use the council-manager system (including Dallas, Phoenix, San Antonio, and San Diego) have moved in this direction, with mayors growing more powerful and prominent and managers fading into the background—or leaving to be replaced by more subservient successors.

A few cities have taken more extreme action, abandoning the council-manager system and returning to the more politically accountable mayor-council form of government. Among the largest cities to make the change are Flint, Michigan; Schenectady and Rochester, New York; Albuquerque, New Mexico; and Pocatello, Idaho. In some cases, the switch was the result of increasing diversity and political conflict that city managers couldn't handle. When Albuquerque made its change in 1974, respondents to a public opinion poll said that "under the council-manager structure they often did not know who could help with a problem or who was responsible for municipal affairs. Many also felt that Albuquerque had outgrown manager government and that a full-time, elected mayor was needed."[28] One researcher actually found that these changes were most common in smaller cities where city managers dabbled in politics too much and "crises in legitimacy" arose.[29] However, outright **abandonment of the council-manager form** of government remains rare. More cities have considered and rejected such a switch than have approved it, largely because of unrealistic but heartfelt fears of autocratic executives and resurrected bosses. Compromise is more common, retaining the manager but gradually increasing the power of the mayor. For if any one has gained in recent city hall power struggles, it is the mayor.

Mayors: Leadership and Authority

Mayors are more difficult to generalize about than other city officials because the powers of the office vary so much from city to city and the personality and skills of particular officeholders count for so much. We can, however, distinguish between the sort of nonexecutive mayors found in the council-manager form of government and the weak and strong mayors found in the mayor-council systems.

Nonexecutive Mayors

Mayors in council-manager cities are members of the city council who preside over meetings and represent the city on ceremonial occasions. Although 65 percent of council-manager cities directly elect their mayors, in the remainder the mayor is chosen by the council from among its members, rotating the position every year or two. In a few cites, such as Cincinnati, the mayor is the top vote winner on the council. Mayors in council-manager cities lack executive authority to hire and fire or propose a budget; only 13 percent may veto acts of the council. The power of such **nonexecutive mayors** comes almost entirely from their title and from being the focus of attention. Beyond that, it's up to individuals to make the most of their positions.

This is difficult but not impossible. The **title of mayor** really means something to most Americans, whatever the formal authority of the office. Out of ignorance or idealism, most people assume mayors are important. This assumption actually gives mayors power, even if it is only symbolic. The public respects and focuses on the mayor. So does the media, which reinforces the public bias, although media concentration on the mayor is probably less out of ignorance than convenience. After all, it is easier to interview one mayor than several council members, and the media doesn't have to explain what a mayor (as opposed to a city manager or city council member) is.

Surprisingly, the symbolic power of the title of mayor carries over to council colleagues who know better. Although council members are in most ways the mayor's equal, many look to the mayor for at least some leadership. Council members tend to give mayors the first opportunity to take the initiative on policies and often expect the mayor to help steer them through controversial issues. Just by **presiding over meetings,** for example, mayors have some control over the meeting's agenda, not so much as to whether or not an issue is heard as to how and when it is considered and how it is resolved. The mayor may recommend referral to administration or to a committee or force a vote. As presiding officer, the mayor also calls on speakers and so can choose those who will say what she or he wants said or make the motion the mayor wants at the appropriate time.

Like council members and the public, administrators also look to mayors for at least some leadership even though few answer to the mayor alone. Managers and department heads work closely with mayors on the agendas of public meetings and rely on mayors to move programs through the council, to communicate with the public, and sometimes to mediate. In return, the mayors expect to see their priorities reflected by the administration. **Partnerships between mayors and managers** are not unusual, especially in the larger cities using the council-manager form of government. "This awkward arrangement can work remarkably well," writes Alan Ehrenhalt, "in the presence of a charismatic mayor and a detail-minded, self-effacing city manager, as was the case in San Antonio for most of the 1980s with Mayor Henry Cisneros and manager Louis J. Fox."[30] Besides his leadership skills, Cisneros, now U.S. Secretary of Housing and Urban Development, had the added advantage of being in the national spotlight as the first Latino to be elected mayor of a major U.S. city.

James Svara, an authority on local leadership, observes that nonexecutive mayors such as Cisneros assert influence by facilitating and coordinating the actions of others, including the city administration, council, and community groups. "The council-manager mayor," Svara writes, "is not limited in his or her leadership but rather is different in the kinds of leadership provided."[31] Instead of being the dominant power, this sort of mayor is first among equals, a potential facilitator with a chance to guide programs and policies. Playing such a role, however, takes more than a title. Considerable skill is required, so the real power of a mayor in a council-manager system is very much dependent on the personality of the mayor.

Nonexecutive mayors can easily lose when there are conflicts. Council members can out vote them. City managers can go around them to the rest of the council or even to the public; they can also slow the process down, manipulate information, and delay implementation. When such conflicts arise, however, they are far more apocalyptic than these tactics imply. If the mayor is no pushover, the result may be gridlock or the factions may take their fight to the public, sometimes to be resolved in elections. Public esteem for their title gives mayors an advantage in these confrontations, at least in comparison to the commonly held stereotypes of bickering council members and bureaucratic managers. But again, the personality and skills of the individual mayor are crucial for success.

Maximizing the Power of Nonexecutive Mayors

In pursuit of leadership, some council-manager cities have strengthened the office of mayor. Sometimes such change is sought by community organizations frustrated by unresponsive managers or by business interests that want a mayor who can sell the city to investors. More often, the instigators are frustrated mayors themselves. If they are sufficiently popular, greater power may be their reward, although the public, despite its expectations of mayors, is usually reluctant to increase executive authority.

In most council-manager cities, strengthening the mayor starts with **direct election** rather than selection by the city council. Election gives the mayor no added authority, but it makes public support clear and may indicate a mandate. It also ensures that the mayor is the center of media and public attention and raises expectations, since candidates universally promise to get things done rather than admitting that without executive authority the mayor is only a member of a team.

In accordance with the basic premises of the council-manager form of government, most nonexecutive mayors are expected to work only part-time and are paid accordingly. San Antonio, for example, pays its mayor $50 per council meeting; the mayor of Dallas earns $2400 per year, and the mayor of Oklahoma City gets $2000 (see Table 7-1). Some council-manager cities, however, pay something closer to a full-time salary: Phoenix pays

$37,500 per year, while Cincinnati pays $40,738, and the mayor of San Jose, California, gets $72,500.[32] As with council pay, more money means the mayor spends less time earning a living elsewhere and more time on his or her public duties, which can translate into power.

Mayors have also enhanced their stature by acquiring the authority to hire and fire their own personal aides rather than working with city staff through the manager. Nonexecutive mayors in small and middle-sized cities usually have no staff except a civil service secretary, but in larger cities, mayors employ one or more aides. These may include a press spokesperson, a speech writer, and aides who help the mayor analyze recommendations from the manager.

In addition to presiding over meetings and controlling agendas, nonexecutive mayors have gained power as **leaders of the council.** When Pete Wilson (now governor of California) was mayor of San Diego, he organized the city council into committees to specialize on various subjects and took the power to appoint the committees and their chairs for himself as mayor. Other mayors have copied Wilson, gaining a modest set of rewards for council allies as well as a little more influence over policy. Some mayors have also expanded their powers of appointment of advisory committees and commissions, again gaining a little more patronage and a little more influence over policy. The shift to district council elections in some cities has also enhanced the stature and leadership role of the mayor as the only citywide elected official.

Executive Mayors

In rare cases, council-manager mayors actually gain powers beyond these. San Jose's mayor, for example, is directly elected, earns a good salary, hires a large personal staff, presides over a districted city council, and appoints its committees. But the voters of San Jose also approved a charter amendment giving the mayor power to propose the budget and nominate the city manager. Perhaps San Jose's mayor is now more like the mayor in a weak mayor form of government rather than the traditional nonexecutive mayor in council-manager systems.

In fact, the powers of mayors vary by degree. In earlier chapters we distinguished between the weak and strong mayor forms of government, and in this chapter, we have considered nonexecutive mayors, but while these distinctions are useful for grasping the differences among forms of government, mayoral powers vary so much that once the basic forms are understood, we almost need to look at particular cities. Figure 7-1 presents a **hierarchy of mayoral powers,** ranging from the purely titular to the substantial authority of the executive mayor, culminating in the powers of appointment, budget, and veto. Council-manager mayors have the first few powers listed, but beginning with salary and staff, mayors

FIGURE 7-1   Hierarchy of Mayoral Powers
Source: Susan Ronder, City College of San Francisco.

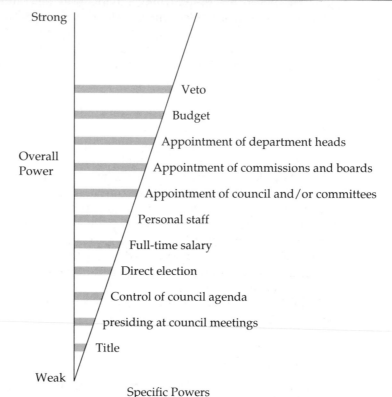

become more executive, gradually shading from weak to strong depending on how completely the different powers are held by the mayor. We should remember, however, that while executive mayors have greater official power, their personalities still count, too.

Like most of their nonexecutive counterparts, **executive mayors** gain prestige from the title of mayor and credibility from being elected. Unlike most council-manager mayors, however, they are expected to work full-time and are paid accordingly. As of 1990, the salaries of executive mayors in large cities ranged from $100,000 in Boston to $133,004 in Houston (see Table 7-1).[33] These mayors also employ sizable personal staffs. But three other powers are essential for the making of an executive mayor: **appointment, budget, and veto.** A strong mayor has the authority to hire and fire department heads and often a chief administrative officer as well as to appoint members of boards and commissions. The mayor, supported by an extensive staff, proposes the budget, which must be approved by the council. The mayor may veto council action subject to override only by a two-thirds vote of the council, which may be hard to get. Additionally, the mayor may issue executive orders, reorganize city departments, and make appointments to fill vacancies when elected offices fall vacant. Some mayors have special powers over agencies that are associated with the city but are somewhat independent, such as redevelopment or housing authorities. Strong mayors, by definition, have all these powers, but they are diluted in a weak mayor form of government (remember this is distinct from nonexecutive mayors in council-manager systems). Weak mayors may appoint some city officials, but budget authority is shared with the council and other executives, and the veto is usually denied. However, the powers of a weak mayor are still greater than those of council-manager mayors.

These powers make it clear that the executive mayor is an administrator, not just a political leader. Overseeing the day-to-day operations of city government, choosing department heads, putting together a budget, and proposing programs all require considerable management skills, yet most mayors get their jobs through their political rather than administrative ability. This suits a city's need for political leadership, but may fall short on the effective and efficient management of a large organization. Some cities try to balance these executive needs through the use of a **chief administrative officer (CAO)** or by deputy mayors appointed by the mayor (sometimes with council approval) specifically for their management skills. An increasing number of cities seem to be moving in this direction, seeking to balance political leadership with professional management.[34] Like city managers, CAOs oversee the daily operations of local governments and often assemble budget proposals, but while managers answer to councils, CAOs answer to mayors. Unlike managers, they do not appoint department heads, and they play a lesser role in developing policies, deferring to mayoral leadership on both.

Executive mayors are also distinguished from nonexecutives in their relations with the city council. Executive mayors are separate from city councils; they do not preside over and rarely attend council meetings. Instead, the council chooses its own presiding officer, and the relationship between the two branches of local government is often more antagonistic. Mayors lose some control of agendas and meetings, although they still shape what happens by the proposals they pass along to the council, and any loss of influence is compensated for by budgetary and veto powers. The council, like legislative bodies elsewhere, spends most of its time reacting to executive proposals, while mayors, like city managers, benefit from their control over city staff and information. A singular executive—whether mayor or manager—also always has the advantage of being one while multi-member councils are inherently prone to disunity.

Whether executive or nonexecutive, mayors use their political skills and resources to win council approval of their programs. They lobby council members and give their allies electoral support, including endorsement and fundraising. Moreover, executive mayors even more than other sorts of mayors have the advantage of being in the media spotlight. An effective mayor uses that spotlight to further his or her program with the council.

Who the Mayors Are

Mayors, like council members and city managers, are mostly white and male. As of 1991, about 12 percent of all mayors were female, 2 percent were African American, and 1.5 percent were Latino.[35] Minorities do a little better in larger cities, which are more likely to have substantial minority populations. Available data on mayoral backgrounds do not distinguish between executive and nonexecutive mayors, but given the sorts of communities that adopt the different forms, it is likely that **minority mayors** are more common in cities with executive rather than nonexecutive mayors. A study of cities with populations over 100,000 reported that 13.1 percent of the mayors were African American, while 2.5 percent were Latino, and 0.8 percent were Asian. Women, at 10.2 percent, are about as successful in these cities as they are in all cities, but the researchers noted that while the mayors of 32 percent of western cities with populations of over 100,000 were female, not one of the northeastern cities in their sample had a woman mayor. The same study found that 80 percent of mayors had a college degree and the same percent had business or professional backgrounds.[36]

Despite the preponderance of white businessmen among mayors, women and minority candidates have achieved striking successes since the 1960s. Women have done particularly well in the West and in suburban cities, although several large cities have also elected women mayors, including San Antonio, San Francisco, San Jose, and Houston. Currently the largest city presided over by a woman mayor is San Diego, where Susan Golding was elected in 1992. African Americans have also done well in mayoral contests, especially in large cities (see Table 7-2). Latino mayors have led many small southwestern towns as well as large cities such as San Antonio, Miami, and Denver. Asians, a smaller minority, have elected fewer mayors, although a Japanese American won the office in San Jose in 1971, and in 1993 a Chinese American ran second in the mayoral race in Los Angeles, which is just 9 percent Asian. Otherwise, only a few small cities have elected Asian mayors. They represent a relatively new and diverse immigrant group, only now emerging as a political force.

In office, women and minority mayors are usually expected to pay more attention to social welfare and neighborhood issues while their white male counterparts are expected to focus more on business and development. These expectations are often accurate, but women and minority candidates almost always have to reach out to white male voters, leaders, and campaign contributors. To gain such support, they often emphasize

Table 7-2   **Largest Cities with African American Mayors, 1994**

City	Mayor	Population	Percent African American
Detroit	Dennis Archer	1,027,974	76
Memphis	Willie Herenton	810,337	55
Baltimore	Kurt Schmoke	736,014	59
Washington	Sharon Pratt Kelly	606,900	66
Seattle	Norman Rice	516,259	10
Cleveland	Michael White	505,616	50
New Orleans	Marc Morial	496,938	62
Denver	Wellington Webb	467,610	13
Kansas City	Emanuel Cleaver	435,146	30
Atlanta	Bill Campbell	396,017	67
Minneapolis	Sharon Sayles Belton	368,400	13
Oakland	Elihu Harris	364,040	44

Source: Black Elected Officials, Washington, DC: Center for Political and Economic Studies Press, 1993 xxxiii and U. S. Bureau of Census.

law and order, managerial competence, and/or economic development over programs that might more obviously benefit their own groups. In doing so, women and minority mayors may alienate their basic constituencies and face bitter criticism as sellouts. The vast majority of minority groups nevertheless continue to support their own.

In recent contests, however, this has often not been enough to elect their candidates. Except in cities where a single minority has become the majority, as have Cuban Americans in Miami, Mexican Americans in San Antonio, and African Americans in Atlanta, Detroit, and Washington, D.C., coalitions with other groups are essential for victory.[37] The election of several African American mayors in the 1970s and 1980s resulted from the solidarity of black voters as well as the support of Hispanics and white liberals, especially Jews. But in the 1990s, these coalitions fell apart in some cities. Black and Hispanic mayors retired or were defeated and were succeeded by whites in New York, Los Angeles, Philadelphia, Chicago, Miami, and San Antonio, despite large minority populations in all those cities. In some cases, the coalition between African Americans and Hispanics split, while the growing Asian population often did not identify or ally with these minorities. Elsewhere, African American candidates lost the support of Jewish voters, who had been crucial to their initial victories, because of antagonism between the two groups. In other places, white voters shifted their loyalties because of worries about the economy or the environmental impacts of growth (usually supported by minority coalitions). Although African American mayors were elected with broad support in Seattle and Kansas City, where blacks are a minority, stable electoral coalitions are rare among large, diverse cities today and candidates must cobble together their support bases, drawing on their own groups and others, including business leaders.

Mayoral Style

Once elected, the formal powers of executive and nonexecutive mayors determine their behavior in office to a substantial degree. But anyone who has observed two or three different mayors of a single city knows how different they can be. Holders of a particular office all possess the same formal powers, but how they use these powers varies because they are different people. Race and sex, as noted above, affect how mayors do their job. So do previous experience, occupation, and education. More personal characteristics, such as knowledge, political instinct, ability to handle people (and the press), and star quality or charisma also play a part. Mayors may be lazy or dynamic, stupid or intelligent, foolish or shrewd. Some are willing to devote more of their own time and energy to their jobs than others. For some, being mayor is the pinnacle of a career, while for others it is the beginning, a stepping stone to higher office. Those without such ambitions may focus more on strictly local issues; they may also be lackadaisical. Those hoping to move upward may be more aggressive about making their mark; they may also spend more time broadening their constituency, cultivating the media, and traveling to the state or national capital. Like other local officeholders, however, most mayors are homebodies. Only a few seek or win higher office.[38]

In addition to the formal powers of the office and personal characteristics, the local political culture also affects mayoral power. Some communities, for example, accept a high level of political conflict and rely on their mayors to provide leadership. Others emphasize professionalism and expect mayors merely to keep things moving while deferring to the experts on policy development and implementation. Still others value broad participation and resent domineering mayors. In some places, the mayor is a god; in others a joke (the attitude of the press has a lot to do with this). Public expectations, in other words, affect both a mayor's power and conduct in office.

These elements—formal powers, personal characteristics, political culture, and others—combine to shape the way a mayor does her or his job. Political scientists have developed various categories of **mayoral styles,**[39] including:

The ribbon cutter: Concentrates on ceremonial aspects and makes no effort to influence policy.

The caretaker: Attempts to solve problems as they arise; has no personal program; seeks to survive and help the city get by.

The promoter: Spends time selling the city to investors and hustling state and federal aid, initiating only those policies that facilitate this.

The broker: A more aggressive version of the caretaker, seeking to put together coalitions to resolve issues, but still not an initiator of policy.

The individualist: Seeks solutions through personal leadership rather than broker-style coalition building; may initiate selective policies.

The executive: A city manager–style mayor who emphasizes good administration and may initiate discrete projects but not broad change.

The oracle: Good at talking, at media manipulation, and at using the symbolic powers of the office, but weak at developing policies and at administration.

The entrepreneur or innovator: A strong leader with a clear, sometimes ambitious program and the ability to initiate it and carry it out.

Most mayors are easy to slot into one of these categories, although some combine the traits of several. Nonexecutive mayors rarely manage to get beyond being ribbon cutters, caretakers, or promoters. By skillful use of their limited resources they can develop into most of the other types, but their powers are too limited to enable them to act as executives or entrepreneurs. Mayors with more extensive authority can fill any of the categories. Staffing of the mayor's office and clear command of the city's budget and bureaucracy are crucial, of course.

City Characteristics and Mayoral Styles.   As we learned in earlier chapters, when cities grow, they become more diverse and political conflict increases. Seeking leadership to resolve this conflict, larger cities tend to opt for the mayor-council form of government and to give their mayors executive powers. **Expectations of mayors** may be great in such cities, and disappointment is common. Weak mayors do not have the authority to do much, and when stronger mayors take action, they often upset more people than they please. Whatever their powers, mayors may not be able to meet the high expectations of them (produced partly by their own campaign promises) because U.S. cities have become increasingly ungovernable.[40] The very diversity that demands leadership may fracture a city into irreconcilable components. Conflicts such as the ethnic antagonisms that exploded into the 1992 Los Angeles riots may be beyond the ability of mayors to resolve. The impoverishment of cities produced by suburbanization also means urban problems and needs are greater while the resources are less. State and federal budget cutbacks have further limited local funds. Even skilled leaders with substantial official powers cannot solve problems without resources. As a consequence, many mayors are happy just to get by as caretakers.

Another option for mayors of cities with intractable problems is to spend their time promoting rather than governing the city. This means lobbying the state and federal governments for grants and aid and trying to recruit business and industry. In the 1970s, some mayors built up formidable power through federally funded programs, but the cutbacks of the Reagan-Bush years severely limited this option. Promoting economic development to bring in jobs and taxes, however, seems to have become a primary mayoral activity, making some mayors seem like cheerleaders for the growth machine. Although this offends environmentalists in some communities, most mayors find promoting their cities a politically safe activity—unlike trying to find other ways to solve difficult urban problems.

Some mayors accept their reduction to caretakers and promoters while others, even in strong mayor cities such as San Francisco and Boston, have demanded greater power and authority to meet public expectations, cope with diversity, and solve increasing urban problems. As James Svara warns, however, "The elected executive leadership model is no panacea for resolving urban problems."[41] Even with the powers of the strong mayor, effective leaders must build a solid base of political support. This is particularly difficult in communities with nonpartisan electoral systems, but even in those with partisan elections, weakening parties mean mayors must rely more and more on their own personal organizations. Until recently, some were able to use jobs provided by federal grants to build support, but these have been eliminated. Now ambitious mayors must spend their time hustling the media and stitching together alliances of interest groups and powerful individuals as a support base, but these alliances are unstable and putting them together diverts the mayor from dealing with the problems he or she was elected to solve. Increasingly, this is true for mayors in both mayor-council and council-manager systems. Politics play their part, whatever the powers of the executive.

Converging Forms: Representation, Administration, Leadership

The balance of representation, professional administration, and leadership is still being worked out in U.S. local governments. The trend is toward more representative councils through district elections and more leadership through stronger mayors, particularly in council-manager cities. But many mayor-council cities are concerned enough about professional administration to have introduced chief administrative officers or their equivalent. Are the forms of government converging? Each community works out its own balance. The pattern suggests **converging forms,** although the trend is modest. The voters almost always reject radical change but they are more tolerant of small, gradual reforms that seem to be consistently in the direction of greater leadership in council-manager cities and more professional administration in mayor-council cities. However much they long for leadership, voters today are almost as skeptical about strong executives as was their revolutionary forebears.

ESSENTIAL
TERMS

city council
district elections
at-large elections
trustees
delegates
council dependence
council pay
council committees
professionalized councils
work the halls
open meeting laws
city manager
profession of city
  management
hiring managers
manager's powers
political resources of city
  managers

abandonment of the
  council-manager form
nonexecutive mayors
title of mayor
presiding over meetings
partnerships between mayors
  and managers
direct election
leaders of the council
hierarchy of mayoral powers
executive mayors
appointment, budget, and veto
chief administrative officer
  (CAO)
minority mayors
mayoral styles
expectations of mayors
converging forms

FIELDWORK

1. Go to at least two meetings of your city council and write a short essay on your observations, testing some of the observations made in this book. Consider the roles played by council members, administrators, citizens, and interest groups as well as relationships among the council members themselves. Does anyone seem to dominate the process? Are decisions made at council meetings after careful deliberation or do they appear to have been made in advance? Why?

2. How are your city council members elected? What sorts of people are on your city council? Are they representative of your community? Check the records on council members for the past 10 years or more at your city clerk's office. Check their backgrounds at the library if these are not available at the clerk's office. Then compare these to census data on your community (available at the library). Has representation changed over time?

3. What sort of a mayor does your city have? Find out the mayor's formal powers by checking the city charter at the office of the city clerk or at the library. Observe the mayor at a meeting if possible. Do some interviews or read old newspapers to ascertain your mayor's leadership style. (Your library will have the newspapers, but unless they're indexed, finding articles on the mayor will be laborious; ask whether the library keeps a file of news clippings.)

NOTES

[1]*The Municipal Year Book* (Washington, DC: International City/County Management Association, 1988), pp. 15–16.

[2]Susan Welch and Timothy Bledsoe, *Urban Reform and Its Consequences* (Chicago: University of Chicago Press, 1988), p. 42.

[3]James H. Svara, *Official Leadership in the City* (New York: Oxford University Press, 1990), p. 126.

[4]Welch and Bledsoe, note 2, p. 78.

[5]Ibid., pp. 77, 102, 105.

[6]Susan A. MacManus, "Mixed Electoral Systems: The Newest Reform Structure," *National Civic Review* 74, no. 10 (November 1985): 490.

[7]Rodney E. Hero, "Hispanics in Urban Government and Politics," *Western Political Quarterly* 43, no. 2 (June 1990): 413.

[8]Ed Goldman, "Out of the Sandbox," *California Journal,* May 1993, p. 15.

[9]Figures are for 1990, from *Governing,* December 1990, p. 66.

[10]Cristine A. Killam, "Salaries of Municipal Officials," *The Municipal Year Book* (Washington, DC: International City/County Management Association, 1992), p. 80.

[11]Hero, note 7, p. 411.

[12]See, for example, Kenneth Prewitt, *The Recruitment of Political Leaders* (Indianapolis: Bobbs-Merrill, 1970).

[13]Svara, note 3, p. 52.

[14]Clarence E. Ridley and Orin F. Notling, *The City Manager Profession* (Chicago: University of Chicago Press, 1934).

[15]Tari Renner, "Appointed Local Government Managers: Stability and Change," *The Municipal Year Book* (Washington, DC: International City/County Management Association, 1990), p. 41.

[16]Ibid., p. 49.

[17]Killam, note 10, p. 80.

[18]*The Municipal Year Book* (Washington, DC: International City/County Management Association, 1992), p. 201.

[19]Renner, note 15, p. 45. Percentages based on a 1989 survey.

[20]Svara, note 3, p. 53.

[21]Renner, note 15, p. 46.

[22]Ibid.

[23]Ibid., p. 50.

[24]Clifford J. Wirth and Michael L. Vasu, "Ideology and Decision Making for American City Managers," *Urban Affairs Quarterly* 22, no. 3 (March 1987): 468.

[25]David N. Ammons and Charldean Newell, "'City Managers Don't Make Policy': A Lie; Let's Face It," *Public Management* 70, no. 12 (December 1988): 15.

[26]Alan Ehrenhalt, "The New City Manager," *Governing,* September 1990, p. 43.

[27]Goldman, note 8, p. 16.

[28]David R. Morgan, *Managing Urban America,* 3rd ed. (Pacific Grove, CA: Brooks, Cole, 1989), p. 53.

[29]Greg J. Protasel, "Abandonments of the Council-Manager Plan," *Public Administration Review* 48, no. 4 (July–August 1988): 809.

[30]Ehrenhalt, note 26, p. 46.

[31]Svara, note 3, p. 87.

[32]*Governing*, December 1990, p. 66.

[33]Ibid.

[34]Eric Anderson, "Two Major Forms of Government," *The Municipal Year Book* (Washington, DC: International City/County Management Association, 1989), p. 25.

[35]*The Municipal Year Book*, note 18, p. 201.

[36]Harold Wolman, Edward Page, and Martha Reavley, "Mayors and Mayoral Careers," *Urban Affairs Quarterly* 25, no. 3 (March 1990): 502–506.

[37]See Rufus B. Browning, Dale Rogers Marshall, and David H. Tabb, eds., *Racial Politics in American Cities* (New York: Longman), 1990.

[38]Wolman et al.'s study of mayors of cities with populations over 100,000 found that only 25 percent ran for or won higher office, note 36, p. 511.

[39]See Svara, note 3; or John P. Kotter and Paul R. Lawrence, *Mayors in Action* (New York: Wiley), 1974.

[40]See Douglas Yates, *The Ungovernable City* (Cambridge, MA: MIT Press, 1977).

[41]Svara, note 3, p. 120.

8

Bureaucracy: The Rest of the Iceberg

C ity councils, managers, and mayors are central to local government, not least because they are visible and accountable to the public. But they are often described as the tip of the local government iceberg since, like icebergs, only a tiny bit of government shows, while the bulk lurks beneath the surface. About 500,000 elected officials head U.S. cities, counties, and other local governments. They employ twenty times that many people—nearly 10 million (see Figure 8-1). Almost half of these work for school districts. Cities employ 2.6 million and counties about 2 million. These constitute the hidden, some say dangerous, part of the iceberg.

Workers in local government are variously referred to as administrators, civil servants, public employees, and bureaucrats. The term of choice often depends on the user's point of view. *Bureaucrat* is customarily a derogatory term for public workers applied by those outside of government, while *public employee* is usually the term such workers bestow on themselves. *Administrators* and *civil servants* are more neutral terms, but they are also more narrow. The former applies only to the top echelon of local government, not workers on the streets or at the desks, and the latter omits local government workers who are not covered by a civil service system. For lack of better terms, *bureaucrat* and *public employees* must suffice. We should try, however, to set aside their vernacular bias (bureaucrat = bad, public employee = good) and use them as neutrally as we did city council, mayor, and city manager. Neutral does not mean uncritical or unanalytical, however. As with the other institutions of local government, bureaucracy needs to be dissected as well as described, for like these others, bureaucracy has its strengths and weaknesses, advantages and disadvantages, and powers and biases.

Perhaps the contempt most Americans feel for bureaucracy comes from the erroneous assumption that it should not have "strengths and

Figure 8-1   Increase in Government Jobs

Source: San Jose Mercury News, 19 April 1991. Reprinted by permission of Tribune Media Services.

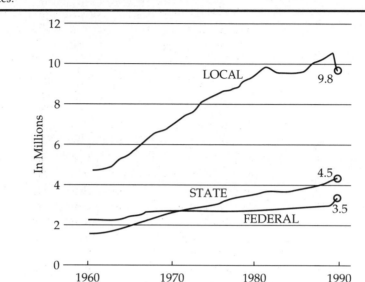

weaknesses, advantages and disadvantages, and powers and biases." Local bureaucrats are expected to be impartial public servants under the direction of elected officials. This is an ideal, however, and it is hard to achieve in practice. Many political activists and analysts believe bureaucracies have become the most important and powerful single element of local governments, perhaps beyond the control of elected officials. How much power bureaucrats have is debatable, but few deny that it is substantial. The real issue is control, by both elected officials and the public. Making public bureaucracies accountable and responsive has long been a major concern in local politics and remains so today.

Building the Iceberg: Patronage versus Civil Service

The bureaucracy of local government runs from the policy makers at the top, who are supposed to be in control, to the workers who put the policies into effect, providing services or regulating activities in their communities (see Figure 8-2). The chief policy makers are elected officials, mainly the city council and mayor, along with the highest ranking appointed officials,

Figure 8-2 The City Bureaucracy

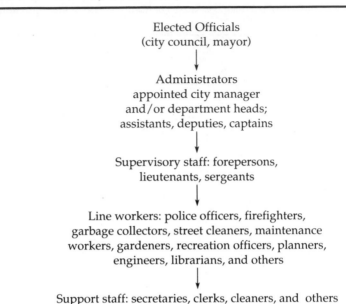

Elected Officials
(city council, mayor)

↓

Administrators
appointed city manager
and/or department heads;
assistants, deputies, captains

↓

Supervisory staff: forepersons,
lieutenants, sergeants

↓

Line workers: police officers, firefighters,
garbage collectors, street cleaners, maintenance
workers, gardeners, recreation officers, planners,
engineers, librarians, and others

↓

Support staff: secretaries, clerks, cleaners, and others

including the city manager and department heads such as the police chief. The latter are also administrators who oversee operations along with their appointed assistants and deputies. Then come the bulk of the workers, the ones we deal with as citizens. Less visible is a vast army of support staff, including clerical workers.

These workers get their jobs through either a patronage or civil service system. Under **patronage,** election winners distributed the spoils of victory, including lots of jobs, to their supporters. If control of local government changed hands, all the old workers were out and the winners hired their own supporters. Government workers were responsive to their allies, but ignored or persecuted people who did not support the machine. The spoils system ensured political control of the bureaucracy, but the machine's interest in control was to accrue rewards for its supporters, not to provide good local government services.

Civil Service

The reformers were more worried about good services than controlling bureaucracy. To them, machine control of local bureaucracies was at the heart of the problem. They therefore developed a system designed to increase not only the competence and fairness of government employees, but also their independence. Under the **civil service** or merit system, all city workers except department heads and their assistants are supposed to be hired, retained, and promoted on the basis of their ability to do the job, as measured by educational qualifications, written exams, interviews, and on-the-job evaluations. Employees who perform well gain job security or tenure and may be fired only for proven incompetence at their job, not because political control of local government changes hands.

Although civil service systems are not universal, they operate to some extent in most local governments. In some cases, only a portion of the workers are covered, depending on rank or department. In others, the system is corrupted or abused in various ways. New York City's civil service system, for example, puts more emphasis on seniority than merit in promoting workers. Elsewhere, qualifications or test scores may be manipulated to accommodate preferred applicants or discretion may be exercised when the final choice among those qualified is made (usually from the top three candidates). A variant of the affirmative action system may be used for buddies and political allies. Even if such favorites are not chosen, bureaucrats (like all humans in groups) tend to select people like themselves, people who will "fit in." This may produce bureaucracies that do not represent the communities they serve.

The variety of ways to subvert a merit system is illustrated by Chicago, home of one of the U.S.'s most famous and long-lasting political machines. Reformers managed to introduce civil service in Chicago in 1895, making it one of the first U.S. cities to adopt such a system, but the city's machine survived partly by its ability to accept reform when it had no alternative and then to find ways of getting around the reform or gaining advantage from it. For a long time, Chicago's civil service was little more than a front. At the peak of his power, the city's last great boss, Mayor Richard J. Daley, controlled 30,000 to 50,000 jobs, both inside and outside of government.[1] Chicago's civil service system did not extend to some departments, and even within the civil service system, machine supporters could get false qualifications recognized, cheat on examinations, or buy passing scores. Additionally, thousands of jobs were classified as temporary or seasonal, so workers could be hired and fired at will. Chicago's employees challenged the patronage system in the courts in the 1970s and 1980s and won reductions in its scope,[2] but its manipulation enabled that city's machine to outlast most others.

Chicago is an extreme case, but most cities and counties have evolved toward a civil service system rather than going through an instantaneous transformation. Reform was often nominal to begin with, taking hold only gradually. This evolution toward a merit system eased the pain and accommodated the residual power of machines. Besides, in the early days of civil service, the sorts of professionals the reformers hoped to recruit to local government were few. But gradually, as training and educational programs developed and local government jobs became more secure and professional, a pool of civil servants emerged.

Civil service systems are still not universal, however, and merely giving the title "civil service system" to a local government personnel program does not mean that it functions properly as such. The vast majority of local government employees are now covered by civil service, but the system is abused in some places, and particular departments or categories of employees may not be included. Civil service coverage is most thorough among local governments in the Sunbelt, where reform was most popular; those in the Frostbelt (like Chicago) tend to be more lax.

Pros and Cons of Civil Service

As the reformers hoped, civil service workers are better trained and more skilled at their jobs than their amateurish machine predecessors. They also do their work with greater fairness and impartiality and much less corruption. Their professionalism is generally agreed to have increased the efficiency and effectiveness of local government, although this is sometimes disputed. Many urban analysts thought Chicago under its political machine was as well run as any other big city. Civil service systems don't necessarily save money, either. They may not waste it through corruption, like the machines, but they still find ways to spend it. Like other reforms, however, civil service has its own shortcomings, foremost among which are representativeness and control.

By imposing the not unreasonable requirements of educational or other appropriate qualifications for employment, the reformers immediately excluded many recent immigrants and their children. These groups had been well represented in machine bureaucracies because the only job qualification was support for the machine. (Many minorities, however, were excluded because of prejudice.) Civil service bureaucracies, particularly in their upper-echelon, white-collar jobs, tended to be dominated by the same white, middle-class males that had instigated the reform movement. By the 1960s, this lack of **representativeness** became a major grievance for minorities and women, who felt local bureaucracies did not adequately reflect and/or adequately respond to the diversity of their communities. Making bureaucracies more representative and responsive thus became part of the counterreform effort.

Similarly, the control and accountability of civil service bureaucracies have become issues. In civil service systems, the job security public workers gain through tenure reduces control by elected officials and may make workers less responsive to the clients they serve. Under the spoils system of the machine, they could easily be fired, so the political bosses had great power over their workers, who cheerfully bent or broke rules to keep their clients happy in return for the support for the machine. Under civil service, however, political control and responsiveness to citizens is not so simple. To protect workers from political interference and the favoritism and corruption it may entail, civil service systems make firing them difficult.

Incompetence on the job must be clearly proven, but this can be very hard to achieve except in extreme cases. Workers have gained further protections through their unions and through contractually agreed grievance procedures for complaints about unfair treatment. Supervisors may prefer to avoid the hassle and the confrontation of trying to fire a worker. Instead, unsatisfactory workers may be kept on or shunted to different positions. They call it "paving over" in New York, where "it is near impossible to fire a city employee for incompetence—or even criminality," according to journalist Joe Klein.[3] Such practices are inefficient, costly, and infuriating for managers and coworkers as well as for the citizens who still have to deal with the unfit workers. Even competent employees sometimes offend their citizen clients because as civil service employees they feel so secure in their jobs that they do not respond as quickly or politely as they should. Yet, although we grumble to our friends about such treatment, how many of us make formal complaints about rudeness or incompetence? Like citizens, elected officials, city managers, and department heads may feel frustrated at their inability to control their own bureaucracies. Civil service systems contribute to this frustration, but the very nature of bureaucracy is also a factor.

The Nature and Inherent Powers of Bureaucracy

Beyond the practical workings of civil service systems, to which we will return, local government bureaucracies share the characteristics and powers of large-scale organizations—of bureaucracies—of all sorts. These universal characteristics and powers of bureaucracies are another element in the constant struggle for **control,** as those officially in charge seek to assert authority over their minions who, in turn, try to protect their autonomy. Although control is a primary goal in the organization of bureaucracies, their scale and other characteristics make it almost impossible. Even some mechanisms of control may be turned to the advantage of the bureaucracy.

The Characteristics of Bureaucracy[4]

The classic conception of bureaucracy is a pyramidal **hierarchy** or **chain of command,** as suggested in Figure 8-2. The goal of the hierarchy is for the democratically elected and accountable officials to control and direct, through a series of intermediary supervisors, a large number of workers.

The supervisors are there to make sure that the workers carry out policies and programs as intended. They can't watch all the workers all the time, though, so they usually devise elaborate **rules and regulations** to tell them how to do their work—how often streets should be swept, for example, or how long library books can be checked out. Parking and traffic regulations tell police officers when to issue tickets; construction codes tell building inspectors when to approve a building as safe. Without such rules, bureaucrats might do as they pleased, favoring their friends and discriminating against enemies or people who are different from themselves—as the political machines did.

As a further check, the actions of the workers may need approval by their superiors, which may be part of the infamous bureaucratic red tape most people hate so much. Approval can take time, and it also usually requires lots of paper work like application forms and reports. Even when approval by higher-ups isn't needed, a lot of paper work can be involved because workers have to report what they've already done to their superiors who, in turn, use the reports to review and control their workers. All this paper work and supervision is a pain, hated by both citizens and bureaucrats (most of whom would really rather just get on with their jobs), but its purpose is to enable those who are responsible (ultimately elected officials and the voters) to make sure that workers are serving citizens as the decision makers intend. In most cases that means fairly and impartially, so that all people or neighborhoods are treated alike. Streets in every neighborhood, rich or poor, should be swept regularly; police should treat all citizens the same way; any one who is legally eligible should receive welfare benefits. In practice, the attainment of such **fairness and impartiality** may be rare, but the point is that, contrary to popular perceptions, the purpose of regulations and red tape is usually intended to achieve these goals and to help, rather than to annoy us; the aim is control of the bureaucracy.

Specialization is another, sometimes exasperating characteristic of bureaucracies. As large organizations with lots of workers dealing with varied and complex problems (like governing cities), it makes sense for bureaucracies to divide up responsibilities and for some members of the organization to specialize in certain tasks, from policing to sanitation or library services. Specialization enables workers to develop expertise to a greater degree than if they performed a wide variety of tasks. Theoretically, that should mean the job is done better because an expert does it. Once the areas of specialization are defined, each specialist is assigned a jurisdiction and usually resists interference by others. For example, librarians don't issue traffic tickets and police officers don't select library books. This **division of labor** makes organizational sense, but it may also lead to frustration and anger when citizens are referred from worker to worker or even department to department and no one seems able or willing to deal with a problem. Better known as passing the buck, this phenomenon is built into specialization, for all its good intentions. Condescending, know-it-all experts may also irritate citizens.

Yet another essential characteristic of bureaucracies is the development of their own systems of recruiting and promoting members. People are not born into bureaucracies, nor do they just walk in, volunteer, and start work. Neither is their advance within the bureaucracy random. Some sort of system functions, both for recruitment and promotion. Usually this requires that workers have the qualifications and ability to do the job, that they retain their job and advance on the basis of the competence of their performance. In practice, however, this system may be subverted by favoritism and ill-defined or slack standards but, again, the intent is control and also fairness. Through their recruitment and promotion systems, bureaucracies develop their own cultures and traditions, which are sometimes narrow and exclusive.

These characteristics—a hierarchical chain of command; rules, regulations, written forms, and red tape; specialization; and a well-defined career structure—are inherent to bureaucracies, not only in local governments but in any large organization. Their essential purposes—including fairness, objectivity, and control by those who are supposed to be in charge—are good, but in practice these goals can be subverted and the system abused, for these essential characteristics are as much a source of power as a means of control. We should recognize, however, that bureaucracies are as inevitable as politics, and, like politics, are not necessarily good or bad.

The Practical Powers of Bureaucracy

In the day-to-day activities of local governments, the characteristics of bureaucracies translate into several formidable sources of power: discretion, expertise, legitimacy, and time. Each is rooted in the very nature of bureaucracy; each makes it more difficult for the officials who are supposed to be in charge to maintain control. To these must be added more overtly political sources of power, including interest group support and public employee unions.

Implementation and Discretion

The greatest power of bureaucracies is derived from their responsibility to implement or put into effect the policies and programs approved by the decision-makers at the top of the bureaucratic pyramid. **Implementation** may be quick or slow, rigorous or lax. The same sort of things happen in households when duties are assigned but not always carried out as promptly or thoroughly as intended. In bureaucracies, middle managers might fund or staff a program inadequately, or the employees who are supposed to do the work might ignore it or keep busy doing other assigned tasks. If the decision-makers at the top notice, recalcitrant bureaucrats may get in trouble, but excuses and promises of improvement are easy to offer. It takes very vigilant officials to push a bureaucracy to do things it really doesn't want to do.

The bureaucracy's power of implementation is made even greater through **delegation.** Councils, mayors, and managers cannot make every decision. Much as they might like to, there's too much to do and they're too busy. Some things must be left to subordinates. Decision-makers thus often provide the outlines of a policy and leave their staff to fill in the details and make it work. Delegated responsibilities are usually carried out as the policy makers wish, but they nonetheless add to the powers of bureaucracy.

Bureaucrats enjoy another form of delegation that also enhances their powers—**discretion** on the job. A social worker or a land-use planner in an office, a teacher in a classroom, or a police officer on the beat all make choices as they carry out the duties prescribed for them by their superiors. They have a finite amount of time and many things to do: should they worry more about helping people or saving money? Preserving the environment or fostering economic development? Teaching facts or analytical skills? Arresting speeders or drug dealers? Should drivers going 5 miles per hour over the limit be ticketed or only those going 10, 15, or 20 miles per hour too fast? Should the social worker, planner, teacher, or police officer serve as many citizens as possible, or take the time to be courteous and thorough with each one? The policy makers at the top occasionally set priorities like these but, generally, they leave the workers to get on with their jobs, trusting them to use their discretionary powers appropriately. Usually they do. If they don't and enough people complain, those in charge may try to do something, but although the whole bureaucratic hierarchy is created to supervise and control what the workers do, it is impossible for every worker to be watched all the time. A supervisor would be needed for every worker—and then a supervisor for every supervisor!

Expertise

Another practical source of bureaucratic power is **expertise** and the associated command of information. On the front lines of bureaucracies, where services are delivered and policies enforced, workers specialize and develop expertise at their jobs. Higher in the bureaucracy, the expertise becomes a little more general in nature, so instead of adjusting stoplights, a higher ranking traffic manager analyzes traffic flow and coordinates the lights. Still higher in the bureaucracy, the expertise may be in management and administration rather than particular policy areas. At the top of the hierarchy, however, specialization and expertise are rare. Here are the generalists—the council members, mayor, and manager—who must deal with the whole range of local government programs. They need to know at least a little about a lot of subjects, although some may have special expertise developed from previous training or occupations and others develop impressive mastery of particular policy areas over time.

Mostly, however, the top decision-makers remain generalists and are therefore dependent on the bureaucracy for advice and information on policies and programs. The politicians may (or may not) initiate discussion of an issue, but when they do, it is usually framed by information and recommendations from the experts on the city staff. Many items on the agendas of city council or county board meetings have been placed there by the bureaucracy through department heads or the city or county executive. Most are accompanied by reports from "staff" or "the administration"—the bureaucracy. At the meetings, the appropriate staff members will be called on to speak, perhaps orchestrated by their department heads or the city or county executive. Their presentations will be accompanied by masses of data and probably by charts and tables. They will usually recommend a course of action—or explain why what the council or community groups want to do is not feasible. The decision-makers almost always follow their recommendations. Why shouldn't they? After all, these are the experts: civil servants, working for the public good. The decision-makers know and trust them. And where else can they get information and advice? Citizens and interest groups may supply it at public hearings or when they lobby elected officials, but they are not experts—except perhaps in their own self-interest, which makes them suspect as informants. In contrast, the local government bureaucracy is supposed to be made up of objective professionals, with no axes to grind.

Bureaucratic Objectivity

Most of the time the information supplied by staff and bureaucrats is objective, but not always. Like the rest of us, bureaucrats have opinions and biases that may affect their recommendations, perhaps unconsciously. They also try to protect themselves and their agencies and to justify their existence and expansion. Whether acting out of bias or for self-protection, it is easy for the experts to manipulate or withhold information, or to lie with statistics. Expert advice may also be unintentionally biased by the narrow perspective that comes with bureaucratic specialization. Take, for example, the case of a neighborhood group that wants to have a pair of busy one-way streets turned back to quieter, two-way streets. The neighborhood advocates will object to the noise, pollution, and dangers of the one-way streets and talk about their social impact. Council members will nod in sympathy. Then the bureaucrats who are in charge of streets and traffic will present their computer projections of traffic flows with charts and slides. The council will almost invariably bow to the superior information of the experts they know and probably trust, despite their sympathy for the neighborhood. Part of the neighborhood's problem is that their concerns are unlikely to be the focus of a government agency (planning departments concentrate more on new developments than on the quality of life in existing neighborhoods and rarely have the clout of their counterparts in traffic management). Another shortcoming for the neighborhood is that its concerns aren't as easy to count as cars, so their data can never be quite so hard and convincing as that of the traffic experts.

The ultimate issue here isn't only information, of course. It's also specialization in terms of what components of community life are judged to merit bureaucratic staff—in this case, traffic, but probably not neighborhood quality of life.

This specialization and compartmentalization is typically bureaucratic; but in the case of local governments, the values of the reform movement have had an additional influence. Foremost among these are the way the reform movement defined what local governments should do in terms of physical rather than social services (traffic management rather than neighborhood quality of life) and stressed the common good (traffic flow) over partial interests (neighborhoods). With some justification, bureaucrats can point out that what helps one neighborhood may hurt others.

It can be extremely difficult for the generalists on the council and the citizen novices to argue with the factual and often abstruse data of the experts. Those who do may be seen as irrational or dense. Consequently, the bureaucrats usually get their way. Besides their expertise, bureaucrats gain power from their image as objective professionals, which gives them a legitimacy that citizens, interest groups, and politicians lack. Bureaucrats can use their status to their own advantage, virtually wrapping themselves in a protective cloak of professionalism. This is particularly true in reform cities, where professionalism is so highly valued and respected and where the staff of the local government is accordingly trusted and deferred to rather than seen as bureaucratic hacks, as they may be in communities where reform values are less dominant.

Time

Bureaucrats also have the advantage of **time.** Except where patronage still applies, public employees generally stay around for a long time. Job security was a goal of the reformers and remains one of the primary attractions of public employment. Local government workers devote whole careers of 20 to 40 years to their specialties and their departments, developing estimable expertise, not only in their own specialization, but also in the structure and process of local government. Elected officials, in contrast, come and go, serving one or two but rarely more than three terms of office. By the time they master policies and process, they may well be on their way out. Professional city managers and department heads may face similar disadvantages. They move from city to city to advance their careers—the average tenure of a city manager is 5.4 years—and may have difficulty gaining command of well-entrenched, long-serving bureaucracies.

Time is on the side of bureaucracies in a more immediate way, too. Council members and executives have lots to do, both in terms of policies and politics. They can concentrate on particular issues and programs only for a little while and then are diverted by other issues, a crisis, an election, or a budget deadline. Citizens have their lives to lead and can devote little time to politics. Bureaucrats, however, are paid to focus on their responsibilities full-time. They know more and have more time to think of ways to do things or avoid doing them. One tactic of bureaucrats under pressure is to ask for a delay on an issue so they can try to find a satisfactory solution. They can then use that time to make their own case better or to allow citizen or council interest to dissipate.

Clientele Groups and Unions

Besides these inherent powers of bureaucracies, more traditional forms of political support are also available. **Clientele groups** (made up the people who are served by particular departments or agencies) sometimes organize to back up their bureaucracy in budget battles or when it is under attack. Police departments most commonly benefit from such support groups, but many communities have their "Friends of" the library or symphony, too. Recreation programs often enjoy the political support of their clients, with uniformed teams of softball players packing council chambers.

    Public employee unions are the latest enhancement of bureaucratic power. A relatively recent phenomenon, they have achieved widespread success and gained great influence. Through their unions the workers can bargain with their employers (the city or county) over both wages and working conditions. The former affect local budgets and the latter infringe on policy making since they may include such issues as work loads for social workers, class sizes for teachers, weapons and training programs for police officers, and much more. Besides bargaining over contracts, public employee unions affect local government by supporting candidates for office to determine who their bosses will be.

    The characteristics and inherent powers of bureaucracies and their political resources add up to a formidable force in local politics. So great is this force that some analysts consider bureaucracies dangerously independent, a subject to which we will return later.

Public Employee Unions and Bureaucractic Power

Perhaps in recognition of the power of bureaucracies, union rights were denied to public workers until the 1960s. Private sector workers had begun to unionize in the nineteenth century although they struggled through the 1930s to see their rights firmly established in law. The predominance of political machines, which performed some of the functions of labor unions, probably diverted public workers from organizing and at the same time made lawmakers cautious about granting them union rights. But the prohibition on public employee unions out-lasted the machines because opponents argued that public workers are distinct from private sector workers. They have greater job security and usually better benefits than private sector workers, which makes unions seem less necessary but, more importantly, public workers are unique in their monopoly control of services that affect public health and safety. These services, the opponents of public sector unions argue, should not be bargained over or jeopardized by strikes.

The Right to Collective Bargaining

Public workers accepted the prohibition for a long time, perhaps appreciative of their job security in times of economic uncertainty. But they felt left out of the private sector economic boom that followed World War II, and as government grew, the workers at the bottom—police officers, firefighters, librarians, and teachers—began to feel alienated and mistreated by the impersonal bureaucracy of which they were a part. Like their colleagues in the factories a century earlier, they began grumbling and agitating for union rights. Private sector unions moved in to organize public workers as some traditionally unionized industries like railroads and steel began to decline.

At the urging of the new organizations of public workers and private sector unions, governments in the United States began recognizing their workers' rights. The state of Wisconsin was first, passing a collective bargaining law for public employees in 1959. The federal government and other states soon followed. Although still a contentious issue in some places, forty states now recognize their public employees' right to collective bargaining (seven southern and three western states do not). **Collective bargaining** means that employees negotiate wages and working conditions with their employers as a group (or union) rather than as individuals. The group is supposed to be stronger than individuals, so everybody gets a better deal. Once public workers gained the right to collective bargaining, unionization proceeded rapidly. By 1982, 40.8 percent of all local government workers belonged to a union or professional association (see Table 8-1), while only about 15 percent of private sector workers were unionized. In 1992, however, the figures had declined to 37 percent and 12 percent, respectively, due to a combination of factors that included a recession, the tax revolt, and the antiunion attitudes of the Reagan administration.

The Process of Collective Bargaining

Normally, a single union represents a particular group of workers in negotiations with management (local government). This union is selected by the workers in an election and is recognized as their bargaining agent by the local government. In most cases, workers are not required to belong to

Table 8-1 Public Employee Unions in U.S. Local Governments, 1982

Total full- and part-time employees	9,249,000
Employees belonging to employee organizations	3,771,000
Percent	40.8
Percent of employees belonging to an employee organization by function	
Education	46.4
Hospitals	14.5
Police	45.3
Fire	51.7
All other	33.5

Source: U.S. Bureau of the Census, *Statistical Abstract of the United States* (Washington, DC: U.S. Government Printing Office, 1987).

the union, although this is sometimes an issue because union members view nonmembers as free riders who get the benefits negotiated by the union without paying dues. Most local governments deal with several unions representing different groups of employees, such as police officers, firefighters, middle management, or general workers. On average, cities negotiate with five such bargaining units, but larger cities (such as New York with over two hundred unions) face many more. Such fragmentation of the work force was once encouraged by local governments to weaken unions, but now it is seen as an inconvenience that makes collective bargaining more difficult and complicated.[5]

In the actual process of collective bargaining, representatives of unions and local government meet and negotiate an agreement on wages, fringe benefits, working conditions, grievance procedures, and other matters. The unions are represented by their elected officers and professional staff, while the local government is represented by a team that may include the city manager, CAO, a full-time labor relations specialist, a department head, or an outside attorney or consultant who specializes in negotiations.[6] Elected officials such as mayors and council members usually stay out of the process, although they confer with their representatives. Labor negotiations seem to require greater technical expertise than most elected officials possess. They direct their negotiators, however, and when an agreement is reached, it must be ratified by these officials on one side and by the union's members on the other. If both approve, the agreement becomes a contract and is binding for a specified time—usually 1 to 5 years. The public may have a say in a hearing at the time of ratification, but negotiations are conducted in private except in a few states.

Deadlock. Negotiators usually reach agreement, but what happens if they fail? In the private sector, the result may be a strike by workers or sometimes a lockout by management. Strikes occur in the public sector, but in most states they are illegal on the grounds that strikes by public workers hurt not only their employers but the citizens they are supposed to serve. Public safety workers such as police officers and firefighters are prohibited from striking everywhere, although a few states permit strikes by some other sorts of government workers. Public employees are sometimes disgruntled enough to break no-strike laws and face the consequences, although sick outs or epidemics of "blue flu" (police officers calling in sick) are more common. Work slowdowns are another alternative in which workers rigidly follow every formal rule and procedure, which delays action and inconveniences clients. Public employee strikes and other such actions are rare, however, and most disagreements are resolved by a neutral third party accepted by both sides who mediates or arbitrates. In mediation, the third party tries to revive communications between the disputing parties and help them reach a settlement. In arbitration, the contending parties usually agree in advance to accept the recommendation of the third party (this is called binding arbitration).

Clout

But negotiating contracts is just one way organized public employees assert their clout. They are also a formidable electoral force. According to journalist Joe Klein, New York City's 350,000 employees mostly live in the city and are reliable voters, making up 15 to 25 percent of the vote in the Democratic primary.[7] In other places, the numbers may not be as high, but they are nonetheless substantial. Besides voting, public employee unions also provide campaign contributions and volunteers. The **electoral clout** of well-organized workers may be particularly great in nonpartisan elections, where few other groups are as interested or active, and in communities with low voter turnout in local elections. Most candidates find the promise of such block support irresistible, but, of course, the unions expect the support to be mutual. If their efforts are successful, they end up with friends on the council and/or in the mayor's office, with whom they communicate regularly and from whom they can expect sympathy. Such activity can backfire if the unions endorse losers, however, and since incumbent officials are often reelected with little opposition, endorsement options may be limited, leading some unions to back away from electoral activity.

Public employee unions also lobby decision-makers and testify (often backed up by masses of members) at public hearings on issues that concern them between elections. Such issues might include complaints about police practices, new building or fire safety codes, banning library books, no smoking ordinances, or almost anything. Additionally, union representatives make sure their hard-won contract is enforced and defend workers subject to discipline or firing.

The Impact of Unionization

Public employee unions have improved the lot of their members with higher wages, better fringe benefits, and even greater job security. Some studies suggest that unorganized workers don't do much worse,[8] but that may be because union contracts set the standard and the managers of unorganized workers cleverly avoid unionization by giving their workers almost as much. Beyond the direct benefits to workers, however, the unionization of public workers has increased the power of bureaucracies. Unions increase job security, which is already great enough in civil service bureaucracies to cause concern. The merit system may also be weakened by unions, which advocate promotion by seniority (time served rather than quality of work) and oppose merit pay (based on job performance). Top-level officials are limited by union agreements on issues like these and others. Their budgets may be predetermined by collective bargaining agreements, their workers are even harder to fire with contract-guaranteed grievance rights and union advocates, and their actions may be challenged by union representatives citing the contract. But while managers may not like unions much, they add balance to local government bureaucracies, protecting individual workers in large and impersonal organizations and vigilantly defending public services.

Limiting Bureaucratic Power

Much as they benefit local government workers, public employee unions only add to already serious concerns about the inherent and practical powers of bureaucracies. Even before unionization, elected officials and political activists on both the left and right were searching for ways to make bureaucracies more responsive and accountable. Most of these efforts were part of the reaction to reform governments—the counterreformation.

Some of the counterreforms were aimed at increasing the power of elected representatives so they could assert their authority in the chain of command more effectively. Many mayors won higher salaries, expanded personal staffs, and greater budgetary and appointment powers, enabling them to dominate more bureaucratic city managers or even to replace them. Some local legislators were given full-time salaries and support staff of their own, so they could be less reliant on the bureaucracy. Some organized themselves into committees, so they could develop expertise to counter that of the bureaucrats. Legislators and executives also experimented with new budgeting systems designed to push bureaucracies to justify their spending.

A few local governments went much further, attempting to reduce the range of city jobs covered by civil service and thereby to gain more control over the services and the workers themselves. In some places, this took the form of removing some jobs from the civil service system on grounds that greater flexibility in hiring was necessary. This ploy seldom succeeded, however, because the public reacted to it as a revival of machine-style patronage. Another tactic was the introduction of **sunset laws,** which set a fixed life span of a few years for new bureaucratic agencies on the theory that none should be permanent (as most bureaucracies tend to become). At the end of this period, the agency must defend its existence to win legislative approval to continue, usually for another fixed period. Sunset laws are a useful way to keep a rein on new agencies, but their application is limited since most of the functions of local government, such as police and fire protection, are sensibly carried out by on-going departments and new agencies are rarely created.

Empowering Communities

While elected officials have sought to control bureaucracies by increasing their own powers, community groups have attempted to gain influence by other means, sometimes with the support of local officials and the federal government. Bureaucracies in some cities, for example, have been decentralized to make them more responsive and accessible with "little city halls" in neighborhoods. More radical **community control** advocates have demanded the devolution of some decisions to the groups most immediately affected, usually through some sort of elected boards. This has most commonly been attempted in schools and on neighborhood planning issues. Birmingham, Dayton, Portland, St. Paul, and New York City, for example, all have elected neighborhood boards or councils. Due to the cost and the resistance of both bureaucracies and central decision-makers, however, such programs have not gotten very far. Much more common are small boards, committees, and commissions of appointed or sometimes elected citizens who advise the local government on selected issues. Federal grant programs often require such citizen involvement, and most local governments have numerous boards and commissions to allow for citizen participation. Such entities may bring pressure on bureaucracies and force them to confront their own clienteles, although citizen participants are also sometimes seduced or co-opted by the bureaucracies they deal with and end up being sympathetic supporters rather than critics.

Citizen Complaints

When citizens have complaints about bureaucracy, they usually take them to their city or county councillor. Local legislators spend a lot of their time dealing with constituent problems, providing advice, helping with red tape, or giving the bureaucracy a prod with a phone call or letter. This service has rightly been used to justify paying council members for full-time work and providing them with personal staff. Helping citizens with problems may seem mundane and even unnecessary (shouldn't the bureaucracy do it right in the first place?), but it gives citizens a useful means of appeal and also helps council members discern problems in the system.

Some communities provide more structured complaint systems with an ombudsman (sic) or citizen review boards. The **ombudsman** is an independent and neutral employee of the local government who hears and acts on citizen complaints and reports to the council. **Citizen review boards** serve the same function, but they usually deal with only one policy area (like police) and, as their name suggests, they are made up of citizens appointed by the council. Most common (but still rare) are police review boards. They hear and investigate grievances against the police, but usually have little real authority. San Francisco, New Orleans, Washington, and Baltimore, however, are said to have relatively independent police boards.[9]

Without an ombudsman or review board, citizens are left to lodge their complaints with the bureaucracy that has offended them unless a busy council member takes up their cause. Many citizens are suspicious of bureaucracies investigating complaints against their own members, not only because of the inherent impersonality of bureaucracy or the tendency of any group to protect one of its own, but because they think the bureaucracy is unrepresentative and unsympathetic. This is particularly true for minorities. Although the idea of an ombudsman seems to have fallen out of fashion, arguments over citizen police review boards continue to arise in communities experiencing tension between racial minorities and police, as in Los Angeles.

Affirmative Action

Another response to such tensions has been to press for a more representative bureaucracy. Civil service bureaucracies have traditionally been dominated by white males. The sorts of professional skills required by merit systems were most accessible to white males, and once employed, they were entrenched by job security. Like other social groups, they also tended to recruit in their own image. In many cities, as the population grew more diverse, the local bureaucracy did not. Minorities wanted access to jobs, but they also complained that unrepresentative bureaucracies were unresponsive to their needs. Police practices were often the central issue, but the same concerns applied to other departments.

Minority groups therefore demanded special hiring programs to broaden the representation of the bureaucracy. Women later made similar demands. The federal government added to the pressure with the 1972 Equal Employment Opportunities Act and requirements for **affirmative action** plans for all institutions accepting federal funds. Local governments responded with affirmative action programs designed to increase minority hiring. Bureaucracies had to learn to make a conscious effort *not* to discriminate against minorities and women. Most had to find new ways of recruiting to attract people who might not have known about the availability of jobs or who might have felt they would be unwelcome applicants. Testing and interviewing procedures were reviewed and revised to make sure they were not in themselves discriminatory, as they were often alleged to be. Middle-class verbal skills were said by minorities to be too heavily weighted while women charged that physical standards were sometimes higher than the job required. Besides changes in recruitment practices, testing, and job standards, the composition of interview panels was changed to better reflect the community rather than the bureaucracy. Even so, minority candidates often have a tough time competing, so to further facilitate affirmative action hiring, applicants who speak a language other than English may be given extra points or those hired might be chosen from the top ten instead of only the top three test scorers.

Many local governments now have well-established affirmative action programs, and the employment of women and minorities has advanced greatly in many communities, although their movement into the higher echelons of the bureaucracy has been slow. Affirmative action programs have been most extensive and successful in communities where minorities have established themselves politically, as in Denver, where minorities have actually been overrepresented in city government in proportion to their share of the population since 1973.[10] Big city mayors also often embraced affirmative action along with some federally funded programs as a way of building support in minority communities. In the 1970s, for example, aggressive mayors in Boston and San Francisco increased minority employment from 6 to 20 percent and from 11 to 38 percent in their respective cities. "A substantial percentage of these increases," political scientist Barbara Ferman points out, "was due to federally funded jobs,"[11] for which hiring rules were more flexible than for the civil service bureaucracy. In other big cities, especially those that elected black mayors (see Table 7-2), substantial improvements in integrating the public work force were also made, with or without federal funds.

But despite some successes, most affirmative action programs are pretty mild, usually involving just a little more active recruitment of minorities and women and the setting of some hoped-for hiring goals rather than strict quotas with fixed numbers. Figure 8-3 reports the use of various methods among cities and counties responding to *Municipal Year Book* surveys in 1984 and 1989. Note that despite increasing controversy about affirmative action, the number of local programs actually declined over these years, probably due more to budget cuts and minimal hiring than to political pressure.

About 26 percent of the cities and counties in the survey reported setting "numeric goals" for hiring. Such goals are distinct from widely

Figure 8-3 Methods Used to Attract Minority and Female Employees in U.S. Cities and Counties with Populations of over 50,000

Source: Evelina R. Moulder, "Affirmative Action: The Role Local Governments are Playing," *The Municipal Year Book* (Washington, DC: International City/County Management Association, 1991), p. 51. Reprinted by permission. Respondents to 1984 and 1989 surveys were not necessarily identical; the data may therefore be skewed.

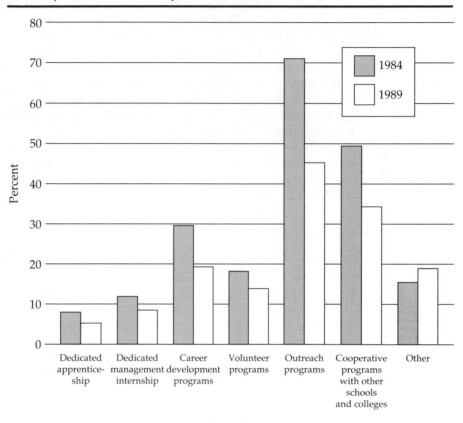

denounced quotas, according to *The Municipal Year Book,* in that they are "ideals to be strived for" rather than rigid "quotas to be attained" at the risk of penalties.[12] Few local governments have set such quotas. In a few extreme cases, however, local governments have been ordered by federal courts to hire only minorities until the composition of their workers is brought into reasonable balance. Such cases usually involve police and fire departments, which have been particularly resistant to affirmative action and which are often politically powerful. In most places, mild affirmative action programs have brought modest and much-needed improvements in the representativeness and sensitivity of bureaucracies. Unfortunately, budget cuts due to reduced federal funds and the tax revolt (see below) capped such programs by stopping new hiring. In some cases, budget cuts worsened the employment balance because they required layoffs, which are usually done on a "last hired–first fired" basis so that recently hired women and minorities were the first to go.

Recent studies suggest that affirmative action still has a long way to go. A study of cities and counties in the liberal San Francisco Bay Area, for example, found that minorities and women were still underrepresented in local government jobs, particularly in higher ranking positions and in smaller, suburban communities.[13] In New York City, blacks are 11 percent of the police force and 29 percent of the population, even after years of affirmative action.[14] But despite its modest impact, affirmative action remains controversial, with conservatives and white males charging reverse discrimination while minorities and women continue to complain about the prejudice of white male bureaucracies. Quotas have been widely condemned and resisted, and in 1989, the U.S. Supreme Court recognized the issue of reverse discrimination and somewhat relaxed court pressures for affirmative action.

The Tax Revolt

Minorities, women, and liberals were not the only ones discontented with bureaucracies in the 1970s. Landlords, small businesses, and homeowners fed up with high taxes also rebelled in many communities, using the initiative process to set strict limits on local revenues. Although primarily motivated by saving themselves money, the **tax revolt** campaigned against "government waste" and "bloated bureaucracy." The bad popular image of bureaucracies, the flawed structure of local taxation, and recession gave the campaign impetus. Launched in 1978 by California's Proposition 13, which slashed local property tax revenues, the movement quickly spread.

Local governments scrambled to find other sources of revenues, but many were forced to cut workers and services, becoming leaner and meaner. Taxpayers enjoyed their savings, but many objected to reductions in local services. Critics condemned the tax revolt as ill-considered and even irrational for cutting revenues without even considering appropriate service levels, but some of the belt-tightening may have been overdue for many of the nation's rapidly expanding local governments. Unfortunately, the belt was tightened so much in some communities that life became considerably more difficult for their residents. Police were cut as crime rose, streets got dirtier, library hours were reduced, class sizes in the schools rose. But while local employment dipped in the late 1970s and early 1980s, it was soon on the rise again (see Figure 8-1). Many of these jobs, however, were in schools and social services, both largely funded by state rather than local revenues, or in growing suburban communities, not the still-deteriorating central cities. Only as the recent recession took hold did the overall number of jobs in local governments decline again.

Contracting Out

Partly in response to general complaints about bureaucracy but largely due to the revenue cuts imposed by the tax revolt, many local governments have turned to **contracting out.** That is, instead of providing services with their own employees, many local governments have begun contracting with private businesses to do the job. Trash collection is the service most commonly contracted out, but recreation programs, maintenance, cleaning, transit, and other services have been handed over to private companies in some places. Parking tickets have recently been contracted out in Chicago, freeing police officers for more urgent tasks. Such services are either paid for out of tax revenues or by directly billing users in the case of trash collection or parking tickets. Contracts for services as basic as police and fire can also be entered into with other governments.

Contracting out generally cuts costs, thus saving tax funds, and gives decision-makers more options. The inflexibility and relatively permanent employment of the civil service system are circumvented and unions are often eliminated by private contractors. Some studies affirm that private contractors provide services more cheaply and efficiently than government,[15] but, overall, the evidence is mixed. Critics of contracting out assert that private companies often bid low to get contracts and then raise their prices later. They also insist that the system is used to pay lower wages, break unions, and get around affirmative action hiring.[16] Local governments and taxpayers may benefit from contracting out, but workers surely suffer.

Controlling Bureaucracy

Some analysts worry that attempts to control bureaucracy have gone too far. "Political control in the form of interference with service delivery or hiring decisions," writes James Svara, "may diminish fairness and obstruct sound management," not to mention efficiency. "The tightly controlled and fully accountable agency," he continues, "may be the most rigid and clogged with red tape, since every action is done by the book."[17] Svara has a point, and we should remember that the initial intent of civil service systems was good government produced by independent workers free of political interference.

Yet many civil service bureaucracies had become too rigid and many were unrepresentative. Those who introduced the controls on bureaucracy discussed above had a point, too. Their efforts have somewhat altered the balance of power in local governments, yet, as noted, local bureaucracies continue to expand, and bureaucracies in general have an astounding capacity to survive.

New Machines or Public Servants?

Analysts of local politics used to debate whether elected officials or private economic elites like the growth machine were most powerful in their communities. It was assumed that bureaucracies were subordinate. Bureaucratic powers have grown so much, however, that some recent power researchers see bureaucracy as a third force, unconstrained by the other two. Stephen Elkin writes that "urban political economies, beneath their diversity, have in common the three axes of a land-use alliance, a complex electoral coalition, and relatively autonomous bureaucracies."[18]

The New Machines. Political scientist Theodore Lowi argues that local government bureaucracies are **"the new machines."** Their "functional fiefdoms" (departments or agencies with allied unions), recruit like-minded members, protect their self-interest rather than that of the public, and are beyond the control of elected officials whose selection they influence.[19] The new machines seem to put more emphasis on survival and expansion than on doing a good job, resisting any intrusions on their own control of their agencies (or turfs), including coordination with other departments. Managers and department heads may actively resist control by elected officials and even go around them to seek support from power holders outside of government.

Lowi's new machines are most common in places like New York City, where public employee unions are particularly strong, but bureaucratic power in general is also great, if less blatant, in the middle-sized reform cities of the Sunbelt and suburbia. One study concluded that "nonpartisan, at-large city councillors . . . treat the interests of municipal workers with greater consideration than . . . ward or partisan councillors. They will provide greater job security through larger work forces and higher levels of compensation"[20] because bureaucracies are an important source of political support in a system where parties and other interests are limited.

Constraints. The autonomy of bureaucracies can easily be overstated, however. Their discretion may be substantial, but in all but a few cases, it is constrained by broad boundaries set by elected officials and private power holders. Bureaucratic leaders, whether managers, department heads, or union officials, have a pretty good idea where these boundaries lie. They may test or push the limits, but those who go too far usually end up looking for employment elsewhere. Their experience sends a message to others.

Some analysts see bureaucracy more positively. Svara insists that these professionals "promote equity" or reasonably fair treatment for different people and neighborhoods, while more allegedly "responsive" systems might show favoritism and bias.[21] Political scientist Peter Lupsha goes further, asserting that civil servants are "a voice of moderation, future orientation and professionalism" and "the key guardians of the public interest," filling "the vacuum and the role of public representation vacated by elected politicians."[22] Michael Lipsky, another political scientist, writes about "street-level" bureaucrats on the front lines of local government, such as teachers, police officers, and social workers. Lipsky recognizes that these workers often hide behind the impersonal structures of bureaucracy and treat those they serve coldly and even rudely, but he points out that they are under stress themselves, poorly supported by superiors, under funded, under staffed, and often facing public antagonism.[23]

Public Servants. Implicit in the views of these writers are motivations for bureaucratic behavior other than pure self-interest. Although concerns about bureaucracies are valid, most bureaucrats see themselves as public servants and try to behave as such. Any of us who are personally acquainted with public workers know this is true and respect them. Most are dedicated to their jobs and try to do their best under adverse circumstances, including meddling politicians, a hostile public, inadequate funding and staffing, and unclear responsibilities and guidelines for doing their work. Besides the commitment of public workers to do their jobs professionally and properly, bureaucrats have individual and collective ethics that typically emphasize democratic accountability, honesty, equity, and professionalism. Inculcated by U.S. society and by the bureaucratic professions themselves, these ethical standards may be imperfectly adhered to in practice, but their abuse is surely no worse than the abuse of ethical standards in other professions—and is probably less than in most. Of course, we may have a right to expect higher standards from public servants.

This takes us back to the issue of control because the professional and ethical values of bureaucracies are a major source of tension within government, as politicians, interest groups, and citizens press for policies and programs that professional bureaucracies view as inequitable, inappropriate, or infeasible. The reaction of bureaucrats to such proposals isn't necessarily selfish; in fact, it may reflect what they perceive as the larger public interest. Svara contends that these professionals are "service oriented and committed to serving the public . . . [through] rational approaches, the orderly management of affairs, and reasonable resolutions of conflict," as well as a "long-term perspective" that elected officials lack.[24]

Bad Rap for Bureaucrats

Although they sometimes earn it, bureaucrats in general have a bad rap. Most are well-meaning people doing their best in big, impersonal organizations. Some elements of bureaucratic behavior are inherent to the nature of the beast itself. These characteristics were enhanced by reform efforts to insulate local government bureaucracies from the insidious influence of politics. Most of us would endorse this goal, although we might say that reform went too far, and a few might even argue that the spoils system had its good points. Most would also agree that efforts to make bureaucracy more representative, responsive, and accountable are healthy, even though specific methods may be disputed.

ESSENTIAL TERMS

patronage	time
civil service	clientele groups
representativeness	public employee unions
control	collective bargaining
hierarchy	electoral clout
chain of command	sunset laws
rules and regulations	community control
fairness and impartiality	ombudsman
specialization	citizen review boards
division of labor	affirmative action
implementation	tax revolt
delegation	contracting out
discretion	"the new machines"
expertise	

FIELDWORK

1. Research the bureaucracy in your city or county. Go to the city clerk's office and get an organization chart to see how the hierarchy is arranged. Ask to see the budget or other appropriate documents to find out how many employees or positions are allocated to various functions, from managers to service workers.

2. Investigate the civil service system in your city or county. You can look at the civil service rules and procedures at the clerk's office and you can examine job descriptions and application procedures at the personnel department. Try to assess how rigorous the system is and how hard it would be to fire an employee.

3. Research public employee unions in your city or county at the city clerk's office and the library. Try to interview a union representative (look under unions in the phone book) and someone in local government who deals with unions.

4. If your city or county has a Human Rights Commission, Women's Rights Commission, or Civil Service Commission, attend a meeting and note the issues that are considered. Who brings complaints or issues to the commission? In whose favor were they resolved.

NOTES

[1]See Mike Royko, *Boss* (New York: Signet, 1971) on the Chicago machine and Mayor Richard J. Daley in their prime. Daley died in 1976; despite defeats in subsequent mayoral elections, the formidable remains of his machine helped elect his son, Richard M. Daley, mayor of Chicago in 1989.

[2]Anne Freedman, "Doing Battle with the Patronage Army: Politics, Courts, and Personnel Administration in Chicago," *Public Administration Review* 48 (September-October 1988): 847–859.

[3]Joe Klein, "The Pinochle Club," *New York Magazine*, 29 October 1990, p. 19.

[4]See Max Weber, *From Max Weber: Essays in Sociology*, translated by A. M. Henderson and Talcott Parsons (New York: Free Press, 1946).

[5]See David R. Morgan, *Managing Urban America*, 3rd ed. (Pacific Grove, CA: Brooks, Cole, 1989), p. 252.

[6]Timothy David Chandler, "Labor-Management Relations in Local Government," *The Municipal Year Book* (Washington, DC: International City/County Management Association, 1989), pp. 89–90.

[7]Klein, note 3, p. 19.

[8]Morgan, note 5, p. 251.

[9]Katherine Bishop, "Police Attacks: Hard Crimes to Uncover, Let Alone Stop," *The New York Times*, 24 March 1991.

[10]Rodney E. Hero, "Hispanics in Urban Government and Politics," *Western Political Quarterly* 43, no. 2 (June 1990): 411.

[11]Barbara Ferman, *Governing the Ungovernable City* (Philadelphia: Temple University Press, 1985), p. 173.

[12]Evelina R. Moulder, "Affirmative Action in Local Government," *The Municipal Year Book* (Washington, DC: International City/County Management Association, 1991), p. 51.

[13]*San Jose Mercury News*, 12 May 1993.

[14]*The Washington Post*, 22 October 1992.

[15]Lori M. Henderson, "Intergovernmental Service Arrangements and the Transfer of Functions," *The Municipal Year Book*, (Washington, DC: International City/County Management Association, 1985), pp. 194–202.

[16]See, for example, C. J. Hech, "Contracting Municipal Service: Does It Really Cost Less?" *National Civic Review*, June 1983, pp. 321–326; Ronald Moe, "Exploring the Limits of Privatization," *Public Administration Review* 47 (November/December 1987): 453–460; and Harold Sullivan, "Privatization of Public Services: A Growing Threat to Constitutional Rights," *Public Administration Review* 47 (November/December 1987): 461–466.

[17]James H. Svara, *Official Leadership in the City* (New York: Oxford University Press, 1990), p. 168.

[18]Stephen L. Elkin, *City and Regime in the American Republic* (Chicago: University of Chicago Press, 1987), p. 60.

[19]Theodore Lowi, "Machine Politics Old and New," *The Public Interest* 9 (Fall 1967): 86.

[20]Jeffrey S. Zax, "Reform City Councils and Municipal Employees," *Public Choice* 64, no. 2 (1990): 169.

[21]Svara, note 16, p. 173.

[22]Peter Lupsha, "Structural Change and Innovation: Elites and Albuquerque Politics in the 1980s," in Clarence Stone and Heywood T. Sanders, ed., *The Politics of Urban Development* (Lawrence: University Press of Kansas, 1987), pp. 237, 242.

[23]Michael Lipsky, *Street-Level Bureaucracy* (New York: Russell Sage, 1980).

[24]Svara, note 17, p. 188.

PART **III**

Outside City Hall: Elections, Influence, and Power

Thus far we've studied the socioeconomic and intergovernmental environment of local politics and the formal decision-makers and institutions of local governments, noting the interplay among them. Now we turn to the elements of local politics that connect them. In terms of the model introduced in chapter 1, these are the inputs of the political system. Many players outside city hall and the formal institutions of government influence or perhaps even control what goes on there. We've already seen their power in the shaping of the insitutions of government themselves.

We begin with those outside local government with the most legitimate claim on influencing it—the voters. Their input is shaped by both community demographics and, more formally, by the electoral structures through which they express their will, a part of the political system shaped and reshaped by reform and counterreform. We will also examine the roles of campaigns and the media in local politics. In the following chapters we'll consider interest groups and the informal or extragovernmental power structures of communities, a subject that summarizes and reviews all that we've studied before.

9

Elections and Campaigns: The Voters (and the Media) Have Their Say

I n a democracy, voters should be the most important influence on government, yet in local politics their interest and participation are often lamentably low. Some people blame such apathy on the voters themselves, but other factors also play a part, including community demographics, electoral structures, local campaigns, and the media.

Local elections were more radically altered by the progressive reform movement than any other element of local government except perhaps the bureaucracy. The reformers introduced electoral structures that affect who votes, how they choose their representatives, and who those representatives are. Not resting at that, the reformers also instituted direct democracy, giving voters the power to make policy and to discharge officials through the processes of initiative, referendum, and recall. Not all communities adopted these systems and not all have been content with their results. But reform electoral structures operate in a majority of U.S. communities, and few have not used parts of the package or at least debated them, often more than once. Controversial when first introduced, the reforms remain controversial in many places. The argument is not abstract. These electoral structures control who has influence in and over local governments. They allocate power. They connect the public to its government, either loosely or closely.

Elections and the act of voting are also shaped by the way local candidates campaign for office. Reform structures caused a different sort of campaigning to evolve in local, as compared to state and national, politics, although professional campaign consultants and communications technology are again changing the nature of local campaigns. As at the higher levels, the media play a part in local politics, especially in election campaigns. Contrary to the national pattern, however, newspapers are much more powerful than the electronic media in most communities. Reform structures have something to do with their influence, too.

Who Votes

Anyone over 18 years old is eligible to vote in local elections providing they have resided in a community for a minimum time specified by law (30 days is common) and are not confined to prison or a mental institution. To exercise this right, citizens must **register to vote,** which involves filling out forms usually available at public places such as post offices and libraries or from the county registrar of voters. Some states once made registration difficult to discourage minority voters, but federal voting rights laws and state legislation have now simplified procedures.

Many people nevertheless decline to register, and many who do register don't vote. Some don't register because they think voting doesn't matter; others just haven't gotten around to it, can't be bothered, or don't know how. Although some are eager voters, many recent immigrants who are new to democracy don't participate now that the machines aren't around to organize them. Some people don't vote because they're apathetic or unaware, especially about local as opposed to national elections. Some can't see how elections will affect them. Others think voting is a sham because the system is rigged or the candidates are all alike anyway.

The Voters

Most of us know which sorts of people are most likely to vote: white, Anglo-Saxon, Protestants (WASPS) head the list, although some other ethnic groups are also highly probable voters, including, for example, Jews, Cuban Americans, Japanese Americans, and middle-class African Americans. In all groups, greater affluence or higher class status makes people more likely to vote, and the higher the class, the greater that probability. In the poor, black neighborhoods of South Central Los Angeles, site of the 1992 riots, for example, only about 5 percent of the registered voters participate in council elections.[1] Education is associated with class and has an identical effect on voting. Older people are more likely voters than the young. Republicans are more likely to vote than Democrats. Especially in local elections, stability is a factor in voting: the longer people have lived in a place, the more likely they are to take part in its elections, because they know and care more about the community and also are more likely to see how local politics affect them. Other, more temporary factors may also influence the propensity of individuals to vote.

Belonging to an interest group, like a neighborhood association or labor union, could be a stimulant or the issues in a particular election may hit home and turn a nonvoter into a voter, as may the candidates, usually by drawing members of their own ethnic group out. Political campaigns can make a difference, too, by making a special effort to get certain people to vote.

Of course, these are generalizations, reflecting tendencies among different sorts of people. They vary from person to person and from community to community, but they generally hold true and they have proven highly accurate in predicting voter participation or **turnout** for state and national elections. Voting in local elections is a little more complicated, however. Some communities have higher turnout than others, but not necessarily because they have a large number of the sort of people who usually vote. Other characteristics of communities also influence participation.

Electoral Structures

We're already familiar with one set of these variables: structures and forms of government. In general, **reform structures** depress voter turnout. Nonpartisan elections, used by about three-fourths of U.S. cities,[2] pull fewer voters than partisan contests, where the party label provides cues for voters and motivation for people with party loyalty. The effect of at-large city council elections on turnout is less clear, although district representation may be a modest stimulant for voters because the candidates are more likely to be known personally and to be more like their constituents. In Buffalo, which uses a mixed system of district and at-large elections, a study found that "proximity rather than prestige encourages participant activity" and concluded that at-large elections "may reduce the incentive for participation."[3] Electing a mayor rather than having an appointed city manager as executive also stimulates voting. However trivial the office of mayor may really be, it has a certain glamour for most voters as well as for the media, which pay more attention to mayoral races.

But the single biggest structural influence on voting is whether local elections are **isolated or concurrent.** In many communities, reformers shifted local voting to a time separate from national elections because they thought the parties and candidates for office at the higher levels drew voters who otherwise wouldn't participate and probably weren't very knowledgeable about local politics. Of course, they also hoped to discourage the lower-class ethnic supporters of the political machines. They succeeded. Voter turnout is dramatically lower in isolated than in concurrent elections. San Jose, California, is an instructive example. The city used isolated elections from 1916 to 1974 when, to save on election costs, it shifted to concurrent elections. Voter turnout in San Jose's last isolated election in 1973 was just 16 percent; its first concurrent election in 1974, which also featured a hotly contested mayoral race, nearly quadrupled turnout to 60 percent. More generally, turnout in isolated local elections averages around 30 percent,[4] although some communities, such as New Orleans (75 percent), San Francisco (68 percent), and Miami (49 percent) achieve much higher rates. Others fall below the average, including even Chicago (28 percent). Los Angeles hit only 11 percent in its 1991 council election and even after the 1992 riots, a contentious 1993 mayor's race drew only about one-third of the voters. Turnout for school board elections can fall even lower—Dallas scored 2.6 percent recently, and New York managed just 9.4 percent in its 1993 board elections.[5]

Overall, turnout is roughly double in cities without reform structures of government. With parties, elected mayors, district representatives, and the added stimulus of concurrent state and national elections, participation is much higher. Yet a majority of U.S. cities use some components of reform. Defenders of these structures argue that although voter turnout is lower, those who vote do so more intelligently. Something else important also happens, however. The electorate is not only smaller, its composition is different and it elects different sorts of people. The factors associated with making some individuals more likely to vote than others (ethnicity, class, education, and so on) mean that the die-hard voters in reformed systems will be more white, more affluent, better educated, older—and more conservative and Republican.[6] Winning candidates, reflecting these characteristics, will be more upper class and Republican, too. The electorate and the elected will be less representative of the community. Moreover, incumbents and candidates with well-known names win more easily because challengers lack the legitimizing influence of the party label or the assistance of the party organization. The dominance of incumbents could be broken by challengers with sympathy from the media or the money to publicize their names in the campaign, but campaign contributors and the media usually support incumbents anyway, making the task of the challengers even more difficult.

Reform structures, in short, depress voter turnout and alter the composition of the electorate and the sorts of people who are elected. They load the deck in favor of the sort of people who created the reform movement in the first place. A more conservative electorate elects more conservative representatives.

Community Characteristics

Other **community characteristics,** especially size and diversity, also affect voter turnout, and sometimes these are strong enough to overcome the bias of reform. Larger cities tend to be more diverse, which means many elements of the community compete for influence. The more they come into conflict, the more they stimulate voter turnout—and broaden representation. Communities with strong political parties (San Francisco, for example), also tend to have higher voter turnout even with nominally nonpartisan elections because the parties are out there working and organizing, even if their labels aren't on the ballot. Stable communities also have higher turnout because when people stay put for a long time they are more likely to become informed and organized. Voting is much lower in mobile communities such as many suburbs and most edge cities.

Voter turnout in communities is a tricky subject, not only because we need to generalize so broadly, but also because of the contradiction between individual and community factors associated with voting. The characteristics of individual voters (ethnicity, class, education, and so on) suggest the likelihood of one person voting. But characteristics of their communities (electoral systems, size, diversity, and so forth) also stimulate or depress turnout. The paradox is that larger, more diverse communities with many minority, lower income, less well educated voters often have higher voter turnout than those with predominantly affluent, well-educated voters. The latter communities are more likely to be smaller and more homogeneous. Since their citizens are pretty much like one another, they have less to disagree about and so less encouragement to participate in local politics (they still vote in high numbers in state and national elections). Low participation may also indicate general satisfaction with the governance of their community—partly because those who do vote and those who are elected are pretty much like those who don't bother to vote. In homogeneous communities, reform structures probably provide adequate representation; in heterogeneous communities, however, where large groups within the population do not vote and are not represented, reform structures suppress the expression of different points of view and can lead to great frustration.

Thus, we find a rough pattern among U.S. cities. Larger cities, particularly those in the Frostbelt, tend to reject reform structures and consequently attain higher voter turnout. Smaller cities and suburbs, as well as many large Sunbelt cities, operate with reform electoral systems and lower turnout. Increased size and diversity have led some Sunbelt cities to return to electoral structures that predated reform, such as elected mayors, district council elections, and concurrent elections. Turnout in these cities has risen, as has voter satisfaction with representation, especially among minorities.

Direct Democracy

In addition to the reforms already discussed, the progressives countered the power of political machines by introducing **direct democracy** to ensure that people had a say in their governance through the processes of recall, referendum, and initiative. A majority of cities now enjoy some form of direct democracy (see Table 9-1), but like other elements of the reform

Table 9-1   U.S. Cities with Initiative, Referendum, and Recall
Processes, 1986

Form of Government	Initiative (percent)	Optional Referendum (percent)	Petition Referendum (percent)	Recall (percent)
Mayor-council	36.8	71.4	39.3	52.9
Council-manager	58.8	82.9	45.1	70.4
Commission	36.5	76.1	46.5	59.4

Source: 1986 survey (all cities not included). *The Municipal Year Book* (Washington, DC: International City/County Management Association, 1988). Reprinted by permission.

package, these devices are most common in Sunbelt communities rather than those of the Frostbelt.

The Recall

Local officials may be removed between scheduled elections through the **recall** process in thirty-one states. The advocates of the recall circulate a petition with a statement of their reasons (which need not be substantial), and must collect a certain number of voter signatures within a specified time; both the number and time limits are fixed by law and vary from community to community and state to state. A number of signatures equal to anywhere from 10 to 30 percent of those who voted in the last election might have to be collected over periods of 40 to 160 days. If enough signatures are collected and verified by the city or county clerk, an election is held. The ballot reads something like: "Shall X be removed from the office of Y?" The official is recalled if a majority of voters vote yes, and the vacant office is filled by either an election or an appointment, as appropriate. About half of those facing recall are removed from office; if recalled, they cannot be candidates to replace themselves in most cases.

Recalls are most frequently used by angry parents against school boards, although council members and mayors are also challenged and voters have recalled mayors in Detroit, Los Angeles, and Seattle. When she was mayor of San Francisco, now-U.S. Senator Diane Feinstein faced a recall organized by a right-wing radical group of Hell's Angels look-alikes who objected to her support for a moderate gun control law. This group found unlikely allies in liberal gays and lesbians discontented with the mayor's positions on their issues. Mayor Feinstein took advantage of the confusion about the reasons for the recall and the relative marginality of its supporters to win a smashing victory and ensure her reelection the following year.

The recall system is easy to use and abuse since clear standards justifying recall are seldom specified in state law. Recall was intended by reformers as a way of removing incompetent or corrupt officials, but it is now more often used to express disagreement about policies such as school curriculum or city growth plans, requiring costly ballots between regular elections. Several states, including Idaho and Georgia, have recently tightened their laws on recall to curtail its misuse.[7] Overall, recalls are rare, but recently attempts at recall have increased. The frustrated (usually conservative) voters who instigated the tax revolt and campaigned for term limits have also sometimes played the recall card, with mixed success.

The Referendum

Far more common on local ballots is the **referendum.** These measures or propositions are mostly placed on the ballot by the city council or county board. Borrowing money (bond measures) and amending charters must almost always be referred to the voters. For example, the Los Angeles City Council responded to citizen discontent after the 1992 riots by placing two referendums on the ballot, one amending the charter to limit the term of office of the city's police chief and another increasing taxes to pay for more police officers. By state law, the council could take neither action without a referendum. The voters approved the charter amendment but rejected the tax increase. In most cases, a simple majority is needed to approve charter amendments, but in many states, taxing and borrowing measures must be approved by 60–67 percent of those voting. Such majorities are difficult to attain, however, so local governments may not attempt to win elections on tax proposals—or they may look for ways around a referendum.

Another form of referendum allows voters to nullify acts of local government. When a local law they dislike is passed, advocates of a protest referendum have a limited time (specified in law) to collect a number of voter signatures (also specified in law). If they meet the deadline and the quota, the measure is put before the voters, either at the next regular election or, occasionally, at a special election. A simple majority is required to overturn the legislation. Protest referenda are rare. In recent years, they have most often been used by homophobic, fundamentalist Christians attempting (often successfully) to overturn local gay-rights ordinances.

The Initiative

Recalls and referenda are reactions to what local officials do, but the **initiative** process allows voters to take a positive policy-making role. They may do so by drafting a new law or a charter amendment and then putting it on the ballot by obtaining a specified number of voter signatures (usually 5 to 10 percent of those voting in the last election) in a specified time (usually around 90 days). The initiative is put to the voters at the next election and takes effect if it wins a majority.

The subjects of initiatives vary widely, from reform of city government to controlled growth to whether a city should be a nuclear free zone, and they are sometimes the most controversial measures on the ballot. Besides referenda, antigay fundamentalists have also taken advantage of the initiative process to further their cause. In 1993, for example, two Oregon cities and four counties passed initiatives prohibiting their local governments from enacting gay-rights ordinances.

The Politics of Direct Democracy

Most local ballot measures or propositions are pretty trivial and boring, however, merely tidying up the charter or dealing with minor, technical matters. Many citizens who go to vote don't bother with this part of their ballot. This **drop-off in voting** can be as much as 15 to 25 percent. Voters who complete their ballot, who are usually more affluent, better educated voters, and more conservative, thus gain greater influence. Tax measures attract more interest and excitement, although voter antagonism has made local governments shy away from such proposals. Sometimes individual politicians get a pet cause on the ballot, often to further their own careers. Interest groups also occasionally use the technique to further their causes. Group endorsements and newspaper support are particularly important on ballot measures since voters lack many other sources of information.

Perhaps disappointingly, direct democracy has not lived up to the expectations of those who introduced it. More often than not, it is used by special interests, politicians, or governments to get what they want rather than by citizens. The rising cost of campaigns only strengthens this tendency. Still, direct democracy offers hope to the relatively powerless by enabling them to take their case to the public over the opposition of elected officials. But whether instigated by citizens or special interests, direct democracy may not result in good law. With the drafting of the legislation often left to self-interested sponsors, and campaigns placed increasingly in the hands of professional political consultants, careful and rational deliberation is rare. Confused by the maze of contradictory language, bewildering issues, and intentionally deceptive campaigns, the disgusted voters often, and probably sensibly, respond by simply voting no.[8]

Local Campaigns

Whether choosing leaders or voting on ballot measures, elections wouldn't be elections without campaigns, and electoral structures do not absolutely determine the election results. Campaigns are crucial intervening variables that attempt to inform and motivate voters. Like other factors, they, too, may stimulate or depress voter turnout. Although far smaller in scale, much of what goes on in a race for mayor, city council, or county board is similar to what goes on in campaigns for state or national office. Some things, however, are different, most notably the potential for grassroots or volunteer activity.

The Candidates

Where do political candidates come from? Some people would say out of the woodwork, and they might be right. If you get a chance sometime, ask a candidate how she or he came to be running. Some seem to be self-generated while others are recruited.

Self-generated candidates are people who decide pretty much on their own that they should run, although sometimes they consult friends or political leaders. It's easy to run for local office in most places—only a small fee and/or a few signatures on a petition are required, so almost anybody can do it. (No wonder we get a lot of eccentric candidates in local politics!) But even the most serious candidates may also be virtually self-nominated. This sort of candidate is most common in homogeneous communities such as suburbs and in places with reformed political structures, weak parties, and weak interest groups. Self-generated candidates are thus more numerous in Sunbelt cities.

In cities with stronger parties and interest groups, greater diversity, and unreformed electoral systems—usually larger, Frostbelt cities—**recruited candidates** are more common. A party organization, interest group, or clique of community leaders puts them forward or encourages them to become candidates and campaigns for them. Where local parties remain strong, as in New York City, they are crucial for candidate recruitment. But even in nonpartisan systems, partylike organizations of community leaders such as San Antonio's Good Government League (now defunct) or Cincinnati's City Charter Committee select and support candidates, usually successfully. Less elite groups may also be active recruiters. The candidates are usually members or at least sympathizers of the group that selects them.

Self-generated candidates reflect relatively open political systems, with opportunity for all, but they often campaign more on personality than policy and when elected, their behavior can be unpredictable because they've managed to get there more or less on their own. They are directly accountable to no one except perhaps their own campaign organization, which probably disintegrates after the election and which, in any case, is personally loyal to the candidate. Recruited candidates, in contrast, are found in more closed and rigid political systems, where they need to work their way up through existing organizations. They will probably have some sort of record, having paid their dues by serving in lower level offices or on commissions. They are more likely to be policy-oriented than self-recruited candidates because to get support, they will have had to satisfy their backers, and once elected, these backers will hold them accountable. The disadvantage of recruited candidates, however, is that they may be accountable only to a narrow constituency rather than to the people who they are elected to represent. Categorizing candidates as self-generated or recruited is a little arbitrary, of course, and many are a little bit of each sort. Nevertheless, these types exist and whether one or the other predominates in a community reveals something about its politics.

Candidates vary in other ways as well, most notably by sex and race. Lately, women have done well as candidates in suburbs and other small communities and in large cities that elect their councils by districts. At least until they become majorities in particular communities, minorities have been less successful except in cities with district elections where minority populations are geographically concentrated. Prejudice has proven hard to overcome for African American, Latino, Asian, and other minority candidates, especially in reformed cities where, besides at-large councils, elections are isolated so interest in the campaign and information are minimal and minority turnout is low. Voter turnout in the most recent city council elections in the Los Angeles neighborhoods that were the center of the 1992 riots, for example, was just 5 percent. Nonpartisan elections also deny minority candidates the legitimizing blessing of a party label telling majority voters that the candidate is okay because he or she is a Democrat or Republican. Nevertheless, minority candidates such as Latino ex-mayor Federico Pena of Denver and African American mayors Norman Rice of Seattle and Emanuel Cleaver of Kansas City have won elections in cities where people of their background remain minorities.

The People in the Campaign

Candidates are not the only people involved in the campaign, of course, and one of the first things a candidate needs to do is put together an organization. This is easier for recruited candidates because the people and groups that encouraged them to run form the nucleus of the campaign team. Self-recruited candidates start with friends and associates, and as their campaigns gain credibility they add other community leaders, activists, and organizations.

In small communities and even in many large ones, volunteers are the heart of the campaign. Candidates draw on family, friends, individual supporters, and members of groups whose endorsement they win. These campaign **volunteers** staff the headquarters, address mailings, canvas door to door, and staff phone banks. Some spend their time recruiting other volunteers, working from the candidate's Christmas card list or membership rosters of churches, neighborhood groups, labor unions, or other sympathetic groups.

Key staff must also be selected. The **campaign manager** is essential. Managers must be planners and strategists, working intimately with the candidates, but leaving them free to spend time in the community winning votes rather than at headquarters overseeing the organization. The larger the campaign, the more the staff grows, often including an office manager, volunteer coordinator, fundraiser, scheduler, media specialist, and sometimes a press person, although the manager usually assumes this function.

Although many of these jobs can be done by volunteers, paid professionals are more and more common. Dependence on such professionals has become greater as campaigns have become more technically complex with opinion polls, direct mail, and television and radio advertising. **Campaign consultants** are now so specialized that candidates can contract for particular services, such as polling, mailing, signs, or TV ads, from different firms or hire just one firm to do it all (usually with subcontractors). Sometimes these services are provided by party organizations or interest groups.

Once one campaign in a community goes professional, others soon follow, and the days of amateur campaigning become history. Volunteer campaigns are still most common in small communities, but professional consultants predominate in larger cities and their influence has reached many small ones as well. Many would-be consultants serve their apprenticeship in smaller places as volunteers or with nominal pay. The availability of professional guns-for-hire (for many do not care who they work for) makes it easier for self-generated candidates with money to succeed. Indeed, the professionals give an advantage to any well-funded candidate, whether self-generated or recruited. Their high prices have made money more crucial in local elections.

The Money

Campaigns in small cities or in districted council races used to cost just a few thousand dollars. Now they can cost anywhere from $10,000 to $200,000 and more, depending on how competitive the race is and how dependent local candidates have become on professional campaign techniques and consultants. At-large council races in big cities are the most expensive, but the money is spread thinly, so district candidates may actually spend more per voter than their at-large counterparts.[9] Mayoral candidates in big cities spend from $300,000 upward. San Diego Mayor Susan Golding spent $1.1 million—nearly $5 per vote—getting elected.[10] That's a likely budget in any of the fifty largest cities in the United States, with several times that amount spent in some (such as Los Angeles, where candidates spent more than $11 million in the 1993 mayoral primary election).

Candidates can get by with less money if they can generate lots of volunteers to do what they might otherwise have to pay for, although campaigns don't really save a lot of money with volunteer public opinion polls of questionable accuracy or with hand-addressed mailings (recipients are more likely to read these, however). Candidates can spend less on other forms of advertising, however, if legions of volunteers work phone banks or canvas door to door. Unfortunately, such volunteers are becoming rare as Americans lead busier lives.

Money is essential, then, and getting it is a major activity of most campaigns. Fundraising specialists may be hired and the campaign manager and candidate may spend more of their time raising money than contacting voters. Family, friends, and associates of the candidate are early contributors. Banquets, picnics, wine-and-cheese receptions, and other events with ticket prices ranging from a few dollars to hundreds are held. Group endorsements are eagerly sought—to add their names to lists of supporters—but also because the groups supply volunteers and their political action committees (PACs) are a major source of funds. Public employee unions are particularly active, providing both money and workers to the candidates they endorse.

But the bulk of **campaign contributions** come from individuals and businesses with a vested interest in local governments: those who stand to benefit or lose from who is elected. Because so much of what local governments do involves land and development, the growth machine—landowners, builders, construction trade unions, attorneys, architects, and related businesses—is prominent in lists of campaign contributors. Companies that contract with local governments to provide services such as garbage collection, street paving, or towing chip in, as do other beneficiaries of local policies and programs, ranging from hotels to big industry. Businesses licensed by local government, such as taxis, cable TV, or tow trucks, also pay up. Campaigns that cost big money get it from big money. Some businesses contribute to candidates who seem opposed to their interests (for example, builders giving to environmentalists) in hopes of making them more friendly should they win. A few even give to rival candidates to cover all bases.

Given these sources of campaign contributions, a candidate needs to be well connected to the local business community. White businessmen are more likely to have such connections and so do better at fundraising than working-class, women, and minority candidates. Because of this disadvantage, minority, gay and lesbian, and women's groups have worked to redress the balance with contributions of their own, with some success. Many of their candidates still operate at a financial disadvantage, however. Neighborhood groups are even less likely to give money, but they often compensate with volunteers.

Worried about the influence of money, many state and local governments have introduced requirements for disclosure of all contributions and expenditures. Such **sunshine laws** help voters measure the rhetoric of candidates against the interests of their supporters. A few communities buy space in local newspapers to publish these reports but in most, the voters won't know what the reports contain unless the news media or opposing candidates publicize them, which they usually do. Over half the states and many local governments go further than disclosure, limiting the dollar amount of contributions to, say, $250 for a council candidate and $500 for a mayoral candidate, or prohibiting contributions from specially formed PACs.

Twelve states and a few large cities, including New York and Los Angeles, have gone one step further, to **public financing of campaigns.** In New York City, where the average cost of running for an open city council seat exceeded $200,000 in the 1980s, the city gives candidates one dollar for every dollar they raise themselves up to $40,000. Candidates must disclose the amount and source of their private contributions and accept a spending limit to qualify for funds. They can spend more if they refuse public funding, but then they look dependent on fat-cat contributors. If most candidates accept public financing and spending limits, the playing field will be more level for candidates without ready access to big money. Other cities have considered public financing of campaigns, but budget crises have made the public and some decision-makers reluctant to spend tax money on campaigns and critics have pointed out that partial public funding did not stop lavish spending in Los Angeles' 1993 mayoral election. Of course, many of those who benefit from the current system are happy to leave it as it is.

The Campaign Strategy

Probably the least visible but most important element of electioneering is the **campaign strategy.** Simply put, this is a framework for using the candidate, people, and money available to the best possible effect. Each of these is a limited resource. The candidate only has so much time, energy, and ability. The campaign only has so many people, all with limits on their time, energy, and ability. Money, too, is finite. The principal task of campaign managers and the major skill they provide is to work out a way to maximize the use of these limited resources. Instinct plays a part in this, and most gifted campaign managers have excellent political instincts, giving them the ability to make snap judgments that are right.

But strategy comes from careful research, too. This is another area where volunteers can help—or where data can be bought from consultants. Such data include voting patterns in past elections in which the candidate, the opponent, or similar candidates and issues have been involved. Census data also are useful in constructing a profile of the city or district and its problems. Opinion polls may be carried out, but usually only in larger cities and high-profile races, because most voters know too little about local politics to say more than "don't know." If either candidate has held office before, the records are checked for past votes and positions. Further research may be carried out on the opposition candidate in newspapers and other public records in hopes of finding something embarassing if the campaign descends to mudslinging, as is increasingly common, especially with the increased involvement of political consultants.

As all the information comes together, the campaign manager, the candidate, and their advisors and top staff lay out a strategy for using their resources. This will include what areas or groups the candidate should concentrate on, where and how to allocate volunteers, and what messages to convey as well as how they are to be sent and to whom they are to be addressed. At the heart of the strategy is the judicious use of available media.

The Media

Although the news media are important in elections, local campaigns rely heavily on other means to achieve their primary function, communicating with voters. These **campaign media** are essential to their success.

Because the scale of local races is so much smaller than that of state and national contests, the most basic local campaign medium is the candidate talking to voters in person. Candidates walk door to door, lurk in shopping malls, and attend neighborhood coffees and small meetings organized by their supporters. Many community groups also invite candidates to their meetings or organize debates or candidates' nights at schools or community centers. In small communities, campaigns may amount to little more than such candidate appearances, local news reports, and a few signs. In larger places, however, a wider variety of media come into play.

Signs.   Because local politics and candidates have such a low profile in most communities, campaigns must first let people know an election is coming and develop name familiarity for their candidate or issue. That's why we see so many tacky signs all over the place when an election is coming. Notice that statewide and national candidates don't use them as much. They benefit more from news coverage (especially TV) and are probably already well known. But particularly in nonpartisan local campaigns, signs along the road, on lawns, and in windows are a fundamental starting point. Lawn and window signs are thought to be most effective because they suggest the endorsement of the household where they are placed. Such signs may be produced and placed by professionals or volunteers. The former do a better job, of course, but they can also be expensive.

Brochures.   The other ubiquitous media item in campaigns from little to large is some kind of pamphlet or brochure about the candidate or issue: a few photos (coat over shoulder; talking to cop; smiling with family), a little text (antidrugs, anticrime, antigrowth, proneighborhood), maybe a little color, depending on campaign finances. Some are glossy and elaborate, others are awkward and amateurish; either kind can work or backfire, depending on the campaign and the community. The brochure will be backup material for another essential campaign medium: candidate appearances, where the candidate or campaign staff will hand it out to whoever will take it. The brochure will probably also be left by volunteers at voters' houses just before the election.

Canvassing.   Such **canvassing** used to be the primary campaign medium, and it still is in small communities. In many places, however, it has been replaced by **phone banks** staffed by volunteers or paid workers. Like canvassers, they hope to talk with the voters and, if possible, find out how they'll vote. These calls may be followed up with a mailing and, if the voter supports the candidate, another call or visit on election day to make sure she or he actually votes. In big cities and suburbs, however, campaigns are finding it more and more difficult to recruit volunteers and those going door to door often find no one at home while those telephoning are more likely to talk to an answering machine than a human being these days.

Direct Mail.   Local campaigns have therefore turned increasingly to a relatively new medium that seems to ensure better access to voters. Targeted or **direct mail** involves sending a selected message to specific voters. Thanks to computers, campaigns can do mailings to members of just one political party or to independents; to men or women; to homeowners or renters; to residents of different neighborhoods; to members of different ethnic or religious groups; or to many other types of people, such as elders or homosexuals. Volunteer campaigners can develop some of the lists (party affiliation and neighborhood are easy) and address envelopes, but professional direct mail consultants can target just about any special group and get a piece in the mail overnight telling them whatever the campaign wants. Campaign managers love direct mail because they can tell different groups different things. They don't necessarily take contradictory positions on issues (although some do), they just put the progrowth stance in their union mailing and play up crime prevention in the neighborhood piece. Managers can also include endorsements from individuals and groups that they know will be effective with the targeted voters. Besides all these advantages, direct mail can be tailored very nicely to the amount of money a campaign can raise. A mail piece can always be added or deleted, while using TV and radio involves higher production costs and advance buying of time. No wonder direct mail has become the dominant medium in contemporary campaigns. It has brought increasing dependence on professional campaign consultants and driven up campaign costs, however.

Advertising.   Local campaigns do advertise in newspapers and on radio and television but, although patterns vary, these media are used less than the others discussed thus far. In big cities, political ads in newspapers are ignored by readers and are a waste of campaign funds. Most candidates don't bother. But in the daily or weekly newspapers of small communities or in weekly neighborhood newspapers in larger cities, such ads can be as helpful as street signs. Television and radio are another matter. In small to medium-sized cities and in district council races, the expense of TV is out of the question and radio, while cheaper, is of doubtful utility. The problem is that, in either case, candidates are paying to communicate with people who can't even vote for them, since TV and radio are broadcast media that reach well beyond most local constituencies. Most campaigns conclude that their money can be better spent on targeted mailing. Except for some isolated communities where the broadcast media reach mostly local voters, radio and especially TV are used mainly in mayoral races in big cities.

Publicity and Endorsements.   Besides advertising, campaigns also seek free publicity in the local news media. Press conferences are a little pretentious for most local candidates and are usually ignored by the media, except in big-time races. Press releases and staged events are common, however, and many candidates and campaign managers work the media by cozying up to local reporters and sharing gossip with them. Most news coverage focuses on mayoral elections, with spotty reporting on council races. This applies especially to TV. Small town newspapers, however, provide more thorough, if sometimes more biased, coverage. Beyond the news pages and especially in small cities, the campaign is waged in letters to the editor, a well-read part of every newspaper and a good place to get free publicity.

Candidates also eagerly seek the endorsements of local newspapers. In some cases this may mean more favorable news coverage, but increasingly, endorsements are confined to editorial pages. Publishers, editors, and/or an editorial board make the endorsements from their personal knowledge of the candidates in smaller cities or from questionnaires and interviews in larger cities. These endorsements are highly prized and considered quite influential because people usually know little about local races (unlike those for higher and/or partisan offices) and take their cues where they can. Researchers estimate that newspaper endorsements are worth 10 to 20 percent of the vote in nonpartisan, at-large races, and can be particularly helpful for women and minority candidates and for ballot measures.[11]

Getting Out the Vote

As election day approaches, campaigns begin to focus on turning out their supporters to vote, a special challenge in local races. **Get-out-the-vote** drives are an essential element of campaigns for minority, liberal, and Democratic candidates, whose supporters are less likely to vote than those of whites, conservatives, and Republicans, although many of the latter also work to get out their voters. Nonpartisan organizations such as the League of Women Voters and more partisan groups such as labor unions and minority groups also work to get people to vote. To prepare for these efforts, campaigns and groups like these often do **voter registration drives** months before the election, hoping to recruit new voters who are likely supporters. To assure this, they target certain neighborhoods or shopping centers, or perhaps colleges and universities if they expect student support. Then, during the campaign, door-to-door and telephone canvassers identify probable supporters. On election day, volunteers again phone or visit these voters to make sure they've cast their ballots. Child care and transportation to the polls are often on offer. Despite such efforts, voter turnout continues to decline—which only makes getting out the vote and the votes of those who do turn out more important.

Campaigns in Perspective

These elements of campaigns are aimed at the basic goal of communicating with voters. The main task is to get the candidate known, building name familiarity. Campaigns can then move on to persuading people to support the candidate by creating a favorable image. Finally, they must motivate supporters to actually vote. Like all forms of advertising, this requires much repetition or cumulative reinforcement, especially in nonpartisan races where name identification and image are all.

Much of what goes on in local campaigns is similar to contests for state and national office, particularly in mayoral races in big cities and in partisan elections. But local campaigns differ from state and national campaigns in important ways. They rely on different media—more mail, less TV—and grassroots, volunteer campaigns are far more common. Newspapers and campaign contributors, however, are even more important because nonpartisan elections generally keep party organizations out of the game. (These elements also apply to campaigns for recall, referenda, and initiatives.) Campaigns, or course, vary considerably from community to community. In big cities with partisan elections—mostly in the Frostbelt—they are far more structured and more like statewide races. In most large Sunbelt cities with reformed electoral systems, they are a free-for-all where money and media count a great deal. In smaller communities, local elites sometimes dominate, but grassroots campaigns have considerable success, too. The professionalization of local campaigns and the higher costs it brings bodes ill for grassroots campaigns, however. Professional consultants also aid and abet the propensity, especially in nonpartisan elections, to emphasize the personalities of the candidates over the issues as well as increasingly negative campaigning. Higher costs and professionalization will not help women and minority candidates, either. Still, local elections are where grassroots campaigns by ordinary people have their best remaining chance and also where campaigns count most since people know least—partly because of the news media.

The News Media in Local Politics: "Shrill and High the Newsboys Cry/ The Worst of the City's Infamy"[12]

In most communities, "news media in local politics" means newspapers because television and radio cover local news minimally and superficially. Television and radio are **broadcast media** and usually have audiences well beyond the boundaries of any single city. Their news editors believe that these audiences are not interested in one community's issues or candidates, so they allocate more time to stories of broader interest (or very narrow human interest). Besides, local news is not very visual or glamorous. The programmers know we have our fingers on the remote control and think we'll switch channels when the local news comes on. Television and radio news teams are also usually understaffed and unable to designate a city hall reporter to specialize in local politics. As a consequence, when their reporters, by necessity generalists, are assigned to cover a local issue, they sometimes misinterpret it because they don't know very much. In some big cities where local politics is more dramatic and glitzy, the electronic media make more of an effort—New York and San Francisco are notable examples—but these are the exceptions to the rule and greater effort doesn't necessarily mean good news coverage.

Newspapers

Although their influence has declined, newspapers are still the most important news medium in local politics. Studies of power in particular cities consistently find the publishers and editors of local newspapers in the top ranks of local power holders.[13] Before TV, newspapers were even more powerful because they were the only source of news. Now more and more of us choose to get our news from TV rather than newspapers. Television doesn't tell us much, but by converting readers into viewers it decreases the power of newspapers.

Most newspapers used to be locally owned and operated by powerful families. Their news coverage was highly biased, usually conservative, and progrowth. Candidates who received their blessing won not only editorial praise, but also favorable news coverage. When communities had more than one newspaper in competition, this wasn't such a problem because alternative views could be expressed. But as competition faded and one-newspaper towns became common, the bias became alarming. Many communities—especially small ones—find themselves in this situation.

Corporate Journalism.   In others, even where one newspaper predominates, the balance has improved. A majority of U.S. newspapers, including small town and suburban newspapers, are now owned by national or regional corporations. Instead of being run by a local family, they are managed by professionals with fewer local axes to grind and ambitions to move on to bigger and better jobs. Reporters, too, are more professional. Their professionalism means greater efforts to provide objective reporting of local politics. Objectivity may be a bit of a myth, but it is a laudable goal that means better coverage of local politics than that produced by the shameless bias once so common.

Professional objectivity doesn't mean the power of newspapers has declined, however, only that it has changed. Newspapers still frame the issues by choosing what to report and what to ignore. Whether they play a story as serious or a bit of a joke (easy to do with lots of local issues) also matters, as does the timeliness of the coverage, which may merely report events as they happen or give enough advance notice to people who might be affected so they can organize and do something. Newspaper power is further enhanced by the laziness or understaffing of TV and radio newsrooms, which rely on newspapers for their coverage of local politics.

Endorsements.   **Newspaper endorsements** of candidates and issues are another way the papers exercise clout. Many readers ignore these recommendations, and in some places people conscientiously vote against whomever the newspaper endorses, but others—10 to 20 percent of the voters according to one study[14]—are influenced by them, especially in nonpartisan, at-large races and on ballot measures. Moreover, newspaper endorsements give candidates credibility with campaign contributors. Candidates and officeholders also pay attention to editorial positions on community issues, knowing they will influence the public—and knowing they will want an editorial endorsement for themselves one day.

In fact, the power of newspapers is probably greatest on nonelectoral issues such as civic projects, proposed developments, or local policies on affirmative action or contracting out. Few other voices are heard throughout the community on these issues and those that are must be filtered through the newspaper anyway. Merely by choosing to cover an issue, the newspaper makes it important, but the manner of coverage as well as editorial opposition or support also matters. Most newspapers are conservative in their endorsements of both candidates and issues, although many take the part of reformers or crusaders for good government. The reformist impulse is often compromised, however, by the newspapers' interest in promoting their cities, which may lead them to ignore or gloss over some issues, especially if they concern social problems or minorities. Most newspapers are big boosters of growth and an integral part of the local growth machine. Growth is in their business interest, of course, because it increases their circulation and advertising revenues. "Trees don't read newspapers," said one publisher whose newspaper supported housing development on orchard land.[15]

Clout.   The most powerful newspapers are probably not major metropolitan dailies as one might expect, but those of smaller communities, where readership is more common and alternative news sources are few. Big city dailies face more competition as well as some of the same problems as the broadcast media: they want to reach a metropolitan audience larger than any single city and their readers are not interested in any one city either. Most big newspapers have responded with zoned editions in which one section (often just its front page) is targeted to a particular area. Zoned editions have actually improved coverage of suburban politics.

However much they may have changed, newspapers retain their clout in local politics, not least because the politically active community elite reads the paper. To be a player in local politics, you have to read what everybody else is reading, even if you don't much like it. Equally importantly, the others most likely to read the local paper are the people who are most likely to vote. Lacking other sources of information—ward heelers are extinct in most places and we have less time to talk to our neighbors—we rely on newspapers more. Their endorsements of candidates and ballot measures carry great weight, especially in nonpartisan elections, but their greatest influence is in framing local issues on their news pages.

Voters and the News Media

Outside city hall, nothing is as important or as influential as the voice of the voters, despite the fact that it is only occasionally heard and is usually muffled because so few participate and because it is so hard to hold elected officials accountable in between elections. A vigilant press is essential both to encourage participation and ensure accountability. Unfortunately, neither press nor the voters are always alert. Electoral systems that dissipate interest and discourage participation do not help.

Voting is not, however, the only way that citizens express their concerns in local politics. One alternative is to move to another city. This exit option is not so readily available in state and national politics, but in most urban areas in the United States (unlike other countries), different communities are near enough for people who can afford it to move fairly readily and still be near work and friends.[16] The phenomenon of white flight to the suburbs is a case in point. Alternatively, people can voice their concerns individually or through interest groups, although this can be costly and exhausting and most don't bother. Many do, however, and as we'll see in the next chapter, some are much more successful than others.

ESSENTIAL TERMS

register to vote
turnout
reform structures
isolated or concurrent elections
community characteristics
direct democracy
recall
referendum
initiative
drop-off in voting
self-generated candidates
recruited candidates
campaign volunteers
campaign managers

campaign consultants
campaign contributions
sunshine laws
public financing of campaigns
campaign strategy
campaign media
canvassing
phone banks
direct mail
get-out-the-vote
voter registration drives
broadcast media
newspaper endorsements

FIELDWORK

1. Does your community conform to this chapter's generalizations about voter turnout? Collect data on voting and the electoral system from your city or county clerk and census data from the library, and make an assessment.

2. Research campaign financing for selected offices in your community by going to the city or county clerk and checking the records. What are the major sources of campaign contributions? If available, what are the major ways candidates spent their money? What is the average cost of a city council campaign?

3. Identify coalitions that formed around ballot measures and candidates in your city's last election. Which coalitions won and which lost? Do you have any explanations for the results?

4. Working in teams, select a few blocks in one area of the city. Determine who is not registered to vote and organize a voter registration drive in anticipation of the next local election.

NOTES

[1]The Economist, *Pocket USA* (London: The Economist Books, 1993), p. 65.

[2]James H. Svara, *Official Leadership in the City* (New York: Oxford University Press, 1990), p. 133.

[3]Michael Haselswerdt, "Voter Reaction to District and At-Large Elections: Buffalo, New York," *Urban Affairs Quarterly* 20 (September 1984): 42.

[4]Paul E. Peterson, *City Limits* (Chicago: University of Chicago Press, 1981), p. 119.

[5]*The New York Times*, 6 May 1993.

[6]Peterson, note 4, p. 115; see also Svara, note 2, p. 137.

[7]David R. Berman, "State Actions Affecting Local Governments," *The Municipal Year Book* (Washington, DC: International City/County Management Association, 1990), p. 56.

[8]Eugene Lee, "The American Experience: 1778–1978," in Austin Ranney, ed., *The Referendum Device* (Washington, DC: American Enterpise Institute, 1981), p. 58.

[9]Haselswerdt, note 3, p. 40.

[10]David Beiler, "The Carpet-Bombers," *Campaign*, January/February 1993, p. 35.

[11]Susan A. MacManus and Charles S. Bullock, III, "Minorities and Women DO Win At Large!" *National Civic Review* 77, no. 3 (May-June 1988): 233.

[12]William Vaughn Moody, "In New York," quoted in James A. Clapp, ed., *The City* (New Brunswick, NJ: Center for Urban Policy Research, 1984), p. 169.

[13]Philip J. Trounstine and Terry Christensen, *Movers and Shakers* (New York: St. Martin's Press, 1982), pp. 131–138.

[14]MacManus and Bullock, note 11, p. 233.

[15]Richard Reinhardt, "Joe Ridder's San Jose," *San Francisco Magazine*, November 1965, p. 66.

[16]See Albert O. Hirschman, *Exit, Voice, and Loyalty* (Cambridge, MA: Harvard University Press, 1970).

10

Interest Groups in Local Politics: Types, Tactics, and Targets

Individual citizens participate in the politics of their communities when they vote or actively campaign for favored candidates and causes. They are also involved in governing their communities between elections. Some write, phone, or meet with their representatives to talk about issues that concern them. Others attend meetings, give public testimony, or serve on committees and commissions, of which most local governments have many. But perhaps the most common and substantial way that citizens take part in community politics is through interest groups.

Interest groups result when individuals get together and organize themselves to attempt to influence the policies and programs of government by applying whatever political resources they have. Although most people correctly assume that interest groups are more active in state and national politics than in local politics, a variety of such groups take part in community politics, too. Sometimes they are a little harder to see because they are people we know rather than slick lobbyists in alligator shoes. Often they are organizations we don't think of as interest groups, such as businesses and corporations or even churches. Although their primary purposes are not political, they sometimes function as interest groups when their concerns are at stake. Businesses or churches, for example, may act like interest groups when a local land-use decision will affect their property, or on issues such as parking and traffic. More generally, businesses want low taxes, good services, and growth in their communities, and churches may seek to protect what they perceive as public morality on issues such as homelessness, homosexual rights, or abortion. In fact, this is a common pattern in interest group activity in local politics: many groups organized for purposes other than politics sometimes operate as interest groups. Politics is the primary purpose of many, however. In larger cities, such groups are increasingly common and some say even dominant.

Types of Interest Groups

To get an idea of what sorts of groups are active in a particular local jurisdiction, study the agendas of the meetings of its governing body. States divide the responsibilities for local governments among cities, counties, and sometimes other governments. The week-to-week decisions of city councils and other governing bodies revolve around these responsibilities, which are readily apparent in their agendas. When items of concern to particular groups are on the agenda, representatives of the groups generally show up at the meeting itself. So when you read the agenda for a meeting, its subject matter will pretty much predict who will be there. Better yet, attend a few meetings and you'll see the groups in action. Of course, every group will not be there every week. Groups—and individuals—show up when their own interests are at stake, take part in deliberations on the specific items that concern them, and leave the meeting immediately after their item has been heard. Nothing could better illustrate the narrowness of their interests. Go and watch.

The sorts of groups active in local decision making vary, not only according to the responsibilities assigned by the state to a particular unit of local government, but also by the social and economic composition of the community. Nevertheless, some types of groups are commonly involved in community politics all across the United States.

Business Groups

Probably the most commonly active groups are **business groups** representing business interests. Individual businesses may be active on a land-use decision that affects their company or on broader issues that concern them, such as taxes or regulations on signs or parking. In general, the more local the business is, the more active it is in community politics. Multinational corporations tend to focus on state and national politics, taking scant interest in particular communities. But businesses that are locally headquartered or exclusive to a single community tend to take what goes on there very seriously, indeed.

Businesses with a common specialty, such as builders, manufacturers, or merchants, often form groups to represent their interests. The most ubiquitous business organization in U.S. communities is the local chamber of commerce, which is usually dominated by retail merchants, although many chambers try to represent the full spectrum of business interests.

Small business associations are active in most communities, and big businesses such as manufacturers often form organizations of their own in larger cities.

Because a primary power of local government is land use, perhaps the most active of all business interests in city and county politics are those related to land and development—the growth machine. Landowners, builders, and their suppliers and associates (lawyers, architects, surveyors, realtors, advertising agencies) are active and powerful in most communities, usually successfully promoting growth and thus furthering their own interests. Builders and realtors often form organizations of their own, but the growth machine as a whole operates more as an informal alliance rather than a structured interest group.

As with all categories of interest groups, it is important to remember that business interests are not homogeneous. Indeed, they vary considerably and may well come into conflict. Downtown merchants may oppose suburban shopping malls or hotels; manufacturing companies may express caution about growth when it brings traffic congestion that hurts their business; realtors may be less enthusiastic about new development because their business is to sell homes, not build them, and limiting the supply may raise prices and thus their commissions. In general, business is antitax, but small business groups are more vehement in their opposition (and generally more conservative) than big businesses, which may accept or even support tax increases when persuaded that such increases will improve services, especially transportation. Like any other group, business will first protect its own well-being or self-interest, and the bottom line is profit. More than most other groups, however, businesses are likely to push for the broader goal of growth, which to them means economic expansion and more business for themselves. The more local the business is—as opposed to being part of a multinational corporation—the greater its enthusiasm for growth.

Labor Groups

Labor groups or unions are powerful interest groups in some large cities in the East and Midwest and in a few elsewhere, such as San Francisco. In the Sunbelt and suburbia, however, membership in unions is low and their influence is limited. Private sector unions such as autoworkers or retail clerks take part in city politics when issues that affect them arise, but such organizations usually focus on state and national rather than local politics because more of their concerns are dealt with at those levels. If they are active locally, it is usually in support of associated unions with more at stake.

The most commonly active local unions are the building trades and public employees. The construction trade unions—carpenters, electricians, plumbers, and so forth—have as big a stake in the politics of land use and growth as their employers, the landowners and builders do, and they are solid political allies of local growth machines. Union support for growth proposals gives them a legitimacy (jobs and housing) that wealthy landowners or corporate developers don't have and may win the support of more liberal-minded decision makers. Public employee unions, which are the most rapidly growing sector of union membership, attempt to influence decision-makers on wages and working conditions for their members, and in so doing, they often shape the delivery of public services, from police and fire protection to parks and libraries.

In most counties, individual unions come together in an umbrella organization called a **labor council,** usually under the auspices of the national American Federation of Labor and Congress of Industrial Organizations (AFL/CIO). Through these councils, unions are connected to state and national labor organizations and support one another—or work out their differences. As with business interests, unions do not always agree. In political endorsements, for example, public employee unions tend to be liberal, while the construction trades tend to be conservative. And while the construction unions are unequivocally progrowth, public employee unions (and others as well) worry about growing so rapidly that the quality of public services and the environment decline. With private sector union membership shrinking and public employee unions growing, the balance of power within the labor movement is shifting.

Neighborhood Groups

Almost as common as business interests in local politics are **neighborhood or homeowner groups.** These organizations are territorially based, speaking for a particular section of the community, ranging in size from a few square blocks to a few square miles. Typical concerns are new developments of almost any sort, traffic, crime, and local amenities such as parks and libraries. These groups usually find themselves trying to prevent something from happening to their area that they perceive as a threat, either to their local quality of life or to property values. Neighborhood opposition to proposals coming from developers or from city hall is so common that these groups have earned the acronym **NIMBY** (*not in my backyard*). Often this involves objections to particular projects considered locally unacceptable land uses, from dumps and factories to community care facilities and low-income housing. Politically, neighborhood or homeowner groups are often on the defensive, opposing changes in their areas, but their activities are not all negative. Many play a productive part in building community and even in providing some local services.

Some—often those that refer to themselves as homeowner rather than neighborhood groups—have extremely narrow interests, however. Urbanist Mike Davis reports that homeowner groups first formed in the

1920s in Los Angeles "as instruments of white mobilization against attempts by blacks to buy homes outside the ghetto," with "white homeowners band[ing] together as 'protective associations.' "[1] Others in California and elsewhere were formed for other reasons, all involving protection, although not all necessarily racist. Recently, California has led the way in the emergence of a new variation of these protective associations. **Common Interest Developments** or **CIDs** are the mandatory organizations that provide services in condominiums and some other housing developments. More than 150,000 such organizations now operate across the country, with 20,000 in California alone. They collect fees (like taxes), provide services such as maintenance and security, and function not only as interest groups, but also as minigovernments.

Homeowner groups and CIDs are most common in white, middle-class areas, where they concentrate mainly on the property values and homogeneity of their communities, opposing developments they think might lead to decreasing home prices or to the arrival of different classes or ethnic groups (also perceived as lessening property values). (Minority and working-class neighborhoods often behave in the same way when they sense similar threats.) Although this NIMBY mentality is widely condemned, critics sometimes forget that their home is the biggest investment most families make. Naturally, they want to protect their investment, even if that means being seen as class- or race-biased. Mixing cheaper homes or different class and racial groups in a neighborhood does not always lead to lower property values, however. The impact of such changes depends on the strength of the neighborhood, the specific projects, and the extent of commingling. Nevertheless, the fears of the NIMBYs aren't purely paranoid in a society in which most neighborhoods are not mixed and in which property values often supersede social values.

Opposition to Growth.   On a broader level, neighborhood/homeowner/ NIMBY politics often extend to antagonism to growth, pitting these interests against business and labor. But while neighborhood opposition to growth may align these groups with environmentalists, their opposition to growth has less to do with open space or clean air and water than with its impact on local services. Growth may generate economic activity in an area, but it doesn't necessarily pay for itself. Somebody has to foot the bill for new roads, fire stations, parks, libraries, and the like. Until the 1970s, when they started saying no, existing neighborhoods paid much of the cost of growth. Since then, however, local governments have shifted more of the bill to the new developments themselves (and thus to the consumers). But even if older neighborhoods don't have to pay for new infrastructures, existing services such as streets, police, and parks must be shared with new developments so service levels in older areas decline. When that happens, neighborhoods may join environmentalists to forge a formidable antigrowth coalition.

Proactive Politics.   Whether narrow NIMBYism or broadly antigrowth coalition, the politics of these groups are mostly negative and defensive. Some territorial groups go beyond this, however, to a more positive and even proactive politics. Homeowner groups may evolve in this way, although many such groups refer to themselves as neighborhood rather than homeowner groups, taking a broader, more generous, and inclusive view of their territory and expressing concerns about its various components. Some such groups, for example, form neighborhood watch programs to fight crime, helping each other and the police. Some organize neighborhood cleanups or tree plantings—again, helping both themselves and their local government. Many get involved in the operation of local libraries and community centers, making them more responsive to their clients and better integrated with their service areas. Many now cooperate with their local governments in planning new developments to avoid NIMBY confrontations. Some, like The Woodlawn Organization (TWO) in a predominantly low-income, African American neighborhood of Chicago, work to improve or build housing and/or to encourage small businesses and create jobs. All these are examples of **coproduction** or neighborhood efforts in cooperation with local government that can improve services, cut government costs, and build community. Newsletters, festivals, and street parties are also part of their community-building, addressing the need of urban dwellers to feel a sense of identity and belonging. All of these are things any of us can do and feel good about and they make our neighborhoods better and more pleasant places to live.

Groups that take on these more positive functions tend to be long-lasting (TWO is over 30 years old) and may attain considerable clout.[2] This power is narrowly confined to issues specific to their territories, but such narrowness is true of most interest groups, and although neighborhood groups aren't always apparent as major players in community power structures, many have confronted and faced down big powers such as developers—or at least given them a run for their money.

Tenuous Organizations.   Most neighborhood or homeowner groups, however, are tenuous organizations at best. They commonly emerge in response to a crisis—some threat to their territory—and fade away when the crisis is resolved. The chief disadvantage for these groups, then, is that they are reactive—and often their reaction comes too late. Only a few neighborhood groups manage to achieve the stability and on-going vigilance that are common to business and labor groups. More common, Mike Davis asserts in his study of Los Angeles, are "individualistic " groups "dominated by cranky personalities, consorting in temporary coalitions and then, inevitably, remolecularizing around their own back yards."[3]

The stability of neighborhood groups is further challenged because their self-interest is not always as easy to define as the self-interest of businesses and unions. Although they tend to be homogeneous, most neighborhoods contain some diversity—Republicans and Democrats, liberals and conservatives, middle- and working-class households, members of racial minorities, and others—and may not readily reach consensus on issues not involving a direct threat. Dissent and even opposing groups within neighborhoods are common. In addition, the mobility of U.S. life as we move from community to community and even spend parts of our day in different areas makes the emergence of such groups less likely. If anything, traditional neighborhood groups may be on the decline.

Minority Groups

Another very common sort of group represents ethnic or racial minorities. Almost every wave of immigrants since the first English settlers of North America has, at one time or another, felt itself a minority and suffered discrimination. In the cities, at least, various newly arrived immigrants often formed protective associations that acted, partly, as interest groups. Depending on the city and the time, these have included the Irish, the Germans, the Italians, and many others. Some of these groups worked their way into mainstream U.S. politics through political machines. And because they were white, many individuals merely melted into the larger society.

Other groups—blacks, Asians, and Latinos in particular—have had a harder time. Nonwhites or people with cultures distinctly different from that of the community majority have had to struggle even harder for political recognition. Shunned by the political machines and denied the right to vote or even own property in some states, it was not until the middle of this century that racial minorities began to win the right of political participation. A great surge of political organizing during the civil rights movement of the 1950s and 1960s, supplemented by federal support for community organizing during the War on Poverty and the Great Society programs of the 1960s, brought visibility and eventually clout, particularly for African American groups in big cities. Latinos and, a little later, Asians organized similarly and began to achieve success in the 1980s and 1990s.

From European ethnic groups to African, Asian, and Latino Americans, people have formed associations that are active in local politics. Those most integrated socially and economically generally concentrate on sustaining their cultural heritage, with St. Patrick's Day parades, Octoberfests, or Italian festas. Those less well integrated and less well off, still fight discrimination and struggle for basic rights, including housing, jobs, and political representation. When **ethnic and racial groups** are territorially concentrated, they overlap with neighborhood groups. This can be an added source of strength, making organizing easier since people live closer together and have more in common. But more often than not, the concentration of a particular group in a specific area is the result of discrimination, so the group has more to struggle against.

As with other types of groups, minority groups are far from unified or uniform. Their interests vary depending on how well they are integrated socially and economically with the larger society. They often compete with one another for community resources or representation. When their interests coincide, coalition makes sense, but racism and ethnocentrism prevents such unity. The antagonism between the Korean shopkeepers and the black residents of South Central Los Angeles during the riots of 1992 illustrates both this competition and racism, when the groups might do better to cooperate. Even within some racial and ethnic groups, competition and conflict may occur. For example, the differences among Japanese, Chinese, Koreans, and Vietnamese, or among Mexicans, Cubans, and Puerto Ricans may be both substantial and politically debilitating.

Nor do minority groups always find easy allies among other sorts of groups. Minority leaders denounce businesses for discriminating and unions for denying them jobs. Even though they frequently represent neighborhoods themselves, and so might share a concern for basic services and community control, minority leaders often denounce other neighborhoods for housing discrimination and elitism. On growth issues, minority groups usually line up with business and unions on grounds that growth means jobs and housing.

Environmental Groups

On the other side of the growth issue are **environmental groups.** Mostly white and middle- or upper-class, well-educated professionals, their self-interest is not tied to growth like that of business, developers, unions, and minority groups pushing for jobs, although they are often liberal enough to show sympathy for these concerns. Besides fighting local growth machines, many environmental groups have also been active on such issues as airport expansion, highway siting, building heights, architectural design, public transit, footpaths, bike lanes, parks, and open space. They gained extra leverage when some states began requiring local governments to consider environmental impact reports (EIRs) on development projects. These EIRs may be challenged at public hearings, an opportunity many environmental groups eagerly seize.

Local politics can be difficult for environmental groups however. The growth machine attitude on land use held by most local governments means environmentalists are fighting the mainstream. The rhetoric of jobs rather than owls is especially leveled against environmentalists at the local level. (As we have seen, however, neighborhood groups concerned about the adequacy of city services may be allies in an antigrowth coalition.) Another difficulty for environmental groups is that many of their concerns, such as air and water quality and open space, overlap local government boundaries and so are beyond the ability of individual communities to control. Environmental advocates must therefore take their case to a higher level of government—if an appropriate one exists. Despite growing public concern, these factors limit the influence of environmental organizations in local politics.

Women's Groups

The involvement of **women's groups** in local politics goes back to the social reform movements of the nineteenth century. They also played a prominent part—even before women could vote in most places—in the Progressive movement. In recent decades, women's groups have campaigned on a variety of issues and have had a significant impact.[4] Local groups as well as chapters of the National Organization for Women and the National Women's Political Caucus have worked to elect women to local offices, with great success. These groups and many women elected officials have changed hiring policies in most communities, introducing affirmative action programs to further the recruitment, employment, and promotion of women. At their instigation, police, courts, and social service bureaucracies have changed their policies on the treatment of rape victims and on domestic violence. Women's groups have also impacted the education system and campaigned for child care. Although the red-hot issue of abortion rights is mainly a matter of state and national policy, women's groups are active on that issue with local health and social service agencies and lately in protecting access to abortion clinics being blockaded by protesters.

Other Groups

Although the groups discussed thus far are the most common ones in local politics, a variety of others take part in many communities. In big cities and some small ones as well, gay and lesbian groups, like other minorities, campaign against discrimination and often complain about police practices. In some places, religious groups have gotten involved in such issues as gay rights and abortion. More liberal church groups have been active with AIDS projects, providing food and shelter for the homeless, and improving race relations. Church groups also take an interest in local education policy since many operate schools themselves. Age groups have also become active in community politics in recent years. Some church groups work with senior citizens, another group that has become more active and vocal recently as the number and needs of elders have increased.

Reform groups have played a significant role in most cities at some point in their history, particularly in the movement against political machines. Their vestiges remain in many communities, continuing the fight for good government. Those words are often in the group's name. The League of Women Voters is perhaps the most common reform group found in U.S. cities. Reform issues for the 1990s include ethics, campaign funding, opening meetings to the public, controlling bureaucracies, and sometimes changes in government structures such as stronger mayors or district elections. Reformers in many metropolitan areas advocate the creation of a regional government to deal with issues that can't be solved by the current fragmented array of cities and counties.

More conservative reform groups have campaigned to limit elected officials to two or three terms of office to increase turnover and hopefully responsiveness. This reform is particularly popular among taxpayer associations, which normally concentrate on fighting tax increases of any sort. Most common in suburbs and the Sunbelt, these groups are usually small and often eccentric—some seem to consist of just a couple of old guys who like to harangue elected officials at public meetings and are often dismissed as cranks. Yet by opposing taxes when more established groups will not, they often strike a chord with the voters, as the national tax revolt proves.

Housing groups are active in some communities, although housing is a transient issue for most people. That is, once they have their own, most people quit worrying about it. Realtors and landlords (business groups, really) are organized in most communities, however, and in some, so are renters. Rent control (limits on how much landlords can charge) was a hot issue in many communities in the 1970s and 1980s. Less common are groups advocating the construction of housing for low-income people. Builders and unions may advocate development, but rarely for those most in need of shelter. Groups campaigning for the homeless, however, emerged as that problem grew in U.S. cities in the 1980s and 1990s.

Cultural and recreational groups supplement all these participants in local politics. Many communities fund activities ranging from opera to square dancing or from soccer to tennis. Often such allocation of funds is the result of group advocacy, and the continuation (or expansion) of funding is actively pursued by groups formed to do just that, giving important clientele support to the bureaucratic agencies that oversee or provide the service. The interests of these groups are, of course, quite narrow, yet they can marshall considerable resources when they feel threatened.

Many other sorts of groups operate in communities, although often only briefly. Sometimes other governments even act like interest groups, seeking to influence a local governing body through the use of group tactics such as lobbying. Urban areas in the United States are characterized by multiple governments and a high degree of fragmentation. Sometimes one government needs to petition another to coordinate policies. School districts, for example, often address city councils on proposed developments since they have to provide schools for the new growth. But while they may be acting like groups, the range of tactics available to these governmental petitioners is limited.

Interest Group Tactics

The groups we've just surveyed have varying political resources and apply them in a varying ways with varying degrees of success. Groups with substantial and diverse resources, such as money, prestige, leadership, and organization, are able to use more of the **tactics** described below and are more likely to succeed, while those with more limited resources find themselves limited in the range of tactics available and, often, in their efficacy as well. But groups have to use what they've got, and use enough of it to get what they want—or lose. They also need to make careful strategic decisions about which tactics to use, avoiding both overkill and overconfidence.

Public Hearings

The most common and visible group tactic is attendance and testimony at **public hearings** by the city council or other appropriate local governing body. This is also the group tactic that we can most readily observe and evaluate.

Effective groups systematically monitor council agendas to watch for items of interest to them. Contacts inside city hall (sympathetic representatives or staff) often give groups notice that such items are coming up. Occasionally, groups manage to take the offensive and place items on a council agenda themselves, thus gaining the advantages of framing the issue and controlling timing. But, usually, groups learn that a subject of interest is coming up a week or two in advance and must quickly decide how to respond.

Well-established groups confident of victory may only need to send a representative or two to observe the meeting and perhaps speak on the issue. But no matter how confident they are, it is important that their representatives be present and visible. To fail to attend insults the decision-makers, leading them to conclude that the issue is insignificant to the group and even that they might be able to make concessions to the opposition (if there is one).

Less confident groups need to send not only representatives but troops. Packing the chambers is a time-honored group technique to show both the strength of feeling within the group and its numerical (voting) strength. Once a group is well established, turning out the troops is not always necessary, but decision-makers grow suspicious of advocates who pretend to speak for many when they represent only themselves, so shrewd group leaders will get their members to meetings now and then just to remind the decision-makers that the group has "legs" (people willing to work). Packing the chambers is also a good way to keep up the internal morale of the group, especially when victory is assured.

At the meeting, groups balance factual argument with emotion and sometimes veiled political intimidation. The testimony of a really angry citizen can be just as persuasive as the most factual presentation because it shows intensity of feeling. Overt political threats, however, usually back-fire. Able groups often choose a few speakers who represent the range of their membership (old/young, majority/minority, male/female, and so on), delegating each to emphasize a particular point and instructing them to be brief. Groups that go on at length and repeat points gain no advantage, but leaders cannot always control their followers when a forum is available. The presentation of petitions, circulated by group members in their neigh-borhoods or elsewhere, is often a feature of public hearings. Well-organized groups will also prime decision-makers in advance with phone calls, postcards, or letters from supporters.

A public hearing is sometimes a real decision-making forum, but more often the meeting is a performance, with decision-makers going through the motions of listening while citizens and interest groups go through the motions of giving testimony. This is because most issues have been kicked around long enough that the decision-makers already have their minds made up. Effective interest groups will have talked to them and counted their votes in advance. That doesn't mean that the perfor-mance at the public meeting is irrelevant. It is an essential part of the decision-making process in most communities; groups that disdain it will lose.

On the other hand, citizens and groups that rely solely on what happens at the public meeting are likely to lose, too—unless they are totally unopposed. The public hearing is the end of the process. Leaving their participation to this point often means it comes too late. The sight of disgusted citizens shaking their heads as they leave a meeting is all too common. They are disappointed to have lost, but they may well have been naive (or idealistic), assuming that decisions really are made at meetings. To assure their influence, groups must find ways of taking part before the public hearing—or risk losing.

Lobbying

The expression *to lobby* comes from the activity of group representatives in the lobbies of legislatures, including those of the local government. You can see it happen in the corridors of city halls before meetings. But, more often, **lobbying** is done in private meetings between group representatives and decision-makers. Designated group members meet with the decision-makers in their offices and talk about issues that are coming up. Sometimes they invite a decision-maker to come to a meeting of the group, a good way to show numerical strength as well as concern about the issue.

Such lobbying almost invariably focuses on the merits of the issue, with groups presenting factual arguments. Political threats (support in coming elections) can easily backfire, so groups generally avoid making them explicit. Besides, politicians are shrewd enough to figure out when they risk alienating groups—taking into account both how strongly a group seems to feel about a particular issue and the alternatives available to the group. As with the public hearing tactic, able groups carefully choose their delegations to lobby decision-makers. They also tailor their arguments to suit the person they are lobbying. Most lobbyists also provide the decision-maker with a succinct written summary of the group's arguments.

Schmoozing

Groups also gain influence through social contacts between their leaders and decision-makers. Such **schmoozing** happens before and after meetings, over coffee or drinks, and at political events such as fundraisers attended by both officials and group leaders. It also happens when paths cross, which they often do. Most communities have a bar or restaurant frequented by political insiders, including elected officials, administrators, and group representatives. These insiders also frequent community institutions such as the symphony or sports teams.

Group representatives knowingly exploit these opportunities, although they do not necessarily engage in explicit persuasion. Schmoozing mostly enables them to show knowledgeable sympathy with the decision-makers and to keep relations friendly, even if they disagree on issues. Sometimes, schmoozing shortcuts the process of influence. A group representative might point out that an issue is coming up soon and ask if the decision-maker has any problems with it or if a meeting is needed. The decision-maker will indicate agreement or difficulty, and the lobbyist can decide whether to shift into a higher gear (but probably not where the schmoozing is in progress).

Campaigns

Groups prime their contacts by supporting sympathetic candidates in **election campaigns.** Financial contributions are a key element of campaign support, but groups also endorse and provide volunteers for candidates. Endorsement is usually done by a committee, based on knowledge about the candidate or, often, on questionnaires and interviews. Group endorsements are much valued by candidates desperate for support from any quarter—especially in nonpartisan elections. Endorsements usually mean money and volunteers, but they also help legitimize candidates and are often used in campaign literature. Volunteers help get the word out and cut the costs of campaigns, so groups such as labor unions and minority or feminist organizations that can turn out their members may compensate for their lack of money (although all these groups also raise funds for their chosen candidates). Giving money nevertheless remains the major campaign tactic of interest groups and as the costs of local campaigns have risen, so has the influence of group contributors. In small communities, however, money doesn't count for quite so much.

Some groups—notably neighborhood and homeowner associations and reform groups such as the League of Women Voters—avoid campaign activity, remaining strictly impartial. Often, however, individual members of such groups will support candidates, thus assuring access while preserving the group's neutrality.

Direct Participation

Most local governments have numerous boards and **commissions** made up of citizens who advise them on various issues and sometimes even make final decisions. Some of these **citizen participation** mechanisms date back to the progressive reform movement and more were established during the 1960s and 1970s to counteract the power of bureaucracies, often in response to group pressure. Some, such as planning, transportation, human rights, or senior citizens commissions, are relatively permanent; others, such as a committee to review a city's general plan or a task force on gangs, might be temporary working groups. Some cities, including Birmingham, Dayton, New York, Portland, and Saint Paul, have district boards or councils to advise on neighborhood issues.[5] Although a few of these are elected positions, most are appointed by city councils or county boards.

Naturally, interested groups lobby hard and compete vigorously with one another to get one of their members appointed to citizen participation bodies that deal with their concerns. Various neighborhoods, environmental groups, business interests, and labor unions might vie for a seat on the planning commission, for example, while groups representing homosexuals, women, business, or different neighborhoods and minorities might contend for a place on the police commission. The winners assume a more formal role in making decisions that affect them as well as increasing their credibility and their access to other decision-makers and to information.

A few groups get even more involved by contracting with local governments for the coproduction of particular services, such as running a community center or a homeless shelter. Chambers of commerce sometimes operate convention or tourist bureaus for cities in this way.

Public Relations, Direct Democracy, and Litigation

Besides all these sorts of insider tactics, groups sometimes resort to other means, including public relations, direct democracy, litigation, and protest politics. All of these, however, are riskier, more difficult, and costlier, either in dollars or in public sympathy.

Public relations involves going over the heads of the decision-makers and trying to win public support for the group's case. Ads in newspapers or on television, mailings, and public meetings might be used. Press releases and staged events can gain free news coverage. If all else fails, most newspapers assiduously publish letters to the editor. Groups also try to lobby the editorial boards of newspapers to win their endorsement. Public relations tactics are rarely used, however, because it is so difficult both to win public sympathy and motivate action (letter writing or attending public hearings). Besides, decision-makers don't like it when groups go over their heads.

In many states and communities, the progressive reformers gave the voters a direct say in their governance through the devices of the initiative, referendum, and recall. Actually, voters rarely take any of these actions spontaneously. Most of the time, the tools of **direct democracy** are used by interest groups with the organization, skills, and money to conduct sometimes rigorous petition drives and the expensive election campaigns that follow. Interest groups prefer the easier, insider techniques discussed above, but direct democracy offers them one more option that they have proven adept at using.

Similarly, groups litigate, or take issues to court, when they can and when they must. Failing to get their way by other means, groups may find ways of questioning the legality of a governmental action. A court case could, at best, reverse the action. But astute groups know that legal action may usefully delay implementation of a policy. Even the threat of **litigation**—with all its delays and expenses—may be enough to win compromises useful to the group.

Protest

A less socially accepted though common means of exercising group influence is through **protest** actions such as demonstrations, marches, rallies, sit-ins, and strikes. Such actions may be about dangerous crosswalks, closure of popular public facilities, police practices, abortion, or civil rights. Protest sometimes escalates to civil disobedience, which entails the intentional violation a law with the expectation of arrest. Such actions may be taken because the law itself is held to be bad (segregation, for example), to show intensity of feeling (parading without a permit), or to prevent an event (blockading abortion clinics). At its most extreme, protest may involve violence. Abortion clinics have been attacked, for example, and some community activists and political leaders emphasize the political significance of the 1992 Los Angeles riot by describing it as an uprising. Such violence is condemned by most practitioners of protest politics, however.

As the distinction between a riot and an uprising suggests, protest is not always an effective group tactic because the message and its targets may be unclear even when the protests are peaceful and lawful. Also, protests often express general discontent rather than focusing on specific policy goals that decision-makers can act on. Decision-makers may feel threatened by the protesters, who may be aiming more at public opinion anyway. Even then, their message may be unclear because the organizers can't control the way their message is filtered by the media, which may focus on the most bombastic speakers rather than the real leaders, or which may present the protest in a negative way to an already suspicious or hostile public.

Despite the role protest has played in U.S. history since before the Boston Tea Party, it has never been accepted in mainstream politics. Protest is an outsiders' tactic and often the last resort of groups that have no alternative. It may be ineffective because of its ambiguity and public hostility, but it can also be effective, at least over the long run. The civil rights movement is the best example of successful, long-term protest, but not the only one. Saul Alinsky, the renowned community organizer, was a flamboyant advocate of protest politics, not least because such events can be fun and can help build essential solidarity in a group, a result he thought as important as any policy outcome.[6]

The Targets of Group Influence

Interest groups try to influence whoever makes decisions that affect them. The primary **targets of group influence** are formal decision-makers such as mayors and city councils, but discerning groups are well aware of alternative and supplementary targets. In addition to elected officials, groups try to influence aides, administrators, and appropriate commissions and committees. Outside city hall, their targets may include other groups, the media, the public, and powerful individuals.

Inside City Hall: Staff, the Bureaucracy, Commissions, and Committees

In large cities, mayors and, increasingly, council members, hire their own personal staffs to assist them. Groups soon learn that these aides have an important influence over their bosses, and court them assiduously. Bureaucrats are also prime targets, although they are often and wrongly thought to be beyond group influence. Some group tactics are not applicable to them, but appointed administrators such as city managers and department heads may be as much politicians as elected officials are. Civil servants, secure in their jobs, are even less susceptible but are still subject to influence. Bribery is possible, though increasingly rare. More often, groups try to win the sympathy of administrators by persuasion, playing on the expertise of the administrators with their own expertise. Many groups also manage to find sympathizers inside the bureaucracy who help them with both tactical and factual information.

Groups also target commissions and committees. Dozens of these citizen participation bodies operate in most local governments, advising elected officials on a wide range of issues. Groups may pave the way to victory when the issue reaches these elected officials by winning the support of the commissions and committees (as well as appropriate administrators) early in the process. Tactics for influencing these bodies include public hearings, lobbying, and schmoozing. As previously noted, groups also try to get their members appointed to commissions that concern them (builders on the planning commission, public employee unions on the civil service commission, for example).

Some groups, especially those representing economic interests, also hire former elected officials, aides, administrators, and commissioners to represent them. The **revolving door** between city hall and interest groups has resulted in what political scientist Peter Lupsha calls a mediator/ consultant class, providing access to developers and corporations and "linking" them to elected officials.[7] Fearing payoffs and conflicts of interest, some local governments have tried to inhibit this phenomenon by prohibiting, for a fixed period of time, ex-officials from working for groups whose interests they formerly decided on.

Outside City Hall: Other Groups, the Media, the Public, and Community Influentials

The broader the support for an issue, the more likely it is to win approval, so groups often court one another to win endorsements for causes or active participation. Sometimes one group (a labor union or the chamber of commerce) will have better access to particular decision-makers than others, so alliance also increases lobbying and schmoozing opportunities. The most ubiquitous **coalitions** in local politics are the growth machine (landowners, developers, and related businesses) and the opposing anti-growth coalition (environmentalists and neighborhood groups). In big cities, minority groups have formed coalitions with one another and with liberals and sometimes with Jewish voters to elect African American and Latino mayors.[8] Women's groups, neighborhoods, and unions have joined them in some places to campaign for district elections. Where a coalition cannot be created, one group may lobby others to neutralize their opposition by making a proposal seem less threatening or even by tactful compromise.

The support of the local media, public opinion, and powerful individuals may also help. Reporters and editors can be schmoozed and lobbied, encouraging positive news coverage and sympathetic editorials. Visual events can be staged and timed for television. Sound bites can be called in to radio stations. Such coverage gives an issue urgency, makes the group and its cause more credible to decision-makers, and may also win public support. Such support is usually a mushy source of group clout at best, but sometimes groups need public opinion behind them to push decision-makers to act. Public relations or protest tactics may be used, or sympathetic media coverage may be sought. The problem, as previously noted, is that even a sympathetic public is hard to move to action. Lastly, groups try to win support from powerful people in their communities, outside as well as inside government.

Allies, whether other groups, the media, the public, or powerful individuals, help interest groups achieve their short-term goals and integrate them with the larger community, making them players in its decisions and assuring their long-term interests. Mayors, council members, and other elected officials will always be the primary targets of interest groups, but we should be aware of these others as well—successful interest groups certainly are.

Patterns in Group Politics

All groups are not equal and all tactics are not equally effective. Nor is the activity of interest groups identical in all communities. Particular groups or tactics may succeed in some communities but not in others, and while some communities are fraught by group politics, others are almost free of group activity. Still, despite wide variation, some **patterns in group politics** can be discerned.

Variation among Communities

Better-off and better-educated people are more likely to belong to interest groups. They are more likely to know how local politics affects them because of their education and access to information and because they possess the resources to participate, including time and money for dues and baby-sitters. In any community, they are the most active participants and, in any community, those who are active are most likely to get what they want. The unorganized and inactive are safely ignored by decision-makers.

But while the better off and better educated are more likely group activists, as with voting, this generalization does not predict the pattern of group activity among communities. Places populated predominantly by the affluent and well educated tend to have low levels of group activity because of a lack of competition and a high degree of consensus. Communities with more varied class and ethnic interests have considerably more vital group activity, for even though the poor and minorities are less likely to organize than the affluent and well educated, they sometimes do so and, faced with competition, those normally likely to organize assuredly do.

Like so much else in local politics, group activity in a community reflects its demographic, social, and economic makeup. Larger, dense, diverse cities have more group activity than smaller, less dense, homogeneous communities. Density—sheer proximity—makes organizing easier and may also create problems that precipitate organization, such as traffic congestion or poor sanitation. Diversity, which is closely related to size, is an even greater factor in group formation, providing a variety of sources of organization ranging from class and occupation to race, ethnicity, sexual orientation, and life-style. What's more, when one interest in a diverse community organizes, others follow, either to protect their interests or to pursue their piece of the pie. Group organizing has a proliferating or snowball effect.

The highest levels of interest group activity, then, are found in large, dense, diverse communities, especially those with high degrees of ethnic and economic diversity. Stable communities (those where people stay put for a long time) also have more group activity, simply because people have to live in a place for a while before they begin to perceive how local politics affects them and make connections with others with shared interests. Since all these characteristics are strongest in Frostbelt cities, group activity there tends to be greater than in their Sunbelt counterparts. Whether Frostbelt or Sunbelt, however, communities in economic or social crisis tend to have more group activity, although it may be ephemeral. Interest groups are less active in smaller, lower density, homogeneous communities. Because they are less diverse, these communities have fewer competing interests and their shared interests are easier for their local government to reflect. Most suburban communities fall into this category. Because they are more consistently affluent than big cities, they also have fewer problems. "Local politics is groupless politics," Paul Peterson wrote, with organized groups having only a "marginal impact," but the sort of local politics he was writing about is in "nonpartisan suburbia," not big cities.[9]

Winners and Losers

Within these patterns of group politics in communities, some groups are consistently winners, confident and successful in obtaining their goals, while others feel frustrated and marginalized, consistently losing. **Political resources** and their skillful use determine a group's success. Such resources include leadership, organization, number of members, status (the esteem in which both individual members and the group itself are held in the community), contacts (in and out of local government), information, and, of course, money. The greater and more diverse the resources of the group, the more tactics they can apply. Such tactics as public relations, direct democracy, campaign contributions, or litigation are not available to most grassroots groups, for example.

Of all these group resources, money is the most important because it can buy the others and because it widens the range of tactics available. Money also gives a group staying power, the ability to persist over a long period of time. While some groups fade away as soon as their issue is resolved, persistent groups are able to protect their victories or outlast their opposition when they lose. For these reasons, economic groups, from chambers of commerce to small business associations and big corporations, are most successful. They have greater financial resources and social respectability than other groups, so they can build access and maintain it more easily. And because they are founded on the fundamental human motivation of greed, they are persistent. The membership of grassroots organizations, such as neighborhood, minority, or environmental groups, may outnumber that of economic groups, but the shared interests that glue these groups together are almost never as strong or as lasting as those of business. The fact that their interests overlap those of the local government gives business groups an added advantage. Local governments gain additional taxes from growth and business expansion, so all these interests have to do is show that their proposals add to the local economy and thus the tax base. No wonder the growth machine and other economic interests are so successful in local politics.

Groups, Communities, and Power

Interest group activity, like so much else we have considered in local politics, both reflects and influences communities. The pattern of group activity in a particular community reflects its very nature, while at the same time the activity of groups shapes the community, especially when they successfully promote growth. As we have seen, some groups are more powerful than others. In the next chapter, we will consider power in communities more generally.

ESSENTIAL
TERMS

interest groups	lobbying
business groups	schmoozing
labor groups	election campaigns
labor council	commissions
neighborhood or homeowner groups	citizen participation
	public relations
NIMBY	direct democracy
Common Interest Developments, (CIDs)	litigation
	protest
coproduction	targets of group influence
ethnic and racial groups	revolving door
environmental groups	coalitions
women's groups	patterns in group politics
tactics	political resources
public hearings	

FIELDWORK 1. Attend a series of city council or commission meetings (on your own or as part of a research team) to observe and inventory interest group activity. What sorts of groups are most active? Which are most successful?

2. Interview interest group leaders (found at council meetings or through library research). What local policies affect the groups? What are their resources and tactics? What sorts of groups do they say are most active and successful in your community?

3. Attend a meeting of an interest group such as your local labor council, chamber of commerce, or neighborhood association. Which issues discussed are related to local politics or policies?

NOTES

[1]Mike Davis, *City of Quartz* (London: Vintage, 1992), p. 161.

[2]See Matthew A. Crenson, *Neighborhood Politics* (Cambridge, MA: Harvard University Press, 1983); or Jeffrey M. Berry, Kent E. Portney, and Ken Thomson, *The Rebirth of Urban Democracy* (Washington, DC: Brookings Institute, 1993).

[3]Davis, note 1, p. 210.

[4]See Joyce Gelb and Marilyn Gittell, "Seeking Equality: The Role of Activist Women in Cities," in Janet K. Boles, ed., *The Egalitarian City* (New York: Praeger, 1986), pp. 93–109; or Janet A. Flammang, ed., *Political Women* (Beverly Hills, CA: Sage, 1984).

[5]See Berry et al., note 2.

[6]See Saul Alinsky, *Rules for Radicals* (New York: Vintage, 1971).

[7]Peter Lupsha, "Structural Change and Innovation: Elites and Albuquerque Politics in the 1980s," in Clarence Stone and Heywood T. Sanders, ed., *The Politics of Urban Development* (Lawrence: University Press of Kansas, 1987), p. 236.

[8]See Rufus Browning, Dale Rogers Marshall, and David Tabb, *Racial Politics in American Cities* (New York: Longman, 1990).

[9]Paul Peterson, *City Limits* (Chicago: University of Chicago Press, 1981), pp. 116, 118.

11

Community Power Structures: Official and Unofficial Decision-Makers

P ower is the ability to make something happen—or to stop it from happening. Power is an element of politics that has come up in almost every chapter in this book, from the formation of local governments to their structures and the roles of voters and interest groups. As we have seen, many struggles within local politics are as much about who will exercise power as they are about what will be done with it. At this point, we need to pull back from studying particular elements of community politics to look briefly at their relative influence in terms of power.

The arrangement of power within a community is called a **power structure.** This differs from the structure of government in that all power is not held by the public officials. Interest groups, for example, play a part not only in decisions about policy, but also, through their involvement in campaigns and elections, in choosing who makes those decisions. Even the formal structures of local government that allocate power have been fought over by those affected outside government, from the municipal reformers to minority groups and progrowth and antigrowth coalitions. These formal structures of government reflect informal local power structures, with unofficial powers (economic, class, or ethnic groups, for example) seeking to shape the official structures of power to their lasting advantage. The most powerful (and able) elements win, shoring up their informal power with formal, or official power. Once a set of governmental structures is in place, it is frozen for years, even decades. But almost inevitably, it is challenged when the informal balance of power within the community shifts. As new forces emerge, seek influence, and face frustration, they conclude that they must contest the formal structure of power, demanding changes that will enable them to advance their own causes. The battle over district and at-large elections, from reform to counterreform, is a case in point. But the forces of change could never succeed in altering the formal structures of government if they had not already taken their place in the informal power structure.

Power, then, operates both inside and outside government. Most of us know intuitively that some people and interests have more power than others. Which are most powerful in our own communities? Are there patterns among communities? These questions have been addressed and argued over by social scientists for decades and, while their conclusions are far from final, they offer rich insights. Their theories and findings are not merely of esoteric, academic interest, however. Citizens also need to know who really rules their communities. We need to know not only in order to understand local politics, but also to participate, since knowing who holds power will shape our tactics and strategy. The study of community power gives us clues.

The Phenomenon of Power

Although defining power is easy enough, studying it is not, for power is complicated and multidimensional. Consider, for example, the varied sources of power. One might be physical strength, including muscle, guns, and armies. But official positions like those of monarchs and mayors are also a source of power, as are money, prestige, command of information, and personal charisma. A related but distinct dimension of power is the means by which it is exercised. Brute force—the power of a mugger—is the most obvious such means. Authority might be seen as institutionalized force. It is the ability of those in an official position of power (parent, teacher, police officer, city council) to order us to do something and penalize us if we refuse or if we do something they have prohibited. A more subtle means of exercising power than force or authority is influence. It means you do what others want you to do not because they make you do it but because you respect or fear them enough to comply. Influence is partly the result of socialization, the process by which parents, schools, and the media teach us the basic values and acceptable behaviors of our society. Among the ideas communicated are who has power and who should be respected and obeyed. Socialization is most effective when it teaches us to anticipate the responses of those in power so we act as they would wish without being asked or ordered. Related to the means of exercising power, and particularly to the accumulation of power, are two additional dimensions, scope and cost. Each of us has some power, although some have more than others. Those with the most power may influence a wide range of issues (scope) at little cost to themselves. Only a word, a gesture, a signature on a check may be necessary. Those with little power may influence a narrow range of issues, perhaps concerning their neighborhood or job, at greater sacrifice (in time, money, energy, and so on) to themselves.

With varying sources, means, scope, and cost, power is clearly a multidimensional phenomenon, and thus hard to study. Although researchers agree that patterns in the exercise of power emerge, forming a power structure, no one has yet invented an infallible method to measure it. There is no machine, like a Geiger counter, which can be pointed at an individual or institution to gauge their power. Social scientists have developed plenty of theories about power, explaining how it works and predicting patterns. But the next step is to develop methods to test these theories by collecting factual data. If the method is objective, it will prove or disprove the theory, but methods can be flawed. The wrong questions may be asked or the wrong sources used. The method may even be slanted or biased to prove the theory. Of course, if the method is imperfect, so are the findings. This is especially a problem with a subject as complex and multidimensional as power. No wonder social scientists have argued about it for so long. But we need not resolve the social science dispute about how to study power. For our purposes, reviewing the various approaches lends insight to the workings of power in communities in general as well as in specific communities.

One common element of the study of power has been the focus on individual communities, or case studies. Researchers initially tried to generalize from particular communities to the universe of communities but later came to see that power structures varied from community to community and even in one community over time. Thanks to hundreds of studies of single communities, we can now make some generalizations and even predictions about patterns of power in communities. But in addition to increasing our understanding of local politics and power in general, power studies help the residents of our communities understand their own local political systems by revealing who holds power, whether inside or outside government.

The Evolving Study of Community Power

For centuries, political scientists mainly studied the formal structures of government and tended to overlook the forces that shaped and influenced those structures. In terms of the multidimensional nature of power, traditional political scientists concentrated on authority rather than the other, more subtle manifestations of power. This focus began shifting when Marxist and other theorists on the left asserted that power was found in the class structure and that government was only a tool of the dominant classes. Then, when some political machines survived or adapted to reform, social scientists (many of whom were active reformers) learned that changing the structure of government does not necessarily change the distribution of power in a community. Later, systems theory gave social scientists impetus to examine power in a broader sense. **Systems theory** is based on the idea of a political system as an organism with interdependent parts interacting within a larger environment. Governmental structure is only one part of the system, acted upon and in turn acting upon the society in which it functions. By opening the door for the inclusion of virtually anything that affected political decisions, systems theory took political scientists considerably beyond government structure. At about the same time, behavioralism—the study of how and why people behave as they do—also encouraged social scientists to examine politics outside of government.

Elitism

The first studies of community power were done by sociologists applying what came to be called **stratification theory,** the idea that societies are stratified into layers or classes and that these strata are distinguished by such characteristics as wealth, prestige, and power. Since these resources are not distributed equally, some have more than others. Early researchers, most notably Robert and Helen Lynd who did pioneering studies of Muncie, Indiana, in the 1920s and 1930s[1], found that stratification did reflect the power structures of their subject communities. The upper class had a virtual monopoly on prestige and money and, with these, ruled the community. Political officeholders were controlled by those with economic power, and the public was passive. The elite, the Lynds wrote, maintained its power through "the pervasiveness of the long fingers of capitalist ownership" and "the thick blubber of custom that envelop[ed] the city's life."[2] Other sociologists soon did similar studies and came up with similar findings.

Then, in 1953, Floyd Hunter's *Community Power Structure*,[3] a study of power in Atlanta, Georgia, was published. Undoubtedly the most influential work ever written about power in U.S. communities, social scientists are still both criticizing and imitating it. While power and politics had been only one component of the broad studies of community life done by earlier researchers (including the Lynds), Hunter chose to focus exclusively on power. He also tried to develop a rigorous method for researching power—one that could be used by anyone—to replace the subjective interviews and observations of earlier researchers. What came to be called the **reputational method** basically consists of the researcher asking a carefully selected series of local leaders who they think has power, why they have it, and how they use it.[4] Connections are then mapped to reveal the community's power structure.

Based on the power structure he unveiled, Hunter developed a theory that has been labeled **elitism.** Shaped like a pyramid, Atlanta's power structure was topped by a small group of businessmen, an elite upper class. Dominating the city's economy through a web of interlocking directorships, they lived in the same neighborhoods and belonged to the same exclusive clubs. According to the study, only four of Atlanta's forty most powerful people were public officials; the rest were bankers, manufacturers, and other business leaders. The members of the elite rarely held office and were not visible to the general public. Their power operated informally, with elected officials carrying out their bidding. Hunter and the sociologists who preceded him were pointing to a layer of power that had been ignored by other academics, particularly political scientists.

Pluralism

Not surprisingly, it was political scientists who led the reaction against Hunter and elitism. Alarmed that the subjects of their study—politicians and elected officials—were relegated to a secondary role by the sociological studies of power, political scientists dismissed Hunter's elite theory of power by criticizing his methodology. They disputed the way Hunter selected his interviewees as well as his questions. Instead of asking whether an elite existed, they asserted, Hunter asked who the elite was, making his study a self-fulfilling prophecy. Labeling his method reputational, the critics charged that Hunter relied too much on opinions and too little on the actual and observable exercise of power.[5] But while these charges have some merit, they oversimplify Hunter's method and overlook the fact that reputation is itself a political resource and may be the best indicator of the more subtle manifestations of power.

Not content with denouncing Hunter, the critics went on to develop an alternative method and theory. Robert Dahl and a group of fellow political scientists at Yale argued that nothing could be assumed about the distribution of power and that it should be studied by examining specific decisions on specific issues. Their **decisional method** of research relied on interviews, observation, and documentary evidence to discern who influenced decisions on selected controversial or key issues. If an elite ruled, the Yale researchers insisted, its preferences would consistently prevail.

Robert Dahl reported their 1958 research on New Haven, Connecticut, in his book *Who Governs,*[6] concluding that no power elite ruled New Haven. Rather, Dahl reported, power was widely distributed. Economic leaders were only one active group among many, and they were not particularly active at that. Dahl also found that the holders of power varied over time and from issue to issue. No single group dominated in all issue areas. In fact, different groups and individuals were active in different issue areas. The only common figures were the mayor and the appropriate bureaucracy for each issue, not the elite. Dahl recognized that some individuals and groups had more power than others and that business leaders had great potential power, but he argued that much of that power was unused. His theory came to be called **pluralism,** reflecting the idea of multiple points of power specialized by policy area.

Thus, political scientists produced a theory about power, a method for studying it, and a set of findings that differed substantially from those of sociologists. Where elitists saw power as centralized, pluralists saw it as diffused. Where elitists believed power was based on class structure, pluralists believed it was centered on the formal political structure. Where elitists studied power through opinion, pluralists studied it through behavior.

Naturally, the elitists defended themselves and attacked the pluralists and their methods. The pluralists selected the wrong decisions, their antagonists argued, choosing controversial issues that are the exception to the rule rather than decisions that are taken without public notice. The elite is most powerful, they insisted, not all powerful. They have more power than others in a community, but others have some, too. Sometimes, therefore, they are challenged and they may even lose—usually on precisely the sorts of controversial issues that the pluralists chose to study. Furthermore, the elitists argued, focusing on observable events and behavior provided only a simplistic and superficial view of the complicated exercise of power. The elite operates behind the scenes or through anticipated reactions, so its influence is not always readily observed. Perhaps more seriously, some decisions that affect a community are taken privately rather than by government, yet these were not included in the pluralist studies. Even more subtle is the elitist concept of the **nondecision,** whereby issues are kept off the public agenda entirely because of the anticipated reaction of elites (or sometimes voters). Particularly in communities with a single dominant industry or group of industries, local decision-makers may anticipate the reactions of these interests and so avoid decisions that would offend them.[7] Matthew Crenson's study of Gary, Indiana, for example, illustrates how local officials failed to confront the problem of air pollution out of fear of that city's main employer, the steel industry.[8]

Needless to say, the pluralists defended themselves against these charges, saying the elitists' views were based on self-deception and ideological bias. Dahl felt his critics were saying that if the overt rulers were not members of the economic elite, then researchers had to dig deeper to find the covert economic rulers, the true elite. But how, Dahl asked, could researchers study things that could not be studied—unconscious actions, anticipated reactions, and nondecisions?[9] The pluralists insisted that the exercise of power be empirically proven and that theories of power that could not be proven be discarded as unscientific. The elitists scoffed and said the pluralists had been duped by the politicians. Each lamented the other's bias.

Synthesis

By the mid-1960s, the two schools of thought appeared to be in stalemate, yet both had contributed to our understanding of power. The elitists alerted us to the less visible holders of power and its subtle exercise through informal consultation, anticipation, and socialization. The pluralists shifted the focus somewhat to behavior, insisting on the need to study specific actions. This insistence stimulated both adherents and antagonists of elite theory to be more explicit about how actual decisions were made. The pluralists also alerted us to the possibility of power varying over time and by issue. Their discussion of inertia, or unused resources—power held but not applied—helped explain why the upper class was sometimes not visibly active as well as why the general public often loses in a system that is ostensibly democratic.

But an irreconcilable gap remained between the two theories and their respective methods. Hundreds of communities have been studied by elitists or pluralists or both, yet the dispute has not been resolved. Indeed, the different methods may produce different results, as research applying both techniques has revealed.[10] These studies found that each method unveiled slightly different influentials. The reputational technique discovered the concealed leaders, while the decisional method found the nominal decision-makers, although there was substantial overlap in the names on the lists. Increasingly, researchers tried to combine the methods, reaching toward synthesis.

The achievement of synthesis, however, was limited by another aspect of community power studies: for practical reasons, most focused on just one community. Such case studies are instructive, but are they applicable to more than the community in question? Can researchers generalize and develop theories that pertain to other communities? The best way would be for a single research project to study many communities, but this has never been feasible, even if agreement could be reached on methodology.

Instead, scholars of community power have reached a sort of compromise by accepting that all communities may not have identical power structures and that power may vary from community to community. Perhaps Hunter's Atlanta really was elitist, and Dahl's New Haven really was pluralist (both studies are, after all, convincing). Other cities—as other studies have told us—might be more or less elitist or pluralist or somewhere in between. One might conceive of a **continuum of power,** then, at one end of which is a typical pluralist power structure and at the other a typical elitist power structure (see Figure 11-1). Communities might be placed at any point on the continuum (at either end, in the middle, or slightly closer to one end than the other), depending on the shape of each one's particular power structure. They might also move across the continuum over time, perhaps becoming more pluralist (as some people think Atlanta has done since Hunter's original study). Various social scientists

FIGURE 11-1   A Continuum of Power

PLURALIST ■■ELITIST

New Haven		City A		Atlanta
1958	City B	1957	Atlanta	1953
	1988		1980	

have generated such continua, sometimes with four or five different types or categories of power structures.[11]

Some political scientists believe that the power of the bureaucracy has grown so great that it constitutes a third alternative to the elitist and pluralist theories. With civil service job protection, public employee unions, technical expertise, and the exclusive power of day-to-day implementation of policy, bureaucracies may have attained power independent from both economic leaders and elected officials. Political scientists Robert Lineberry and Ira Sharkansky formulated a **triangular model of community power** with economic elites at one point, political leaders at another, and bureaucratic administrators at a third (see Figure 11-2).[12] Cities, they suggest, might gravitate toward one of the points in the triangle, depending on their historical situation.

The concept of a continuum, whether linear or triangular, is useful because it enables us to generalize broadly about power and communities and to include many theories and findings. We should bear in mind, however, that such generalizations may be simplistic, and that those who subscribe to traditional elite theory would be skeptical because the continuum tends to accept pluralist assertions that power varies in structure, over time, and between communities. Elitists insist that the only thing that varies is the composition of the upper class.

Explaining Variation in Community Power Structures

If we accept the idea of **variation in power structures** from community to community and/or over time, we are still left with the questions of why one

FIGURE 11-2   A Triangular Model of Power

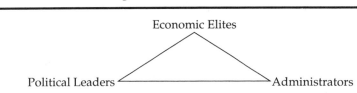

community is pluralistic while another is elitist or why a community grows more or less pluralistic over time. Past studies of communities and a measure of common sense provide some answers. Various researchers have developed the generalizations that follow,[13] but we should remembered that they point out tendencies that are not necessarily universal truths.

Size and Diversity

Size seems to be a major determinant of a city's power structure. Larger cities are more likely to have pluralistic power structures, not so much due to size per se but because largeness is associated with an increased potential for competition and conflict among varied groups. Smaller cities are less diverse and more easily dominated by a single major economic force. As cities grow, they diversify. The class structure grows more complex, the ethnic composition of the city becomes more elaborate, and special interest groups emerge. Some cannot be controlled by the dominant elite and may even challenge it, so competition and pluralism increase.

Economic Development

In general, as economic development increases, so does diversity and pluralism. If the community is dominated by a single industry, its power structure reflects this domination, tending to elitism, while economically diversified communities tend to pluralism. As economies develop beyond locally based commerce to include service and industrial sectors, new interests are introduced, bringing competition and greater pluralism. As communities industrialize, workers organize, and unionization may add another challenge to the ruling elite. Communities with strong unions tend toward pluralism, although it should be noted that unions, in general, have grown weaker rather than stronger in recent years.

Another element of the economic structure of communities pertinent to their power structures is **absentee ownership** or management of local industries. The managers and executives of branch operations of national corporations are less active in community politics than locally resident owners of local operations. The lives and careers of the executives of absentee-owned corporations are not connected to the community but to the corporation. They will advance by moving on, not staying in the community. Their political involvement will mostly be confined to issues of direct and specific concern to their corporation, such as getting necessary zoning approvals or gleaning goodwill. These executives tend to stay out of many local issues or to confine their political activity to support for the chamber of commerce or other locally based organizations. Home-owned industries, on the other hand, are led by locals. They have stakes in their community that go well beyond zonings and goodwill. They are part of the community and they won't be transferred to Houston or Tokyo next year, so their involvement in local politics is broader and more intense.

Corporate executives have great power when they choose to use it—especially if they threaten to move their operation elsewhere (a threat that lacks credibility coming from a locally owned business)—but because their interests are mainly outside the community, they exercise their power less. This leaves more room in the power structure for other interests, so communities with a high degree of absentee-owned, corporate industries tend to be more pluralistic. Those with predominantly locally owned industries whose owners and executives are more politically active tend to be more elitist.

The Structure of the Local Government

Another set of characteristics that indicates a city's location on the continuum of community power is the structure of its government. Cities with a reformed, council-manager form of government and nonpartisan, isolated, at-large elections tend to elitism, while those with an unreformed, mayor-council form of government with partisan, concurrent, district elections tend to pluralism. This may seem counterintuitive, because reform systems should be more open and democratic and unreformed cities usually had political machines that could be seen as a form of elitism. But reform structures often insulate government from the public. The chief executive is appointed rather than elected, and voter turnout is usually low. Traditional elites easily dominate or control such structures. A pluralistic power structure is more likely where the old-style structures bring higher voter participation and more accountable and diverse elected officials. Strong political parties help, too.

It is important to remember, however, that governmental structures do not appear out of thin air. At some time, somebody decides whether a city should be governed by a city manager or a mayor and how the city council should be elected. When those decisions are made, choices about power, access, and accountability are also made. Government structure thus reflects the community power structure.

The Political Culture

The shared values, traditions, myths, and accepted behaviors of a community constitute its **political culture.** These are maintained and passed on by socialization or the inculcation of ideas that affect our behavior. Included among these are such notions as "You can't fight city hall," or "The X family (or corporation) runs this town," or "What's good for business is good for the city." The values of the community affect which people are acceptable as leaders and who the leaders listen to and care about, as well as whether or not the public is active or passive in community decision making. In most U.S. communities, the people with the most prestige, and so the most power, are successful in business. Politicians and the public react to them with respect and thus give them power.

In pluralistic political cultures, a high value is placed on public participation, while elitist cultures may actively discourage participation. Pluralistic political cultures also accept and even welcome conflict and competition, while more elitist communities suppress them.

Patterns of Power

The combined characteristics of size, diversity, economic development, structure of government, and political culture all contribute to the shaping of a community's power structure and are in turn shaped by that structure. Knowing these characteristics of a community, we can make some good guesses about its power structure. But these variables also suggest **patterns of power** among cities across the country.

Larger cities tend to be more pluralistic, due to diversity and competition. Smaller communities incline to elitism, although this doesn't necessarily mean they are dictatorial or undemocratic. Often, such communities are homogeneous and have a high degree of consensus—agreeing on their leaders and supporting what they do. Dissident interests, however, are not welcome.

Sunbelt and Frostbelt

Besides size, a pattern is discernible in the power structures of central cities in the Sunbelt and Frostbelt. Dozens of formal and informal community power studies suggest that power in older Frostbelt cities is largely held by elites, while the newer Sunbelt cities are more pluralistic.[14] In the 1970s and 1980s, for example, elite leaders in the Frostbelt city of Indianapolis rammed through a transit system, a sports stadium, and a consolidated city-county government with no public vote and little consultation. Meanwhile in Sunbelt San Jose, an antigrowth coalition challenged the ruling elite, voters repeatedly rejected proposals for a stadium, and plans for regional government never got beyond the talking stage. This contrast is typical of Frostbelt and Sunbelt cities, but it is not simply a product of geography. It is related to the timing of the maturation of communities, their economic development, and the unique features of Sunbelt cities.

The key element is change: power structures are less entrenched in the Sunbelt because they are still new and in flux. Sunbelt central cities are young. Most were small and dependent on agriculture or oil, with few manufacturing or service industries, just 40 years ago. They grew explosively from the 1950s onward, not only because they had a good climate and room to grow, but more significantly because of the expansion of sectors of the economy such as energy, electronics, aerospace, and defense. Federal spending, Sunbelt boosterism, cheap land and energy, low taxes, and nonunion workers helped, too. Frostbelt cities, with higher costs on every count, lost out.

In the 1940s and 1950s—and well into the 1960s—most Sunbelt cities had well-established elitist power structures.[15] These were the boosters who brought growth and, ultimately, their own demise. For growth brought change—new interests and, eventually, new elites. Neighborhood, minority, and environmental groups challenged the old elite, often demanding changes in the (reformed) structures of government or control of growth. But while new grassroots interests gained influence and old elites faded away, new elites also emerged. Many were associated with the new energy, aerospace, electronics, and defense industries—national corporations heavily dependent on federal contracts and lacking local ties. Other new economic leaders emerged as national companies bought out department stores, banks, newspapers, television stations, and industries. These changes meant that much of the decision-making power of these communities, at least in terms of economics, was elsewhere. Old elites declined and grassroots groups gained. The communities, at least briefly, became more pluralistic. The new economic interests settled in, however, and began to assert their power. A new, corporate-based elite emerged, but although their potential power was great, they used it less because so many of their interests were beyond the community. The net result was a somewhat more pluralistic distribution of power. Frostbelt central cities, with more locally based economic interests, remained more elitist, although national corporations played their part in these communities as well.

The Movement Toward Pluralism

As this Sunbelt/Frostbelt contrast suggests, the cumulative effect of the characteristics associated with the shaping of community power structure—especially size, diversity, and economic development, which all increase together—seems to indicate movement in the direction of pluralism, or at least power structures in transition from relative elitism to relative pluralism. Virtually every change in these characteristics broadens participation; and nearly every one is related to growth, which may be the single strongest summarizing factor in altering a city's power structure. The irony is that although it is usually old guard elites that force growth on a community, they sow the seeds of their own destruction by facilitating the development of competing interests. Cities that are shrinking and decaying, however, may also grow more pluralistic because of the departure of economic elites. On the other hand, almost anything the remaining or new businesses want is eagerly granted.

As the foregoing suggests, most changes bring a decline in the power of the elite, and most are brought about by forces outside the community. New industries, new immigrants, new organizers—which may precipitate the reactive organizing of previously passive interests—all may challenge elites and, in so doing, push the power structure toward pluralism. Local elites have also been weakened by the federal government and its courts, which have extended the rights and electoral prospects of minorities, while states have regulated and limited the fiscal and land-use power of cities. The increasing autonomy of bureaucracies has eroded elite control, and the organization of minority and neighborhood groups has challenged elite policies on growth, government structure, and other issues.

But how pluralistic have power structures become when so many decisions are out of the control of individual communities? In a national corporate economy, industry locates where it pleases, with little commitment to particular communities. Federal, state, and regional authorities—all of which assert more and more control over local governments—are surely more susceptible to the influence of corporate economic interests than they are to that of communities. Such pluralism as U.S. communities enjoy may be merely the dregs of power.

Beyond Power Studies

Journalists and local researchers still do community power studies, but despite all they have taught us, power studies have fallen out of favor among social scientists, partly because of the methodological problems previously discussed. Additionally, social scientists criticize the tendency of community power studies to **focus on personalities** (naming names) rather than on the economic, social, and political institutions and structures that are the source of the individual's power. Moreover, since the heyday of power studies in the 1960s and 1970s, freeways, instant communications, and suburbanization have blurred the boundaries of once clearly self-contained communities so that it is now hard to know what case to study: the city? the county? the metropolitan area with its many governments?

But power studies are also somewhat out of fashion because of new ways of looking at local politics, especially that of political economy. Theorists who take this approach set aside the issue of whether communities are elitist or pluralist and focus on the question of why economic interests usually win in local politics. The expectation that economic interests prevail makes it tempting to dismiss these writers as neo-elitist, but their arguments are more subtle than that, and their major contribution is putting community power and politics into the broader framework of the national economy and relations between states and local governments. We are already familiar with Harvey Molotch's assertion that cities are growth machines through which local, "land-based" elites, "profit through the increasing intensification of land use of the area in which [their] members hold a common interest."[16] They compete for growth and investment with elites in other communities and use government to facilitate growth, usually supported by local businesses and newspapers. Molotch differs from elite theory in his suggestion that the main economic interest of community power holders will be land development. Other economic interests pursue benefits elsewhere, in state or federal tax, trade, or employment policies, for example. But land-based interests must act through local government because decision making about land is delegated to local governments by the states. Hence various economic interests are most active at that level of government that can benefit them most. "Some groups, more than others," observes Clarence Stone, "have strong and immediate incentives to play an active and on-going part in" local politics, and, equally significantly, "some groups, more than others, are valuable to city officials in meeting their governing responsibilities."[17]

Local officials are sympathetic to growth advocates because economic development is in their interest, too. As Paul Peterson points out, "economic prosperity is necessary for protecting the fiscal [tax] base of local government."[18] This diverts local governments from social programs such as job training or building low-cost housing, although many justify growth on the grounds that it will broaden the tax base and provide potential funding for just such programs. But as with land-use powers, the state structures the fiscal base of local governments, strictly limiting the sort of taxes they can collect. Primary among these is the land-based property tax. No wonder communities become growth machines. Not only is land use their major power, it is the major way that they can increase their tax base. The propensity to go for growth is given further impetus by competition from other cities pursuing the same developments. Cities across the country compete with one another for major industrial or governmental projects. Even cities that try to plan growth carefully often make exceptions to their own rules when a local industry threatens to move to a more cooperative venue or when nearby communities recruit developments that might well cause them traffic or other problems without benefiting their tax base. State laws on incorporation and annexation generally encourage such competition. But the competition extends beyond metropolitan areas, states, or even the nation. The internationalization of the economy now means that multinational corporations seek cheap labor, low capital costs, and access to larger markets all over the world—putting individual cities at an even greater disadvantage.

But like Floyd Hunter's power elite, the forces of growth are not omnipotent. Pluralists can take comfort that in many places an antigrowth **"countercoalition"**[19] of neighborhood groups, environmentalists, and sometimes minority organizations emerges to resist growth. Such counter-coalitions have had some success in the Sunbelt cities of San Francisco, New Orleans, Denver, and San Diego.[20] Increasingly autonomous local bureaucracies may also join the fray. Observing Albuquerque, political scientist Peter Lupsha notes that professional public administrators and bureaucrats "seek to provide a voice of moderation, future orientation, and professionalism" opposed to the short-term profit-seeking of the growth machine.[21] Countercoalitions often lose because the forces aligned against them and the way states structure the conflict are so overwhelming, but sometimes, if only briefly, they prevail or win a compromise. Such coalitions do best in rich, small communities (usually suburbs and often university towns such as Palo Alto and Austin) that can afford to let growth happen elsewhere. Most large cities cannot afford such a luxury.

Power in Perspective

These theorists sometimes make it sound as if local politics are pre-determined by larger forces, but none of them writes off the role of real people in communities. The early theorists focused on elites, while their latter-day counterparts concentrate more on how the economy and the state-imposed structures of local government affect community politics. But all acknowledge that these forces are not omnipotent; what elected officials and ordinary people do makes a difference, too. We've seen in earlier chapters that various elements play a part in local politics and power: the city council, the mayor and/or city manager, administrators and the bureaucracy, the voters, the media, and interest groups, from businesses and unions to neighborhoods and minority groups. Community power studies add to these by turning our attention to the informal, nongovernmental aspects of politics and power, and by putting all these in perspective, suggesting their relative influence. We gain not only a better understanding of politics in our own communities, but also of what we're up against if we want to achieve change.

ESSENTIAL TERMS	
power structure	triangular model of community power
systems theory	
stratification theory	variation in power structures
reputational method	absentee ownership
elitism	political culture
decisional method	patterns of power
pluralism	focus on personalities
nondecision	countercoalition
continuum of power	

FIELDWORK 1. Do an informal power study by asking people at a city council or other public meeting who the most powerful individuals or organizations in your community are. (Bear in mind that where you ask the questions, as well as who you ask, may bias your survey.)

2. Apply the community characteristics (size, diversity, economic development, structure of government, political culture) associated with power structures to your community by doing library research or asking appropriate people. What sort of power structure would the characteristics of your community predict?

NOTES

[1]Robert S. Lynd and Helen Merrell Lynd, *Middletown* (New York: Harcourt Brace and World, 1929); and *Middletown in Transition* (New York: Harcourt Brace Jovanovich, 1937).

[2]*Middletown in Transition*, p. 490.

[3]Floyd Hunter, *Community Power Structure* (Chapel Hill: University of North Carolina Press, 1953).

[4]See *Community Power Structure;* or chapter 2 of Philip J. Trounstine and Terry Christensen, *Movers and Shakers* (New York: St. Martin's Press, 1982).

[5]See Robert Dahl, "A Critique of the Ruling Elite Model," in Willis D. Hawley and Frederick M. Wirt, eds., *The Search for Community Power*, 2nd ed. (Englewood Cliffs, NJ: Prentice-Hall, 1974); or chapter 2 of Trounstine and Christensen, note 4.

[6]Robert Dahl, *Who Governs* (New Haven, CT: Yale University Press, 1961).

[7]See Peter Bachrach and Morton S. Baratz, *Power and Poverty* (New York: Oxford University Press, 1963).

[8]Matthew A. Crenson, *The Un-Politics of Air Pollution* (Baltimore: Johns Hopkins University Press, 1971).

[9]See Dahl, note 5.

[10]See Robert Presthus, *Men At the Top* (New York: Oxford University Press, 1964); or Delbert Miller, *International Community Power Structures* (Bloomington: Indiana University Press, 1970).

[11]See, for example, Frederick M. Wirt, *Power in the City* (Berkeley: University of California Press, 1974).

[12]Robert Lineberry and Ira Sharkansky, *Urban Politics and Public Policy*, 2nd ed. (New York: Harper & Row, 1978), p. 179.

[13]Ibid., pp. 182–186; and Terry Clark, *Community Structure, Power, and Decision Making* (Scranton, PA: Chandler, 1968).

[14]See Trounstine and Christensen, note 2, chapter 6.

[15]Ibid., chapters 4 and 6.

[16]Harvey Molotch, "The City as a Growth Machine," *American Journal of Sociology* 82, no. 2 (1976): 309.

[17]Clarence Stone, "The Study of the Politics of Urban Development," in Clarence Stone and Heywood T. Sanders, eds., *The Politics of Urban Development* (Lawrence: University Press of Kansas, 1987), p. 284.

[18]Paul E. Peterson, *City Limits* (Chicago: University of Chicago Press, 1981), p. 29.

[19]See Molotch, note 16, p. 328.

[20]See Richard E. DeLeon, *Left Coast City: Progressive Politics in San Francisco* (Lawrence: University of Kansas Press, 1992); or Susan S. Fainstein, Norman I. Fainstein, Richard Child Hill, Dennis Judd, and Michael Peter Smith, eds., *Restructuring the City* (New York: Longman, 1986).

[21]Peter Lupsha, "Structural Change and Innovation: Elites and Albuquerque Politics in the 1980s," in Stone and Sanders, note 17, p. 237.

PART IV

Budget Politics, Public Policy, and Regional Government

The community power studies discussed in the previous chapter give us a different perspective on local politics, as do the three broad and diverse subjects considered in the chapters that follow. Like power structures, budget politics, public policy, and regional government also summarize and review much of what we have studied so far. In terms of the model introduced in chapter 1, these might be seen as the outputs of the political system, the things that it does and the ways that it affects our lives. These outputs are produced by all the elements of local politics discussed thus far, but the process does not end here. The impact of these outputs on our lives and on the environment of the political system produces a response, or feedback, which is carried back to decision-makers, bringing the process full circle. This, too, is illustrated in the chapters that follow.

We begin with budget politics—or the getting and spending of money by local governments. Although the budget is a part of the formal political process, environmental factors, including local economic conditions and the actions of other governments, shape its possibilities and, as we will see, substantially constrain local options. And, of course, the spending set forth in local budgets comprises a set of outputs that affect not only life in the community but future budgets. The public policies examined in the following chapter, including education, welfare, crime, growth, and transportation, are more purely outputs, but again we will see how local governments are both influenced and constrained by their economic and intergovernmental environments and how their actions affect their circumstances. We conclude with a look at metropolitan regional government and politics. Properly speaking, this is not an output of local political systems, but more the sum of their parts. The current situation regarding regional governments—or their absence—is central to many issues in local politics, from the needs/resources dichotomy described in chapters 3 and 4 to the growth and transportation policies discussed in chapter 13. Regional government is appropriate to conclude with, not only because it sums up so much of what we have considered thus far, but because in one form or another, it is the future of local politics.

12

Budget Politics: The Getting and Spending of Money

N o single document tells more about a local government than its budget. A careful or even cursory examination of the annual budget of a city or county reveals its sources of funds and the way the money is spent. We can see what they do and to some extent how they do it. We can extrapolate aspects of local politics, including how a community's political energies are exerted in acquiring revenues and which programs have political support. Much about relations with other governments is also revealed. Budgets are, in general, a good way to get an overview of local government and politics anywhere.

But as crucial as they are, neither budgets nor budget politics are transparent or instantly comprehensible. They tell us where the money comes from and where it goes and give clues about the politics involved in both, but how easily the money is acquired and how well it is spent are not readily discernible, even to those directly involved. Often obscure and highly technical, budget politics are an insiders' game, best played by bureaucrats, experienced elected officials, and lobbyists. The public, community groups, and even the media tend to take little interest in budget making. When they do take part in the public hearings at the very end of the process, it is usually to object to cuts in their favored programs and it is generally too late.

But while the public rarely plays a major part in the budget-making process itself, it has had a significant impact on budgets through the tax revolt that swept the country over the last 20 years, rejecting new taxes, capping old ones, and electing budget-cutters such as Ronald Reagan to state and national office. Local revenues from taxes and intergovernmental aid shrank as a result of voter action, but other fiscal pressures also hit. The roller-coaster effects of inflation and recession in the national economy, which were beyond the control of local governments, cut into their tax bases and expanded their payroll costs as well as demands for social and other services. Partly in response to their own fiscal problems, the state and national governments passed on or mandated programs without providing adequate funding, even while the tax base for many local governments contracted, with industry shifting to the suburbs, Sunbelt, or other countries. Some cities and counties, especially in the Frostbelt, faced rising costs and declining revenues because of decay; others, mostly in the Sunbelt, found themselves unable to contend with rapid growth. Meanwhile, despite contracting revenues, continuing urbanization brought rising demands for local services, from transportation to public safety and social welfare.

Like other elements of local politics, the extent to which these pressures were felt varied greatly from place to place, as did their responses. This is partly because the tax resources of communities vary so much, both in their tax bases and the types of taxes states make available to them. Service demands vary, too, depending on the responsibilities allocated to different sorts of local government (see Table 4-2) and the characteristics of the communities themselves. As we know, the needs/resources dichotomy means that service needs and tax resources are not always congruent.

To further complicate matters, local governments often work with more than one budget, dividing their money into separate pots according to its sources and what it can be spent for. Primary among these and our focus here is the **operating budget,** which covers salaries, maintenance, and on-going expenses. Most local governments also have a **capital budget,** which allocates funds for major infrastructure projects such as roads, bridges, and buildings. Sometimes special programs such as redevelopment have separate budgets and funding sources as well. But whatever the budget's designation, the same officials usually decide how to spend it—and it all comes from the taxpayers.

Where the Money Comes From

Local governments get money for their operating budgets from three basic sources: taxes, charges and fees, and intergovernmental aid (see Figures 12-1, 12-2, and 12-3). They also obtain money by borrowing, although this is almost always restricted to capital expenditures and must be paid back from one of the three basic revenue sources. Each of these basic sources includes its own variations.

FIGURE 12-1   General Revenues of All U.S. Local Governments, 1990

Source: Advisory Commission on Intergovernmental Relations, *Significant Features of Fiscal Federalism*, vol. 2 (Washington, DC: U.S. Government Printing Office, 1992), p. 119.

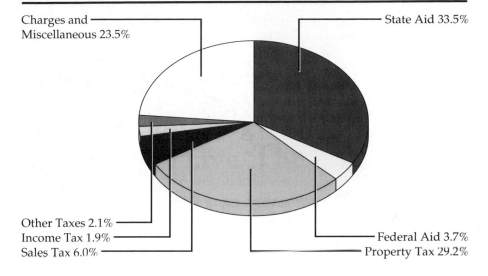

Charges and Miscellaneous 23.5%

State Aid 33.5%

Other Taxes 2.1%
Income Tax 1.9%
Sales Tax 6.0%

Federal Aid 3.7%
Property Tax 29.2%

The Property Tax

Historically, the biggest single source of local revenues was the real estate or property tax, which accounted for more than half of all local income and sometimes much more. Today it contributes considerably less, due to increased intergovernmental aid and to the tax revolt, which made the property tax its primary target. Nevertheless, the property tax accounted for 26.9 percent of local revenues in 1990. Its significance varied considerably, however, as Tables 12-1 and 12-2 reveal. School districts and counties, which are allowed little fiscal flexibility by states, depended on it most. Cities, however, relied on it for just half of their local tax revenues and for only 17.3 percent of their total income because they were able to generate funds from other taxes and from charges and fees. Nevertheless, the property tax remains a crucial source of local tax revenue. It is also controversial and unpopular.

Although in some places the **property tax** once extended to household goods and even pets, today it is generally limited to buildings and land. It works through state-regulated formulas that combine the estimated or assessed value of real estate with a tax rate. Valuations are usually done by a county tax assessor, who is often elected. The **assessed value** of property may reflect its approximate market value or only a percentage of it, depending on state rules. The **tax rate** is then applied to this, usually on the basis of a certain amount per $100 of assessed value

FIGURE 12-2   General Revenues of U.S. Counties, 1990

Source: Bureau of the Census, *City Government Finances, series* GF, no. 8, annual; *Statistical Abstract of the United States,* 1992, p. 297.

Charges and Miscellaneous 24.3%

Intergovernmental Revenues 39.8%

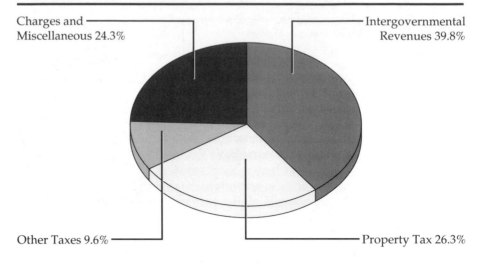

Other Taxes 9.6%

Property Tax 26.3%

FIGURE 12-3   General Revenues of U.S. Cities, 1990

Source: Bureau of the Census, *City Government Finances,* series GF, no. 4, annual; *Statistical Abstract of the United States,* 1992, p. 302.

Charges 16%

Property Tax 22%

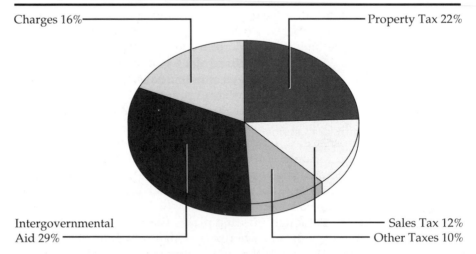

Intergovernmental Aid 29%

Sales Tax 12%
Other Taxes 10%

(AV). A $100,000 home assessed at 100 percent of market value, for example, might be taxed at $1.95 per $100 AV, for a total of $1950 in property tax. The same home assessed at 40 percent of market value might be taxed at $5.20 per $100 AV for a property tax of $2080. Assessments are subject to state guidelines, while tax rates are set by local governments—within limits

Table 12-1 Property Taxes as Percent of General Revenue by Level of Government

Year	All	Counties	Municipalities	Townships	School Districts	Special Districts
1962	48.0	45.7	44.2	65.3	51.0	25.0
1972	39.5	36.5	31.3	64.9	47.3	17.3
1982	28.1	26.6	21.4	52.1	35.8	9.5
1990	25.8	26.9	17.3	51.3	36.5	8.0

Source: Bureau of the Census, *Governmental Finances*, 1989–1990 and earlier years (Washington DC: U.S. Government Printing Office, 1990). Figures are for fiscal years ending in June.

imposed by states. The tax collected on a property is apportioned among the local governments with jurisdiction over it—usually a city, county, and school district.

Problems with the Property Tax. The most obvious problem that arises with this complex system is the **fairness of assessments.** This was a major issue in the past, when assessors affiliated with political machines used their evaluations to reward friends and punish enemies. Such worries have been resolved in most states by regulation and appeals procedures introduced by the progressive reformers, more frequent turnover of property, and computerization of real estate transactions. In others, such as Indiana, infrequent and amateur assessments are still a problem. Complaints still arise elsewhere, too, especially about the accuracy of assessments of industrial or other large properties that change hands less frequently than houses. If such properties are underassessed, the burden of the property tax falls more heavily on homeowners. Their burden is also increased by the exemption of some properties, such as churches, educational institutions, and government offices, from paying property taxes

Table 12-2 Property Taxes as Percent of Taxes by Level of Government

Year	All	Counties	Municipalities	Townships	School Districts	Special Districts
1962	87.7	93.5	93.5	93.3	98.6	100.0
1972	83.7	85.6	64.3	93.5	98.1	94.9
1982	76.1	77.2	52.6	93.7	96.8	79.6
1990	74.5	73.3	50.9	92.4	97.5	70.0

Source: Bureau of the Census, *Governmental Finances*, 1989–1990 and earlier years (Washington DC: U.S. Government Printing Office, 1990). Figures are for fiscal years ending in June.

even though they use city services. This is usually a minor problem, but it can be serious in capitol cities with many such institutions, such as Boston and Washington, D.C., where over half of all property is exempt. Tax delinquency is also a problem in inner cities and some poor suburbs where landlords sometimes abandon slum properties. Nonpayment averages 3 to 4 percent among large cities, rising to as much as 9 percent in Detroit.[1] Cities may take over and resell these properties, but they often have difficulty disposing of them.

Another concern with the property tax is that it is a **regressive tax**— the less affluent pay a higher proportion of their incomes in property tax than do the rich. A **progressive tax,** in contrast, falls more heavily on the rich; the income tax is intended to be such a tax. Of course, the less affluent pay smaller property tax bills in absolute terms because their homes are not as valuable as those of the rich. The regressivity results from the fact that the poor devote a bigger proportion of their income to housing and therefore to the property tax than do the rich. Half or more of the incomes of poor, working, and many middle-class people go to mortgages or rents. Those who are renters, as most low-income people are, may not even know they are paying the tax, since their landlords, who are responsible for it, merely calculate it into the rent. Higher income people may allocate a quarter or less of their income to housing. More are homeowners who are very conscious of their tax bill, even though it hurts them less. Many people think its regressivity makes the property tax unfair even when the homes of the rich and poor are fairly assessed. Others argue that its regressivity is balanced by the greater reliance of lower income residents on city services. More affluent people, however, are usually better organized and more able to achieve the services or tax cuts they want.

A more serious problem with the property tax as a primary source of local revenue is the way the governmental fragmentation of metropolitan areas structures the **needs/resources dichotomy,** with more affluent taxpayers and higher value property in independent suburban enclaves and the less affluent in central cities or inner suburbs. Each taxes the property within its boundaries, so a suburb with expensive homes but low service needs can tax lightly and still cover its expenses. Communities with lower value properties and higher service needs tax more heavily, raising their rates to generate enough revenue. Higher rates and bigger tax bills, however, drive businesses and affluent homeowners to the suburbs, necessitating even heavier taxes. The combination of fragmented government and the property tax also structures the **fiscal zoning** of land and helps make local governments into growth machines. Developing land is the way they generate property tax revenues, and the higher the value of the development, the greater the tax benefits. Local governments thus have a vested interest in growth, particularly if the projects are high in tax value but low in service requirements. They compete with one another for such projects—and to avoid low-cost housing for which service costs outweigh the taxes paid.

The Tax Revolt. According to public opinion polls, the property tax has long been the most hated of all taxes, making it the main target of the **tax revolt.** A combination of factors led to this targeting and ultimately to reduced property tax revenues for local governments.

In the 1970s, real estate speculation encouraged by federal tax laws combined with inflation was driving up home prices by 20 percent or more each year in some places, particularly in the Sunbelt. Modern assessment practices meant that these increases could be almost instantly included in tax calculations, so property tax revenues also rose with inflation in home prices, which was well above the overall inflation rate. Local governments could have avoided or softened the tax increases by lowering their tax rates so they got enough revenue to keep their own budgets in line with overall inflation, but not so much as to arouse taxpayers. Many local governments did lower their rates a little, but rarely in proportion to the rising tax revenues generated by the inflation in home prices. By announcing their slightly lowered rates with great fanfare, they may have increased taxpayer anger when big tax bills arrived. Most local governments, however, cheerfully increased their spending in accordance with their increased income.

Rapidly rising property tax bills both hurt and annoyed people. Low-income and elderly people on fixed incomes from welfare, Social Security, or pensions were hit hardest. Property tax bills could rise by hundreds or even thousands of dollars a year, but their incomes did not. Elders hoping to live out their lives in family homes long since paid for were put under great stress. But people who could afford to pay the property tax were also angered by the precipitant rises, and the way property tax is collected intensified their anger. We pay sales tax a bit at a time, hardly noticing. Income tax is deducted from our monthly or weekly paychecks and many of us don't even notice our pretax wages; we may be surprised at the total we've paid when we file our income tax forms on April 15, but even then the system dupes us into celebrating a refund of a few dollars. We are eased into paying these taxes, but the property tax slaps us in the face with a single big bill that comes in the mail. In the late 1970s, with the nasty surprises of bigger bills every year, many got mad enough to say they weren't going to take it any more.

Some of their frustration was with the overall burden of combined local, state, and federal taxes, but the property tax was singled out as the most hated and least predictable of all. It was also relatively vulnerable because it could be attacked locally through a referendum, a means that could not be used against federal or, in some cases, state taxes. By the early 1970s, voters were regularly saying no to bonds and increases in property tax rates in referenda. State and local governments, conscious of both the problems and the unpopularity of the property tax introduced reforms, including improved assessment practices, rebates, exemptions, and deferrals for the elderly and the poor, and even alternative taxes in some places.

These reforms were too little, too late, however, and the tax revolt exploded, particularly in Sunbelt states where inflated house prices were driving up property taxes most rapidly. In 1978, the voters of California led the way with the passage of initiative **Proposition 13.** This measure fixes the property tax rate at 1 percent of market value, based on the most recent sale of the property or its 1975 value if it has not been sold, with assessments rising by only 2 percent a year. When property is sold, however, it is assessed at its market value (usually a steep rise); then it falls subject to the 2 percent annual increase. By cutting the rate and rolling back assessed values, Proposition 13 reduced property tax bills by a total of 57 percent. Moreover, the burden on the taxpayer was lightened and made predictable by the 2 percent limit on increased assessments.

The measure saved people lots of money and forced local governments, which had been getting a little sloppy and self-indulgent, to trim fat and shape up. But while Proposition 13 remains so popular as to be sacrosanct in California, it wasn't all good, and it certainly wasn't fair. State aid and belt-tightening helped local governments get over the initial shock of losing 57 percent of their primary source of revenue, but eventually services declined and, in the long term, counties and school districts became less independent because of their reliance on state assistance, which always has strings attached. Cities with more varied revenue sources did a little better. The main beneficiaries were big businesses, elders, and other homeowners who stay put, since property is only reassessed when it is sold. Property taxes are thus higher on houses purchased more recently. Someone who has stayed in a $30,000 home bought in 1975 might be paying one-seventh the property tax of the next-door neighbor living in an identical house bought for $300,000 in 1990 and getting exactly the same services. The courts have thus far judged Proposition 13 constitutional, although in 1989, the U.S. Supreme Court struck down a similar "welcome neighbor" tax in Webster County, West Virginia, on the grounds that it violated the equal protection clause of the Fourteenth Amendment.[2]

Besides its unfairness, this reassessment procedure reduced the mobility of Californians, who now move a little less frequently because they fear bigger tax bills. Even so, California homes, on average, change hands every 4 or 5 years. Big business, however, stays put longer, thus enjoying the same benefits as the 1975-homeowner. Before Proposition 13, business carried more than half of the total property tax burden; within 2 years of its enactment, homeowners carried more than half, a proportion that has grown since then. In all, business gleaned two-thirds of the $120 billion saved in property tax up to 1988.[3]

Other states soon followed California's lead, and the tax revolt swept the nation. In 1980, voters in Massachusetts passed Proposition 2 ½, limiting the property tax to 2 ½ percent of a community's total assessed value and annual increases in assessment to 2 ½ percent. The state's local governments slashed their budgets and cut staff. Similar measures were put to the voters in several states and, although a few were rejected, most were approved. All around the country, state and local governments backed away from tax increases and tightened their budgets as the message of the tax revolt sunk in. As of 1989, all but seven states had enacted some sort of limits on property tax rates or assessment increases (see Table 12-3), although many of these predated the tax revolt.[4] Perhaps to drive their point home, the voters elected tax-bashing candidates like Ronald Reagan and George "no new taxes" Bush.

Although tax increases were back on the agendas of governments at all levels by the 1990s, the tax revolt was not necessarily over. In 1992, Colorado voters passed a law requiring voter approval of new taxes or increases in existing taxes other than those justified by inflation and population growth. And in March 1993, the schools in Kalkaska, Michigan, were closed for the year when local voters rejected a tax increase for the third time. But while the tax revolt may have assuaged the public, dissipated antagonism to the property tax, and decreased what some viewed as overdependence on it as a source of local revenue, the serious problems of that tax remain, including its regressivity and its impact on the needs/resources dichotomy and fiscal zoning.

Other Taxes

Nationally, no other tax equals the property tax as a source of local revenue, although since the 1970s, other taxes have become increasingly important and now raise more money in some localities than the property tax.

Thirteen states allow their local governments to levy a **local income tax,** but its use is extensive only in Kentucky, Ohio, and Pennsylvania. As of 1991, 3697 local governments collected the tax, but 2824 of these were in Pennsylvania alone.[5] Large cities levying an income tax include New York, Yonkers, Baltimore, St. Louis, Kansas City (Missouri), Indianapolis, Columbus, Toledo, and Cincinnati. The tax is usually set at a flat rate (such as 1 percent of wages), although the rates of New York and Washington, D.C., are progressive, with higher rates for those with higher incomes.

Cities levy income taxes on their own residents, but a few central cities charge a **payroll tax** on everyone who works in the city, thus taxing suburbanites who use their services and partially redressing the needs/resources imbalance. Philadelphia even applies its payroll tax to visiting athletes. Cleveland gets 61 percent of its total budget from its payroll tax, and 77 percent of that amount comes from nonresidents.[6] Altogether,

Table 12-3   Restriction on U.S. Local Government Tax and Expenditure Powers, 1988

Region	No Limits	Property Tax Rate Limits	Property Tax Revenue Limits	Revenue Rollbacks	General Revenue Limits	Expenditure Limits	Limits on Assessment	Full Disclosure
Alabama		X						
Alaska		X	X					
Arizona			X			X	X	
Arkansas		X		X				
California		X				X	X	
Colorado			X					X
Connecticut	X							
Delaware				X				C
Florida		X		X				X
Georgia	X							
Hawaii								X
Idaho		X	X					
Illinois		X	X					X
Indiana			X					
Iowa		X					X	X
Kansas				X				
Kentucky		X		X				X
Louisiana		X		X				
Maine	X							
Maryland							X	X
Massachusetts		X	X					
Michigan		X		X				X
Minnesota		X			X			X
Mississippi		X	X					
Missouri		X		X				
Montana		X		X				M
Nebraska		X						
Nevada			X		X			
New Hampshire		X						
New Jersey			C				M	
New Mexico		X	X				X	
New York		X					X*	
North Carolina		X						
North Dakota		X	X					
Ohio		X		X				
Oklahoma		X						
Oregon			X					
Pennsylvania		X						
Rhode Island			M					X
South Carolina	X							
South Dakota		X						
Tennessee								X

Table 12-3 *continued*

Region	No Limits	Property Tax Rate Limits	Property Tax Revenue Limits	Revenue Rollbacks	General Revenue Limits	Expenditure Limits	Limits on Assessment	Full Disclosure
Texas		X			X			X
Utah		X						X
Vermont	X							
Virginia					X			X
Washington		X	X					
West Virginia		X						
Wisconsin	X							
Wyoming		X						
U.S. Total	7	30	15	12	2	3	6	16

C—designates counties only; M—designates municipalities only. *Selected cities only.
Source: Steven D. Gold and Martha Fabricius. *How States Limit City and County Property Taxes and Spending* (Denver: National Conference of State Legislatures, 1989), p. 9. Reprinted with permission.

however, income or payroll taxes generate less than 3 percent of local revenues. Cities might prefer a local income tax because it would be more fair, but it is not politically feasible. Taxpayers now hate the income tax almost as much as the property tax and will not hear of a further increase, even if it saves them elsewhere; nor are jealous states, themselves turning increasingly to the income tax, prepared to share it with local governments. Meanwhile, critics believe that cities with income or payroll taxes are driving jobs and middle-class people away and losing their economic competition with the suburbs.[7]

Sales taxes are a little more common means of raising local funds, generating 6 percent of all local revenues in 1990 and rising—local sales taxes increased by 150 percent between 1978 and 1987 (the years of the tax revolt).[8] Thirty-one states allow cities, counties, and sometimes transit districts to charge sales tax. In some cases, such as California, a percentage of the state sales tax is shared with cities and counties, which may also add local sales taxes for special purposes such as transportation. The sales tax is a primary source of revenue for only a few cities, however, including Denver, where it generates nearly half of local revenues, and Oklahoma City, where it supplies almost 60 percent of revenues.[9] Most cities resist such reliance because, like a local income tax, the benefits of a sales tax are limited by the fear of driving businesses to adjacent jurisdictions without the tax and by the fact that most states already collect a sales tax and cities can't add much to it without causing a political uproar.

Although schools rely almost exclusively on money from the property tax and counties have few additional local taxes, states generally allow cities more flexibility. Besides the sales tax, many collect an assortment of minor taxes on hotels, rental cars, gambling, cigarettes, liquor, admissions, entertainment, and utilities. Most of these produce little revenue, but cities welcome whatever they can get and particularly like some of these because they come from tourists and commuters. The exception is the utility tax, which hits local residents and businesses and which generates more than 10 percent of local revenues in some places.

Charges and Fees

Following the tax revolt, local governments turned not only to these other taxes, but to **charges and fees,** now the most rapidly growing source of local funds. A *Municipal Year Book* survey reported that cities with populations over 10,000 raised 21 percent of their general revenues from charges and counties with populations over 25,000 raised 23 percent.[10] Unlike taxes, which everybody pays whether they use a service or not, charges and fees are paid only by users. "You should make services pay for themselves," says an Oklahoma City council member. "You know what the cost of water is; people who use water ought to pay for it."[11] Besides water, local governments charge for garbage collection, sewers, transit, airports, parking, and admissions to public facilities such as parks, zoos, golf courses, and swimming pools. Cities that own their own utilities do particularly well. Austin, Texas, for example, gets 46 percent of its revenues from its electric utility company, relying on property taxes for just 10 percent (as compared with 59 percent in Fort Worth).[12] Additionally, local governments make money on fees for business licenses, building permits, and franchises for private companies to provide city services. In theory, charges and fees should pay for the cost of providing a service and no more, but critics assert that cities desperate for funds may set prices too high and actually make money on their charges, in which case they are taxes. Critics also point out that charges reduce the access of low-income people to local services and facilities.

Intergovernmental Aid: The States

Taxes and charges are the two major means by which local governments generate their own revenue, but they are also heavily dependent on aid from the state and federal governments—or **intergovernmental aid**—which now contribute nearly 40 percent of local government budgets. As with other funding sources, this is not evenly spread among different types of local governments. School districts and counties are most heavily dependent on intergovernmental aid, while many cities receive very little.

This is because state funds concentrate on education, which, in many places, is not a city function. States also contribute to welfare and health care, which are the major services receiving federal funds. These are county functions in many states so, again, cities are not direct beneficiaries. *The Municipal Year Book* points out that while total state aid to local governments "jumped from $83 billion in 1980 to $130 billion in 1986 . . . when allotments for education and welfare are taken out, cities and towns received just about $15 billion in 1986 . . . up from about $8 billion in 1978."[13] In some states, however—particularly in the Northeast—cities perform one or more of these functions and so are the recipients of considerable intergovernmental aid. New York City, which handles education, welfare, and health, gets a third of its budget from the state and federal governments. Counties and school districts, however, rely on intergovernmental aid even more.

Although states provide much more aid than the federal government, the amount varies greatly among the states. California, for example, gives its local governments over five times more money per resident than New Hampshire does.[14] In all, about one-third of state funds are passed on to local governments, where they comprise about one-third of all local revenues and over half of general revenues for school districts. Some of the money is allocated on a formula basis and designated for the provision of specific services, mainly education, welfare, and health. Some are **shared revenues,** usually a fixed percentage of state sales, gasoline, or other taxes which may be **earmarked,** meaning it must be spent for a designated purpose. This is almost always the case with gas taxes, for example, which usually must be used for roads or sometimes other forms of transportation. States are stingy about giving funds with no strings attached—only 10.9 percent of state aid to local governments is "unrestricted"[15]—and such money is usually eaten up by state-mandated programs anyway. Local governments complain that such **mandates** requiring them to do certain things cost them more than they get in aid, so the states are actually allocating local revenues.

Local governments nevertheless welcome state aid, although they might also welcome fewer restrictions on how they spend it. Central cities and poor school districts and counties particularly appreciate the equalizing or leveling effect of state aid. With a broad and inclusive tax base, the states have the capacity to at least partially resolve the needs/resources dichotomy, although to date efforts in this regard have mainly been confined to education. But state funds are not unlimited and local governments have recently been reminded that what the state gives it can take away. In California, for example, a 1993 budget crisis impelled the state government to shift more than $2 billion in property taxes from cities and counties to schools in order to reduce the state's own spending on education.

Intergovernmental Aid: The Federal Government

Like state aid, federal funds have traditionally had an equalizing effect and have recently been cut. Categorical **grants-in-aid** for specific projects have been disproportionately awarded to big cities, usually by Democratic presidents seeking to reward or win friends. Funds for social programs, including welfare and Medicaid, also go disproportionately to big cities, where most of those in need are concentrated. Also like state aid, most federal funds have strict strings attached.

Overall, the federal government contributes about 5.4 percent of all local funds (compared to state aid at 33.3 percent). The bulk of this is for social programs and entitlements distributed on a formula basis according to need. In 1993, health and welfare entitlements absorbed half of the $184 billion in federal aid to state and local governments. These funds to the states are supplemented by the states and passed along to local governments, where they are further supplemented by local money and actually administered. As noted, this is usually a county function, although cities carry it out in some parts of the country. In either case, little local discretion is allowed, so the local government is essentially an administrative agency of the state and federal governments.

Unlike grants for social services, local governments must apply for categorical grants-in-aid, and they are awarded selectively. More than four hundred different sorts of grants are available, funding projects ranging from airports to transit, housing, sewers, and parks. Local governments are happy to receive the money, although they complain about red tape, inadequate funding, and categories that may not include their top-priority projects. The federal government responded to these criticisms by loosening restrictions on some funds through block grants and (briefly) revenue sharing.

Federal aid to local governments rose dramatically through the 1970s, but the declining power of big cities, the rise of suburbia, a succession of conservative presidents, and the massive federal deficit led to change in the 1980s, particularly under President Ronald Reagan. Whereas federal payments to state and local governments rose by 45 percent between 1975 and 1980, they increased by only 10 percent between 1981 and 1985 and by less thereafter.[16] Although the dollar amount increased, the total portion of the federal budget allocated to local governments shrank steadily from 15.5 percent in 1980 to 10.7 percent in 1989,[17] while the portions for defense and debt retirement increased. Such increases in local aid as occurred went for welfare and health programs, although the Reagan administration trimmed these wherever possible. The biggest cuts, however, came in categorical grants-in-aid. Dozens of programs were eliminated and funding for others was greatly reduced. The budget of the Department of Housing and Urban Development was halved, and grants to cities were slashed by one-third even without allowing for inflation. "Over the 1980s,"

The Municipal Year Book reports, "the percent of the average local government budget provided by federal funds was sliced in half—from around 16 percent to 8 percent," while "federal dollars for priority municipal programs—including housing, public transit, and job training—are now less than half of what they were a few years ago."[18] Large cities lost the most. The U.S. Conference of Mayors reports that federal contributions to the budgets of the fifty largest cities fell from 17.7 percent in 1980 to 6.4 percent in 1990.[19] Suburban and Sunbelt cities, however, lost less because most had not relied so heavily on federal largesse.

President Clinton and his administration, which includes two former mayors in charge of key urban agencies, have increased federal aid to cities slightly. Efforts to reform the health care system could also help local governments. The budget deficit, however, has prevented a major turnaround in federal aid programs, and cuts in defense spending have knocked the economic props out from under some communities, especially in the Sunbelt. Federal aid to local governments may yet rise, but the on-going problem of the deficit makes it unlikely that aid will attain its past levels.

Borrowing

While all the sources of funds discussed thus far may be used to pay for the operating budgets of local governments, covering on-going costs such as salaries and maintenance, **borrowing** is usually allowed only for long-term infrastructure projects.

Local governments are required by law to balance their operating budgets so, in general, they must get by on revenues from the sources discussed above and may not borrow for these on-going expenses. But because revenues arrive in lump sums at different times of the year when particular taxes are collected or state and federal funds are distributed and operating expenses are on-going, income and spending may be out of synch. Some states therefore allow local governments to engage in short-term borrowing by issuing **tax or revenue anticipation notes (TANs or RANs),** which investors purchase and which the local governments repay with interest in 30 to 120 days. Cities can get in trouble by abusing this system, as New York City did in the 1970s. Philadelphia was so hardup in 1993 that lenders refused to loan the city money on the grounds that projected revenues were inadequate to cover its expenses and repay its debts.

Most—97 percent—of local borrowing is long term rather than short term, however, and goes to capital rather than operating budgets. Larger amounts are involved and they are repaid over a period of years rather than months, rather like a home mortgage. Such borrowing is justified on the grounds that capital projects such as roads, bridges, and buildings will last for a long time and so may be paid for over a long period, at the end of which the borrower still has the facility. In contrast, borrowing for operating costs such as salaries, which are recurring and must be paid every month, could lead to an endless cycle of debt.

Long-term borrowing is done by issuing bonds, or IOUs, which are purchased by investors and repaid at a fixed rate of interest over a specified period of years. Traditionally, this was done in the form of **general obligation (GO) bonds,** which, under state law, are guaranteed by the local government borrower. If a local government goes broke and defaults on its loans, the state takes it over, slashes local services, and pays off the bondholders. Actually, several cities went bust in the 1930s, and a few local governments go bankrupt every year. Cleveland went into default in 1978, and only state intervention saved New York City from the brink in the 1970s. Bridgeport, Connecticut, faced bankruptcy in 1991. Such desperate straits are rare, however, and the guarantees for GO bonds give them a security that makes them an attractive investment. Interest on these bonds is also exempt from federal taxes, which adds to their allure as an investment and helps out local governments by enabling them to offer lower interest rates.

Guaranteed GO bonds are regulated by the states, many of which set borrowing limits. Most also require voter approval, usually by 60–67 percent of those voting. In the 1970s, some cities hit their borrowing limits, and in others, voters rejected the bonds, which are generally paid for by the unpopular property tax. Thus, local governments turned increasingly to nonguaranteed bonds, which are subject to fewer state regulations and generally do not need voter approval. These are usually **revenue bonds,** paid for by income from the facilities they provide, such as airports, stadiums, or toll bridges. Revenue bonds are easier to issue, but because they are nonguaranteed, investors are more cautious and expect higher interest rates.

Despite state restrictions and voter rejections, borrowing by local governments has continued to rise. Cuts in federal grants for capital projects gave impetus to local indebtedness, and nonguaranteed revenue bonds have provided means. In 1980, local borrowing was about equally split between guaranteed and nonguaranteed bonds; as of 1990, two-thirds was nonguaranteed.[20] Not all voters have rejected bonds, however. According to a survey by *The Municipal Year Book,* between 1977 and 1986 (the height of the tax revolt), three-fourths of all bond measures won approval.[21] Undoubtedly, local governments became more cautious about balloting on bond measures, but where they could be persuaded of need, voters were willing to authorize borrowing and taxes.

The Bottom Line

Bond elections are not the only way voters have their say about local revenues. States also require **voter approval** of some other tax measures. The tax revolt exploited these opportunities and used the initiative process as well. Such democracy is praiseworthy, yet it is also unfair, in that local governments are singled out for referenda on taxes while the states are less restricted and the federal government is exempt. Discontented taxpayers may vent their anger with taxes in general on local governments in particular, simply because they are allowed to do so. If we could vote on taxes at all levels, local governments, which provide visible and necessary services, might come off best. Perhaps the voters have perceived this. The image of local governments seems to have improved, perhaps due to post-tax revolt belt-tightening or because the revolt supplied the public with a needed catharsis. A 1990 Gallup poll reported that more people felt they were getting more "for their money" from local than from the state or federal governments. Asked "which level of government spends your money best?" 35 percent chose local, compared to 14 percent for state, and 12 percent for federal.[22]

Nevertheless, local governments have born the brunt of the tax revolt. When it reached higher levels of government, they responded by cutting local aid, especially to cities. The last two decades have seen local governments scrambling for revenues. Schools have grown more dependent on the states. Counties have increased charges and fees while relying on intergovernmental aid to pay for social programs. Cities have raised charges, imposed new taxes, and increased indebtedness. As *The Municipal Year Book* puts it, the "money chase continues unabated, and apparently uninhibited."[23]

How the Money Is Spent

Patterns of spending among local governments vary as much as their revenue sources. This is partly because of the way states allocate responsibilities to different sorts of local governments. Education, for example, is usually, but not always, the responsibility of school districts, and counties often provide social services, while cities concentrate on public safety and a mix of other tasks. Spending also reflects community characteristics. Central cities, with dense, needy populations generally spend more, while suburbs, although richer, spend less, and Frostbelt cities tend to spend more than Sunbelt cities, both because of greater need and because their states assign them more responsibilities. Richer communities may, however, spend more for amenities such as parks, libraries, and lighted tennis courts simply because they can afford to without taxing themselves heavily to do so. Spending patterns are thus determined by both state-imposed obligations and by community characteristics. But local budgets also reflect community priorities and history. Some communities have paternalistic attitudes, providing extensive services, while others are more laissez-faire in style, minimizing government. The former are more likely to be central cities in the Frostbelt; the latter are usually suburban or

Sunbelt cities, which coincidentally are better off and so can afford to do less. Here again, community characteristics and the demands they generate come into play.

In turn, expenditures have an impact on communities, their politics, and their environments. Local spending makes urban places, with all their problems, more liveable—and spending usually rises as these problems increase. Spending also has an impact on the local economy. Businesses may encourage local spending as an economic stimulus, and local governments often see spending as a form of investment. If such spending works, it increases revenues, which makes further spending and further stimulation possible. If increased spending necessitates higher taxes, however, it can have the opposite effect, depressing the economy and driving business away. The balance is tricky, and local governments spend a lot of energy trying to get it right, although most seem to have a propensity to tax and spend as much as they can, hoping to satisfy their constituents while stimulating the local economy.

Spending Patterns

Education is the single largest local expenditure, followed by social services, public safety, and transportation (see Figure 12-4). Separating school districts, counties, and cities, however, reveals different **spending patterns**

FIGURE 12-4   Spending by All U.S. Local Governments, 1990

Source: Advisory Commission on Intergovernmental Relations, *Significant Features of Fiscal Federalism,* vol. 2 (Washington, DC: U.S. Government Printing Office, 1992), p. 149.

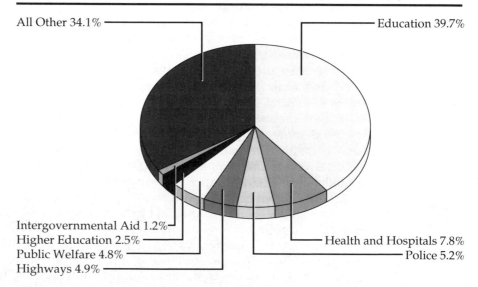

All Other 34.1% — Education 39.7%

Intergovernmental Aid 1.2%
Higher Education 2.5%
Public Welfare 4.8%
Highways 4.9%

Health and Hospitals 7.8%
Police 5.2%

FIGURE 12-5 U.S. County Spending, 1990

Source: Bureau of the Census, *City Government Finances*, series GF, no. 8 (Washington, DC: U.S. Government Printing Office, annual); *Statistical Abstract of the United States* (Washington, DC: U.S. Government Printing Office, 1992), p. 297.

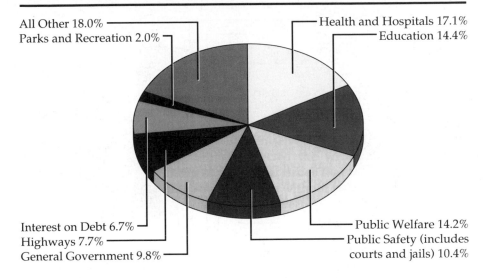

All Other 18.0%
Parks and Recreation 2.0%
Health and Hospitals 17.1%
Education 14.4%
Interest on Debt 6.7%
Highways 7.7%
General Government 9.8%
Public Welfare 14.2%
Public Safety (includes courts and jails) 10.4%

(see Figures 12-5 and 12-6). Health and welfare rank high in county budgets, while public safety and sewers and sanitation are the big spending categories for cities. Education still ranks second in both cases because some cities and counties have that responsibility; most, however, do not.

Spending also varies wildly among cities, again influenced by state-assigned responsibilities and community characteristics. Among the nation's seventy-five largest cities, annual spending per capita in 1988 ranged from as low as $354 in El Paso and $456 in Mobile to as high as $5889 in Washington, D.C., and $3545 in New York City. San Diego, San Jose, Oklahoma City, Pittsburgh, Omaha, Virginia Beach, Sacramento, Wichita, Louisville, Fresno, Mesa, and Arlington all spent less than $800 per capita, while San Francisco, Indianapolis, Boston, Denver, Nashville, Buffalo, Norfolk, Rochester, Anchorage, Jersey City, and Richmond all spent over twice that amount. The big spenders, however, are mostly consolidated city-counties and most have responsibility for education; the low spenders—mostly in the Sunbelt—do not.

The Budget Process

Each year local governments go through a long and complex process to put together a budget for the next year. Although this process arguably involves the most important decisions local governments make about public

FIGURE 12-6   U.S. City Spending, 1990

Source: Bureau of the Census, *City Government Finances*, series GF, no. 4 (Washington, DC: U.S. Government Printing Office, annual); *Statistical Abstract of the United States* (Washington, DC: U.S. Government Printing Office, 1992), p. 298.

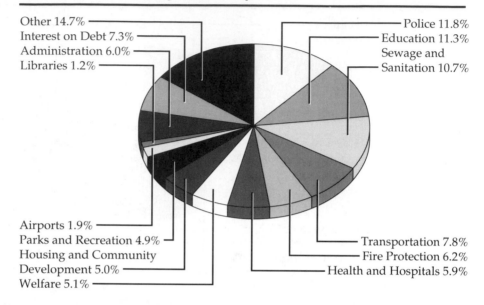

Other 14.7%
Interest on Debt 7.3%
Administration 6.0%
Libraries 1.2%

Police 11.8%
Education 11.3%
Sewage and
Sanitation 10.7%

Airports 1.9%
Parks and Recreation 4.9%
Housing and Community
Development 5.0%
Welfare 5.1%

Transportation 7.8%
Fire Protection 6.2%
Health and Hospitals 5.9%

policy, it takes place mostly out of the public view, with its own special set of political actors, most of whom are bureaucrats rather than elected officials. Yet even though much energy is expended on the budget, each year's budget is much like that of the preceding year except for tinkering at the margins.

A local government's chief executive officer (CEO), whether mayor, city manager, county executive, or superintendent of schools, is usually in charge of the process, although in some local governments independent fiscal officers such as controllers or treasurers play a part. The **budget process** begins with the CEO's budget staff or agency developing a projection of revenues for the coming year, so the budget-makers will know how much they will have to spend. This is easier said than done given the complex and varied sources of local revenues discussed above. Budget projections must not only predict what other governments will do, since local governments are so dependent on intergovernmental aid, but also how boom or recession in the national and local economies will affect local taxes: Will retail sales increase or decrease sales tax revenues? Will property values generate more or less income from property taxes? Will users pay more in charges and fees, or cut back on their use of services? In volatile economic circumstances, such predictions are difficult and risky. They are a particular challenge for small communities with limited staff resources, but even large ones with sophisticated computer projections have difficulty.

Revenue projections are next analyzed by the CEO and his or her executive staff, who develop overall guidelines for spending and sometimes for increases or decreases in particular programs. Normally, this is accomplished with only informal consultation with city councils or county commissioners. Although the CEO will want their support eventually, the CEO will try to keep them from interfering in the early stages. Recognizing the significance of the budget and seeking to break into the process, some councils and commissions insist on formal consultation at this point and even issue their own budget guidelines. These are usually less effective than those of the CEO, however, because multimember legislative bodies rarely agree on a single, clear set of priorities.

Budget directives from on high next proceed to departments and agencies, whose heads, along with their own budget aides, put together proposals for their fiefdoms. These may or may not follow the directives. Some department heads, counting council votes and public support, may ask for considerably more than the CEO's guidelines would suggest. Police departments seem particularly able to do this. Most departments ask for a little more than their allocation for the previous year and even a little more than they really need, so they can absorb expected cuts. Few departments trim their budgets as much as they might because they are competing with other departments that will not and because they know further reductions are ahead. Most department budgets are therefore padded, at least a little.

The department budgets go back to the CEO and the executive budget staff, where they are reconciled and combined into a complete budget to be recommended to the city council or county commission. At this point, the CEO exercises maximum power, balancing various programs, rewarding or punishing departments and their heads, expanding or contracting her or his preferred services and possibly even introducing new ones.

Once this is done, the mayor or manager's draft budget is published, at which point the process becomes public, although few citizens show much interest. Most budget documents are hundreds of pages long, highly detailed, and, perhaps intentionally, incomprehensible. Within a few weeks of publication, the budget will be subject to one or more public hearings and a final vote by the council or commission. During this time, the legislators, few of whom have expertise in budgeting, grapple with this complex document, mostly individually, although sometimes in committees. Some have their own budget analysts or personal staffs to help, but most do not. Lobbyists, however, will offer help. Among these will be the executive, department heads, other bureaucrats, and public employee union representatives, all trying to persuade legislators to favor their programs and interests. In addition to all this in-house lobbying, a few community groups may also assert pressure. These generally include the clienteles of particular bureaucracies hoping to retain services and chambers of commerce and other business organizations worried about taxes and fees as well as the maintenance of services they view as good for business. Other community groups may be activated if they perceive a clear threat or opportunity in the budget. The local newspaper will run a story or two and an editorial on the budget; TV news will mention it only if dramatic (and visual) cuts or tax increases are projected.

This largely behind-the-scenes activity culminates in public hearings at which most of these players give formal public testimony and the council or commission makes a final decision. Besides a few lobbyists, public attendance at the hearings is almost nonexistent except for city hall regulars, a couple of members of local antitax groups, and clients of particular bureaucracies who may be present when their department's budget is discussed after which they'll leave. Council members and commissioners continue their struggle to assert themselves, but have difficulty changing so authoritative a document presented by an often-domineering CEO and his or her experts who have been working on it for most of a year and when an increase in funds for one program involves cuts in others. The legislators may fiddle with the details, possibly affecting 1 or 2 percent of the total budget, but in the end, with a fixed deadline impending and other business pressing, they will approve the CEO's budget more or less intact. Their vote and the public hearing that precedes it often amount to little more than a rubber stamp.

The Budget Process in Perspective

The budget process is a little like a runaway train in a tunnel, out of control and unstoppable. It is hidden from most voters, offering few opportunities for public input—and then usually after key decisions have already been made. Decision-makers try to reassert their mastery of the process, but usually just get run over by it. Some local governments have improved their budget controls, but most are still controlled by the process. Several problems, some of which are not strictly local, are built in.

Local budgeting, probably like our personal budgeting, is revenue driven, incremental, fragmented, insulated, and uncontrollable.[24] The process is **revenue driven** because local governments begin with an estimate of how much money will be coming in and then decide what they can do. Alternatively, they could decide what they need to do and then figure out ways to come up with the money. Most local governments do not have enough control over their own revenues or even spending to budget in any other way, however. Do you? So they start with revenues, which are usually a little more or a little less than they got in the previous year. Accordingly, they increase or decrease spending for their programs a little. When revenues were constantly rising, scholars called this **incremental budgeting;** lately, however, decreasing income has made

decremental budgeting more common. In either case, the point is that no major change occurs: the process is conservative. No programs are eliminated and new ones are rarely introduced. The government and its budget go on more or less as before, often without very serious scrutiny, which may lead to waste and inefficiency. But this is the easiest and least controversial way to make a budget, and the budget process itself makes it inevitable. As we have learned, the process is fragmented, with multiple participants, most of whom are insiders and bureaucrats protecting their own interests. The mayor, manager, and council members could introduce concerns about the more general good and they sometimes do, but the insulated nature of the process usually keeps their attention focused on the fragments (specific programs) rather than the whole.

These are criticisms of which local officeholders are well aware; many have learned of the problems through firsthand frustration. Elected officials and top managers have tried various means of gaining better control of budgets and the budgetary process. Traditional line-item budgets (which allocate funds department by department and then by personnel, operating expenses, equipment, and other costs) are, budget expert David Morgan writes, "good for accounting but not so good for measuring the effect of spending on service delivery or quality."[25] Incrementalism and fragmentation are inherent to this process. Budget reformers have therefore attempted to impose more analytical and evaluative systems. Cost/benefit analysis, for example, requires departments to justify their budgets in terms of services rendered, with the benefits expected to outweigh or at least equal the costs; "zero-based budgeting" is the opposite of incrementalism, forcing every program to be constructed from scratch and to justify every element; planning-programming-budgeting (PPB) shifts the focus from budget items like supplies and wages to broadly defined programs such as public safety and emphasizes goals and actual outputs. Table 12-4 reveals the variety of budgeting tools employed by cities. Note that while larger cities used more of these tools, many were used by cities of all sizes.

The current trend in budget management is **performance evaluation** of individuals and departments. Phoenix, for example, does elaborate internal performance evaluations and even sends questionnaires to people outside the government. Portland and San Jose audit departments, require a formal department response, make the reports public, and review improvements annually. Seattle "looks at what the city wants to accomplish across department lines" and opens the budget process "to citizen involvement."[26] Whatever the system, the point is to connect expenditures with their impact or actual services. This shift in focus better enables elected officials and the public to understand what the budget is about and it puts bureaucrats on the defensive, justifying their costs. In other words, it opens up the process a little. Unfortunately, reforms like these usually sound better than they work. Budget items do not easily crunch into new

Table 12-4 Budgeting Tool Use by City Size

Population Group	No. of cities reporting (A)	Program budgeting Percent of (A)	Zero-based budgeting Percent of (A)	Trend monitoring Percent of (A)	Revenue and expense forecasting Percent of (A)	Strategic planning Percent of (A)	Management by objectives Percent of (A)
Total, all respondents	451	66	33	70	68	60	62
500,000–1,000,000	9	89	67	100	78	78	67
250,000– 499,999	28	68	43	82	68	71	82
100,000– 249,999	58	83	29	71	76	71	67
50,000– 99,999	123	63	42	78	74	63	64
25,000– 49,999	233	61	28	63	63	54	57

Note: A = all. *Source: The Municipal Year Book* (Washington, DC: International City/County Management Association, 1989), p. 47. Reprinted by permission.

categories, and bureaucrats—the main budget players—still find ways of protecting their interests.

But whatever local governments do, much of the budget process is beyond their control. Revenues are subject to state regulation as well as the political tolerance of the taxpayers and voters. Spending can be almost as inflexible. Many programs are locked in by entrenched bureaucracies, labor contracts, and public expectations. Some, particularly police, are popular and so can be tampered with only at great political risk. Others are mandated by state or federal law. Some of these are paid for by intergovernmental aid, in which case the mandates are even more rigid and may require the expenditure of local matching funds. Counties, which mainly deliver mandated programs and rely particularly heavily on intergovernmental aid, have the least budgetary freedom. New York State's counties have local control over only 40 percent of their budgets[27] and California's typically have discretion over less than 20 percent of theirs. Cities, which receive less intergovernmental aid, have more freedom, but complain because programs are mandated without funding. "We don't get any help from the state," said New Orleans Mayor Sidney Barthelemy, "and they keep piling programs on us."[28] Responding to complaints like these, a third of the states now reimburse local governments for any programs the states mandate.[29] Federal mandates, meanwhile, cost state and local governments $100 billion a year. "The idea," declared the National Governors Association, "is that they get the credit, we get the bills."[30]

Management information systems	Performance monitoring	Program evaluation	Productivity improvement	Employee incentive program	Productivity bargaining	Quality circles
Percent of (A)	Percent of (A)	Percent of (A)	Percent of (A)	Percent of (A)	Percent of (A)	
76	67	77	54	64	16	32
89	78	100	100	78	56	56
75	67	77	54	64	16	32
83	83	81	60	64	12	41
81	69	82	59	68	18	33
71	60	76	44	61	13	26

Fiscal Stress

"Over half of America's cities no longer can pay current expenses out of current income," reported *Financial World* in 1991.[31] The reference was to large cities, but communities of all sizes have suffered severe **fiscal stress** since the late 1970s, and most have had to find ways of cutting spending or increasing revenues, neither of which is easy. State and federal mandates and budget cuts are only part of the problem. Other fixed or rising costs, including labor contracts, have impacted local budgets. Recession and inflation, well beyond local control, have depressed revenues and increased expenses. Major demographic and economic trends have drained resources from central cities and the Frostbelt and concentrated them in the suburbs and the Sunbelt, isolating needs from resources. In the 1990s, migrating industry and recession brought Frostbelt strains even to the relatively affluent central cities of the Sunbelt. Meanwhile, strict state limits on local taxation were made even stronger by the tax revolt. Local revenues were legally or politically capped, even as all the other factors cited above put them into decline. To further exacerbate matters, the public, worried about crime, schools, traffic, and the environment, demanded increased services from local governments. Big cities found themselves in a particular bind, with business and middle-class taxpayers leaving as a social under-class grew, new waves of immigrants arrived, and racial tension increased. Suburbs were better off, but older, inner suburbs faced problems not unlike those of the central cities, and newer ones were often overwhelmed by rapid growth they could not control. Many local governments exacerbated these external and structural problems by their own behavior. Decades of easy income caused some to become lax in their budgeting and the budget process itself is fragmented and conservative, resisting tough decisions and innovation. Its limitations are indicated by the annual shock with which projected deficits are greeted. Outright mismanagement made matters worse.

Despite all these sources of fiscal stress, local revenues have not generally declined in absolute terms. Most local governments get more money every year. The increases, however, have not kept pace with increased costs and demands for services. Many cities and counties thus face **deficits** almost annually. Their deficits, however, are not like that of the federal government, because they cannot simply borrow to get what they need. Every state requires its local governments to balance their budgets every year, so they must cut expenditures or raise taxes.

Coping

Nevertheless, many local governments have responded to chronic fiscal stress with imagination and innovation. While some merely cut spending department by department in proportion to the overall loss of revenues, others introduced the new methods of budgeting discussed above, attempting to evaluate what they do and to maximize what they get for their money. Some have found new ways of paying for services and others have found new sources of funds; some have even won voter approval of tax increases.

In some cases, responsibilities for funding of particular services have been shuffled around, usually with state governments taking on greater burdens. Several states, for example, have begun assuming the costs of operating the courts, previously a city or county obligation. The state role in funding education has expanded even further. At the local level, some counties now bill cities for services. For example, counties usually run the jails used by city police to incarcerate those they arrest; now some counties expect to be paid for providing these facilities.

Perhaps the most common solution has been **privatization of services** or **contracting out.** Instead of providing some services with their own employees, local governments contract with private businesses to do the job, usually by a process of competitive bidding. Services are still paid for by tax funds or user fees and charges, but local governments can usually get more for their money. They also avoid building up their bureaucracies and when budget time rolls around, they can deal with private contractors much more firmly than with their own in-house departments. Among the services now commonly contracted out are rubbish collection and disposal, vehicle towing and storage, maintenance of buildings and grounds, data processing, recreation programs and facilities, and snow removal. Towing and disposing of abandoned cars once cost Chicago $25 per vehicle even after deducting the sale of the car for scrap metal; after privatizing, Chicago gained $25 for each vehicle, generating an annual income of $2 million.[32] Although major local services such as police and fire protection are generally not thought suitable for privatization, Scottsdale, Arizona, privatized fire protection and reported an annual savings of 47 percent.[33] But while privatization is increasingly popular, especially in large cities, the evidence of its benefits is mixed. Critics point out that it does not always save money. Unions charge that it leads to lower wages and loss of jobs. Elected officials worry about loss of control and public accountability for services provided by private companies. Strict regulation is necessary to manage these problems and to prevent privatization from turning into machine-like patronage.[34]

Another increasingly common response to budget problems is to allow alternative institutions to take responsibility for what once were city or county services. Special assessment districts have long enabled neighborhoods or business districts to impose small taxes for local improvements the city cannot provide, such as sidewalks or sewers. This mechanism was enhanced in the 1980s by the creation of **business improvement districts (BIDs).** About 1000 BIDs operate around the country, collecting their own taxes to enhance city services in a particular area. In New York City, the Grand Central Partnership BID provides security, landscaping, street cleaning, and even a shelter for the homeless. Altogether, New York's twenty-five BIDs are providing $30 million a year in services.[35] BIDs and assessment districts are also common in St. Louis, where *The Economist* reports "many streets have 'gone private.' "[36] **Common interest developments (CIDs)** similarly provide services for fees, but while BIDs are created with the approval of those who pay them taxes, membership in CIDs is a condition of residence. BIDs and CIDs relieve local governments of some service costs, but often at the expense of public accountability and the fragmentation of communities into bits with different levels of service according to their ability to pay.

As noted earlier, many local governments have generated additional income by introducing or increasing charges and fees and minor taxes. Dade County, Miami, now levies a 1 percent tax on meals to fund programs for the homeless. Indianapolis even launched a local income tax. More surprisingly, some cities asked voters to approve tax increases and won. Voters in various parts of the country have passed bond measures and approved tax increases. The key to winning such approvals seems to be in the packaging of the taxes, which must be clearly linked to voter-perceived needs, such as for transportation or police. In 1989, for example, Oklahoma City voters rejected a tax increase half of which was not earmarked but later gave 80 percent approval to a similar increase earmarked for public safety.[37] **"Special-purpose taxes,"** writes journalist William Schneider, "are the suburban ideal—not just private government but private taxes."[38] What has long been true for tax-sensitive suburban voters may now apply more broadly.

Other local governments have become entrepreneurial. Chicago and San Diego, for example, have "city stores" that sell old signs, fire helmets, and even bricks from Comiskey Park, once home to the Chicago White Sox. Elsewhere, cities recycle lawn waste to sell as mulch or convert sewage for marketing as fertilizer. Riverview, Michigan, sells methane gas recovered from a landfill it owns to the local utility company.[39]

But while many local governments have tried one or more of these methods of coping with fiscal stress, the almost universal response has been to gear up the local growth machine. No fewer than 15,000 local governments host economic development agencies, each hustling projects that will add to their community's tax base, thus increasing revenues without, they hope, costing too much in services. The governmental and tax structures of local governments in most states already impel them to act as growth machines. The fiscal stresses of the 1980s and 1990s have only added to this imperative. But even if it works, economic development is no panacea. Sometimes communities give away more in benefits than they gain in taxes. And even if they are net winners, economic development is a competitive process; their win may be another community's loss.

Running Cities on the Cheap

"Much of the urban problem in the United States is the result of trying to run cities on the cheap," economist John Kenneth Galbraith wrote years ago. "The one thing we have never understood was how expensive the . . . city is."[40] But we are not just stingy with money, we are stingy with power, which prevents local governments from raising the funds they need and which many of their citizens might like them to spend. Some of this stinginess comes directly from local voters, which is democratic and appropriate, although as noted above, discontented taxpayers may be venting their anger about taxes in general on local governments in particular because they are the most readily available and vulnerable target. But local voters are only one factor in the fiscal limitations on local governments, and perhaps not a crucial one at that. "The control of city finances," political economist Mark Gottdiener gloomily writes, "has passed over into the hands of state, federal, and private interests and out of the grasp of local residents."[41]

| ESSENTIAL
TERMS | operating budget
capital budget
property tax
assessed value (AV) | borrowing
tax or revenue anticipation
    notes (TANs or RANs)
general obligation (GO) bonds |

tax rate
fairness of assessments
regressive tax
progressive tax
needs/resources dichotomy
fiscal zoning
tax revolt
Proposition 13
local income tax
payroll tax
sales tax
charges and fees
intergovernmental aid
shared revenues
earmarked taxes
mandates
grants-in-aid

revenue bonds
voter approval
spending patterns
budget process
revenue-driven
incremental budgeting
decremental budgeting
performance evaluation
fiscal stress
deficits
privatization/contracting
  out
business improvement
  districts (BIDs)
common interest
  developments (CIDs)
special purpose taxes

FIELDWORK 1. What does your own city or county budget tell you? Where does the money come from and how is it spent? How does your city or county compare with the patterns described in this chapter? (Budgets will be available at your library or at the offices of the city or county clerk.)

2. Compare the budgets of several cities in your area. How do they differ in terms of funding sources and spending?

3. Compare the budgets of your city, county, and school district. How do their funding sources and spending differ?

NOTES

[1]Katherine Barrett and Richard Greene, "American Cities," *Financial World*, 19 February 1991, p. 36.

[2]*Allegheny Pittsburgh Coal Company* v. *Webster County Commission, West Virginia,* 485 US 976, 1989.

[3]*The New York Times,* 4 June 1988.

[4]Advisory Commission on Intergovernmental Relations, *Significant Features of Fiscal Federalism* (Washington, DC: U.S. Government Printing Office, 1992), p. 18.

[5]Ibid., p. 73.

[6]David R. Morgan, *Managing Urban America,* 3rd ed. (Pacific Grove, CA: Brooks/Cole, 1989), p. 266.

[7]*The Economist,* 9 May 1992, p. 23.

[8]Frederick D. Stocker, ed., *A Look at State and Local Tax Policies* (Cambridge, MA: Lincoln Institute of Land Policy, 1991), p. 17.

[9]Barrett and Greene, note 1, pp. 29, 35.

[10]Victor S. DeSantis, "Profiles of Individual Cities and Counties," *The Municipal Year Book* (Washington, DC: International City/County Management Association, 1990), p. 184. Figures are for 1987.

[11]Barrett and Greene, note 1, p. 29.

[12]Ibid., p. 32.

[13]David R. Berman, "State Actions Affecting Local Government," *The Municipal Year Book* (Washington, DC: International City/County Management Association, 1989), p. 130.

[14]*Governing*, December 1990, pp. 70–71.

[15]U.S. Department of Commerce, *Statistical Abstract of the United States, 1992* (Washington, DC: U.S. Government Printing Office, 1992), p. 296.

[16]Advisory Commission on Intergovernmental Relations, *Significant Features of Fiscal Federalism, 1989*, vol. 2 (Washington, DC: U.S. Government Printing Office, 1989), p. 18.

[17]U.S. Department of Commerce, *Statistical Abstract of the United States, 1991* (Washington, DC: U.S. Government Printing Office, 1991), p. 282.

[18]David R. Berman, "State Actions Affecting Local Government," *The Municipal Year Book* (Washington, DC: International City/County Management Association, 1992), p. 51.

[19]*The New York Times*, 21 June 1992.

[20]Advisory Commission on Intergovernmental Relations, *Significant Features of Fiscal Federalism*, vol. 2 (Washington, DC: U.S. Government Printing Office, 1990), p. 253.

[21]Roy Green and Randall Crane, "Debt Financing at the Municipal Level: Decision Making during the 1980s," *The Municipal Year Book* (Washington, DC: International City/County Management Association, 1989), p. 97.

[22]Advisory Commission on Intergovernmental Relations, *Changing Public Attitudes on Government and Taxes* (Washington, DC: U.S. Government Printing Office, 1991), pp. 7–8.

[23]Green and Crane, note 21, p. 106.

[24]See Robert Lineberry and Ira Sharkansky, *Urban Politics and Public Policy*, 2nd ed. (New York: Harper & Row, 1978), pp. 243–244.

[25]Morgan, note 6, p. 275.

[26]Barrett and Greene, note 1, p. 24; other examples are also from Barrett and Greene.

[27]*The New York Times*, 31 March 1991.

[28]Barrett and Greene, note 1, p. 24.

[29]Berman, note 18, p. 53.

[30]David R. Berman, "State Actions Affecting Local Government," *The Municipal Year Book* (Washington, DC: International City/County Management Association, 1990), p. 55.

[31]Barrett and Greene, note 1, p. 22.

[32]Ibid., p. 22.

[33]Morgan, note 6, p. 191.

[34]See for example, C. J. Hech, "Contracting Municipal Service: Does It Really Cost Less?" *National Civic Review* (June 1983): 321–326 or Harold Sullivan, "Privatization of Public Services: A Growing Threat to Constitutional Rights," *Public Administration Review* 47 (November/December 1987): 461–466.

[35]*The Economist*, 25 April 1992, p. 48.

[36]*The Economist*, 25 July 1992, p. 46.

[37]Barrett and Greene, note 1, p. 29.

[38]William Schneider, "The Suburban Century Begins," *The Atlantic*, July 1992, p. 39.

[39]*The New York Times*, 6 September 1993 and 10 February 1994.

[40]Quoted in *The Los Angeles Times*, 4 October 1970.

[41]Mark Gottdiener, *The Decline of Urban Politics* (Newbury Park, CA: Sage, 1987), p. 15.

13

Politics and Public Policy: Some Local Issues and Battles

A ll of the elements of local politics discussed thus far, from its environment to its formal institutions and informal influences, come
together to shape the programs and policies of local governments. After
all, the local government exists to provide certain services and make certain
kinds of decisions. We have referred to these throughout this book, but
mostly in terms of which governments do what rather than how they do it.
Yet political battles in local politics are usually over the latter and only
occasionally over whether or not something should be done at all.

In this chapter, we will consider a few of the major policies local
governments deal with and some of the issues they confront in doing so, as
well as the political forces involved. In terms of the systems model introduced in chapter 1, the decisions or policies of local government are
outputs, regulating behavior or providing services. These outputs affect
the environment of local politics positively or negatively, which, in turn,
produces reaction, or feedback. Those who like or dislike the policies
support or oppose those who made the decisions. The process goes full
circle when the policies, filtered through the environment, return to the
political agenda to affect the system that created them, reminding us of the
interdependence of the components of both political systems and communities.

We will see some of this played out in the public policies discussed in
this chapter and we will also gain a different perspective on local politics.
Focusing on policy helps us understand the real and human impacts of
what local governments do. It also puts the elements of local political

systems into perspective, suggesting which are significant and which are marginal. Many social scientists start with public policy rather than the institutional and environmental forces we've concentrated on because they think a policy focus best reveals the workings of politics. So, now that we've mastered the basics of local politics, we can move on to sample a policy perspective.

A Policy Sampler: Education, Welfare, and Crime

Local governments provide a variety of services, each of which comprises a policy area. We can't consider all of them here, but we will briefly examine the three that eat up the most money—education, welfare, and crime—before going into greater detail on land use and transportation, policies on which local governments spend less but have more power.

Education

Although education is by far the largest single spending category for all local governments combined, it is primarily a state service that is locally provided. States supply the largest share of education funds and also regulate much of what goes on in schools, including testing, curricula, textbooks, conditions of employment of teachers, and more. Although a few states delegate the actual operation of the schools to cities or counties, most assign this responsibility to **school districts,** which are separate local governments. The districts supplement state funding through local taxes, but state regulations often mean they have little discretion about either the taxes or the sort of education provided. Despite much national debate about education, the federal government provides less than 10 percent of the money spent on schools, although President Clinton has proposed increasing this amount.

The nation's 15,000 school districts are generally governed by small elected **school boards.** Most board members are concerned parents rather than education experts. They serve only part-time and generally leave the management of the schools to the professional educators they appoint. Usually called superintendents, these administrators are very powerful, so their selection is often hotly contested. Besides this choice, other local education issues include the curriculum, testing, teacher hiring and evaluation, truancy, dropouts, drugs, and sex education, although state regulations often limit the options available to school boards. The main participants in local education politics are parents, administrators, and teachers and their unions. Those not directly involved show little interest, which is a problem when school districts take tax proposals to the voters (as they must). As noted in the previous chapter, the schools of Kalkaska, Michigan, closed their doors in March 1993, after voters there turned down a tax increase for the third time. Schools have particular difficulties with referenda on taxes because although everyone pays, only a few benefit directly. Single people, childless couples, empty-nesters whose children have left home, and those whose children are in private schools may be reluctant to pay higher taxes for the benefit of others, particularly where the sense of community has grown weak. Yet as support declines, the burden on schools is increasing because of such social problems as crime, violence, drugs, and cultural conflict exacerbated by increased immigration. All of these, along with the even bigger issues of segregation and funding, touch most of the school districts in the United States.

Segregation. **Racial segregation** of schools was common and legal until the 1954 U.S. Supreme Court decision in *Brown* v. *Board of Education of Topeka*, which ruled that *de jure* or intentional segregation by law was unconstitutional.[1] Many school districts were ordered to find ways of integrating their schools. Some could simply change attendance boundaries, but in other communities the problem went beyond the schools themselves. Many were segregated not because of formal school board policies, but because neighborhoods in their communities were segregated. Such de facto segregation by practice rather than by law was common not only in the South, but in big cities elsewhere as well. Recognizing this segregation, courts ordered schools to integrate, often by busing students across town.

Busing proved highly controversial and resulted in hundreds of court cases, referenda, and electoral defeats for school board members and other officials, as well as protests, violence, and even riots, not only in southern cities, but in traditionally liberal northern ones such as Boston, where working-class Irish and Italian families deeply resented the forced busing of their children to schools in black neighborhoods.[2] But although racism was the main reason for local resistance to busing, opponents also argued in favor of the traditions of neighborhood schools and local control. The federal courts, they asserted, had placed the constitutional rights of individual students above the rights of communities to decide how to run their schools. Busing was also highly disruptive for schools and students, especially where it was forced or court ordered. Perhaps in recognition of these problems, the courts eventually softened their approach somewhat, allowing school districts to develop voluntary busing schemes often centered around magnet schools with specialties designed to attract a mixture of students. Although these actions improved integration in some school districts, many urban areas, especially in the North and in the suburbs, are fragmented into internally homogeneous school districts that make integration impossible without crossing district lines. Court-ordered busing may have actually increased this sort of segregation by accelerating white flight from cities to suburbs. The Supreme Court has overruled cross-district busing or other integration schemes unless district lines were drawn with the intention of segregation, but this is difficult to prove, so integration plans generally stop at district boundaries.

After decades of attempted desegregation, a 1993 Harvard study reported that 66 percent of African American and 73 percent of Hispanic students were attending schools that were over half black or Latino or both and that these figures were slowly rising, not falling. According to the study, this was due not to white flight but to immigration and higher birth rates among minorities along with the isolation of minorities in certain school districts.[3]

Funding.   **School funding** is a closely related issue. The fragmentation of urban areas into multiple local jurisdictions produces segregation not only by race, but also by class, resulting in a needs/resources dichotomy, with the poor and minorities concentrated in some districts and the more affluent in others richer in tax resources. Since the property tax is the primary local source of funds and since the tax base is not evenly distributed, some districts are richer than others and can spend more on education. Detroit spends about $5000 per pupil each year, while its rich suburb of Bloomfield spends twice that amount. A north Chicago school district set a 1992 tax rate of $7.33 per $100 assessed value, but because of low property values, generated only $1638 per student while in Lake Forest, an affluent Chicago suburb, the tax rate of $1.32 per $100 AV raised $14,143 per pupil. The richest districts in Texas averaged $11,801 per student in 1992 compared to $3109 in the poorest.[4]

But the problem is not only unequal funding. Besides having less money, central city school districts have more expensive problems and less discretion over how to spend their limited funds. Inner-city schools must cope with the expenses of court-ordered integration, for example, while homogeneous suburban districts need not. Inner-city schools also enroll more than their fair share of children with learning disabilities and disadvantaged kids who require expensive and often state-mandated compensatory education. Moreover, increased immigration in the 1970s and 1980s, mostly to central cities, brought many pupils who speak little English. More than a third of the students in big city schools in California, New York, and Texas, for example, are not native English-speakers. The courts have ruled that minority-language students are entitled to special assistance,[5] and although the federal government provides some aid, most of this expensive burden, as with desegregation and teaching the disadvantaged, falls on already underfunded central city schools. Meanwhile richer suburban districts, with fewer problems and mandates and more money, can provide educational enrichment.

This unequal funding has been challenged in the courts and while the U.S. Supreme Court has refused to intervene, several state supreme courts, beginning with California in 1971,[6] have ruled that unequal education spending is in violation of state constitutions. Kentucky and Texas are currently grappling with court orders to that effect. As a consequence of these cases and a general recognition of the problem, several states have moved to equalize education spending, although suburban majorities in state legislatures sometimes resist. Only in Hawaii where state funding is complete is spending per pupil equal but, overall, state spending on education has increased and with it, **equalization.** Whereas states provided 17 percent of education funds in 1900, by 1989 their share was 55 percent; of the remainder, 35 percent was local and about 10 percent was federal.[7] When President Clinton took office, the federal share was down to 6 percent.[8] He has sought to increase federal aid to schools and to concentrate it more in the neediest districts. Funding remains a central issue in education, but with states in charge, courts intervening, and local voters reluctant to raise taxes, school districts can do little about it except spend what they get as best they can. Unlike cities and counties, they cannot expand their tax base by development. Rather, they may be victims of that development, obliged to educate growing populations without much tax benefit.

These issues suggest that although 90 percent of the nation's school districts are nominally independent, their local discretion is severely constrained by the actions of the state, federal, and other local governments, as well as by the voters and by individuals making decisions about where to live and where to send their kids to schools.

Welfare

If health spending for the uninsured poor is included, welfare ranks second to education in local spending, but local governments have even less discretion over these programs. Counties generally administer welfare and health services although in some states, mainly in the Northeast, these are city duties. In either case, the funding is chiefly by the state and federal governments with locals adding matching funds and delivering the services under guidelines from the higher levels.

The biggest welfare program is **Aid to Families with Dependent Children (AFDC),** which costs $23 billion a year and serves nearly 5 million families, mostly headed by single mothers. About 40 percent of AFDC recipients are black, 38 percent are white, and 17 percent are Hispanic.[9] The program is funded by federal grants to the states, which both state and local governments may supplement. States also have some discretion as to who qualifies for benefits and how much they will receive. In 1992, monthly AFDC payments combined with food stamp benefits (another federal program) for a family of three ranged from $412 in Mississippi to $1184 in Alaska, although in most states the figure is closer to $600.[10] This leaves most AFDC families well short of the federally defined poverty level of

$11,280 a year (or $940 a month) for a family of three. Other forms of welfare include Supplemental Security Income (SSI), a direct federal program for the aged, blind, and disabled, and general assistance (GA), a primarily state program for which people without children may qualify. Welfare recipients generally also qualify for **Medicaid,** a program intended to provide medical care for the poor. Medicaid is funded by federal grants to states and, like welfare, is administered by counties or cities. State and local governments set standards under federal guidelines and may supplement funding. Local governments (usually counties) also operate hospitals providing emergency and general services as well as special facilities for the mentally ill.

But while local governments administer these programs, funding and guidelines from above leave them with only narrow choices. Local officials complain that they not only lack discretion over funds provided by the state and federal governments, but also over increasing portions of their own locally raised revenues due to mandates for matching funds and the costs of administration of programs that they are legally obliged to provide. The big issues in welfare and health care are fought in state and national, not local, politics. Worries about a permanently dependent welfare underclass, for example, have led to state and federal experiments with **workfare** or required employment for the able-bodied. The Clinton administration has revived these experiments and is actively searching for ways of weaning people off welfare as well as for ways of reforming health care. With growing welfare rolls—the number of AFDC recipients rose by 1 million between 1991 and 1992—and the budget pressures of the tax revolt and recession, some governments have been crudely cutting assistance. AFDC benefits have declined and many states have cut GA programs. In 1993, Michigan completely eliminated GA, which critics feared would add to its prison and homeless populations.

Despite efforts to reform it, welfare will not go away. Although cheats exist and some honest recipients can be helped to enter employment by training and child care, many are old, ill, or disabled, and a majority are children. Some have been denied employment or training opportunities by racial discrimination. Welfare is a response to these problems, largely brought about by urbanization and the concomitant breakdown of families and communities. If poverty in urban areas seems bad now, imagine what it would be like without public assistance.

Local governments remain at the margins of these debates, although their mayors speak out and they participate through their state and federal legislative representatives and their lobbyists. They push for more funding by the higher levels, but most find welfare eating up more and more of their own discretionary funds and some mostly rural counties allege that mandated welfare spending is pushing them into bankruptcy. With the main issues resolved elsewhere, those dealt with locally chiefly involve the way services are provided and whether social workers should just check on eligibility and see that payments are made or should provide extra services to help people with the problems that put them on welfare in the first place. Cities and counties also debate special programs for the homeless or others in need, but budget constraints often prevent action. Battles over these issues are mostly bureaucratic, fought out within local governments by elected officials, administrators, welfare workers, unions, and private-sector service providers. Welfare recipients have little representation or say, although some advocacy groups speak on their behalf. The general public, while worried about abuses of the welfare system, shows little interest.

Overall, both the economic problems that cause poverty and the welfare programs intended to deal with it are beyond the control of local governments. Many do, however, attempt to address the problem through economic development programs intended to increase local revenues and provide jobs. Unfortunately, many of those on welfare are unemployable and the sort of economic development most cities seek does not provide jobs for unskilled workers other than indirectly, through maintenance jobs, for example.

Crime

"I hate to say it," San Francisco Mayor George Moscone once said, "but crime is an overhead you have to pay if you want to live in the city."[11] As we learned in chapter 2, urbanization breaks down families and communities, the informal agents of social control. Urbanization increases the propensity for crime through proximity brought about by higher density, the social conflict that comes with diversity, and the social psychology of isolation and alienation. But while increased crime is inevitable in cities, only criminals think it is desirable. One of the main reasons local governments exist in the first place is to provide public safety.

Unlike the other policies discussed thus far, public safety is a responsibility of cities, except in unincorporated areas, where it is a county function. Most of the funds are local, too. Except for minor matters, however, the laws enforced by city police or county sheriffs are made by the states. States also organize the courts, which are usually administered by counties with some funding from states. Prisons, where those convicted of serious crimes are incarcerated, are provided by the states, while counties (or cities in some places) run jails for people awaiting trial and unable to make bail or for those serving short sentences for minor crimes.

The Police.   Policing is the job of cities and their biggest single expenditure. Police spending is also usually their most controversial annual budget issue, with almost perpetual community and police pressure on decision-makers to spend more and hire more police officers, even at the expense of other programs. Crime is usually a top item on the list of public concerns produced by opinion polls, and the knee-jerk reaction of government is to hire more cops. Most city police forces are understaffed enough to justify this, although critics say existing staff and funds could usually be better deployed.

Besides funding, a whole array of issues revolves around **police-community relations.** The videotaped police beating of a black citizen in Los Angeles and the 1992 riots following the acquittal of the police officers involved put this issue in the national spotlight, but it is a familiar problem in most communities where minorities live. Police departments have been slow to reflect demographic change in their communities, with many remaining predominantly white and even more not trained to deal with increasing cultural diversity. At the same time, parts of the communities police patrol have given them reason to be hostile, with more dangerous guns, drugs, and gangs. Mistrust and alienation have come to characterize police-community relations in many cities. In a 1991 national survey of Hispanics, for example, no fewer than 48 percent said Hispanics were treated worse than others by police. Reactions varied considerably, however, with only 26 percent saying so in San Antonio as compared with 58 percent in Los Angeles and 68 percent in the San Francisco Bay Area.[12]

Some police departments seem set on exacerbating this alienation by behaving like occupying armies, cruising through neighborhoods in armored cars and treating residents like inmates, a policy that does more to contain than to solve the problem of crime. In many communities, aggrieved minorities have demanded **civilian review boards** composed of people appointed by the city council to hear complaints about police. They argue that an outside group of nonprofessionals is necessary because the police cannot objectively deal with complaints against themselves. Led by police chiefs and unions, the police vigorously resist outside review and such proposals are usually rejected. But by raising the issue, community groups have improved the internal police investigation of complaints, and in some places they have succeeded in establishing review boards. For the most part, these have improved police-community relations and have not been as disruptive as the police departments feared, although their effectiveness varies considerably depending on how much authority, independence, and financing they are given. More commonly, police departments have tried to better community relations by training officers in how to deal with cultural diversity and by hiring more minorities, women, and, in some cases, gays so that they better reflect the communities they serve.

Perhaps more significantly, new leaders such as the African American police chiefs of New York and Los Angeles have replaced the occupying army style with **community policing** which gets more officers away from desks and out on the beat, where they are encouraged to get out of the car to talk to people. Community policing, however, is not only for the sake of police-community relations. It is also viewed as a way of fighting crime by enlisting the support of citizens—something that happens automatically in smaller communities but which is somehow lost in big urban places. Many police departments try to encourage community involvement through advisory boards or neighborhood watch programs in which isolated urban residents are brought together, introduced, and trained to be more aware of one another and the security of their neighborhoods. But the main component of community policing is simply putting more cops on regular beats where they can get acquainted with the locals and help prevent crime rather than just reacting to it. It seems to work. Crime rates and emergency calls decreased in Flint, Michigan, and in New York City following their shift to community policing.[13] But even with better funding and community support, the job of the police is made more difficult by guns, drugs, and gangs, three current problems that are well beyond their capacity to resolve.

Guns and Gun Control.   Widespread possession of guns makes the United States one of the most violent societies in the world and gives police justification for overreacting when threatened. In 1992, handguns were used in the murder of 13,220 people in the United States as compared to just 13 in Australia, 33 in Britain, 60 in Japan, and 128 in Canada.[14] Some police leaders and many big city mayors have campaigned for **gun control** and a few cities have banned or required permits for the carrying of handguns, but constitutional issues and the vigilance of the powerful National Rifle Association make it difficult for local governments to act. Besides, given the multiplicity of governments in most metropolitan areas, banning guns in one might make little difference. Although local law officers face armed and dangerous citizens daily, the issue of gun control is larger than any locality.

Recognizing this, some states have passed modest gun controls such as bans on assult weapons or waiting periods for purchase of handguns. In 1993, the U.S. Congress imposed a national short waiting period by enacting the Brady Bill (named for the press aide who was wounded in the attempted assassination of President Ronald Reagan in 1991). These controls may help cities in the long run but most advocates of gun control feel they are too limited to have much impact.

Drugs.   Drugs, another national problem that hits cities hard and gives cops an impossible task, were designated the number one issue by city officials in 1989[15] and rank at the top of public concerns, too. Drug addiction is partly a social problem, a response to urban alienation, but police only deal with drug use as a crime. That's their job. Besides, drug use is not only a crime itself, it generates crime to pay for the addiction. But while police try to cope with the law enforcement end of the drug problem, experts agree that enforcement alone will not stop drugs. Kids need to be taught the danger of drugs, which requires the cooperation of schools, and addicts need treatment, which is the job of underfunded social service programs (often run by the county rather than the city) or perhaps state or federal prisons. Under President Bush, the federal government fought a $12 billion a year "war on drugs" with the emphasis on law enforcement. The prison population increased and casual use of drugs declined, but the number of heavy drug abusers continued to rise. President Clinton and his drug czar, Lee Brown, an African American and former New York City police commissioner, have increased spending to $13.4 billion and have also increased emphasis on treatment.

Baltimore Mayor Kurt Schmoke and others have urged the legalization or **decriminalization of drugs** by repealing laws that make their use or possession a criminal offense. They argue that, like the prohibition of alcohol, the current policy has only exacerbated the situation and has made drugs big business for organized crime. Decriminalization, they assert, would shift the focus to education and treatment and let police concentrate on more traditional crime. Cities do not make drug laws, however, so this controversial proposal would require state and federal action, which is unlikely. Like guns, the problem of drugs goes beyond the boundaries of communities and the reach of police.

Youth Gangs.   **Gangs** are another contemporary urban problem. Like drugs, they are a social phenomenon and a response to the alienation of urban life. Gangs give young people an identity and a sense of community, however warped these may be. Most gangs are based on territory or turf and on race. In Los Angeles County, for example, an estimated 130,000 teenagers belong to 1000 gangs, and 430 gang-related deaths were reported in 1992.[16] Some of their violence is directed at one another, but gangs are also involved in drug dealing, protection rackets, and other criminal activity. Heavy-handed policing may contain but does not solve the problem. Community policing may help, but gangs are manifestations of wider social problems, beyond the capacity of police or cities to solve.

Crime and Local Politics.   All these issues are fought out on the battleground of local politics. Police-community relations, guns, drugs, and gangs are mostly big-city issues, although many suburbs confront them as well. Crime is a universal worry, however, and most communities fight about funding of police. In big cities, the main political activists on law and order issues are mayors, council members, administrators, minority leaders, social service agencies, and some community groups. The chief of police, the most powerful executive officer after the mayor or manager, and the police union, which is always the most powerful public employee union, are major players and usually winners, thanks to public support. In smaller, suburban communities, participants are fewer—council members, the manager, the chief, and the police union (if any). In budget battles, police do not always get what they want, but they usually do better than other departments, with at least small annual increases. No amount ever seems to be enough to solve the problem, though, because police concentrate on enforcement and containment, which is their job, rather than on the roots of crime, which no other agency of local government seems to have the know-how or resources to address. And despite public support and ever-increasing funds (in most communities), even police enforcement activities seem inadequate or at least unable to keep up with rising crime. As a consequence, many individuals, businesses, and communities have turned to **private security** companies, whose forces now considerably outnumber police,[17] a trend that only increases division and social inequality (in this case, in police protection).

On these issues and others, cities and counties find themselves on the frontline, facing social problems they did not create and that they cannot solve single-handedly. Most attempt to contain the problems, but fiscal and political constraints limit even these activities. Many turn to growth and economic development, over which they have more control, in hopes of mitigating social problems by increasing tax revenues and generating jobs.

Land-Use Policy: The Politics of Growth

Regulating land use and development is probably the greatest discretionary power allocated to cities and counties by states as well as the main way they attempt to affect their own fate and well-being. As such, the politics of land use and growth have cropped up throughout our study of local politics and they often dominate local decision making, particularly for cities.

Zoning and General Plans

Cities have land-use authority within their borders, which they may expand by **annexation.** Counties have fixed boundaries within which they generally regulate land use only in areas that are not part of any city. In either case, the basic mechanisms for land-use control are zoning and general planning. Development was once freely allowed in communities, but problems arose when adjacent projects didn't fit together, like a factory or a slaughterhouse next to homes or a park. **Zoning** was conceived to avoid such problems by setting out districts exclusively for certain kinds of development, ranging from single-family, suburban-style homes to highrise apartments, shopping malls, and industrial areas. Mixed uses, like a 7-11 store in a housing development or apartments above shops in a commercial zone, are sometimes allowed.

Zoning was controversial because it limits the rights of property owners to do what they want with their land, but the U.S. Supreme Court ruled it a constitutional use of local power in 1926,[18] and its use spread rapidly. Property owners nevertheless still bring court cases on alleged unfairness. The courts have ruled zoning restrictions based on race, religion, or national origin unconstitutional, but zoning is generally allowed to segregate by class (which often equals race) through the concentration of homes of a similar value in a particular area so that only people of a certain class can afford to move there. This **exclusionary zoning** has been challenged in the courts, but unless an explicit intent to discriminate can be proven, it is allowed to stand.

General or master plans, another innovation of this century, sum up and aim to rationalize all of a community's zones and to project intended patterns of future development. Sewers, street plans, parks, and other public facilities are also included. The idea of a **general plan** is to project development into the future, although many only reflect what already exists. General plans typically look 10 to 20 years ahead, but as conditions change plans must change. Minor alterations usually are made at annual hearings with reconsideration of the entire plan every 5 years or so.

Once a community's general plan is in place, developments that conform need only formal approval by the local government. Landowners or developers who want to do something different need to apply to the city or county for a change in its zoning or general plan. The city or county's professional planners study the requested change and make a recommendation, which is often considered by an advisory commission before it goes before a public hearing and a vote by the city council or county board. Much of the meeting time of local bodies like these is taken up by such land-use decisions, especially in growing communities.

Capital improvement projects such as roads, sewers, storm drains, and other infrastructure facilities are also essential for development, and local governments must see that they are provided. Traditionally, they were paid for by borrowing, which required voter approval, but when the tax revolt and antigrowth movement challenged such borrowing, private developers sometimes began footing the bill.

Local land-use decisions involve one or more of the mechanisms of annexation, zoning, general plans, and capital improvements and sometimes all four. Tax structures also play an important part. Participants in land-use decisions include elected officials, bureaucrats (both planners and service providers), interest groups, power elites, and sometimes the states, which set the framework for decisions and seem to intervene increasingly frequently.

The Growth Machine

Harvey Molotch's assertion that "the very essence of a locality is its operation as a growth machine"[19] has been a theme throughout this book. In Molotch's view, community elites with an interest in land seek to increase the intensity of land use to maximize their profits. The progrowth coalition usually includes not only landowners, but realtors, lawyers, bankers, investment companies, builders and developers, and the construction trade unions. Newspapers and businesses not directly involved in development also lend their support, foreseeing benefits for themselves in expansion. Local officials become boosters and "ambassadors" to industry, and "governmental authority at the local and nonlocal levels," Molotch writes, "is utilized to assist in achieving this growth at the expense of competing localities."[20]

But local governments are not only responding to powerful interests within their communities. They are also pursuing their own interests. Some local leaders may see growth as a way of furthering their personal ambitions, but a more fundamental force is also at work. "Economic prosperity is necessary for protecting the fiscal base of local government," notes Paul Peterson. "As policy alternatives are proposed, each is evaluated according to how well it will help to achieve this objective."[21] Because local governments depend so heavily on property and sales taxes, they, too, have a vested interest in growth which results in fiscal zoning. The progrowth attitude of local governments is thus not only a response to the political power of the growth coalition, which is formidable, but also to their structural dependence on growth. "Those promoting a policy must show how the plan is consistent with the economic interests of the city as a whole," Peterson asserts. "If a particular policy can be shown to be of long-range economic benefit to the city, its chances for adoption are increased."[22] Among these benefits are increased taxes, profits, investment, and jobs, all of which help sell growth not only to local decision-makers, but also to the public.

Growth coalitions dominated land-use politics in most U.S. cities from the 1940s through the 1970s and beyond, although their power was most blatant in the booming central cities of the Sunbelt and in some expanding suburbs. Growth was not only an unchallenged good, but a major industry itself in many of these communities as they annexed aggressively, won voter approval of bond measures to subsidize infrastructures, and zoned for the convenience of developers. General plans were minimal or nonexistent in most Sunbelt and suburban cities until the 1970s. New industries were eagerly and expensively recruited, with ready-made zonings and capital improvements often lavishly subsidized. Such self-promotion seems superfluous since growth was flowing to the Sunbelt and suburbia anyway, but communities were competing with one another within regions and all over the country.

Many suburbs, however, eschewed growth at any cost. Peterson points out that "in some smaller communities the emphasis is more on status than economic interests." These communities "externalize the negative effects of commerce and industry by zoning these productive activities outside their own jurisdiction."[23] They want them close, but not too close, preferring to remain affluent residential enclaves, which still gives them a rich tax base they can spend on schools and amenities. Combined with exclusionary zoning to keep out low-income residents, this increases land and property values and they still get economic development, albeit of a different sort.

Such an option was not available to the central cities of the Frostbelt, nor were they as aggressively progrowth as their Sunbelt counterparts during this time. Already bounded by independent incorporated suburbs, they had nowhere to annex. Already taxing heavily, bond measures were tough to pass, even though their aging infrastructures needed rebuilding. People and industry were leaving rather than arriving, and developers made few proposals. The growth machine was not dead in these communities, however, it had only fallen on hard times. Land-based interests and developers still exercised great power over land-use issues, particularly those connected to downtown commercial centers in cities such as Philadelphia, Pittsburgh, Boston, New York, San Francisco, and Chicago. To fight decay and decline, these cities instituted urban renewal or redevelopment programs for their downtowns. They established economic development offices to retain and recruit industry. And they launched promotional campaigns like "I ♥ New York." In fact, the desperation of these communities for taxes and jobs may have given economic interests even greater power. If anything, cities in decline could not afford to be choosy about the developments they accepted. Nevertheless, the growth machine was not so dominant as in the Sunbelt and suburbia. Other interests, including well-established businesses and community groups, played a part in local power structures, and other matters, such as social issues, were on the local agenda.

The Costs of Growth

By the 1970s the **costs of growth** were beginning to become apparent in many suburban and Sunbelt communities. The open space of the country-side that had attracted residents and even industries to the peripheries of these cities was disappearing with continued development. Where growth was rapid, infrastructures such as roads and schools had often not kept up, leading to traffic congestion, air pollution, and crowded classrooms. Middle-class workers found their commute time lengthening and their children in schools with double sessions in temporary buildings and class sizes larger than in older areas. Other services, including police, fire protection, parks, libraries, and sewage treatment were stretched to the limit and often judged inadequate. The low taxes that had once been an attraction rose steadily but seemed to pay for continuing growth rather than improving these services. Meanwhile, low-income inner city neighborhoods found themselves threatened by downtowns expanding through redevelopment programs. Yet despite increasing discontent, the growth machine ground on.

Besides a declining quality of life and a deteriorating environment, growth often costs local residents more in taxes to provide for services even as it enriches local elites. Even the claim that growth generates jobs is spurious according to Molotch, who asserts that "local growth does not create jobs: it distributes jobs." Cities merely compete with one another for the limited number of jobs available. Unemployment, Molotch shows, is no lower in fast-growing areas and is often higher than elsewhere.[24]

Peterson points out a different and more subtle cost of this growth orientation. Responding to the pressures of local economic elites and the fiscal structures imposed on them by the states, local governments go for growth, but to get it, they must also keep taxes and therefore spending low or they lose out to competing communities. "To maintain their local economic health, they must maintain a local efficiency that leaves little scope for egalitarian concerns. These limits . . . require that local governments concentrate on developmental as against redistributive objectives"[25] that would require heavier taxation to fund greater spending on education, welfare, mass transit, and other public facilities. But higher taxes stymie growth and often result in the flight of businesses and more affluent taxpayers. So local governments pursue growth in hopes that it will generate money for social programs, but it rarely seems to bring in enough. No wonder the programs discussed at the beginning of this chapter all suffer funding problems. They, too, are victims of the growth machine.

The Antigrowth Movement

But the growth machine sewed the seeds of a challenge to its dominance, not only by the problems it caused but also by the people it brought to communities. The environmental movement that got under way in the late 1960s and some antitax crusaders in the early 1970s raised the issue of growth, but the unlikely rebels who were the mainstays of the antigrowth campaign were middle-class professionals—not the rich, who either profited from growth or had their own securely controlled communities, or the poor and working class, who may have suffered most from growth but who generally lived in declining communities where growth was not an issue. Carl Abbott, author of *The New Urban America*, explains that the engineers, government employees, and managers of

> the "postindustrial" middle class . . . depend on statewide or national markets for their talents rather than on local markets for their goods and services. They therefore tend to see the city as a residential environment rather than an economic machine. As salaried employees who [were] caught in the inflation of the 1970s, they [were] also more interested in the availability of affordable and convenient housing in attractive neighborhoods than in the booster's shibboleth of population growth.[26]

These middle-class professionals were conscious of the environment and high taxes, and they were outraged at poor services, traffic congestion, and air pollution. By the mid-1970s, they were running controlled-growth candidates for local office and putting growth limits on local ballots by initiative—and winning. In San Diego, their organization was called PLAN! (*Prevent Los Angelization Now!*), while the slogan in Seattle was "Have a Nice Day—Somewhere Else." They joined the tax revolt, which decreased subsidies for growth and somewhat reduced its justification as a generator of property taxes. The **antigrowth movement** continued through the 1980s, by which time most successful candidates in the suburbs and Sunbelt cities used the rhetoric of growth control, even if they failed to practice what they preached once in office.

Meanwhile, back in the central cities where decay was more common than growth, similar stirrings were under way. Redevelopment programs had begun extending downtowns into lower- and working-class residential areas, which, to the amazement of many local politicians, organized resistance to this manifestation of the growth machine. The civil rights movement of the 1950s and 1960s had boosted the confidence of minorities and expanded their voting power, as had their continued migration to central cities. Federal antipoverty programs stimulated and even subsidized community organization. Middle-class central city neighborhoods also organized, often to fight threatening projects such as freeways and stadiums. In Sunbelt central cities, they sometimes joined the antigrowth coalition, although minority groups worried about jobs generally did not.

Controls on Growth

Zoning and general planning, the basic tools of growth control, were already in the hands of local governments. Suburban communities had long used them to keep out low-cost housing, apartments, and industrial projects. The growth-control movement gave such exclusionary zoning a new sort of legitimacy—protecting the environment and community services. But these standard controls were exercised at the discretion of elected officials, who were influenced by developers and whose campaigns were often funded by the growth machine. Even controlled-growth candidates were sometimes co-opted by these interests.

Frustrated by the failure of traditional zoning and general planning to limit development, antigrowth and environmental organizations proposed a variety of more rigorous **growth controls,** for example:

- Limits on the number of homes built
- Greenbelt or urban development line
- Limits on population
- Limits on commercial or industrial square footage
- Limits on commercial or industrial height
- Downzoning

- Voter or council supermajority approval for upzoning
- Infrastructure requirements
- Growth management as an element in general plan
- State or regional growth management plans[27]

In the early 1970s, communities in New York and California set limits on the number of housing units that could be built each year. Builders challenged both cases in court and, in precedent-setting decisions, both were upheld as reasonable uses of planning powers.[28] The legal case of Petaluma (just north of San Francisco), was helped by provisions for low-cost housing within annual quotas. Instead of limiting housing construction, some communities, such as Boulder, Colorado, sought to control growth by setting population caps. Others attempted to concentrate growth close to existing services by setting boundaries for development or by designating or in some cases even purchasing land around their city limits for greenbelts in which construction was prohibited or deferred.

Some communities, particularly larger ones, restricted commercial, office, or industrial development rather than housing. Neighborhoods in these cities blamed such developments for declining services and rising taxes and, in some cases, felt directly threatened by commercial expansion. Height limits were one response, as were restrictions on the amount of square footage that could be developed. In San Francisco, for example, a 1986 ballot measure limited new office construction to 950,000 square feet a year (about three 20-story buildings).[29] Elsewhere, both central cities and suburbs attempted to manage growth by **downzoning** areas to less intense uses. Commercial or industrial zones were changed to residential uses and areas zoned for high-density housing were redesignated for lower density, single-family homes. Even in booming Los Angeles, voters gave a 70 percent yes vote to a 1986 initiative that set out a ten-point growth management plan and slashed future commercial development density in half. Some communities instituted requirements for approval of zoning or general plan changes that increase densities (upzoning) by voters or a "supermajority" (more than a simple majority) of the city council.

Where frustration was greatest, communities set moratoriums halting growth either for a fixed period, as in Cape Cod, Massachusetts, or until infrastructures or other services could be supplied, as in Boulder, which drew a "blue line" around the city and would not supply water to housing built beyond it. By the mid-1980s, infrastructures had become a key factor, and many cities began requiring that development be deferred until specified facilities such as roads, transit, sewage treatment, or schools could be supplied. This sometimes resulted in moratoriums on growth since tax revenues, especially after the tax revolt, were insufficient to fund such facilities. With taxpayers no longer willing to subsidize development, many cities turned to **impact fees** or charges on developers to pay for infrastructure improvements. This relieved local taxpayers but since developers passed the cost on to consumers, it raised the price of housing by as much as 18 to 34 percent according to one study[30] and so controlled growth in a different way.

To cap these controls, many communities strengthened their general plans to include comprehensive growth plans, although in some cases this was a way of avoiding more stringent limits. The growth-control movement and environmentalists also pushed for better regional planning, seeing that the problems of growth were larger than any one community. At the same time they were enacting their moratorium on new development, Cape Cod voters approved a regional land-use management agency or special district by an even greater majority, taking a more "proactive and longer-term" approach to growth according to political scientist Scott A. Bollens.[31] That same year on the West Coast, voters in San Diego County rejected stringent growth controls but approved the creation of an advisory committee to recommend policies for regional growth management. Other metropolitan areas moved in the same direction, and a few, including Atlanta, Minneapolis–St. Paul, Portland, and Seattle, established new multipurpose regional authorities.

Local growth issues soon moved to state capitols. States are the source of local land-use powers, so losers in local contests, whether pro- or antigrowth, sometimes take their cases to the higher level. State involvement is also justified by the fact that growth issues overlap local jurisdictions. As a consequence, some states reviewed and revised their laws on annexation, consolidation, and interjurisdictional agreements to facilitate regional coordination and many increased their requirements for regional planning on transportation, air quality control, and other environmental issues. A few, including Florida, Georgia, Hawaii, Maine, New Jersey, Oregon, Rhode Island, Vermont, and Washington, developed statewide plans. Florida and some others imposed **concurrency requirements** limiting development to areas with infrastructure facilities in place or where they could be built concurrently with the development. New Jersey's state planning commission, established in 1988, channels growth to existing cities and suburbs by seeing that state funds for roads and sewers are spent there and by added incentives for new developments within existing cities. Eighteen states enacted **consistency laws** requiring that zoning policies conform with general plans. A California state court ordered downzoning in parts of Los Angeles as a result of that state's consistency law.

State intervention has not, however, always been on the side of controlled growth. In Virginia, for example, the state legislature overturned a 1987 downzoning by a suburban, antigrowth county outside Washington, D.C. Oregon and Massachusetts can override local zoning that excludes low- and moderate-cost housing. Both state and federal courts have also been active on growth issues. Although generally accepting growth controls, some state courts have warned local governments that

they must "take account of the 'extralocal consequences' of their decisions,"[32] and both state and federal courts have proven wary of exclusionary zoning. State courts, for example, have overturned local minimum floor area requirements (causing large, expensive homes). The New
Jersey Supreme Court has ruled exclusionary zoning contrary to the
state constitution and ordered communities to allow the construction of
affordable housing.[33] Federal courts have banned zoning apartments
to only certain areas as discriminatory, whether intentional or not. Both
state and federal courts have also judged some zoning decisions to be
unfair "takings" of property because they denied owners reasonable
development rights. Usually the courts order financial compensation in
such cases.

The Politics of Growth

As this review of the various mechanisms of growth control suggests, the
movement has been both widespread and varied. In California, for example, a comprehensive study by the Lincoln Institute of Land Policy
reported that about 80 percent of all cities and counties enacted some form
of growth control in the 1970s and 1980s. Half established at least two of
the mechanisms discussed above and a fifth imposed four or more. Los
Angeles legislated eight growth-control measures and San Francisco
approved seven, but the smaller city of San Luis Obispo topped them with
no fewer than nine. Among the array of measures, infrastructure and
zoning controls were the most commonly adopted.[34] State and regional
bodies also introduced planning requirements.

     Although press and academic analyses of the growth-control move-
ment often focus on its use of the initiative process, the California study
reports that 85.6 percent of local growth measures were enacted through
the normal city or county law-making process rather than by the voters.[35]
Several factors were at work to produce this result. From the early 1970s
onward, growth-control candidates were winning elections in cities where
growth was an issue. In some communities, the electoral structure was
changed to facilitate their victories. At-large election of council members
became a target of the neighborhood and growth-control movements,
usually in alliance with minority groups. The high cost of these citywide
races enhanced the power of developers, who made major campaign
contributions and helped elect council members who were more concerned
about citywide issues than about neighborhood services. Counterreformers therefore advocated a return to district council elections, which cost less
(thus decreasing dependence on campaign contributors) and resulted in a
more neighborhood- and service-oriented city council. Whether by winning at-large or district elections, as council majorities committed to
controlling growth took hold, initiatives became unnecessary because
policies could be changed by legislative action.

The growth machine also played its part in this shift by adapting to changing circumstances. After losing several initiative contests, corporate developers hired sophisticated political consultants to conduct their pro-growth campaigns. They denounced antigrowth crusaders as "elitists" who were denying young families housing, driving jobs away, and threatening the economic well-being of their communities. In alliance with labor unions, local business, and sometimes minority groups, they presented themselves as "friends of the people"[36] and succeeded in defeating slow-growth measures in many booming areas, including Orange County and San Diego (both in California). Recessions in the 1980s strengthened the developers' economic arguments, which may explain why voters in the state of Washington rejected a statewide growth-control initiative that included supporting funds in 1990.

Developers also adapted by compromise and lobbying. Accepting mild measures like a comprehensive growth element of a general plan could often fend off more radical controls. Impact fees or charges for building permits could be tolerated since the alternative of voter-approved bond measures to fund infrastructures was unrealistic and besides, costs could be passed on to home purchasers. Developers also found that even antigrowth candidates—whether running by district or at-large—needed campaign funds. Controlling growth was politically popular and resulted in bursts of activity but stable groups failed to materialize in most communities so candidates and elected officials, lacking party or organizational support, often turned to those with a long-term interest in local politics and the money to back it up—the growth machine. Developers also applied their lobbying skills to the new officials. In some cases, they cut deals with minority council members, promising jobs or that work would be sub-contracted to minorities. As a consequence, growth measures were often moderated, and neighborhood advocates, environmentalists, and supporters of district elections were disappointed in candidates who, in their view, "sold out."

The Impact of Growth Controls

As the foregoing suggests, in most communities the battle over growth resulted in compromise. Although some opponents of growth were so fanatic that they were labeled BANANAS (*b*uild *a*bsolutely *n*othing *a*nywhere *n*ear *a*nybody), most did not argue that all development should be halted. Rather than no growth, they wanted controlled growth that would not cost them money or harm the environment, local services, or their property values. If projects could be shown to be of net benefit, they continued to win approval—developers just had to work harder to make their case.

Some analysts argue that the battle over growth control is more symbolic than practical. John Logan and Min Zhou assert that growth is so heavily influenced by external factors, such as national and regional economies and corporate decisions about where to locate, that local governments can't control it anyway. Even when they adopt measures to do so, these are often ignored or abused—making exceptions for a major industry, for example. Growth control, they suggest, has more to do with "elitism" and "stability" than with environmental issues.[37] Their argument is supported by evidence that communities that adopt growth control measures are not necessarily experiencing rapid growth themselves. The Lincoln Institute reported that cities with larger populations were more likely to adopt growth controls than smaller ones, but there "was no simple relationship" between the growth rate of individual communities and control measures.[38] They found that growth measures were often a response to regional or statewide, rather than strictly local, growth.[39]

Developers, advocates of low-income housing, and many academic analysts have concluded that growth control amounts to a contemporary manifestation of traditional suburban patterns of exclusionary zoning.[40] Virtually all of the measures discussed above drive up the cost of houses, either by limiting the supply, adding impact fees, or increasing size and land area. Some communities (usually larger ones) try to include mixed-price housing, but lower cost homes are rarely built because they don't offer enough profit to private developers and public funds are limited.

Such exclusivity is not limited to the suburbs. In central cities, growth controls often take the form of downzoning to protect housing in old neighborhoods that have been zoned but not yet developed for high-density residential, commercial, or industrial uses. Such neighborhoods, which may once have been upper class, have usually declined as their original population moved to the suburbs and lower income and minority people moved in, often splitting big homes into flats or boarding houses. In the 1970s, fashion, environmental consciousness, and increasing numbers of couples without children brought some middle-class people back to such inner-city neighborhoods. They bought the grand old houses and fixed them up, formed residents' groups, and sought city assistance, including downzoning to protect their reemerging neighborhoods. Cities usually welcome such requests, happy to see middle-class taxpayers returning rather than fleeing. But the process has been labeled **gentrification** because middle-class homeowners (or gentry) replace poor and minority people, who cannot afford the rising prices in these downzoned and rehabilitated areas. Nor do the new residents always make their predecessors feel welcome, demanding that police move street people on and that community facilities such as alcoholic drop-in centers or homeless shelters be relocated.

Traditionally, neighborhoods of homeowners, whether in suburbs or central cities, resist nonconforming incursions on their territories. On a small scale, this not-in-my-backyard or **NIMBY** phenomenon revolves around objections to particular projects that are considered locally unacceptable land uses or LULUs, from dumps and factories to community care facilities and low-income housing. As a result, the so-called LULUs are located only where they run into little or no resistance, which means they tend to be concentrated in the least well-off parts of central cities rather than distributed evenly throughout metropolitan areas. No regional authority exists to achieve such distribution. But growth controls, with their propensity to exclusion, take NIMBYism to a larger scale. As the report of the presidential Commission on Affordable Housing puts it:

> The personal basis of NIMBY involves fear of change in either the physical environment or composition of a community. It can variously reflect concern about property values, service levels, fiscal impacts, community ambience, the environment, or public health and safety. Its more perverse manifestations reflect racial or ethnic prejudice masquerading under the guise of these other concerns . . . NIMBY sentiment . . . is so powerful because it is easily translatable into government action, given the existing system for regulating land use and development.[41]

Yet it would be unfair and short-sighted to dismiss the growth-control movement as merely an extension of narrow-minded NIMBYism, bigotry, or elitism. These motives play a part in many communities, but so do the issues of rising taxes, declining services, traffic congestion, disappearing open space, and air pollution. These are real and serious issues of great concern to many residents and not just a smokescreen for elitism. Nor are all communities that seek to control growth wealthy and white. This could hardly be the case in California, where 80 percent of cities and counties have adopted growth controls. The Lincoln Institute study of these communities found that those without growth measures had only slightly lower per capita incomes and education levels than those that instituted controls and found no difference in ethnic composition.[42]

The End of the Growth Machine?

With growth controls and resistance to development so extensive and by all evidence still expanding, it might seem that the death knell of the growth machine has been sounded. But while the politics of growth have changed, the imperative remains.

Growth was so widely accepted and supported for so long that resistance came as a shock, not only to development interests but to local officials who had ruled their communities unchallenged. In the beginning, growth machine interests lost many battles, not necessarily because their arguments lacked merit but because their power had declined as their communities changed. In some new suburbs there was no established power structure, so when residents got around to organizing they could dictate to the developers who had created their communities. In central cities in the Sunbelt, new residents felt no allegiance to the old elites. Newly organized minorities and neighborhoods also challenged faltering growth machines in Frostbelt central cities. In many places, locally owned businesses were replaced by multinational corporations whose managers and employees shared few interests with the old guard growth machine.

But although the growth machine was challenged, it was not defeated. Growth controls often merely resulted in the redistribution of growth from communities that could afford to reject it to those that couldn't or to those that ardently welcomed it. This redistribution of growth facilitated the development of the edge cities that sprouted at freeway interchanges, often in areas that lacked single, traditional local governments and were unincorporated county areas with private governments in the form of the owners of office, commercial, or residential complexes. But except for the most affluent and elite suburbs, development also continued in communities with traditional municipal authorities even when constituents worried about growth instigated control measures. The growth was usually different—better planned and paying for itself rather than imposing greater tax burdens on existing residents—but it was still growth.

Cities and counties are growth machines in the first place not just because of the power of development interests, but also because of the fundamental design of local governments. State-dictated dependence on property and sales taxes makes cities and counties seek growth to expand their revenues. Increased revenues might not be necessary, except that the cost of maintaining existing services has risen while their constituents demand more due to rising crime rates or other problems. The tax revolt denied many local governments the alternative of raising taxes on existing development even as declining federal and state aid reduced their income. To many, growth seems a painless way to generate revenue without raising taxes. The growth-control movement altered this bias by demanding clear evidence that the benefits of each new project outweigh or at least equal its costs in services.

Additionally, state laws of incorporation have fragmented metropolitan areas into many independent governments in competition with one another for tax resources. Each wishes to strengthen its tax base, seeking the most lucrative developments while rejecting those that might cost more in services than they would generate in taxes. Resistance to low- and moderate-cost housing is not only NIMBY bigotry, it is economic realism for local governments given the current tax structure. In fact, many cities resist any sort of housing at all, preferring tax-rich industrial and commercial developments. This preference creates regional problems associated with growth, since jobs are concentrated in communities that have managed to attract lots of industry and housing is elsewhere, necessitating heavy commuting and causing traffic congestion and air pollution. Local governments also find themselves presented with offers they can't refuse when a developer wants to build a major project such as a shopping center, hotel, or industry on their territory and credibly threatens to go elsewhere if rejected. In the nightmares of local decision makers, they stand firm on growth control, the development is built in an adjacent community, they lose the taxes, their own businesses suffer, and they still bear some of the problems the development generates, such as traffic. No wonder communities compromise on growth control.

Promoting Development

So powerful are the structural imperatives of growth that local governments no longer leave its pursuit to the private sector. Until the 1950s, committees of local business leaders or chambers of commerce promoted growth. At home, they backed business-oriented candidates and campaigned for bond measures to fund capital improvements and community projects. Beyond the city, they advertised its benefits and recruited development, especially industry. As multinational corporations replaced locally owned companies, big business withdrew somewhat from this activity, although they still support chambers of commerce, which continue as promoters in most communities. Many are partly funded by cities, but thousands of local governments also have their own development programs.

Stimulated by federal grant programs, most large cities, especially in the Frostbelt, launched **urban renewal or redevelopment** programs in the 1950s. Established in the Housing Act of 1949 and extended in subsequent acts, the federal urban renewal program was originally intended to demolish inner-city slums and build new housing, but over the years it was diverted to other forms of development, including offices, hotels, and civic buildings, all justified as boosting the local economy. In most cases, urban renewal programs were used to bolster declining downtown commercial districts, often transforming them into office centers. In the process, low-income neighborhoods were demolished and not replaced; the poor and minorities were pushed out (urban renewal was also labeled "negro removal"); and such housing as was constructed was often for the middle class rather than the poor or working classes who had previously lived in the target areas. Sunbelt central cities copied their Frostbelt counterparts, using urban renewal programs to "sustain the predominance of established business districts against the growing challenge of suburban areas," according to Carl Abbott.[43]

But, in most cases, urban renewal was the last gasp of local business elites. By the 1970s, resistance to redevelopment programs arose and became the big city equivalent of the suburban antigrowth movement. Minority, low-income, and eventually gentrifying middle-class neighborhoods that found themselves in the path of renewal programs led the resistance, but others joined them, criticizing public subsidies for private profits, the costs of projects, their special tax status, their drain on services in other areas, and their elitism (some called them "golden ghettoes"). In

1974, the federal government began phasing out its urban renewal program and as funds dried up and opposition rose, many cities let their programs run down or scaled them back. In some states, such as California, special tax structures funded the continuation of redevelopment programs, however, and even suburbs and small cities took advantage of the opportunity to subsidize development and beat their neighbors. Mike Davis reports that the California law, which had been intended "to allow cities to build low income housing . . . had become totally perverted by the 1970s, wealthy cities and industrial enclaves—from Palm Springs to City of Industry were using [it]."[44] These programs are generally less threatening to neighborhoods, but they are still criticized for diverting tax resources needed elsewhere and for failing to provide the low-cost housing they were created to build.

Even more common than redevelopment agencies are local **economic development offices.** Fifteen thousand cities and counties have such programs, so many that only small rural cities and elite suburbs seem to shun these efforts. Most were established in the 1970s, when federal aid began to decline and local revenues were capped by the tax revolt. These economic development offices have taken over some of the promotional efforts of business groups and chambers of commerce, attempting to attract new businesses and investment to their communities to expand their tax bases. Most do more than merely promote, however. Some offer "one-stop" shopping to developers, helping them win approval for projects by simplifying the planning process. Some put together land packages and arrange for subsidized infrastructure improvements to make their communities more attractive. Tax breaks of various sorts are also available. Forty states, for example, allow their communities to designate **enterprise zones,** where taxes on new development are deferred or reduced. As of 1993, seven hundred such zones had been hopefully established. Most seem to help local businesses rather than attracting much new investment, however. More commonly, cities invest in big projects—convention centers and stadiums are favorites—hoping for spin-off benefits. Denver, which operates a very aggressive economic development program, has built a stadium, a convention center, and a library and is currently completing a new airport larger than the island of Manhattan at a cost of nearly $4 billion. Philadelphia has invested in an "Avenue of the Arts," with concert halls and renovated theaters.

The efficacy of these programs is disputed, however, not only by local advocates of growth control but also by academic studies that suggest that the locational decisions of business and industry are little affected by local incentives.[45] Other factors, such as access to markets and a trained work force, proximity to supporting and related industries, and even the residence of company CEOs, are thought to be more influential than anything local governments can offer. Moreover, most economic development programs have failed to create jobs for those most in need—the poor and unskilled. Local officials, impelled by their lust for tax revenues, nevertheless eagerly pursue economic development. Despite the successes of the growth-control movement and the reduced power of local development interests, the growth machine rolls on, now led by local governments themselves.

Transportation—Policy or Nonpolicy?

Along with growth, the issue that comes up most frequently in opinion polls in both suburbs and central cities is transportation, usually expressed as complaints about traffic. Of course, the two are closely connected, since the way communities grow depends on available transportation, and growth, in turn, affects transportation.

Auto Transit

More than any other country in the world, the United States has opted for the automobile as its primary transportation mode, so however communities deal with this issue, the car is at its heart. Most people do not think of cars as public transportation like buses or subways, but even though individuals pay for and operate their own cars, they wouldn't get far without a vast network of roads and highways—a public transportation system. Most people don't think of the **costs of auto transit,** either—cars seem a cheap way to get around for just the price of a little gas. But as a transportation system, cars are actually very expensive for individuals, governments, and society.

Although gas is cheap in the United States—by public policy that may be changing—the total operating costs for a car driven for an average of 12,000 miles a year have been estimated at anywhere from $4500 to $8000. Of course, it depends on the car and the driver, but besides gas, the bill includes a share of the initial purchase price of the car, insurance, maintenance, parking, taxes, and more. Residents of urban areas with good public transit systems, in contrast, might spend as little as $1000 to $2000 per year, including occasional taxis and auto rentals for weekends away. But these direct costs are only a small portion of the price of our reliance on automobiles. Total annual subsidies for cars have been estimated at $200 billion, of which less than 25 percent comes from gas taxes.[46] In 1989, state, federal, and local governments spent nearly $100 billion on streets and highways. More is spent on parking facilities. Health care and insurance costs also are higher because automobiles are the major cause of air pollution and vehicular injuries. Vast amounts of land are required for auto transportation systems, too, not only for roads and parking, but also for driveways, garages, gas stations, and sales lots. As much as a third of the land in a typical Sunbelt city may be devoted to automobiles, but even their denser Frostbelt counterparts reserve a fifth of their territory for cars. Look around you. Surely this land, which generates no taxes itself, could be put to more productive uses. Instead, it is paved over, which is not only expensive in itself, but which requires further spending for storm drains and flood control, since water runs off the pavement. Some cities are even sinking (or subsiding) because the runoff does not replenish their underground water tables. To all these must be added the social costs of the automobile transportation system. As much as 20 percent of all U.S. households and 33 percent of those in central cities have no car. Children, elders, the disabled, and the poor are denied access to the system. Freeways have built walls through cities, isolating poor and minority neighborhoods. Some of those trapped in poverty can't get out simply because they don't have a car to get to the suburbs, where entry-level jobs are increasingly located. Finally, the segregation and isolation wrought by extensive suburbanization would not be possible without the automobile.

If cars are so costly, why do we continue to rely on them so exclusively for urban transportation? The simple answer is that we love them. Americans are not the only ones; people elsewhere eagerly acquire cars when they can afford to. Yet our love affair with the car is more passionate. In the United States, getting a car is as much a part of coming of age as sex. We give our cars names and see them as an expression of our personalities. Of course, some of this passion is the result of massive advertising by automakers, who sell us cars not just as a means of transportation, but as a life style, a way to make ourselves glamorous. We also love cars for the independence and privacy they give us. We can jump in and go where we want when we want, not relying on some transit system that runs on its own schedule rather than ours and doesn't stop at our doorsteps. In our cars, we can enjoy our own sound systems, talk on the phone, and feel secure, insulated from strangers. For many of us, they are a way of coping with urban diversity.

But on a more practical level, we need cars to get around. Lots of people say they'd use public transit if they could, but viable alternatives are rarely available because our cities have been built around automobile transportation, with low densities and suburban sprawl, especially in the Sunbelt. Our metropolitan areas are highly decentralized, with downtowns, edge cities, and industrial areas scattered, so they have many centers rather than one, and complex rather than simple, singular commute patterns. But to make public transit work, high densities and regular commuter corridors are necessary, with enough people going to the same places and near fixed rail or bus routes to have easy access. Except for our oldest cities, these conditions are rare in the United States. We urbanized— or suburbanized to put it more accurately—mainly in this century, the century of the automobile, and transportation was planned accordingly.

Public Transportation Policy

Our **auto-dependence,** however, was not merely an accident of technology and the popular appeal of cars. Powerful economic and political forces were also at work. In the 1920s, most U.S. cities, including those in the Sunbelt, had transit systems, usually electric trolleys running on rails. "Who needs a car in LA?" asks a character in *Who Framed Roger Rabbit,* "We've got the best public transportation in the world." This is taken as a joke now, but Los Angeles' Red Car trolleys once provided a good service. Then, in the 1930s, automakers, oil companies, and tire manufacturers conspired to purchase and eliminate these systems and replace them with buses and private autos. By the time the companies were taken to court and convicted of criminal conspiracy, a hundred trolley systems in forty-nine cities had been eliminated; by the 1950s, most trolleys in the United States were history. The same corporate interests, along with construction companies, also lobbied the state and federal governments to earmark funds raised by gas taxes exclusively for highway building. In addition to the highway lobby, local growth machines eagerly supported road building to provide access to their land and make development possible. So did the public. The governments responded, concentrating transportation spending almost exclusively on highways, a policy that stimulated suburbanization that, in turn, may have made alternative modes of transportation impossible.

Changing Priorities.   Yet, for the vast majority of Americans, the system worked well until recently. By the 1970s, with the costs of using a car rising and traffic congestion and air pollution increasing, governments and the public began to consider alternatives. A modest antiauto, protransit movement emerged. Environmentalists concerned about sprawling growth and air pollution took the lead, and the antigrowth movement often opposed road building to limit growth. Central city neighborhoods fought threatening freeway projects and won in Boston, New York, San Francisco, and elsewhere, in some cases bringing highway construction to a halt. The tax revolt hindered road building, but only slightly since highway money comes from gas taxes and is usually earmarked for highways only. In many communities, groups organized to lobby for transit. In a few, groups such as WalkBoston, Auto-Free New York, and the Pedestrian Council of Philadelphia even advocated the radical transportation alternative of walking— and better planning to facilitate it.

Federal, state, and local governments have responded by changing policies. The federal government and most states continue to spend most of their transportation funds on roads and highways, but allocations for transit have increased from virtually nothing to more notable sums. By 1989, for example, the states were spending $57.9 billion on highways and $8.7 billion on transit, while the federal government allocated $15 and $2 billion, respectively. President Clinton, however, proposed $8.4 billion for transit in his first budget. In the 1970s, many cities and counties took over failing private bus services, sometimes with state or federal aid or with voter approved tax increases. Sunbelt cities, facing the expense of building new **mass transit systems** to serve their sprawling communities, began to envy older cities with transit systems in place or under construction as in Washington, D.C. (1975), Baltimore (1983), and Buffalo (1985). San Francisco (1973), Atlanta (1979), and Miami (1983) built expensive but fast heavy-rail systems, while San Diego (1981), Portland (1986), Sacramento (1987), San Jose (1990), and Dallas (1995) opted for cheaper light-rail or trolley networks. Los Angeles built both. Other communities improved bus services, sometimes dedicating special traffic lanes for buses only. Often, cars with more than one passenger are also allowed to use such **high occupancy vehicle (HOV) lanes.** Some cities built networks of bike lanes or footpaths for walkers. A few considered tolls or even electronic charges for road use (no electronic system has yet been implemented). Meanwhile, between 1970 and 1990, road building slowed, with urban roads increasing by just 4 percent.[47]

Yet despite all this activity, use of the automobile actually increased. Vehicle miles doubled between 1970 and 1990 while use of public transportation declined from 8 percent of all trips to work in 1980 to 6 percent in 1990.[48] Transit ridership exceeded 10 percent only in a few large, older metropolitan areas with good networks—such as New York City, San Francisco, Chicago, Philadelphia, Boston, Miami, Pittsburgh, and Washington, D.C. In most Sunbelt metropolitan areas, fewer than 5 percent of trips were on public transit and 70 to 80 percent of commuters drove to work alone.

Alternative systems. These disappointing statistics fueled the debate about solutions. Big, heavy-rail systems like San Francisco's Bay Area Rapid Transit (BART) and Washington, D.C.'s Metro, are fast and attractive, but expensive, partly because to attain their speed their tracks must be completely separated from roadways. Critics say they serve mainly white-collar suburbanites commuting to central city business districts, while helping intrasuburban commuters and central city residents little. Trolleys, which can be built along existing streets and use well-tested technology, are cheaper, but much slower, and so are less attractive to long-distance commuters. Those that have been built also tend to serve white-collar, suburban commuters best. Buses are the most flexible form of transit because they are not tied to a track, so routes can be changed easily and a wider clientele can be served. But middle-class commuters seem to have an aversion to buses and personnel costs for buses are higher than for trolleys and trains. HOV lanes and staggered work hours ease traffic congestion, but mostly by spreading it out. Bikeways and footpaths, although attractive, are a realistic solution for few people as yet.

Some transit advocates insist that the best way to get people out of their cars and into public transit is to make driving more expensive and unpleasant. They push for higher gas taxes and parking fees and a halt to road building to allow traffic to grow more and more congested. Some have suggested higher tolls or fees, possibly electronically charged. Such a punitive approach might well get us out of our cars, but most likely it would be to storm the offices of the bureaucratic agency that imposed it.

Land Use and Transportation. Other transit advocates argue that better local land-use planning is needed to make any of these systems work. Instead of taking use of the automobile for granted and planning accordingly, cities need to plan in such a way as to make public transit more feasible by concentrating people and jobs near transportation corridors, whether that means freeways or trolleys. Generally, this means higher densities. One study found that "doubling residential density reduces the annual auto mileage per capita by 25 to 30 percent."[49] Some transit systems, however, require higher densities than others. The Sierra Club estimates that rail systems need densities of forty-three homes per acre within one-eighth of a mile of stations, but a University of Indiana study found eight units per acre sufficed for buses.[50] Central cities in the Frostbelt have been concentrating densities along transportation corridors for decades, but some Sunbelt and suburban cities, especially where the growth-control movement is strong, have only recently begun to do so; many also require a transportation study for any new development.

An alternative to higher densities is planning for a better balance of housing, jobs, and shopping so people need to travel shorter distances. Edge cities are an example of such developments. Instead of dense, centralized urban regions, we could plan for decentralized or multinucleated metropolitan areas with many centers rather than just one. To some extent this is already happening. As early as 1980, twice as many workers commuted to jobs within the suburbs as commuted from suburb to central city. This shift in commuting patterns helps, but it doesn't always solve transportation problems and may merely complicate the building of viable transit systems because commuters take a variety of routes rather than a single one. Commuting within suburbs may also take as long or longer than commuting between suburb and central city. The goal of better land-use planning is not merely to redistribute the commute but to reduce it by bringing jobs, housing, and other facilities closer together.

The Issues—Which Systems, Who Rides, and Who Pays?

Which alternative is best? The answer is that no single system suffices. Big cities not wholly dependent on the automobile rely on a complex network of trains, subways, trolleys, buses, roads, bikeways, footpaths, and even ferries. People have diverse transportation needs and differing tolerances for the various modes, so the systems will attract and serve different clienteles. Many people need to use two or three modes to reach their destinations, perhaps walking or driving to a station, taking a train or heavy-rail system to another, then a bus and a short walk. Few will find that a subway, trolley, or even bus takes them door to door, like their cars can (or could). Until an extensive and elaborate system is in place, with easy and convenient changes from one mode to another, it will be difficult to get people out of their cars. Yet building such a network takes time and despite the great hopes for systems such as San Francisco's BART or all the trolley lines that are being built, each is only a piece in the puzzle—with the solution years away. As systems come on line and the cost of driving rises in money, time, and air quality, more and more people will get on board. Or so transit planners hope. Changes in land-use planning, including higher densities and mixed uses, will also help, but only in the long term.

Who Rides and Who Pays?   The issue, however, is not only which system or combination is best. Other questions arise about who should be served and who should pay. Minority and central city leaders usually push for transit for those most in need—low-income people without cars—arguing that lack of transportation is part of the poverty trap. Environmentalists and most transit planners, however, argue that the primary goal should be getting people out of cars, so their target riders are less needy, middle-class, suburban commuters. Deciding who the riders should be affects the mode of transportation chosen, since the neediest will use buses, while experts say a "sexier" form of transit, like sleek heavy rail or trolleys, is required to get middle-class commuters out of their cars. Of course, low-income, inner-city dwellers can use systems designed for middle-class suburbanites, but they usually need to go to places not served by these systems. A related issue is who should pay—the riders or the taxpayers? Although taxpayers are reluctant, some of the new systems, such as those in California, have been funded by taxes approved by state or local voters. None would have been built without substantial federal subsidies, however. Once built, transit systems continue to require subsidies for operating costs. Fares paid by riders are never enough and raising fares to cover costs would only mean fewer riders. Continuing subsidies will be necessary, but while who pays for public transit remains an issue, we need to bear in mind that automobile transportation is subsidized, too.

Who Decides.   The ultimate issue in transportation, however, is **who decides.** And the answer is no one. Rather, many decide. We each make decisions when we choose where to live in relation to our work—and more people are making this decision consciously and carefully. Transportation is also affected by the land-use decisions of individual cities and counties. Taken together, these decisions structure the transportation needs of a region, yet they are not necessarily made with that in mind. The state and federal governments, which supply much of the funding for transportation, set their own priorities to which cities and counties must adapt decisions about road building and public transit. Some transit or bus systems are operated by individual cities, but most cross city boundaries. Many are managed by counties or special districts that encompass several cities. This is appropriate because transportation is a regional issue—few cities are self-contained and few of us confine our lives to just one city. Recognizing this, most metropolitan areas also have regional transportation planning agencies that operate no systems but which try to coordinate all the transit systems in their areas, including land-use planning—but often with little authority. The answer to who decides, then, is individuals, cities, counties, separate transit systems and agencies, regional authorities, and the state and federal governments. Coordination occurs only by occasional miracles of cooperation and luck.

The absence of coordination and a central authority makes democratic accountability difficult because no one is in charge. Having no central decision-maker also means that the system is biased in favor of the status quo—the automobile—which suits the powerful forces of the growth machine and the highway lobby very well. The nonpolicy is, in fact, their policy. Perhaps it is ours, too. Americans love their cars and although opinion polls report majorities in favor of public transit, most of us mean we support transit for other people—so we can drive in less traffic.

Ultimately, solving the transportation problem will require regional planning and regional authority, not only for transit systems, but also for land use, which takes us back to the issue of controlled growth and on to the subject of our next chapter, metropolitan regional government.

Local Limits

Several themes run through all the policies considered in this chapter. Race and class, although not discussed separately, seem to come up in every policy area and to be central factors in several. The power of bureaucracies—whether in education, welfare, police, or land-use and transportation planning—is also more apparent than it may have been in previous chapters. Perhaps most evident, however, are the limits local governments face in dealing with issues. These limits, as noted in chapter 1, include legal, fiscal, and structural constraints imposed by state and federal governments as well as political limits set by the voters and local power structures. What local governments do still matters, but their choices have narrowed. No wonder they so often function as growth machines. Land-use policy remains a primary local power and a tool to which local governments turn in the face of all their other difficulties. This may change, however, because of the larger problems of fragmentation of metropolitan areas and the needs/resources dichotomy, which also run through all the policies discussed in this chapter and which lead to the next step and the next chapter.

ESSENTIAL TERMS

outputs	general plan
school districts	capital improvement projects
school boards	costs of growth
racial segregation	antigrowth movement
school funding	growth controls
equalization	downzoning
Aid to Families with Dependent Children (AFDC)	impact fees
	concurrency requirements
Medicaid	consistency laws
workfare	gentrification
police-community relations	NIMBY
civilian review boards	urban renewal or redevelopment
community policing	economic development offices
gun control	enterprise zones
decriminalization of drugs	costs of auto transit
gangs	auto-dependence
private security	mass transit systems
annexation	high occupancy vehicle
zoning	(HOV) lanes
exclusionary zoning	who decides (about transit)

FIELDWORK

1. Pick a recent 3 to 6 month period and go through your local newspaper at the library to see which of the policy areas discussed in this chapter are under consideration in your community. What are the issues? Who takes which side? Who will decide?

2. Attend a meeting of a school board, or a police or planning commission. What issues were discussed? How much influence did administrators (superintendent of schools, police chief, or director of planning) and interest groups have?

3. Compare spending per pupil in the school districts in your area. Simply divide the total amount each district spends by the number of pupils it serves. Data will be available from individual school districts or possibly from a county office. You may also wish to investigate tax rates.

4. Go to your city or county planning department and ask to study your local government's general (or master) plan. Does it attempt to control growth? Has your city or county enacted any growth-control measures?

5. Study the transportation system or one mode of transportation in your area. Who is it meant to serve? Who pays? Who makes decisions?

NOTES

[1]*Brown v. Board of Education of Topeka*, 347 US 483, 1954.

[2]See J. Anthony Lukas, *Common Ground* (New York: Knopf, 1985).

[3]*The New York Times*, 14 December 1993.

[4]*The New York Times*, 3 May 1993.

[5]*Lau v. Nichols*, 414 US 563, 1974.

[6]*Serrano v. Priest*, 487 P.2d 1241, 1971.

[7]Thomas R. Dye, *Politics in States and Communities*, 7th ed. (Englewood Cliffs, NJ: Prentice-Hall, 1991), p. 421.

[8]*The New York Times*, 25 August 1993.

[9]*The New York Times*, 5 July 1992.

[10]Ibid.

[11]*Newsweek*, 20 December 1976.

[12]Telemundo poll reported by the *San Jose Mercury News*, 25 May 1991.

[13]See George Kelling, "Police and Communities: The Quiet Revolution," *Perspectives on Policing* (Washington, DC: U.S. Department of Justice, 1988); and *The Economist*, 9 May 1992, p. 26.

[14]*The New York Times*, 2 March 1994.

[15]Randy Arndt, "Drugs and Housing Plague Cities, Towns," *Nation's Cities Weekly*, 18 January 1989, p. 1.

[16]*Time*, 15 June 1992, p. 37.

[17]$52 billion a year is spent on private security companies that employ 1.5 million workers; spending on the nation's 600,000 professional law enforcement officers is half that amount. *The Guardian*, 19 July 1993.

[18]*Village of Euclid v. Ambler Realty Co.*, 272 U.S. 364, 1926.

[19]Harvey Molotch, "The City as a Growth Machine," *American Journal of Sociology* 82, no. 2 (1976): 310.

[20]Ibid., p. 309.

[21]Paul E. Peterson, *City Limits* (Chicago: University of Chicago Press, 1981), p. 29.

[22]Ibid., p. 129.

[23]Ibid., p. 31.

[24]Molotch, note 19, pp. 319–321.

[25]Peterson, note 21, p. 69.

[26]Carl Abbott, *The New Urban America* (Chapel Hill: University of North Carolina Press, 1987), p. 215.

[27]Madelyn Glickfeld and Nick Levine, *Regional Growth . . . Local Reaction* (Cambridge, MA: Lincoln Institute of Land Policy, 1992), pp. 13–15. Reprinted by permission.

[28]*Golden v. Remapo*, 285 N.E.2d 291 (1972) (NY) and *Petaluma v. Construction Industry Association*, 552 F.2d 897 (1975)(CA).

[29]See Richard E. DeLeon, *Left Coast City: Progressive Politics in San Francisco, 1975-1991* (Lawrence: University of Kansas Press, 1992), chapter 4.

[30]David E. Dowall, *The Suburban Squeeze: Land Conversion and Regulation in the San Francisco Bay Area* (Berkeley: University of California Press, 1984), pp. 133–134.

[31]Scott A. Bollens, "Constituencies for Limitation and Regionalism," *Urban Affairs Quarterly* 26, no. 1 (September 1990): 47.

[32]David R. Berman, "State Actions Affecting Local Governments," *The Municipal Year Book* (Washington, DC: International City/County Management Association, 1989), p. 129.

[33]*Southern Burlington County NAACP v. Township of Mount Laurel, I and II*, 336 A.2d 713 (1976) and 456 A.2d 390 (1983).

[34]Glickfeld and Levine, note 27, pp. 21–22, 43.

[35]Ibid., p.33.

[36]Mike Davis, *City of Quartz* (London: Vintage, 1992), p. 211.

[37]John Logan and Min Zhou, "Do Suburban Growth Controls Control Growth?" *American Sociological Review* 54 (June 1989): 461–471; and "The Adoption of Growth Controls in Suburban Communities," *Social Science Quarterly* 71, no. 1 (March 1990): 118–129.

[38]Glickfeld and Levine, note 27, p. 34.

[39]Ibid., p. 58.

[40]See Dowall, note 30; or Bernard Frieden, *The Environmental Protection Hustle* (Cambridge, MA: MIT Press, 1979).

[41]Advisory Commission on Affordable Housing, *Removing Barriers to Affordable Housing* (Washington, DC: U.S. Government Printing Office, 1991).

[42]Glickfeld and Levine, note 27, p. 26.

[43]Abbott, note 26, p. 148.

[44]Davis, note 36, p. 422.

[45]See Logan and Zhou, note 32; or Harold Wolman, "Local Economic Development Policy: What Explains the Divergence between Policy Analysis and Political Behavior?" *Journal of Urban Affairs* 10, no. 1 (1988): 19–28.

[46]David Morris, "For Fiscal and Ecological Health, Take Autos off Welfare," *San Jose Mercury News*, 20 November 1990.

[47]*The Economist*, 6 March 1993, p. 18.

[48]Ibid.

[49]Study by John Holtzclaw for the Natural Resources Defense Council reported in the *San Jose Mercury News*, 6 April 1991.

[50]Ibid.

14

Metropolitan Politics: The Future of Local Government

In previous chapters, we have considered politics and government in individual communities, but as we learned in chapter 3, metropolitan areas are made up of dozens or even hundreds of such entities. Here, we turn our attention to politics in the sprawling urban regions of the United States, including both central cities and suburbs.

The Census Bureau refers to these as **Metropolitan Statistical Areas (MSAs)** (see Figure 3-1) and to adjacent, interrelated MSAs as **Consolidated Metropolitan Statistical Areas (CMSAs).** We have examined the demographics of these areas, emphasizing the differences between central cities and suburbs and among suburbs, and we know that although they are economically and socially interdependent, with none able to stand alone, they are politically independent, or fragmented. For all their interdependence, no metropolitan area in the United States has a single government, although some have regional governments in addition to cities and counties.

The Fragmentation of Metropolitan Areas

The average MSA has 90 local governments, including cities, counties, towns and townships, special districts, and school districts. Large MSAs and CMSAs have many more, with some scoring over 1000. The Los Angeles CMSA covers 5 counties, 160 cities, and hundreds of special districts and school districts. Its population totals 14 million, of whom only 3.5 million live in the city of Los Angeles itself. The example of Los Angeles, as in so many ways, is extreme, but not unique. Other MSAs and

CSMAs also are characterized by a multiplicity of local governments: Allegheny County, Pennsylvania, where Pittsburgh is the central city, has a total of 84 municipalities; St. Louis County, Missouri, has 91, yet 40 percent of its total population lives outside its cities in unincorporated areas. But the **fragmentation of metropolitan areas** into many municipalities is only the beginning. They overlap with counties, towns, or townships, special districts, and school districts. "Even the professionals can't keep track of who does what," says Ann Siracusa, a Los Angeles city planner.[1] Responsibility for governing most neighborhoods is divided among a city, a county (or town or township), a school district, and several special districts. Some metropolitan areas, like the one centering on New York City, spill across state lines and a few, such as San Diego and El Paso, even cross international borders.

These great urban networks of social and economic interdependence are, for the most part, politically fragmented, with dozens or even hundreds of large and small governmental entities sometimes cooperating, but more often squabbling, competing, or ignoring one another. But this arrangement is not inevitable. In most other countries, urban regions have a single government, or perhaps a two-tiered system a little like our national structure, with a large-scale, regional "federal" government and local units with specified responsibilities. But in the United States, state laws of incorporation, much influenced by the politics of suburbanization, facilitate the formation of multiple local governments in metropolitan areas.

Still, fragmented government is not necessarily a problem. Indeed, it is politically popular and conforms nicely with U.S. mistrust of big government, enthusiasm for local democracy, and idealization of small town life. Some analysts assert that the multiplicity of governments in metropolitan areas usefully and democratically decentralizes power and policy and provides citizens with consumerlike choices of public services as packaged by different local governments. Others, including both academics and those active in local politics, argue that these benefits are outweighed by the problems caused by fragmentation. Foremost among these is the isolation of needs and resources. Other concerns include local governments competing with one another for tax advantages, ignoring the impact of what they do on their neighbors, and unable to coordinate policies on regional problems such as transportation or air pollution.

These dilemmas have not been ignored by metropolitan areas, however. Despite their fragmentation and the absence of a single regional government, a wide variety of mostly partial solutions to regional fragmentation is in operation. Ironically—or predictably?—most metropolitan areas have responded to the problems of multiple governments by adding yet more layers of government, which rarely achieve solutions. The future promises worsening problems, a continuing search for answers, and challenges to local government as we know it.

Metropolitan Fragmentation: Some Advantages

With a few exceptions, solutions to governmental fragmentation in metropolitan areas have thus far themselves been fragmentary, as different metropolitan regions patch together what they need to get by or simply accept the disadvantages of fragmentation and muddle through. They do so because the advantages of fragmentation are, at least for some, substantial.

Public Choice

Influential economic analysts of metropolitan fragmentation argue that one benefit of multiple governments is consumer choice. Local governments present packages of services and compete with one another to attract citizens and businesses; the more local governments, the greater the choice. Citizens who prefer low taxes and minimal services opt for one municipality, while those who want more and are prepared to pay for it opt for others, available on almost a sliding scale. Those who are discontented with the tax-and-service package of their communities may try to alter them through participation in the political process, exercising what choice theorists call "voice." Alternatively, they may exit, or vote with their feet, moving to another, more suitable community.[2]

With one or more big cities and a plethora of highly diverse suburbs, most metropolitan areas offer plenty of choices. In recent years, these have been supplemented by thousands of Common Interest Developments and Business Improvement Districts in self-contained housing developments and business districts. In a sense, these private, minigovernments are a refinement of public choice, covering areas that are smaller and more internally homogeneous than most suburbs. But most are ruled almost dictatorially by small committees, an undemocratic arrangement that reduces their residents' voice option and leaves acquiescence or exit as the only genuine choices.

Public choice theory explains, accepts, and even justifies metropolitan fragmentation, but the theory has its shortcomings. Many citizens and businesses make careful choices about where they locate, especially with regard to taxes, schools, housing, and homogeneity. Some do not, however, and even for those who wish to, information may be incomplete or inaccessible. Many citizens do not use or even know about all the services available. Moreover, some factors in our decisions about where to live are not under the control of the communities we choose, such as the amount of time it takes us to get to work or to amenities such as shopping centers or sports or theater facilities in other cities.

The most serious shortcoming of public choice theory, however, is its glossing over or acceptance of limits on individual choices. Racial discrimination, although now illegal and weaker, has long limited the choices available to minorities, while the cost of housing in the carefully zoned suburbs prevents all but the richest from exercising complete choice. What kind of alternatives do poor and working-class people have? They usually end up in the central city, paying the highest taxes. Public choice theorists would point out that in return for their high taxes, they get a bigger package of services, which they need and that they couldn't get by on the minimal services of rich, low-taxing communities. This is true, but many residents of the rich, low-taxing communities take advantage of facilities paid for by poorer central city residents, and disparities in spending on some services, such as education, may mean that the neediest are denied what they need most. Indeed, conditions are such in many central cities that the choice available to the poor may be more of a trap, containing them and condemning them to perpetual poverty.

Most people simply do not and cannot exercise the choices hypothesized by public choice theory. Most people and even many businesses, especially small ones, do not calculate locational benefits as consciously as public choice theory implies. Yet the theory has its merits. Along with other factors, many people and businesses that can afford it probably include tax and service packages at least to some imprecise degree in their deliberations about where to settle. The recent proliferation of residents' associations functioning as private governments suggests ever-greater numbers of people exercising such choices. Meanwhile, local governments compete with one another to present the most attractive package and entice the most advantageous residents and businesses. Although critics dismiss public choice theory as an acceptance of the fragmented and inequitable metropolitan status quo, it nevertheless helps explain the actions of citizens, businesses, and local governments and the political popularity of fragmentation.

Community and Local Democracy

Choice aside, the fragmentation of big urban regions into many local governments has the advantages of enhancing the sense of community and local democracy.

Many Americans identify with small towns much more than with big cities or their neighborhoods. Self-governing suburbs give them some of the feel of a small town, a sense of identity and community. Often, this feeling is illusory because people don't put down roots in a suburb the way they do in a small town. They usually commute to work and move on to other suburbs after a few years. Yet because people long for community, even the illusion offered by most suburbs takes on meaning. Besides, the **sense of community** comes not only from the fantasy of living in a small town but from the hard reality of segregation. As we know, most suburbs are homogeneous due to choice, discrimination, and zoning. Being surrounded by people like themselves gives suburbanites the illusion of community even if they rarely interact. After all, community means having something in common, although many people would like it to mean more.

Like the sense of community, **local democracy** also benefits from the fragmentation of metropolitan areas, at least theoretically. The little governments of small communities are more accessible and easier for citizens to influence than big ones. Instead of competing with lots of other people and groups, there are only a few. Running for office costs hundreds of dollars rather than hundreds of thousands. The voices of individual citizens can be heard. Yet in practice, residents of suburban communities actually participate in local politics less than those of big cities. Homogeneity and the absence of competition mean that others like themselves make decisions, so they get what they want without much participation. Although passive, this is still a sort of democracy, and although relatively few actually participate, the potential for easy access and influence is still greater than in larger cities.

The Politics of Giving People What They Want

The governmental fragmentation of metropolitan areas exists because it is politically popular. Politics created and now sustains fragmentation because it gives people what they want, homogeneous communities and low taxes. As political scientist Gary Miller writes, citizens "voted with their feet for low taxes, low levels of bureaucratic activity, low levels of government spending."[3] Nor is this Balkanized array of insular and independent entities a mere by-product of rapid, unplanned growth. Rather, it is the result of state and local policy. With over half of all Americans now living in suburbs, dealing with the growing problems caused by fragmentation will be politically difficult.

Metropolitan Fragmentation: Some Disadvantages

Several of the problems of the political fragmentation of metropolitan areas have already been mentioned in this and previous chapters, although others are less obvious. Whether obvious or not, however, the problems have become severe enough to impel a search for solutions in most metropolitan areas.

Economies of Scale

One of the most basic problems with fragmentation is that some units of government may be too small to provide some services efficiently and economically. Big cities "can get it for you wholesale," while smaller ones may have to pay more or forgo the service. A large city, for example, can get a good deal on the purchase of a fleet of police cars or can afford to establish a highly professional police academy, while a small city probably pays more for equipment and makes do with less formal training. Smaller departments, such as planning, personnel, or parks, can also be relatively expensive for small communities to provide.

Just how expensive, however, is debatable. One study of local governments in the Chicago metropolitan area found a strong relationship between fragmentation and higher cost government.[4] Other studies have found no such relationship,[5] and some assert that **economies of scale** depend on the particular service in question. In most cases, these economies are probably not major, however, and most small cities seem to make up for such costs with frugality or just making do with a little less. They are usually able to do so because their problems, like crime, are not so severe and they need not offer the range of services most big cities feel obliged to provide. Larger scale projects, however, such as water supply, sewage treatment, or solid waste disposal, cost far too much for a single small city to build or manage, while big cities take them on as a matter of course. Fortunately for small cities, this is often an easy problem to solve. They can cooperate to provide the service or buy it from a larger city, although sometimes the larger city denies the service unless smaller ones agree to be absorbed, as Los Angeles did with water and San Jose did with sewage treatment.

The Needs/Resources Dichotomy

A far more serious and perhaps insoluble problem with fragmentation is the needs/resources dichotomy. Communities within metropolitan areas are segregated by race and class, with needy and dependent populations concentrated in declining central cities while surrounding, politically independent suburbs enjoy fewer problems and stronger tax bases. Metropolitan areas are polarized, with population groups separated from one another and tax resources isolated from needs. Moreover, parts of each urban region do not bear their fair share of its burdens, including low-income housing, temporary shelters for the homeless, and community care facilities for addicts and alcoholics or the disabled and elderly. A regional government, in theory, might distribute—or redistribute—both resources and burdens more equitably.

But metropolitan fragmentation means more than the unfair distribution of needs and resources. It also means outright competition as each jurisdiction strives to attract projects that will generate more tax revenue than they will cost in services and to avoid or clear their communities of any elements that might be a net tax burden. This emphasis on costs and benefits or fiscal zoning in land-use decisions may produce tax advantages and private profits, thus satisfying the growth machine, but it exacerbates the needs/resources dichotomy and other regional problems.

Externalities

Each government in a metropolitan region makes independent decisions, but often these decisions have an impact on others. A housing or industrial development might cause traffic and air pollution, for example, or the flight pattern of an airport in one city might cause noise problems in another. A suburb might persuade a corporation to move its headquarters out of the central city, netting taxes and jobs for itself, but worsening the disparity in needs and resources. These spillovers are called **externalities:** what one does affects others beyond its borders. Externalities may also affect other governments responsible for different services within their borders if, for example, a city zones housing projects where a school or water district cannot provide services.

Externalities are not all negative, however. Positive spillovers occur when cities provide services nonresidents use, such as an airport, shopping center, stadium, or jobs in a business or industrial district. Suburban commuters often enjoy benefits like these (and roads, police protection, and many others) without paying much in the way of direct taxes to support them. But although they pay most of their taxes in the suburbs where they reside, they may pay some sales or entertainment taxes elsewhere, and their presence as workers or shoppers generates business and drives up property values, thus increasing tax revenues.

Whether negative or positive, however, externalities are beyond the control of any but the jurisdiction that makes the decision that generates them, yet they have a regional impact, and harm or help other local governments that have no say.

Regional Problems

As we know, cities within a region compete to avoid projects that entail any sort of social burdens and to attract those that will expand their tax bases. Sometimes their competition for projects such as airports or stadiums can be ridiculously expensive and inefficient. More frequently, their decisions result in externalities that create problems for metropolitan areas that extend beyond the boundaries of any single government.

Local land-use decisions create not only imbalances in tax resources, but transportation problems when jobs are in one part of the metropolitan area and housing is in another. Transportation policy transcends the boundaries of individual communities because residents do not confine their activities to a single city, nor is any city self-contained and self-sufficient. Highways and mass transit systems must cross boundaries.

Land-use and transportation decisions also affect air and water quality. A single city could ban automobiles and every other source of air pollution and still only marginally improve its own air quality because of drift from other cities, sometimes dozens of miles away. The same applies to industrial pollution and underground water tables and the flow of rivers. Nor do most cities dispose of all their solid waste within their own boundaries, relying instead on regional dumps or rural areas. Most of these policies affect the environment, which may be the biggest loser in the politics of fragmentation. Individual governments may consider their own environments, but none may care for that of the region as a whole.

These increasingly obvious and serious problems are almost impossible to solve because in the absence of any regional authority, they can be addressed only by cooperation, which is difficult to obtain from governments accustomed to competing with one another and jealous of their tax resources and land-use powers. Not surprisingly, most metropolitan areas have done little to deal with **regional problems** until recently.

Responsibility, Coordination, and Accountability

Ultimately, the problem in most metropolitan areas is that nobody is in charge. No government is responsible for what goes on or for solving regional problems. Nor do the many governments within a metropolitan area readily coordinate what they do or cooperate on policies and programs. Each does what it considers best for itself and its constituents, none accepts responsibility for regional repercussions. Their actions are usually competitive, sometimes contradictory, and almost always uncoordinated, more often exacerbating rather than ameliorating regional problems.

These problems are increasingly serious, however, and they are also increasingly salient to the citizens, who cite traffic and air pollution as two of their top worries in opinion polls on local issues. Yet who can citizens hold accountable for regional problems? In most cases, the answer is no one, because no one is in charge. Their own local governments might be victims of negative externalities rather than their cause—and if the actions of one city have negative effects elsewhere, its own residents may benefit too much to complain. Much as people care about traffic and air pollution, regional cooperation is rarely a hot issue in local elections.

Although **responsibility, coordination, and accountability** on regional matters are weak or nonexistent in fragmented metropolitan areas, opponents of regional government worry that the big and distant institutions it may require will be no more democratically accountable. In most metropolitan areas, when regional agencies have been created to confront some area-wide problems, they have been invisible—unelected, ignored by the media, lost in the array of local institutions that govern us, and almost completely beyond public control.

Ways of Coping with Metropolitan Fragmentation

Despite the fear of big government and the loss of local autonomy, regional problems have grown serious enough to impel action in most metropolitan areas. Sometimes states impose solutions on fractious regions; sometimes individual communities find their own ways of coping; sometimes they even cooperate. Some of their attempted solutions are simple and straightforward, using available institutions and systems; others are more creative and complex.

Annexation

The most obvious way to solve the problem of fragmentation is to avoid it by having existing cities annex adjacent land as it develops to create one big city rather than allow new developments to form their own governments by incorporation. States may prevent fragmentation by making **annexation** easy and incorporation difficult. Few states do so, however, because suburbanization and fragmentation are so politically popular. Moreover, most big cities are already boxed in by independent suburbs, so annexation is not an option.

At least in some parts of the country, however, **annexation** is still possible. During the 1970s and 1980s, existing cities annexed an average of 800 square miles a year. Much of this was by suburbs, but central cities in the Sunbelt were also active and are only now beginning to be boxed in. Cities in Texas, North Carolina, and Florida, where state laws facilitate annexation, were most active, as were those in California, although incorporation is also easy there. Portland, Oregon, led the country in population added by annexation, with 52,900 residents of already developed areas brought into the city limits in the 1980s.[6] Some big cities, including Oklahoma City and several in Texas, have annexed huge tracts of undeveloped land to ensure that continued expansion falls within city limits and under their control. "If you can't make the neighboring cities help pay your costs," said Fort Worth (Texas) Mayor Bob Bolen, "then you have to expand your boundaries to the point that you take in the growth areas."[7] Texas state law also prohibits the incorporation of new cities within 3 miles of existing municipalities without their permission. Texas cities such as Houston and San Antonio, which have exercised these powers vigorously, have managed to contain their suburbs and prevent fragmentation.

In most metropolitan areas, it is too late for annexation to prevent fragmentation because the suburbs have already incorporated and surrounded the central city. Such annexation as occurs is by outer suburbs, which at least has the merit of preventing further fragmentation. But in most states, residents and property owners in areas subject to annexation have virtual veto power and they usually exercise it to protect their perceived self-interest. Recognizing that this resistance contributes to fragmentation, some states have tightened up laws on incorporation and made it easier for cities to annex unincorporated areas, especially those within their own borders.

Where fragmentation already exists, the traditional alternative to annexation is **consolidation,** whereby two cities merge. Majority approval by the voters and city councils of both cities is usually required and rarely obtained. Central cities are willing, but their suburban counterparts usually are not, preferring to retain their independence, homogeneity, and tax resources. Sometimes "shotgun weddings" occur when one prospective partner has something the other can't do without, such as water or a sewage treatment facility, but more often such situations are resolved by cooperative or contractual agreements to consolidate services rather than consolidate cities, since none wants to surrender its identity.

Contracts

Another way cities can obtain such services is by contracting for their provision by the county or another city. **Contracting for services** is also called the **Lakewood plan** after the city in Los Angeles County where it was introduced by developers seeking to avoid annexation and taxation by nearby Long Beach. Instead, they incorporated the city of Lakewood and then purchased services by contract from the County of Los Angeles, which now offers fifty-eight different services, from tree planting to animal control. A third of Los Angeles County's eighty-five cities do not have their own police force, contracting with the county sheriff instead. By providing so many services, Los Angeles County has become a sort of regional government, although its cities may opt in or out service by service. The Lakewood plan has been widely copied around the country, with over 90 percent of all local governments contracting for some sort of service.[8] The practice is used most extensively in the West.

Contracting for services has proven practical and popular because it allows cities to acquire a wide variety of cost-efficient services without surrendering local control. They can sometimes even seek competitive bids from, say, a county, a large city, and a private provider. "The assumption," management expert David Morgan observes, "is that city administrators no longer have to be concerned with enforcing bureaucratic productiveness. Instead they can concentrate on representing consumer interests in negotiating advantageous price and service contracts."[9] Economies of scale are easily and flexibly obtained and, as cities grow, they retain the option of providing the contracted services themselves. The Lakewood plan makes small, independent suburbs possible and puts the public choice model into effect, at least for some.

This is a somewhat idealized version of contracting, however. Cities usually have little choice about which agencies they contract with and consequently have minimal bargaining power, pushing up costs. Detroit's suburbs, for example, grumble about the price of water and sewage services they purchase from the central city, yet are unwilling to raise the substantial sums systems of their own would require. Another problem with the Lakewood plan, as with public choice theory, is that everyone cannot take advantage of its benefits. Municipal boundaries isolate poor communities from rich ones, so some can afford more than others. As Los Angeles expert Mike Davis points out, the Lakewood plan was instigated not for efficiency but for "self-seeking economic advantage," enabling suburbs to "zone out service-demanding low-income and renting populations and eliminate homegrown union or bureaucratic pressures for service expansion."[10] Rather than solving the problem of fragmentation, contracting for services actually facilitates it by enabling small, autonomous cities to survive.

Cooperation

Another, more positive way of dealing with fragmentation is by cooperation, whether formal or informal. Local governments sometimes consult or even lobby one another to minimize negative spillovers, coordinate programs and land-use planning, and reduce competition. Joint committees of council members, administrators, and/or prominent citizens are often formed to facilitate such cooperation. Out of necessity, **regional cooperation** on a wide range of issues became more common and more formal in the 1980s. Cities banded together through joint-powers agreements and set up new, shared agencies to provide services such as sewage treatment or to build facilities such as airports or stadiums, apportioning costs among them. Sometimes administrators lead the way, with fire chiefs, for example, working out mutual aid agreements for cross-boundary emergency assistance, or police chiefs agreeing on 911 arrangements. In Wake County, North Carolina, for example, local governments cooperate on economic development, solid waste, and libraries. Albuquerque and Bernalillo County in New Mexico built a shared civic center. In Ohio, Greater Cleveland was formed by the central city, suburbs, and county to share the costs of some large projects. More radically, local governments in the Louisville, Kentucky, and Minneapolis–St. Paul areas agreed to share tax revenues, at least to some extent.

Councils of Governments

To further cooperation, particularly on land-use planning, local governments in metropolitan areas (and many rural ones as well) have established voluntary **councils of governments** or **COGs.** The first was organized in the Detroit area in 1954, but other big metropolitan areas soon followed. Originally intended simply to improve communications, COGs got a boost in the mid-1960s when the federal government began to require regional planning and review as a condition of grants to cities to make sure its money was not wasted on duplicate projects in the same region (such as three international airports) or spent on projects with negative externalities (like many airports). The councils took on this task in most areas, gaining a modest power, official status as a regional planning agency, and federal funding for their operations. Thanks to federal policy, the number of COGs burgeoned, reaching 670 by 1980.

As their name implies, councils of governments are made up of representatives of cities and counties, usually council members, commissioners, and/or supervisors. Each member government has one vote, although some COGs make modest adjustments to reflect differences in population. The primary function of COGs is the coordination of land-use planning within their regions, but as voluntary bodies they have no power of enforcement other than the good will of their members. They gained some authority from federal grant requirements for regional review, however, and while grants were rarely vetoed by COGs, projects were commonly revised to minimize any negative regional impact. But the Reagan administration dropped the reviews, denying COGs even this modest power; cuts in grants also gave COGs less to do and made them more reliant on membership dues for funding. Many ceased to function.

Even if they had legislative and taxing powers, however, COGs might not take on regional problems with much vigor because their one government/one vote system of representation means suburbs greatly outnumber central cities and the member governments are loath to interfere in one another's affairs. The COG nevertheless perform useful functions, acting as clearinghouses for information and sometimes helping with the development of other regional agencies and cooperative programs. Primarily, however, they are a forum of communication among local governments in each region, a task that may seem negligible, but which is surely necessary if regional problems are to be addressed.

Counties

Counties have traditionally been the primary local government for rural and unincorporated areas, which are normally (but not always) unurbanized. Traditions have changed, however, with big **urban counties** taking on municipal functions in the past few decades and with a few beginning to act somewhat like regional governments. In some cases, such as Los Angeles County, this is accomplished by extensive contracting and the bargaining power it entails. In others, counties have formally assumed responsibilities previously left to cities, such as transit, emergency communications (911), health, and housing. These transfers of responsibilities are sometimes mandated by the states, but more often cities no longer wish to perform the services or economies of scale make it too costly for them to do so. Transit is a good example of both.

City/county consolidation is a more radical solution to fragmented government. Here, a county and one or more of the cities within it merge to form a single government, with a new county council and executive replacing those of the previous county and cities and previous separate departments such as police and sheriff merged into one. Consolidated city/counties operate in only a few metropolitan areas (see Table 4-1), although these include Baton Rouge, Boston, Denver, Honolulu, Indianapolis, Jacksonville, Nashville, New Orleans, New York City, Philadelphia, and San Francisco. These mergers reduced duplication of services, but most predated suburbanization and involved only one city and one county, thus decreasing the number of governments by only one. New York City's consolidations, however, merged several counties, and latter-day consolidations in Nashville, Jacksonville, and Indianapolis merged counties, central cities, and suburbs.

City/county consolidations seem a simple solution to fragmentation, yet they are rare in the United States, largely due to political resistance in the suburbs and among local officials. Although consolidations have met with some success in the South and West, dozens of proposed mergers have been put before the voters and rejected. Consolidation proposals have been defeated three times in recent years in Sacramento, California, for example. But even if voters were willing, such consolidations would work only where urbanization is contained within one county. This is the case in a majority of MSAs, but all the larger ones sprawl across several counties and even across state and national boundaries. Most city/counties are now surrounded by suburban cities and counties. For city/county consolidation to work as a regional government, multicounty consolidations would be necessary and, given political attitudes about single-city/county consolidations, these seem less than likely to win voter approval.

Special Districts

The most common way of dealing with regional problems is through the creation of special districts or authorities to handle each one, as needed. Single-purpose **special districts** are governments created by states, existing local governments, or the voters, with limited taxing and policy-making powers confined to a specific subject or policy area and a defined territory, which may be a small part of a city, parts of several cities, or all the cities and counties in a region. Some, called authorities, build bridges or other infrastructure facilities. Special districts are the most numerous of all forms of local government, totaling 29,532. Most of these are not regional in scope, however. Those that are most commonly provide such services as transit, water, air quality, conservation, sewage, airports, parks, libraries, fire protection, and flood control. Perhaps the mother of all special districts is the Port of New York Authority, established in 1921 by an interstate compact between New Jersey and New York to manage transportation facilities. The authority, with a board appointed by the governors of the two states, manages tunnels, bridges, three major airports, and the World Trade Center.

Special districts are a highly flexible way of dealing with regional issues, quicker and far less controversial to establish than multipurpose regional governments. They deal only with a commonly recognized and agreed upon regional problem, with clearly defined responsibilities and strict fiscal limitations. They do not threaten existing cities and counties and take away only the minimum amount of power deemed necessary to address a problem. But despite their flexibility and popularity, special districts augment metropolitan fragmentation by adding yet more layers of government and potential new levels of conflict. Worse, these added layers are almost invisible. The governing bodies of most special districts are appointed by other officeholders rather than being elected, so accountability and representation are minimal. Although they have power over us, most voters do not know special districts exist, much less who their nominal representatives are. The media, too busy with other stories, doesn't help.

Perhaps even more seriously, special districts, though intended to deal with regional problems, do so only on a piecemeal basis, with, for example, one special district responsible for air pollution, another for transportation, while COGs make land-use plans and cities make the actual decisions. Air quality, transportation, and land use are interrelated, however, so conflict among the multiple decision-makers is inevitable unless one has power over the others, which is rarely the case except on small and narrowly defined issues. In southern California, for example, the South Coast Air Quality Management District (SCAQMD), a special district covering the 5-county Los Angeles CMSA, has imposed a transportation plan to meet its air quality goals, much to the objections of the Southern California Association of Governments (SCAG), the area's COG, as well as its various transit districts, 5 counties, and 160 cities, all of which see SCAQMD as taking their powers.

Special districts are good at planning regional parks and airports and may achieve economies of scale in the provisions of some services, such as water supply and sewage treatment. They are less effective, however, at solving regional problems that are difficult to isolate, such as transportation and the environment, or at improving regional planning or redressing the needs/resources dichotomy.

Federation

An obvious, but largely untried answer to metropolitan fragmentation, economies of scale, and regional problems is a **federation** of local governments, dividing responsibilities between a large, regional government and smaller units along the lines of the state and national governments in the United States. The province of Ontario, Canada, set up the model metropolitan federation in Toronto in 1953; Winnipeg, Manitoba, also operates a federated system. In Toronto, a regional council, with representation about equally divided between the central city and its suburbs, is in charge of strategic or large-scale planning, transportation, air quality, sewers, water, and police, while local boroughs are responsible for smaller scale, local land use, streets, parks, and other local services, according to economy of scale. Metro government has reportedly helped Toronto build an excellent area-wide education system, good public transport, and affordable housing in mixed-income neighborhoods.[11] Physical, planning, and environmental issues are better handled than in fragmented metropolitan areas, and the needs/resources dichotomy is also largely resolved, although social welfare issues have not been given as high a priority as some hoped, presumably because of suburban representation on the regional council.[12] The chief issue in these systems, as in other federations, is the division of responsibility between the larger and smaller components.

No U.S. metropolitan area has tried a Toronto-style federation, but Miami and its suburbs adopted something similar in 1957, with Dade County taking on even more regional responsibilities than the urban counties discussed earlier. Cities there still provide education, police, and other local services, while the county is responsible for mass transit, water, sewage, and some other functions. Cities have land-use powers, but the county does strategic planning and sets standards. As in the Canadian federations, the division of labor is an issue and has generated hundreds of court cases. Some rich suburbs have even tried to secede from the county. Although two-tiered systems like these have been considered in other metropolitan areas, including Boston, Pittsburgh, and St. Louis, none have yet been adopted.

Emerging Systems

Federation and consolidation are rare, but some metropolitan areas have nevertheless moved beyond the ad hoc hodgepodge of contracts, cooperative agreements, special districts, and urban counties to new forms of regional government. Seattle, Portland, and the Twin Cities of Minneapolis–St. Paul have all done so, and similar plans are being developed elsewhere. In each of these areas, existing cities and counties have been retained, with a new, regional body imposed over them, thus creating a **three-tiered structure.** These new **multipurpose regional agencies** often combine previous single-purpose special districts into one more comprehensive and efficient unit, although their functions are still limited.

The Municipality of Metropolitan Seattle, for example, was created by the voters of King County in 1958 as a special-purpose government to handle water quality and sewage. Garbage collection and public transit

FIGURE 14-1   Seattle Metro Council

Source: Tracy Peterson, "Seattle Metro: Regional Solutions to Local Problems," *Government Finance Review* 6, no. 3 (June 1990): 21. Used by permission of the Government Finance Officers Association.

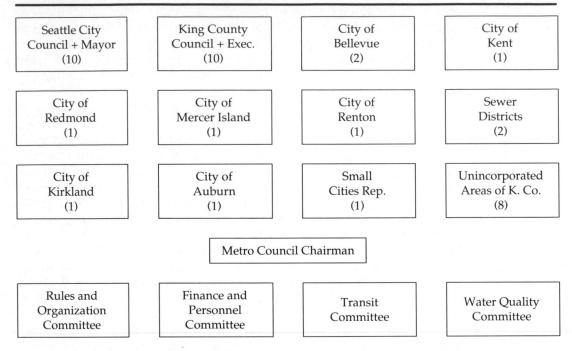

were added to its responsibilities later. The Seattle Metro Council is made up of representatives appointed by its component county, cities, and sewer districts, roughly balanced by population (see Figure 14-1). But while Seattle Metro can address pressing regional issues and the precedent has been set for adding others as needed, Seattle and King County contain only half of the Puget Sound metropolitan area, so it is not yet a comprehensive regional body.

The Greater Portland Metropolitan Service District, approved by voters in 1978, handles a similar range of activities plus a zoo and a convention center, but with three counties under its jurisdiction, its coverage is more comprehensive. Portland Metro's planning powers are strong enough to override local planning decisions if necessary. It has used these powers to contain development, preserve open space, and increase jobs and housing in downtown Portland. Alone among the nation's multipurpose metropolitan governments, Portland Metro's twelve-member council is directly elected—by district rather than at-large.

The most advanced of the emerging metro governments is the Twin Cities Metropolitan Council, created by the Minnesota state legislature (rather than the voters) in 1969. Originating as a regional planning body (or COG), responsibilities have been added gradually and now include sewers, waste management, open space, transportation, airports, sports facilities, public housing, and some social services. Unlike most other metropolitan bodies, which rely on state grants or dues from other governments for funds, the Twin Cities Council has taxing and borrowing powers. Most local services and land-use decisions, however, are left to the cities and counties, with the Metro Council exercising veto power if local plans contradict those of the region. Tax disparities within the region are mitigated by a tax-base-sharing plan whereby any jurisdictions that exceed average growth by 40 percent share the added revenues with the others. But while the Twin Cities Metro Council is probably the most progressive in the nation, local critics find its powers inadequate and allege that cities and counties have "by-passed" it on "important decisions."[13] Another complaint is that the council is appointed by the governor of Minnesota rather than elected. Direct election might be the next appropriate step, although some analysts worry that this would only increase the ability of the suburbs to block needed actions.[14]

Meanwhile, the Atlanta region and California's major metropolitan areas are also moving toward the three-tiered metro model. The Atlanta Regional Commission (ARC) is already asserting planning influence greater than COGS thanks to supportive state legislation, but California's metropolitan regions have not yet got beyond special districts and COGs. In the San Francisco/Oakland/San Jose CMSA, which includes nine counties and ninety-eight cities, a coalition of elected officials, business, and environmental leaders proposed the merger of the region's COG, air quality, and transportation agencies, with water and conservation districts to follow. At the moment, the functions of the five agencies—of which the voters are mostly unaware—overlap and their policies may even contradict one another. Tax sharing and how the new Metro Council's members would be selected were contentious issues, however, and in 1991, the plan was rejected by the region's COG, thanks to the votes of the representatives of the area's small cities and less urban counties. A similar merger of existing regional agencies is being mooted for greater Los Angeles, although the challenge there is even more formidable. San Diego, however, has made some progress. After the voters created a blue ribbon advisory committee to make recommendations on regional growth in 1988, the planning powers of SANDAG, the area's COG, were expanded; transportation planning, handled by separate agencies in the San Francisco and Los Angeles areas, was already managed by SANDAG.

The Politics of Regional Government

As the forgoing inventory of ways of coping with metropolitan fragmentation suggests, any reforms face considerable resistance. Although most metropolitan areas have grappled with the problem, few have made much progress and most make do with partial solutions such as contracting and special districts. The public takes little interest in regional politics despite constant complaints about air pollution and traffic congestion. When asked in referenda, however, the voters almost invariably reject regional government. Perhaps that's why they are so seldom asked and why the issue is usually fought out among elites. But whether the voters or elites make the decision, self-interest seems to be their primary motivation.

Who Favors Regional Government

The main **proponents of regional government** have been central city businesses, newspapers, and politicians and, more recently, environmentalists and corporations. Downtown interests support regional government in hopes of containing expanding shopping centers. Major newspapers support regionalism partly because it is the sort of good government issue that newspapers like to crusade on but also because a single metropolitan government would make their job of covering local news easier, provide bigger stories of wider interest, and cut into readership of their booming suburban competitors. Central city politicians campaign for regional government because they covet the tax resources of the suburbs and justly hope to redistribute some of the burdens of the metropolitan area more widely; some may see regional government as a means of political advancement. Central city interest groups sometimes back their politicians on regionalism as a means of sharing their burdens with the suburbs. Reform or good government groups, such as the League of Women Voters, also often advocate regional government on the grounds of economy, efficiency, and fairness.

All of these are fairly traditional proponents of regionalism, but in the 1980s, some new cheerleaders joined them. Environmentalists, alarmed by air and water pollution and disappearing open space, became avid regionalists, seeing metropolitan government as the only hope for sensible conservation and planning. Corporations also climbed on the regional bandwagon. Most showed little interest until lately, since fragmentation made it easier for them to get their own way. But in the 1980s, many realized that bad regional planning was driving up housing costs and commuting time for their workers, and thus costs and wages for themselves. Some exercised the exit option, abandoning major metropolitan areas for smaller ones or moving their operations out of the country. Others settled in to see if they could make their regions work a little better and came to the conclusion that some sort of regional government might help. Big corporate developers who operate on a regional scale sometimes join them, although businesses that are part of local growth machines generally do not. Over all, however, corporate interest has given regionalism a big boost, although it should be noted that these businesses are worried about planning and transportation, not the redistribution of tax resources, and that they are quite content with unelected regional agencies that they can easily influence—perhaps more economically and effectively than many little governments.

Who Opposes Regional Government

Suburbanites are the principal **opponents of regional government** and, since they outnumber central cities in voters as well as in the number of local governments, however a decision on metro government is made, they usually win. Suburban citizens wish to protect their homogeneous communities, property values, and taxes. They rage about traffic, air pollution, inefficiency, and other regional problems, but when push comes to shove, they protect their own interests. In a 1985 survey of Orange County, California, with 2.2 million people and twenty-six cities, political scientist Mark Baldassare found that despite their expressed frustration with such issues, only 28 percent favored city/county consolidation, while 63 percent were opposed and remained "unwilling to give away local power."[15] Officials of suburban governments usually have a more sophisticated understanding of regional issues and generally accept existing solutions, such as contracts, COGs, and special districts. Of course, these protect suburban autonomy except where limited regional action is absolutely necessary. They balk at more radical (or thorough) solutions, protecting their communities as well as their own jobs and powers.

Suburbanites are not the only antagonists to regional government, however. Conservative and libertarian antagonists to big government are vociferous opponents. Public employees and their unions usually oppose advanced forms of metropolitan government because consolidation of institutions may reduce the number of jobs. Local growth machines also oppose regionalism because they generally get their way in the current, fragmented setup, and they know better planning will restrict them. Perhaps surprisingly, central city minorities that might be expected to support regionalism as a means of tapping suburban tax resources also usually object to regional government. African American and Latino leaders often see regionalism as a means of diluting their political power just as minorities are finally becoming majorities in big cities. And diluting the minority vote was a primary motivation for city/county consolidation in Indianapolis in 1969, when black political clout in that city was growing.[16] As in Indianapolis, metro government would reinstate white majorities almost everywhere. Minority leaders in big cities have concluded that they would rather have power over their decaying, needy communities than share it by being reduced to minorities once more. They also recognize that proposals for metro government do not always include redistribution of tax resources and even if a common pool is established, suburban majorities might demand attention to their concerns rather than those of the central city, as some studies suggest is the case in Toronto.[17]

Both suburban and central city opponents to metropolitan regional government emphasize that they are defending local democracy as well as self-interest, however. Metropolitan fragmentation facilitates public choice, community, and local democracy, they say. Grassroots groups, including central city neighborhoods, minorities, and suburbanites could easily be swamped by a big, regional government operating beyond their reach. They would find themselves competing not just with each other, but with regional power holders such as corporations. However, there is nothing inherently evil in larger units of government and more comprehensive regional planning, although there is a great deal wrong when the move to regionalism disenfranchises the grassroots. The current system of regional governance, with its invisible, unaccountable, mostly appointed bodies, already does that. Stronger regional government does seem necessary and even inevitable. If so, it should not be imposed by economic elites from the top down, as seems likely, but constructed from the bottom up in such a way as to assure representation for the least powerful neighborhoods and cities. This will not happen, however, unless grassroots forces, most of whom take little interest in issues beyond their own communities, overcome their parochialism, accept the inevitability of regional government, and involve themselves in shaping it.

The Future of Metropolitan Regional Government

Some researchers think that the current system is a good and flexible adaptation to the complexity of metropolitan areas,[18] yet as regional problems grow, new forms of metropolitan government seem likely. Local governments are already being pushed to act, particularly in the South and West, where rapid growth has intensified the problems and fragmentation has exacerbated them. Transportation and air pollution are key issues, putting regionalism on the agenda of Sunbelt cities that, unlike their counterparts in the Frostbelt, lack mass transit systems. On these and other issues, local governments all over the country are taking regional action, with more formal cooperation and more county provision of urban services. New special districts and limited multipurpose regional agencies like those in Seattle, Portland, and Minneapolis are also emerging.

Given local resistance, however, the impetus for stronger regional authorities may come from higher levels of government. The federal government under President Clinton is showing greater interest than it did under Presidents Reagan and Bush, and increased funds for regional projects and planning are likely. The states, which actually created the problem in the first place with their laws of incorporation and annexation, are also reasserting themselves. Minnesota, for example, initiated the Twin Cities Metro Council. According to *The Municipal Year Book*, several states have already "reexamined laws that restrict annexation, consolidation, and the ability of localities to enter contracts and agreements."[19] Several have introduced statewide growth plans. Texas and other states have given some of their cities limited "extraterritorial powers" to regulate land use in adjacent unincorporated areas. California has witnessed a flurry of legislative action on regional issues, with fifty bills introduced in 1990 alone, including several plans for regional planning bodies and one for shared development revenues. None has been enacted, but they reinforce local movements in California's metropolitan areas and suggest that change is imminent. Despite these positive moves, however, the suburban majorities of most state legislatures seem more interested in planning than in redressing the imbalance of needs and resources.

The courts, at least in some states, have taken a different line. In California, Texas, and, more recently, Kentucky, state courts have ordered governors and legislators to resolve spending gaps between rich and poor school districts. Many states had begun to equalize spending without court orders; others are under pressure to do so. Thus far court-mandated equalization has been confined to education, which often has special status in state constitutions, but theoretically it could be applied to other services as well.

Public opinion could also be a source of change, and there are some signs that even in highly suburbanized areas, attitudes are changing. "There's a general sense that government has gotten us into a mess," says political scientist Mark Baldassare. "Most people feel there's no game plan, no way to get us out of this mess."[20] According to Baldassarc's 1985 survey of Orange County residents, this view has not yet been translated into support for regional government. But two 1992 surveys of northern California's Bay Area found big majorities in favor of limited regional government.[21] Perhaps public opinion is finally moving on this issue, although reform is usually more benignly viewed in opinion polls than in actual votes on concrete proposals.

The reality of suburban political power suggests that the future of regional government will reflect its past, with patchwork solutions where necessary rather than radical change. Counties will play a bigger role in many states; new special districts will be formed, some of which, as in Portland, Seattle, and the Twin Cities will be multipurpose. But in all probability, the local governments of the foreseeable future will be very much like the ones we have concentrated on through most of this book.

ESSENTIAL TERMS		
Metropolitan Statistical Areas (MSAs)		contracting for services/ Lakewood plan
Consolidated Metropolitan Statistical Areas (CMSAs)		regional cooperation
fragmentation of metropolitan areas		councils of governments (COGs)
		urban counties
public choice theory		sense of community

local democracy   special districts
economies of scale   federation
externalities   three-tiered structure
regional problems   multipurpose regional agencies
responsibility, coordination,   proponents of regional
  accountability   government
annexation   opponents of regional
consolidation   government
city/county consolidation

FIELDWORK   1. How did you and your family come to live where you do? Does your decision conform with public choice theory or put it into question? Test the theory further by asking other people how they picked their places of residence.

2. Do a survey of governments in your area at the library or county office (you could also check out your property tax bill). How many cities are in your county? How many other counties and cities are included in your MSA? How many special districts and school districts operate in your county? How many cover more than one city or county? How many local governments serve you? Do you think it all adds up to choice or fragmentation and confusion?

3. What regional governments or organizations exist in your area? What authority do they have?

NOTES   [1]Quoted in *The Economist*, 13 October 1990, p. 16.

[2]See Vincent Ostrom, Charles M. Tiebout, and Robert Warren, "The Organization of Government in Metropolitan Areas: A Theoretical Inquiry," *American Political Science Review* 55 (December 1961): 831–842; see also Charles M. Tiebout, "The Pure Theory of Local Economic Expenditure," *Journal of Political Economy* 64 (October 1956): 416–423; or Albert O. Hirschman, *Exit, Voice, and Loyalty* (Cambridge, MA: Harvard University Press, 1970).

[3]Gary Miller, *Cities by Contract: The Politics of Municipal Incorporation* (Cambridge, MA: MIT Press, 1981), p. 8.

[4]Drew A. Dolan, "Local Government Fragmentation: Does It Drive Up the Cost of Government?" *Urban Affairs Quarterly* 26, no. 1 (September 1990): 28–45.

[5]See, for example, Advisory Commission on Intergovernmental Relations, *Metropolitan Organization: The St. Louis Case* (Washington, DC: ACIR, 1988).

[6]Joel C. Miller, "Municipal Annexations and Boundary Changes, 1980–1987," *The Municipal Year Book* (Washington, DC: International City/County Management Association, 1990), p. 75.

[7]*The New York Times*, 23 February 1991.

[8]Ronald J. Oakerson and Roger B. Parks, "Local Government Constitutions: A Different View of Metropolitan Governance," *American Review of Public Administration* 19, no. 4 (December 1989): 288.

[9]David R. Morgan, *Managing Urban America*, 3rd ed. (Pacific Grove, CA: Brooks/Cole, 1989), p. 30.

[10]Mike Davis, *City of Quartz* (London: Vintage, 1992), p. 166.

[11]*The Economist*, 19 May 1990, p. 18.

[12]Bernard H. Ross, Myron A. Levine, and Murray S. Stedman, *Urban Politics: Power in Metropolitan America*, 4th ed. (Itasca, IL: F. E. Peacock, 1991), p. 270.

[13]Ibid., pp. 272–273.

[14]Robert E. Einsweiler, "Metropolitan Government and Planning: Lessons in Shared Power," in B. Checkoway and C. V. Patton, eds., *The Metropolitan Midwest: Policy Problems and Prospects for Change* (Urbana: University of Illinois Press, 1985), p. 294.

[15]Mark Baldassare, "Citizen Support for Regional Government in the New Suburbia," *Urban Affairs Quarterly* 24, no. 3 (March 1989): 467.

[16]Philip J. Trounstine and Terry Christensen, *Movers and Shakers* (New York: St. Martin's Press, 1982), pp. 180–181.

[17]Ross et al., note 12, p. 270.

[18]See the public choice theorists cited in note 1; or Advisory Commission on Intergovernmental Relations, *Metropolitan Reorganization: The St. Louis Case* (Washington, DC: ACIR, 1988).

[19]David R. Berman, "State Actions Affecting Local Governments," *The Municipal Year Book* (Washington, DC: International City/County Management Association, 1989), p. 131.

[20]*The Economist*, 13 October 1990, p. 16.

[21]*San Jose Mercury News*, 7 April 1991; *San Francisco Chronicle*, 22 November 1991; see also Larry N. Gerston and Peter J. Haas, "Political Support for Regional Government in the 1990s," *Urban Affairs Quarterly* 29, no. 1 (September 1993): 154–163.

Circleville: The Game

The game of Circleville gives you a chance to apply and test what you've learned about local politics by reading this text and observing your own community. The game requires you to play a role but it only works if you take your role seriously and play as realistically as you know how. To understand Circleville, you should read the description of the city below and then review the text, paying particular attention to the chapters about how the characteristics of a city affect its politics and forms of government. You should also review the parts of the text that are pertinent to your role or to those of people you will be dealing with.

The game has only a few basic but important rules:

1. Keep within the framework of what you know about politics and Circleville; don't make things up or elaborate without consulting the instructor.
2. All the issues that emerge in the game must be resolved by the last class.
3. You must nevertheless play as if the game goes on. You know the game will end, but no end is in sight for most players in real-life politics.
4. The game must take place in the classroom.

As play begins, it is December in Circleville, so the city is midway through its fiscal (or budget) year, which runs from July to June. The budget is thus in place. Each class session represents one week in the life of Circleville. Council meetings are held in each class session, beginning at a time specified by the instructor. Some items have already been placed on the council agenda; others need to be placed there, and still others may be added. Other activities may proceed at the same time as the meeting (as in real life).

Players are responsible for creating their own roles, following the brief descriptions below. By the class session before the game, each player is to write a one-page description of his or her role and goals. These one-page descriptions will be reviewed and evaluated by the instructor. Think about what kind of a person/player you are portraying and what that person/player's goals might be. Think about what issues might interest your character and also who your allies and opponents might be. You might wish to investigate the background of a real-life counterpart to your role.

Play the game according to the role you are assigned and the knowledge you have gained from this class. Think about ways you can show what you know about urban politics through your play. This is a test.

Players will be evaluated on the basis of (1) their initial description of their roles, (2) a written evaluation each will write at the end of the game, (3) grades assigned them by other players, and (4) the impressions of the instructor. Aggressive activity will not necessarily lead to good grades— the way you play your role should depend on the sort of role it is.

The Setting

Circleville is a city of 200,000 people, of which about 20 percent is Hispanic, 3 percent African American, and 2 percent Asian. Circleville's workers are about equally divided between blue collar (manufacturing), white collar (office), and service (sales, restaurants, and so on) jobs. Unemployment is 13.4 percent, double the national average, and includes a disproportionate share of the city's Hispanic residents.

Located at the edge of the Sunbelt, growth in Circleville has been slow but steady until recently, when a high-tech manufacturing company moved to town and stimulated a growth boom for the past 2 years. This growth was concentrated on Circleville's Southside and Westside except for some redevelopment and in-fill downtown, which is part of the Northside council district. Growth has been even more rapid in the dozen middle-class and upper-class suburbs that surround Circleville.

The Form of Government

Circleville, a home rule or "charter" city, uses a council-manager form of government, with a directly elected mayor who is one of seven city council members.

The city manager hires and fires all department heads, supervises a civil service bureaucracy of 1200 workers, proposes and administers the budget, advises the council on policy, and implements council policies and programs.

The mayor is directly elected and acts as a member of the city council, over which the mayor presides. In addition to the mayor, two other members of the council are elected at-large; the remaining four members are elected by district. All serve 4-year terms without limitation. Elections are nonpartisan, concurrent, and staggered (the mayor and two district representatives are chosen in one election and the other members run in the next). Council pay is $12,000 per year; the mayor's is $24,000.

The Players

The Mayor and Council Members

The Mayor. The Mayor is the 35-year-old scion of Circleville's founding family. Once the city's biggest landowners, the family holdings have now shrunken to just one square block of central Circleville. Unlike all of his or her ancestors, the young mayor is a liberal Democrat whose burning ambition is to run for higher office, preferably Congress. Up for reelection next year.

At-large Councilman, Seat 1. Recently elected to his fourth term on the council, the councilman is a small businessman with conservative leanings and faces reelection next year.

At-large Councilwoman, Seat 2. Recently elected, this first-term council member was a League of Women Voters activist for many years. A high school teacher, she was elected on a reform platform, defeating an old ally of the other at-large council member.

District Council Member (Northside). This senior council member represents the downtown and old working-class neighborhoods of the city. Mostly Italian and Portuguese, this area also includes most of the city's black and Asian population and a substantial number of Hispanics as well. Up for reelection next year.

District Council Member (Eastside). Recently elected, this first-term council member, a fiery liberal, represents the city's poorest district, which includes most of its Hispanic population, as well as a very few affluent citizens who live in the foothills along the edge of the district.

District Council Member (Westside). Recently elected, this first-term council member only moved to Circleville 3 years ago when the council member's spouse helped set up the city's new high-tech industry. Many other employees of that industry live in the council member's middle-class district.

District Council Member (Southside). Representing the city's most affluent and stable neighborhoods, this council member is a college professor and an environmentalist. Up for reelection next year.

The Council Aide. Hired by the mayor, subject to approval of the council, the aide assists the council under the direction of the mayor.

The Bureaucracy

The City Manager.   With a master's degree in public administration and 20 years of experience in city government, Circleville is the first city in which this ambitious professional has held the top job. Hired only last year by a 5–2 council vote (the Seat 1 at-large member and the Northside member voted no), the manager hopes to demonstrate such competence in managing Circleville that a larger city will soon beckon.

The Deputy City Manager.   Brought to Circleville by the new manager, the deputy hopes to follow in the manager's footsteps, perhaps even succeeding to the office of manager in Circleville (the sooner the better). The primary responsibility of the deputy is to manage the city budget.

The Assistant Deputy City Manager.   Formerly deputy city manager whose application to be manager was ignored by the council, the new manager has assigned this senior civil servant responsibilities for intergovernmental relations and council liaison.

The City Attorney.   Appointed by the council, the attorney provides advice on the legality of council actions. The incumbent is an aging member of the city's old power elite, which has kept the attorney in office despite the fact that he/she was appointed before any current member of the council was elected.

The City Clerk.   Appointed by the council, the clerk keeps the council records and attends to the agenda. The current clerk is truly a neutral record-keeper with no personal agenda in city politics except to keep the books in order.

The Police Chief.   Passed over as a contender for city manager (only the Seat 1 at-large council member and the Northside member supported the chief), the city's long-time chief is looking to make a move—possibly to a larger city, possibly to a higher post in Circleville.

The Fire Chief.   A 30-year veteran of the fire department, the chief is looking forward to retirement soon and doesn't want to rock any boats.

The Director of Public Works.   An old crony of the mayor's father, the director of public works has many friends among the city's business elite. The Department of Public Works is in charge of the most basic services of the city other than fire and police protection, including street maintenance, refuse collection, sewage treatment, and so on. The press has alleged that this department is bloated and inefficient, perhaps even corrupt, due to lax management.

The Director of Parks and Recreation.   Hired by the current manager, the director of parks and recreation holds a degree in "recreation studies," is an active environmentalist, and is a crusader for public parks and recreational facilities.

The Director of Planning. Hired by the current manager, the planning director is new to Circleville. With a master's degree in planning, the director has 10 years' experience working in smaller, suburban communities.

The Director of Libraries and Cultural Programs. A true lover of the arts, this city administrator runs Circleville's libraries and small museum, and supervises funding of a number of cultural programs.

The Deputies and Assistant Directors. Appointed by department heads, they provide whatever administrative assistance their bosses may require.

Community Representatives

League of Women Voters. A reform group advocating open government, efficiency, and accountability.

Southside Homeowners. A neighborhood group representing the affluent homeowners of south Circleville.

Westside Community Association. A neighborhood group made up mostly of newcomers to Circleville and speaking for the Westside.

People in Neighborhoods (PIN). An Alinsky-inspired community action organization founded recently in central Circleville and represented by a paid organizer.

President, Chamber of Commerce. A paid, full-time spokesperson for local business (mostly retail).

Chairman of the Board, Chamber of Commerce. Owner of a downtown department store.

Police and Firefighters Union. A paid, full-time spokesperson for the city's police and firefighters, who are in the third year of a 4-year contract.

Municipal Worker's Federation (MWF). Part-time representative for other city workers; also in the third year of a 4-year contract.

Women's Agenda of Circleville (WAC). A liberal, feminist group, represented by a young attorney.

Friends of the Environment (FOE). An environmentalist organization, represented by an architect.

Buildmore Homes. Represented by a regional vice president.

Megabyte Multinational. A high-tech manufacturing company new to Circleville and represented by a regional vice president.

Jekyl and Hyde. A consulting agency of experts for hire.

Small Business Association (SBA). Mostly old, downtown retail merchants, represented by a downtown jeweler.

Gay/Lesbian Action Group (GLAG). With a mainly professional membership, GLAG has lobbied the city on police treatment of homosexuals and insurance for the domestic partners of gay city workers. GLAG's president is a counselor at Circleville Community College.

Raza Si.   Mexican American community organization represented by a priest (or nun).

Intergovernmental Council.   A coalition of neighboring suburban communities represented by a suburban council member.

Greater Circleville Employers' Association (GCEA).   A coalition of the major manufacturing employers in the Circleville region represented by a paid, full-time lobbyist.

The Media

Publisher, Circleville Sentinel.   Scion of the local publishing dynasty, now in charge of the local newspaper, which has recently been acquired by Multinational Megamedia, an international chain owned by stockholders elsewhere.

City Hall Reporter, Circleville Sentinel.   Fresh out of journalism school and on his/her first assignment.

Political Columnist, Circleville Sentinel.   An aging reporter, near retirement.

Circleville Evaluation

Your name: _____

Your role: _____

Your grade: _____

Complete this evaluation and turn it in by the next class session. Use the back of this page if necessary.

1. Describe what you did in the game.

2. What did the game teach you about city politics?

3. How do your observations of Circleville compare to your observations of real-life city council meetings?

4. Who were the most powerful players? Why?

5. What were the shortcomings of the game as a representation of real-life politics?

6. What grade would you give yourself? Why? (Remember, A = excellent, B = good, C = average, D = poor.)

7. Grade as many other players as you wish.

BIBLIOGRAPHY

Abbott, Carl. *The New Urban America*. Chapel Hill: University of North Carolina Press, 1987.

Alinsky, Saul. *Rules for Radicals*. New York: Vintage, 1971.

Allswang, John M. *Bosses, Machines, and Urban Voters*. Baltimore: Johns Hopkins University Press, 1986.

Ammons, David N., and Chardean Newell. *City Executives*. Albany, NY: State University of New York Press, 1989.

————and————. " 'City Managers Don't Make Policy': A Lie; Let's Face It." *Public Management* 70, no. 12 (December 1988): 14–17.

Anderson, Eric. "Two Major Forms of Government." *The Municipal Year Book*. Washington, DC: International City/County Management Association, 1989, 25–32.

Andrews, Lynn H. "A Suggested Approach for a City Manager during the First 90 Days in a New City." *Public Management* 71, no. 8 (August 1989): 14–18.

Ayres, Douglas W. "A 21st Century Council-Manager Charter." *Public Management* 72, no. 8 (September 1989): 13–15.

Bachrach, Peter, and Morton S. Baratz. *Power and Poverty*. New York: Oxford University Press, 1963.

Baldassare, Mark. "Citizen Support for Regional Government in the New Suburbia." *Urban Affairs Quarterly* 24, no. 3 (March 1989): 460–469.

Banfield, Edward C., and James Q. Wilson. *City Politics*. New York: Vintage, 1963.

Barrett, Katherine, and Richard Greene. "American Cities." *Financial World*, 19 February 1991.

Beauregard, Robert A. "Tenacious Inequalities." *Urban Affairs Quarterly* 25, no. 3 (March 1990): 420–434.

Bell, Daniel. *The Coming of Post-Industrial Society*. New York: Basic Books, 1973.

Berman, David R. "State Actions Affecting Local Governments." *The Municipal Year Book.* Washington, DC: International City/County Management Association, 1989, 129–144; 1990, 55–70; 1992, 51–57.

Berry, Jeffrey M., Kent E. Portney, and Ken Thomson. *The Rebirth of Urban Democracy.* Washington, DC: Brookings Institute, 1993.

Bishop, Katherine. "Police Attacks: Hard Crimes to Uncover Let Alone Stop." *The New York Times,* 24 March 1991.

Blodget, Terrell, John C. Crowley, and Craig M. Wheeland. "The Position of the Mayor in Large Council-Manager Cities." *National Civic Review* 79, no. 4 (July–August 1990): 332–349.

Boles, Janet K., ed. *The Egalitarian City.* New York: Praeger, 1986.

Bollens, Scott A. "Constituencies for Limitation and Regionalism." *Urban Affairs Quarterly* 26, no. 1 (September 1990): 46–67.

Bowermaster, Jon. "Seattle, Too Much of a Good Thing." *The New York Times Magazine,* 6 January 1991, 24.

Bratt, Rachel G., Chester Hartman, and Ann Myerson, eds. *Critical Perspectives on Housing.* Philadelphia: Temple University Press, 1986.

Browning, Rufus, Dale Rogers Marshall, and David Tabb. *Protest Is Not Enough.* Berkeley: University of California Press, 1984.

———. *Racial Politics in American Cities.* New York: Longman, 1990.

Callow, Alexander B., Jr., ed. *The City Boss in America.* New York: Oxford University Press, 1976.

Chandler, Timothy David. "Labor-Management Relations in Local Government." *The Municipal Year Book.* Washington, DC: International City/County Management Association, 1989, 85–96.

Checkoway, B., and C. V. Patton, eds. *The Metropolitan Midwest: Policy Problems and Prospects for Change.* Urbana: University of Illinois Press, 1985.

Clark, Terry. *Community Structure, Power, and Decision Making.* Scranton, PA: Chandler, 1968.

Clarke, S. E., and A. Kirby. "In Search of the Corpse: The Mysterious Case of Local Politics." *Urban Affairs Quarterly* 25, no. 3 (March 1990): 389–412.

Crenson, Matthew A. *The Un-Politics of Air Pollution.* Baltimore: Johns Hopkins University Press, 1971.

———. *Neighborhood Politics.* Cambridge, MA: Harvard University Press, 1983.

Dahl, Robert. *Who Governs.* New Haven, CT: Yale University Press, 1961.

Davis, Mike. *City of Quartz.* London: Vintage, 1992.

DeGrove, John M. *Planning and Growth Management in the States.* Cambridge, MA: Lincoln Institute of Land Policy, 1992.

DeLeon, Richard E. *Left Coast City: Progressive Politics in San Francisco, 1975–1991.* Lawrence: University of Kansas Press, 1992.

Dodge, William R. "Regional Problem Solving in the 1990s: Experimentation with Local Governance for the 21st Century." *National Civic Review* 79, no. 4 (July–August 1990): 354–366.

Dogan, Mattei, and John D. Kasarda, eds. *The Metropolis Era, Vol. II: Mega-Cities.* Beverly Hills, CA: Sage, 1990.

Dolan, Drew A. "Local Government Fragmentation: Does It Drive Up the Cost of Government?" *Urban Affairs Quarterly* 26, no. 1 (September 1990): 28–45.

Dowall, David E. *The Suburban Squeeze: Land Conversion and Regulation in the San Francisco Bay Area.* Berkeley: University of California Press, 1984.

Dye, Thomas R. *Politics in States and Communities,* 7th ed. Englewood Cliffs, NJ: Prentice-Hall, 1991.

Dye, Thomas R., and Susan MacManus. "Predicting City Government Structure." *American Journal of Political Science* 10 (May 1976): 257–272.

Ehrenhalt, Alan. "The New City Manager." *Governing,* September 1990, 41–46.

Elkin, Stephen L. *City and Regime in the American Republic.* Chicago: University of Chicago Press, 1987.

Fainstein, Susan S., Norman I. Fainstein, Richard Child Hill, Dennis Judd, and Michael Peter Smith. *Restructuring the City.* New York: Longman, 1986.

Ferman, Barbara. *Governing the Ungovernable City.* Philadelphia: Temple University Press, 1985.

Fishman, Robert. "America's New City: Megalopolis Unbound." *Wilson Quarterly* 14, no. 1 (Winter 1990): 25–45.

Flammang, Janet A., ed. *Political Women.* Beverly Hills, CA: Sage, 1984.

Freedman, Anne. "Doing Battle with the Patronage Army: Politics, Courts, and Personnel Administration in Chicago." *Public Administration Review* 48 (September-October 1988): 847–859.

Frey, William. "Metropolitan America: Beyond the Transition." *Population Bulletin* 45, no. 2 (July 1990, entire issue).

Garreau, Joel. *Edge City.* Garden City, NY: Doubleday, 1991.

Gerston, Larry N., and Peter J. Haas. "Political Support for Regional Government in the 1990s." *Urban Affairs Quarterly* 29, no. 1 (September 1993): 154–163.

Glickfeld, Madelyn, and Nick Levine. *Regional Growth . . . Local Reaction.* Cambridge, MA: Lincoln Institute of Land Policy, 1992.

Goldman, Ed. "Out of the Sandbox." *California Journal,* May 1993, 15–17.

Gosnell, Harold F. *Machine Politics: Chicago Model.* Chicago, University of Chicago Press, 1937.

Gottdiener, Mark. *The Decline of Urban Politics.* Newbury Park, CA: Sage, 1987.

Green, Roy, and Randall Crane. "Debt Financing at the Municipal Level: Decision Making during the 1980s." *The Municipal Year Book.* Washington, DC: International City/County Management Association, 1989, 97–106.

Haselswerdt, Michael. "Voter Reaction to District and At-Large Elections: Buffalo, New York." *Urban Affairs Quarterly* 20 (September 1984): 31–45.

Hawley, Willis D., and Frederick M. Wirt, eds. *The Search for Community Power,* 2nd ed. Englewood Cliffs, NJ: Prentice-Hall, 1974.

Hayes, Kathy, and Semoon Chang. "The Relative Efficiency of City Manager and Mayor-Council Forms of Government," *Southern Economic Journal* 57, no. 1 (July 1990): 167–177.

Hech, C. J. "Contracting Municipal Service: Does It Really Cost Less?" *National Civic Review,* June 1983, 321–326.

Heilig, Peggy, and Robert J. Mundt. "Changes in Representational Equity: The Effect of Adopting Districts." *Social Science Quarterly* 64 (June 1983): 393–397.

Henderson, Lenneal J. "Metropolitan Governance: Citizen Participation in the Urban Federation." *National Civic Review* 79, no. 2 (March–April 1990): 105–117.

Henderson, Lori M. "Intergovernmental Service Arrangements and the Transfer of Functions." *The Municipal Year Book.* Washington, DC: International City/County Management Association, 1985, 194–202.

Hero, Rodney E. "Multiracial Coalitions in City Elections Involving Minority Candidates." *Urban Affairs Quarterly* 25, no. 2 (December 1989): 342–351.

———. "Hispanics in Urban Government and Politics." *Western Political Quarterly* 43, no. 2 (June 1990): 403–414.

Herson, Lawrence J. R., and John M. Bolland. *The Urban Web: Politics, Policy, and Theory.* Chicago: Nelson-Hall, 1990.

Hirschman, Albert O. *Exit, Voice, and Loyalty.* Cambridge, MA: Harvard University Press, 1970.

Hunter, Floyd. *Community Power Structure.* Chapel Hill: University of North Carolina Press, 1953.

Jones, Bryan D. *Governing Urban America.* Boston: Little, Brown, 1983.

Kantor, Paul, with Stephen David. *The Dependent City.* Glenview, IL: Scott, Foresman, 1988.

Kaplan, Marshall, and Franklin James, eds. *The Future of National Urban Policy.* Durham, NC: Duke University Press, 1990.

Karnig, Albert K., and B. Oliver Walter. "Election of Women to City Councils." *Social Science Quarterly* 56, no. 4 (March 1976): 605–613.

Kelling, George. "Police and Communities: The Quiet Revolution." *Perspectives on Policing,* no. 1. Washington, DC: U.S. Department of Justice, 1988.

Klein, Joe. "The Pinochle Club." *New York,* 29 October 1990, 19.

Kotter, John P., and Paul R. Lawrence. *Mayors in Action.* New York: Wiley, 1974.

Ladd, Helen F. "State Assistance to Local Governments: Changes in the 1980s." *The American Economic Review* 80, no. 2 (May 1990): 171–175.

La Gory, Mark. "The Organization of Space and the Character of the Urban Experience." *Publius* 18 (Fall 1988): 71–89.

Lee, Eugene. "The American Experience: 1778–1978." in Austin Ranney, ed., *The Referendum Device.* Washington, DC: American Enterprise Institute, 1981, 46–59.

Lineberry, Robert, and Ira Sharkansky. *Urban Politics and Public Policy,* 2nd ed. New York: Harper & Row, 1978.

Lipsky, Michael. *Street-Level Bureaucracy.* New York: Russell Sage, 1980.

Logan, John R., and Gordana Rabrenovic. "Neighborhood Associations." *Urban Affairs Quarterly* 26, no. 1 (September 1990): 68–94.

Logan, John, and Min Zhou. "Do Suburban Growth Controls Control Growth?" *American Sociological Review* 54 (June 1989): 461–471.

———. "The Adoption of Growth Controls in Suburban Communities." *Social Science Quarterly* 71, no. 1 (March 1990): 118–129.

Lowi, Theodore J. "Machine Politics—Old and New." *The Public Interest* 9 (1967) 83–92.

Lukas, J. Anthony. *Common Ground.* New York: Knopf, 1985.

Lynd, Robert S., and Helen Merrell Lynd. *Middletown.* New York: Harcourt Brace and World, 1929.

———. *Middletown in Transition.* New York: Harcourt Brace Jovanovich, 1937.

MacManus, Susan A. "Mixed Electoral Systems: The Newest Reform Structure." *National Civic Review* 74, no. 10 (November 1985): 484–491.

MacManus, Susan A., and Charles S. Bullock. "Racial Representation Issues." *PS* 18 (Fall 1985): 759–769.

——. "Minorities and Women DO Win At Large!" *National Civic Review* 77, no. 3 (May–June 1988): 231–244.

——. "Women on Southern City Councils: A Decade of Change." *Journal of Political Science* 17, no. 1, 2 (1989): 32–49.

Marando, Vincent L., and Robert D. Thomas. *The Forgotton Governments: County Commissioners as Policy Makers.* Gainesville: University Presses of Florida, 1977.

McIlwain, Joy. "Regional Approaches Gaining Ground." *American City and County* 104, no. 8 (August 1989): 38–41.

McKenzie, Evan. "Morning in Privatopia." *Dissent,* Spring 1989, 257–260.

Miller, Delbert. *International Community Power Structures.* Bloomington: Indiana University Press, 1970.

Mladenka, Kenneth R. "Blacks and Hispanics in Urban Politics." *American Political Science Review* 83, no. 1 (March 1989): 165–191.

Moe, Ronald. "Exploring the Limits of Privatization." *Public Administration Review* 47 (November/December 1987): 453–460.

Molotch, Harvey. "The City as a Growth Machine." *American Journal of Sociology* 82, no. 2 (1976): 309–331.

Morgan, David R. *Managing Urban America,* 3rd ed. Pacific Grove, CA: Brooks/Cole, 1989.

Morgan, David R. and Michael W. Hirlinger. "The Dependent City and Intergovernmental Aid." *Urban Affairs Quarterly* 29, no. 2, (December 1993): 256–275.

Moulder, Evelina R. "Affirmative Action in Local Government." *The Municipal Year Book.* Washington, DC: International City/County Management Association, 1991, 47–52.

Nalbandian, John. "The Contemporary Role of City Managers." *American Review of Public Administration* 19, no. 4 (December 1989): 261–278.

Neighbor, Howard D. "How to Win at Charter Revision." *National Civic Review* 74, no. 10 (November 1985): 477–483.

Oakerson, Ronald J., and Roger B. Parks. "Citizen Voice and Public Entrepreneurship: The Organizational Dynamic of a Complex Metropolitan County." *Publius* 18 (Fall 1988): 91–112.

——. "Local Government Constitutions: A Different View of Metropolitan Governance." *American Review of Public Administration* 19, no. 4 (December 1989): 279–294.

Ostrom, Vincent, Charles M. Tiebout, and Robert Warren. "The Organization of Government in Metropolitan Areas: A Theoretical Inquiry." *American Political Science Review* 55 (December 1961): 831–842.

Pecorella, Robert F. "Measured Decentralization: The New York City Community Board System." *National Civic Review* 78 (June 1989): 202–208.

Peterson, G. E., and C. W. Lewis, eds. *Reagan and the Cities.* Washington, DC: Urban Institute Press, 1986.

Peterson, Paul E. *City Limits.* Chicago: University of Chicago Press, 1981.

Peterson, Tracy E. "Seattle Metro: Regional Solutions to Local Problems." *Government Finance Review* 6 (June 1990): 19–21.

Phillips, Kevin. *The Politics of Rich and Poor.* New York: Harper & Row, 1991.

Presthus, Robert. *Men at the Top.* New York: Oxford University Press, 1964.

Prewitt, Kenneth. *The Recruitment of Political Leaders.* Indianapolis: Bobbs-Merrill, 1970.

Protasel, Greg J. "Abandonments of the Council-Manager Plan." *Public Administration Review* 48, no. 4 (July–August 1988): 807–812.

Rakove, Milton. *Don't Make No Waves, Don't Back No Losers.* Bloomington: Indiana University Press, 1975.

Renner, Tari. "Appointed Local Government Managers: Stability and Change." *The Municipal Year Book.* Washington, DC: International City/County Management Association, 1990, 41–52.

Renner, Tari, and Victor S. DeSantis. "Contemporary Patterns and Trends in Municipal Government Structures." *The Municipal Year Book 1993.* Washington, DC: International City/County Management Association, 1993, 57–69.

Ridley, Clarence E., and Orin F. Notling. *The City Manager Profession.* Chicago: University of Chicago Press, 1934.

Riordan, William L. *Plunkitt of Tammany Hall.* New York: Dutton, 1963.

Ross, Bernard H., Myron A. Levine, and Murray S. Stedman. *Urban Politics: Power in Metropolitan America,* 4th ed. Itasca, IL: F. E. Peacock, 1991.

Royko, Mike. *Boss.* New York: Signet, 1971.

Salter, J. T. *Boss Rule.* New York: McGraw-Hill, 1935.

Sato, Sho, and Arvo Van Alstyne. *State and Local Government Law,* 2nd ed. Boston: Little, Brown, 1977.

Schneider, Mark, and Kee Ok Park. "Metropolitan Counties as Service Delivery Agents: The Still Forgotten Governments." *Public Administration Review* 49, no. 4 (July/August 1989): 347–352.

Schumaker, Paul. *Critical Pluralism, Democratic Performance, and Community Power.* Lawrence: University Press of Kansas, 1991.

Schneider, William. "The Suburban Century Begins." *The Atlantic,* July 1992, 33–44.

Shaforth, Frank. "The Reagan Years and the Nation's Cities." *The Municipal Year Book.* Washington, DC: International City/County Management Association, 1989, 115–128.

Sharp, Elaine B. *Urban Politics and Administration: From Service Delivery to Economic Development.* New York: Longman, 1990.

Sokolow, Alvin D. "Legislators without Ambition: Why Small-Town Citizens Seek Public Office." *State and Local Government Review* 21 (Winter 1989): 23–30.

Sparrow, Glen. "The Emerging Chief Executive: The San Diego Experience." *National Civic Review* 74, no. 11 (December 1985): 538–547.

Stephens, G. Ross. "The Least Glorious, Most Local, Most Trivial, Homely, Provincial, and Most Ignored Form of Local Government." *Urban Affairs Quarterly* 24, no. 4 (June 1989): 501–512.

Stocker, Frederick D., ed. *A Look at State and Local Tax Policies.* Cambridge, MA: Lincoln Institute of Land Policy, 1991.

Stone, Clarence, and Heywood T. Sanders, eds. *The Politics of Urban Development.* Lawrence: University Press of Kansas, 1987.

Studlar, Donley T., and Susan Welch. "Does District Magnitude Matter? Women Candidates in London Local Elections." *Western Political Quarterly* 44, no. 2 (June 1991): 457–466.

Sullivan, Harold. "Privatization of Public Services: A Growing Threat to Constitutional Rights." *Public Administration Review* 47 (November/December 1987): 461–466.

Svara, James H. *Official Leadership in the City*. New York: Oxford University Press, 1990.

Tabb, William, and Larry Sawers, eds. *Sunbelt/Snowbelt: Urban Development and Regional Restructuring*. New York: Oxford University Press, 1984.

———. *Marxism and the Metropolis*. New York: Oxford University Press, 1978.

Tiebout, Charles M. "The Pure Theory of Local Economic Expenditure." *Journal of Political Economy* 64 (October 1956): 416–423.

Tobin, Gary A., ed. *Divided Neighborhoods: Changing Patterns of Racial Segregation* (*Urban Affairs Annual Review* 32). Newbury Park, CA: Sage, 1987.

Tonnies, Ferdinand. *Community and Society*. Edited and translated by Charles Loomis. East Lansing: Michigan State University Press, 1957.

Trounstine, Philip J., and Terry Christensen. *Movers and Shakers*. New York: St. Martin's Press, 1982.

Vogel, Ronald K., and Bert E. Swanson. "The Growth Machine versus the Antigrowth Coalition." *Urban Affairs Quarterly* 25, no. 1 (Sept. 1989): 63–85.

Ward, Doris. "Regional Governance Issues in California: Citizen and Policy Implications." *National Civic Review* 79, no. 2 (March–April 1990): 132–137.

Weber, Max. *From Max Weber: Essays in Sociology*. Translated by A. M. Henderson and Talcott Parsons. New York: Free Press, 1946.

Welch, Susan, and Timothy Bledsoe. *Urban Reform and Its Consequences: A Study in Representation*. Chicago: University of Chicago Press, 1988.

Whyte, William H. *City*. Garden City, NY: Doubleday, 1988.

Wirt, Frederick M. *Power in the City*. Berkeley: University of California Press, 1974.

Wirth, Clifford J., and Michael L. Vasu. "Ideology and Decision Making for American City Managers." *Urban Affairs Quarterly* 22, no. 3 (March 1987): 454–474.

Wirth, Louis. "Urbanism as a Way of Life." *American Journal of Sociology* 44 (July 1938): 1–24.

Wolman, Harold. "Local Economic Development Policy: What Explains the Divergence between Policy Analysis and Political Behavior?" *Journal of Urban Affairs* 10, no. 1 (1988): 19–28.

Wolman, Harold, Edward Page, and Martha Reavley. "Mayors and Mayoral Careers." *Urban Affairs Quarterly* 25, no. 3 (March 1990): 500–514.

Wood, Robert. *Suburbia*. Boston: Houghton Mifflin, 1958.

Yates, Douglas. *The Ungovernable City*. Cambridge, MA: MIT Press, 1977.

Zax, Jeffrey S. "Election Methods and Black and Hispanic City Council Membership." *Social Science Quarterly* 71, no. 2 (June 1990): 340–355.

———. "Reform City Councils and Municipal Employees." *Public Choice* 64, no. 2 (1990): 167–177.

Zimmerman, Joseph F. "Alternative Local Electoral Systems." *National Civic Review* 79, no. 1 (Jan.–Feb. 1990): 23–36.

Index

Page references to tables are printed in italic type.